North Korea's Foreign Policy

North Korea's Foreign Policy

The Kim Jong-un Regime in a Hostile World

Edited by Scott A. Snyder
and Kyung-Ae Park

ROWMAN & LITTLEFIELD
Lanham • Boulder • New York • London

Published by Rowman & Littlefield
An imprint of The Rowman & Littlefield Publishing Group, Inc.
4501 Forbes Boulevard, Suite 200, Lanham, Maryland 20706
www.rowman.com
86-90 Paul Street, London EC2A 4NE

British Library Cataloguing in Publication Information Available

Library of Congress Cataloging-in-Publication Data

Names: Snyder, Scott, 1964- author. | Park, Kyung-Ae, 1955- author.
Title: North Korea's foreign policy : the Kim Jong-un regime in a hostile
   world / Scott A. Snyder and Kyung-Ae Park.
Other titles: Kim Jong-un regime in a hostile world
Description: Lanham : Rowman & Littlefield, [2023] | Series: Asia in world
   politics | Includes bibliographical references and index.
Identifiers: LCCN 2022039748 (print) | LCCN 2022039749 (ebook) | ISBN
   9781538160299 (cloth) | ISBN 9781538160305 (paper) | ISBN 9781538160312
   (ebook)
Subjects: LCSH: Korea (North)—Foreign relations—21st century. | Korea
   (North)—Politics and government—2011- | Kim, Chŏng-ŭn, 1984-
Classification: LCC DS935.65 .S693 2023 (print) | LCC DS935.65 (ebook) |
   DDC 327.5193—dc23/eng/20220920
LC record available at https://lccn.loc.gov/2022039748
LC ebook record available at https://lccn.loc.gov/2022039749

∞™ The paper used in this publication meets the minimum requirements of American National Standard for Information Sciences—Permanence of Paper for Printed Library Materials, ANSI/NISO Z39.48-1992.

Contents

Acknowledgments

The production of a multiauthored volume on a topic such as North Korea always entails a high tolerance for uncertainty and risk. We experienced that uncertainty and risk as coeditors of *North Korea in Transition: Politics, Economics, and Society*, published almost a decade ago by Rowman & Littlefield following the death of Kim Jong-il. Kim Jong-il's death and Kim Jong-un's succession generated a wide range of speculation and uncertainty both about North Korea's stability and its future and about the book project, given that authors had already begun to write chapter drafts at the time of Kim Jong-il's passing. More importantly, it required a steady hand and confidence from our editor, Susan McEachern.

Consequently, we were gratified that prior to her retirement from Rowman & Littlefield in 2021, Susan invited us to submit a proposal for a new edited volume evaluating the first decade of North Korea's foreign policy under Kim Jong-un. Susan approached us at the encouragement of Samuel Kim, who has been so prolific in his own analysis of North Korea, China, and globalization for decades. We owe a debt of gratitude to both Susan and Samuel for the opportunity to lead this assessment of Kim Jong-un's impact on North Korean foreign policy following his first decade in power. We dedicate this volume to both of them in recognition of their extensive contributions to the field of Asian studies over many decades.

We primarily owe our thanks to an excellent team of global contributors, all of whom performed ably to provide incisive analysis as well as to meet our deadlines and field our follow-up inquiries. We are pleased that this is truly a global project that includes analysts with a diverse range of backgrounds and perspectives. Financial support for the project came from the Knowledge Partnership Program at the University of British Columbia, under the direction of Kyung-Ae Park. The editors would like to thank Huilin Gao for her administrative support and to acknowledge the excellent editorial and research contributions of Ellen Swicord and Jennifer Ahn in support of the production of the volume. We are grateful to Ashley Dodge, Haley White, and Katelyn Turner at Rowman & Littlefield for their support throughout the editorial and publishing process.

List of Tables

security, the country continues to suffer from economic stagnation and political isolation.

Kim appeared intent on improving North Korea's domestic economic circumstances in the early days of his assumption of power. But despite the promise he made never to ask his people to "tighten their belts" in his inaugural public speech in April 2012, Kim has struggled to bring prosperity to North Korea. Kim's early experimentation with partial privatization, marketization, and establishment of Special Economic Zones (SEZs) raised hopes that he would launch North Korea's economic development by integrating North Korea with the global economy. Under Kim's leadership, relaxed attitudes toward private exchanges enabled North Korean economic growth rates to increase steadily as the government regulated but did not stand in the way of informal markets as the primary means of economic exchange. North Korean traders got rich, and a new class of moneylenders backed new ventures, including cross-border exchanges that integrated North Korea more deeply into the global economy.

But Kim's commitment to military development has limited North Korea's economic growth. The international community has responded to North Korea's missile and nuclear tests with international sanctions, leaving Special Economic Zones (SEZs) to languish, limiting inward capital flows, and imposing a cap on North Korean growth prospects. The COVID-19 pandemic has reinforced economic retrenchment, enabled regime efforts to restore central economic planning by curbing the growing power of markets as a means for social advancement, and restored the primacy of political loyalty as the essential prerequisite for survival and economic prosperity.

The central dilemma that has shaped North Korean foreign policy during Kim Jong-un's first decade in power has revolved around his desire to ensure North Korea's prosperity and security while sustaining the political isolation and control necessary to perpetuate the regime. The preservation of North Korea's unitary system, in which the leader requires absolute loyalty and maintains absolute control, requires a high degree of isolation from the international community. However, the objective of becoming a "strong and prosperous state" requires a willingness to take on the risks that accompany exposure to and interaction with the outside world. A successful North Korean economic transition would entail economic integration and interdependence and adherence to international business norms that would inevitably conflict with the imperative of absolute loyalty to Kim. Likewise, the regime's pursuit of absolute security through expanded nuclear capabilities serves indirectly to reinforce the high degree of political isolation needed to perpetuate the regime, but it also expands the rest of the world's vulnerability to North Korea's nuclear capabilities. North Korea's quest to attain absolute security through nuclear weapons puts the world at risk because it is impossible for the international community to contain and compartmentalize North Korea's capacity to endanger global security.

This volume is divided into three sections, each of which investigates questions critical to the evaluation of North Korea's foreign policy under Kim Jong-un. First, the volume considers the impact of domestic factors that have influenced the formation and implementation of Kim Jong-un's foreign policy, including: Kim's consolidation of power and assumption of his father's titles and roles; Kim's efforts to strengthen the Workers' Party of Korea (WPK) as the main instrument of governance; and the cycle of economic reform and entrenchment that has resulted from contradictions inherent in the simultaneous pursuit of economic reforms and nuclear and missile development. Second, the volume examines Kim's distinctive use of summitry and evaluates the effectiveness of such meetings as an instrument by which Kim has sought to attain his foreign policy goals. Third, the volume considers the impact of international responses to North Korea's pursuit of nuclear capabilities on North Korea's foreign policy, with special reference to international sanctions, cyber programs, human rights, and joint education ventures. This examination underscores Kim's ambition, creativity, and high-risk tolerance in pursuit of long-term objectives designed to transform North Korea and its place in the world, along with his failure to satisfactorily implement *either* of his main goals: economic *or* military development. The volume will further assess the extent to which international backlash generated by Kim's ambitious attempt to pursue both economic reforms and a nuclear deterrent capability has hindered Kim's ability to fully achieve his desired objectives during his first decade in power.

NORTH KOREA'S DOMESTIC ENVIRONMENT AND ITS IMPACT ON KIM JONG-UN'S FOREIGN POLICY

As Kim Jong-un assumed leadership following his father's death in December 2011, external observers debated the sustainability of Kim's leadership, including his ability to consolidate power and assert control over North Korean institutions. There were doubts about whether a twentysomething Kim could successfully assert control over a system full of entrenched interests largely controlled by older subordinates in a rigidly conservative culture that prized respect for elders. Planning for Kim Jong-un's succession had clarified his status as North Korea's next leader, but those plans included the appointment of powerful and experienced senior advisors to guide Kim as he gradually consolidated power. Kim methodically dispelled doubts about his authority, however, by restoring and regularizing the operations of the WPK following his father's reliance on the military as the primary instrument through which he asserted his leadership. Kim additionally dismissed and replaced senior North Korean military leaders and ruthlessly eliminated all possible challenges to his power, including through the execution of his uncle Chang Song-thaek and the assassination of his half brother Kim Jong-nam. Kim's relatively rapid consolidation of power; subordination of the party, military, security services, and government to his authority; and establishment of the WPK as the main institutional mechanism for governing North Korea paint the picture of a ruthless leader capable of decisively defending his power.

External observers debated whether Kim Jong-un, as North Korea's newly established leader, would have the ability to assert independent agency in setting regime priorities. Since Kim's position and power flowed from his lineage, questions have swirled about the extent to which Kim has been captive to the legacies of his father and grandfather versus the extent to which he might be able to independently reform and transform North Korea. Kim's early pursuit of the *byungjin* policy has not settled this question. The policy hearkens back to his grandfather's policy efforts, but the specifics are subject to reinterpretation so as to meet North Korea's current needs. It remains unclear whether Kim can ultimately succeed in achieving long-standing regime aspirations to unify the peninsula under North Korean leadership and/or secure international prestige as a powerful nuclear state invulnerable to the threats of a hostile world.

Chapters by Kookmin University Professor Andrei Lankov, Seoul National University Professor Byung-yeon Kim, and Aston University Professor Virginie Grzelczyk in the first section of this volume highlight the tensions Kim faced as he navigated the unique requirements necessary to achieve regime preservation while simultaneously pursuing the imperative of regime transformation in an effort to achieve long-held regime objectives. Kim initially pursued policies designed to achieve the transformation of North Korea's economic and military circumstances within the constraints imposed by the imperative of regime preservation. These constraints largely shaped Kim's formulation and implementation of domestic economic and security policies and their impact on North Korea's foreign policy. The chapters in this section analyze how Kim navigated between these objectives, needs, constraints, and contradictions as he assumed leadership and took responsibility for sustaining the Kim family regime.

Andrei Lankov explains how Kim's embrace of the *byungjin* policy during 2012–2017 effectively responded to the concerns of the North Korean elite. North Korean elite interests extend beyond traditional objectives of securing and enriching the state to include the perpetuation of the Kim regime. Unlike elites in former communist countries in Eastern Europe and the former Soviet Union, the gap in living standards between North Korea and its neighbors (most significantly, the 25:1 gap in living standards with South Korea) and the extent of elite complicity with past regime repression ensure that North Korean elites would have no future in a post-Kim North Korean state. To meet North Korean elite aspirations for prosperity while minimizing the risks to regime stability that would result from exposure to the outside world, Kim embarked on reforms modeled on elements of Chinese and Vietnamese experiences while maintaining North Korea's isolation by blocking technological or economic measures that would have promoted economic integration or interdependence. Lankov describes Kim's economic policy as "reforms without openness."

Byung-yeon Kim assesses Kim Jong-un's economic development strategy in even greater detail, noting that Kim's only feasible economic reform option is "market-led growth within socialism." This reform pathway is much shallower than Chinese and Vietnamese reform efforts due to Kim's need to mitigate against the risks of intrusion of capitalist influences that would likely erode state controls. Kim analyzes North Korea's adoption of the "field responsibility system" and the "responsibility management system of socialist enterprise" both in terms of their positive impact on North Korea's economic growth and in comparison to the much stronger growth rates unleashed by deeper socialist economic transitions in China and Vietnam. According to Kim, North Korean reforms were intended to use market mechanisms to boost the socialist economy rather than to allow market transformation and the integration of North Korea's economy into the international capitalist system.

Both Lankov and Kim address North Korea's economic retrenchment policies from 2019. Kim presents empirical evidence suggesting that UN Security Council (UNSC) sanctions directly impacted North Korean economic performance from 2019, using North Korean media discussions of "self-reliance" and nocturnal luminosity data to suggest that sanctions on North Korean manufacturing may have reduced production by as much as 20 percent. Kim notes North Korea's further economic retrenchment in the context of the country's economic centralization and self-quarantine measures taken amid the pandemic but expresses openness to the possibility that North Korea may pursue further economic reforms in the aftermath of the pandemic. Lankov analyzes Kim Jong-un's failure to secure relief from UNSC sanctions at the 2019 summit in Hanoi with US president Donald Trump, quarantine measures taken by North Korea in 2020 in response to the pandemic, and growing Sino-US rivalry, concluding that China may provide limited subsidies to North Korea as a low-cost investment to maintain North Korea as a strategic buffer against the US-South Korea alliance.

Virginie Grzelczyk addresses the other prong of Kim's *byungjin* policy, detailing his pursuit of nuclear and missile programs to relieve the country's long-standing sense of vulnerability to the US nuclear threat and the ways in which North Korea's military development has generated international opposition that has impeded Kim's economic development goals. Grzelczyk reviews the history of North Korea's nuclear program, providing context for how and why Kim Jong-un acknowledged the program as his forefathers' legacy and his push to complete it both as a "great equalizer" capable of deterring a US nuclear strike and as a demonstration to domestic audiences of North Korea's strength and the regime's legitimacy. Grzelczyk further details the dramatic expansion of North Korea's nuclear and missile testing under Kim Jong-un and the development of an extensive network of UNSC and unilateral sanctions imposed on North Korea by the international community. Grzelczyk concludes that North Korea's nuclear program will likely persist into the future because it effectively meets North Korea's needs for deterrence and prestige and may even provide a business opportunity to the extent that the country successfully pursues either extortion or the sale of nuclear technology to third parties.

KIM JONG-UN'S SUMMITRY AND IMPLICATIONS FOR NORTH KOREA'S FOREIGN POLICY

Perhaps the boldest feature of Kim Jong-un's foreign policy legacy in his first decade of rule has been his use of summitry with global leaders to attain a measure of international prestige and legitimation for North Korea. Following Kim's consolidation of political control and a year of rapid advancement of North Korea's nuclear and missile capabilities, he pivoted from shows of strength to a diplomatic charm offensive as the centerpiece of North Korea's foreign policy strategy. The shift was striking both because North Korea's pause in testing in late 2017 and turn to diplomacy in early 2018 dramatically reduced tensions around North Korea's sprint toward nuclear strike and survivability capabilities and because the subsequent flurry of international summitry occurred on a scale and frequency unprecedented in North Korean history. In the space of sixteen months from March 2018 to June 2019, Kim Jong-un met on over twelve occasions with the leaders of China, Russia, South Korea, and the United States, easily eclipsing the number of summit meetings with leaders of major powers that his father and grandfather held over multiple decades. Notable for its absence was the failure of Japanese prime minister Abe Shinzo to gain an audience with Kim Jong-un despite his declaration of willingness to meet Kim unconditionally.

The central ambiguity underlying Kim's diplomatic charm offensive was whether his summit diplomacy represented an effort to seek indirect affirmation of North Korea's nuclear accomplishments or an intention to sacrifice

North Korea's nuclear status in exchange for lasting integration with and participation in the outside world. Kim enhanced his country's international prestige and promised as part of his diplomatic offensive to work toward "complete denuclearization" with Trump, Chinese president Xi Jinping, and South Korean president Moon Jae-in. The mixed record of these efforts, Kim's failure to break North Korea out of its economic isolation, and his country's enhanced economic dependency on China for its survival, however, render the legacy of summitry unclear.

While Kim opened the door toward "complete denuclearization" in his statements with other world leaders, that commitment was not part of Kim's internal justification for summitry. Kim sought international recognition on the platform created by North Korea's military development, not as a pathway to North Korea's integration with the rest of the world. But Kim's failure to follow through on his promises has also raised questions about whether Kim's summitry is sustainable, and it has threatened to catalyze North Korea's renewed international isolation.

Kim Jong-un's turn toward summitry marked a dramatic moment for North Korea on the international stage, but it is difficult to evaluate whether summitry proved effective in achieving Kim's objectives. Kim's summitry restored close leader-level relations with China, but failed to generate progress in inter-Korean relations, change the trajectory of the US-North Korea relationship, or loosen the vise of international sanctions on North Korea. Following the failed Hanoi summit with Trump, Kim returned to Pyongyang empty-handed and publicly humiliated to a degree unprecedented in the history of North Korean leadership. Kim's summit with Russian president Vladimir Putin shortly thereafter seemed more aimed at erasing the failure of the Hanoi summit than at achieving any particular foreign policy objective.

Kim's summitry had four impacts, some more positive than others. First, summitry humanized Kim Jong-un. On the dramatic occasion of Kim's first meeting with Moon at the Demilitarized Zone (DMZ) dividing the two Koreas on April 27, 2018, Kim abandoned the veil of indirect diplomacy by subordinates in favor of direct meetings with world leaders. Kim's decision not to work through proxies was arguably more efficient, but it removed the veil of deniability and imposed direct responsibility on Kim both to meet commitments and to ensure the success of summit diplomacy.

Second, Kim's Hanoi summit failure exemplified the risks of his personal involvement in diplomatic negotiations. Kim's failure could not be easily erased because he himself sat at the table. His direct pledges on the international stage also provided a public test of his credibility. Breakdowns or failures to honor pledges, for instance, to work toward "complete denuclearization," would reflect poorly on Kim's credibility as a diplomatic counterpart on the international stage.

Third, Kim's summitry revealed a fundamental disconnect in North Korea's conduct of diplomacy, especially to the extent that Kim's representatives were circumscribed or unable to negotiate on his behalf on particular issues. Both the failure of subordinates to win authorization from Kim to address complex issues in detail and the necessity of leaving important decisions that required working-level consensus to Kim revealed vertical disconnects in North Korea's top-down bureaucratic structure that reduced prospects for productive diplomacy.

Fourth, the experiences with summitry ran the risk of becoming an obstacle to North Korea's ability to effectively pursue future summit diplomacy. Kim's past summitry may have set expectations for North Korea that engagements at such a high level have unsatisfactory results, decreasing prospects or desires for future meetings. To the extent that Kim and his counterparts view North Korea's past summit experiences as unproductive, North Korea's future prospects for needed leader-to-leader communication necessary to avoid miscalculation, especially in moments of crisis, might be circumscribed.

Chapters in this section written by Sejong Institute former president Haksoon Paik, the Stimson Center's Yun Sun, Professor Ramon Pacheco Pardo of King's College of London, and Vladivostok-based Far Eastern State University's Artyom Lukin explore the impact of Kim's summitry on critical North Korean relationships with South Korea, China, the United States, and Russia.

In his review of the Moon administration's pursuit of summitry with Kim, Haksoon Paik points to Moon's desire to reduce tensions and mitigate the risks of nuclear war as major catalysts for South Korean efforts to jump-start diplomacy. The Moon administration sought both to revive inter-Korean cooperation and to serve as an intermediary for the establishment of peaceful denuclearization negotiations in the face of escalating tensions and name-calling between Trump and Kim. By holding three summits in quick succession in 2018, Moon and Kim revived inter-Korean commitments to support peaceful denuclearization and agreed for the first time to a series of military confidence-building measures designed to reduce military tensions in and around the DMZ and the risk of accidental military confrontation.

Moon and Kim opened the way for three historic meetings between Kim and Trump and even tried to facilitate a pathway toward the relaxation of economic sanctions in exchange for North Korean pledges to forestall nuclear activities at the Yongbyon nuclear facility. This was the first occasion on which denuclearization issues were dealt with as a part of the inter-Korean negotiating agenda. But the envisioned end-of-war declaration and resumption of inter-Korean economic cooperation never materialized due to the failure of US-North Korea negotiations in Hanoi, which also resulted in the souring of relations between Moon and Kim.

Paik points to three aspects of Kim's disappointment with Moon and the resulting deterioration in inter-Korean relations: Moon's failure to place South Korea in the driver's seat in determining policy toward North Korea independent of the United States, Moon's failure to fulfill economic pledges contained in the Panmunjom and Pyongyang Joint Statements, and Moon's failure to steer the United States toward a more accommodative response to North Korea's proposals for partial denuclearization. The Hanoi summit failure demoted Moon from intermediary to marginal actor due primarily to Kim's disappointment with Moon and to Trump and Moon's failure to bridge the gap between the denuclearization process and benefits that would accompany North Korea's denuclearization.

The most significant and lasting beneficiary of Kim Jong-un's turn to summitry has been the Sino–North Korean relationship. Summitry between Xi Jinping and Kim Jong-un enabled the restoration of the geostrategic nature of the Sino-North Korean relationship and of North Korea's value to China as a buffer against US and South Korean combined influence on the Korean Peninsula. Yun Sun describes how the restoration of summitry and the frequency of leader-level meetings during 2018 and 2019 enabled both Kim and Xi to restore a shared strategic rationale for nurturing a special relationship while putting aside their ongoing differences regarding North Korea's military development and nuclear status.

Trump's announced intent to meet with Kim provided a clear catalyst for frequent summitry between Kim and Xi in 2018. Yun describes how Kim sought to enhance North Korea's strategic options by capitalizing on the Sino-US rivalry while the continuation of summitry before and after inter-Korean and US–North Korea summit meetings provided both countries with opportunities to coordinate and align their respective strategies. For Xi Jinping, summitry with Kim served to mitigate the risk of strategic surprises that might result from Kim's summitry with South Korea and the United States. For Kim Jong-un, summitry with Xi provided opportunities to both secure tangible economic support from China and to enhance North Korea's strategic depth in anticipation of meetings with erstwhile foes. Most important, summitry opened the door to the restoration of a strategic relationship between Kim and Xi that would prove mutually beneficial against the backdrop of rising Sino-US rivalry.

While frequent Sino–North Korean summitry signaled the restoration of a special relationship between North Korea and China, it also revealed the extent of the disparity in objectives between the United States and North Korea. Ramon Pacheco Pardo describes how summitry with a US president had been an objective of North Korean foreign policy since the 1970s. Amid the inter-Korean competition for legitimacy, both Kim Il-sung and Kim Jong-il sought summit meetings with US presidents to ease their diplomatic isolation and match South Korean diplomatic advancements. In meeting with Trump, Kim Jong-un succeeded where his father and grandfather had failed. Pacheco Pardo attributes Kim's success primarily to his own needs for recognition, normalization, and economic development as well as to the fortuitous circumstances created by the combination of a pro-engagement South Korean leader and an unorthodox US president. While Pacheco Pardo argues that Kim's meetings with Trump may have normalized both the idea of summitry between North Korea and the United States and the idea of Kim as an international leader, he acknowledges that summitry also revealed the extent of the structural gap between the United States and North Korea on denuclearization, diplomatic normalization, and values such as human rights.

If US–North Korea summitry was defined by showmanship and Sino–North Korean summitry was defined by a rediscovery of strategic purpose, the Russia–North Korea summit left an impression of distance and distraction that contrasts with Vladimir Putin's distinction as the only foreign leader to have held summits with both Kim Jong-un and his father Kim Jong-il. Artyom Lukin situates Putin's summitry with Kim Jong-un in the historical context of the ups and downs of the Soviet-North Korean relationship, portraying an interaction akin to that of distant relatives who coincidentally share similar worldviews (primarily in opposition to perceived US imperialism) but share limited common interests. The lack of material inducements that might sweeten those interests and Russia's inclination to defer to China as North Korea's primary patron provide little incentive or prospect for the growth of the relationship. The April 2019 Putin-Kim summit provided moral support for Kim in the wake of Kim's Hanoi failure but generated few tangible benefits for either side. Instead, Putin's solo press conference following the summit appeared to symbolize the limits of the relationship rather than renewed opportunity.

NORTH KOREAN DIPLOMACY TOWARD THE WORLD

Beyond summitry, North Korea in its first decade under Kim Jong-un has also engaged with the United Nations and the international community in a variety of forms. These engagements mainly constituted defensive responses to international sanctions that had mixed effects on North Korea's diplomatic strategies and foreign policy. The establishment of the UN Panel of Experts charged with enforcing sanctions on North Korea added a punitive dimension to North Korea's interaction with the rest of the world. The Panel progressively investigated and revealed North Korean illicit and sanctions-busting behaviors in a relentless attempt to name and shame member states into curbing North Korea's sanctionable behavior. The imposition of sanctions on

North Korea and the extensive efforts North Korea has made to circumvent those sanctions has diverted North Korea's foreign policy profile, priorities, and focus from the conduct of diplomacy to support for the acquisition of tangible resources necessary to sustain Kim's regime and North Korea's military modernization.

As a means of securing hard currency in the face of international financial sanctions, North Korea has launched an extensive cyber capability that has evolved steadily during the past decade under Kim Jong-un in its reach, effectiveness, and aims. North Korean cyber operations have become a lucrative mechanism through which it has secured the billions of dollars in financial resources necessary to sustain the country in the face of international sanctions. Cybertheft has been a critical vector of North Korea's interactions with the outside world because it has provided the regime with an unrecorded stream of income largely beyond the reach of international sanctions. North Korea's use of cyber capabilities to circumvent international sanctions and finance its military development has influenced its diplomatic profile by keeping North Korea a target of ongoing efforts to close the financial loopholes that North Korea has exploited.

The UN General Assembly has long served as the primary forum in which North Korea could assert its grievances with its unfair treatment by the rest of the world and with perceived US hostility. Furthermore, North Korea had long attempted to harvest much-needed technological and scientific information and external goods through engagement with UN agencies such as the World Health Organization, World Food Programme, UN Development Programme, and UNICEF. But the international focus on human rights violations within North Korea has forced the country to expend diplomatic energy to defend itself against the allegations. Efforts to improve the human rights situation within North Korea have occurred through the UN Human Rights Council (UNHRC), nongovernmental activism, and unilateral sanctions imposed on North Korea. The UN has been the only venue at which North Korea has directly contended with international attacks on its human rights record. Because North Korean sanctions evasion, cybertheft, and defense against accusations of human rights violations have had a disproportionate influence on the practice of North Korean foreign policy, this volume devotes special attention to the impact of each of these strictures on North Korea's foreign policy under Kim Jong-un.

This section seeks to better understand how international measures to hold North Korea accountable for its ballistic missile development and human rights record have influenced the conduct of North Korean foreign policy under Kim Jong-un. University of Sydney Professor Justin Hastings, Nanyang Technological University Professor Michael Raska, and Carleton University Professor Sandra Fahy respectively analyze the impact of the

UN sanctions regime and North Korean sanctions evasion efforts on North Korean foreign policy, the evolution and aims of North Korean cybertheft capabilities, and North Korean approaches to UNHRC efforts to uphold minimum human rights standards in North Korea.

Justin Hastings observes that the incremental strengthening of international sanctions not only mobilized Kim to engage in summitry to pursue sanctions relief, but also redirected much of North Korean diplomatic activity away from conventional diplomacy and toward economic and business functions in support of sanctions evasion efforts. Hastings further concludes that despite North Korea's pursuit of an independent foreign policy, the imposition of sanctions has increased North Korea's dependence on countries such as China and others that have lagged in their enforcement of UN sanctions.

In his analysis of the evolution and purposes of North Korea's cyber capabilities, Michael Raska reviews the evolution and organizational structure of North Korea's cyber programs, details the types of international cooperation and assistance required by North Korea to enhance its capabilities, and assesses the evolution of both these capabilities and the international responses designed to counter them. Raska concludes that North Korea's development and use of cyber operations to exert international influence, evade economic and political restrictions on its access to financial resources, and secure a stream of funding to sustain the regime constitute a relatively low-cost strategy that has yielded a favorable return on investment in North Korea's ability to procure hard currency and enabled North Korea to secure valuable information on emerging technologies.

Sandra Fahy assesses the human rights dimension of North Korea's confrontation with the international community at the UNHRC with special reference to North Korean responses to the 2014 report of the UN Commission of Inquiry (COI). Fahy observes that although the UNSC has primarily concerned itself with North Korea's nuclear proliferation and development of weapons of mass destruction, it has also served as the main venue for investigating allegations of crimes against humanity in North Korea. The 2014 UN COI report on North Korea's human rights situation in particular has addressed these allegations. Fahy finds that North Korean state media has traditionally responded to UN critiques of North Korean human rights practices with a mixture of "deflection, obfuscation, and whataboutism," but that following the publication of the 2014 report, North Korea participated in the UN's Universal Periodic Review (UPR) process out of a desire to deflect the COI recommendation that the International Criminal Court indict Kim Jong-un for crimes against humanity. Although North Korea has primarily dismissed UPR recommendations for human rights improvement as meddling in North Korea's internal affairs motivated by Western hostility, the North has implicitly accepted the UN body as sufficiently legitimate by presenting a line of defense that responded to the recommendations.

Finally, North Korea has engaged in Track II diplomatic activities to secure knowledge, technology, and international engagement opportunities in areas not yet completely blocked by sanctions. These engagements provide possible new insights into the regime's thinking about its pursuit of economic development and suggest possible future forms of North Korean engagement with the outside world. The Canada-DPRK Knowledge Partnership Program (KPP) constitutes an example of North Korean efforts to gain knowledge and skills that might enhance North Korea's economic integration into the global economy through the development of international knowledge partnerships.

In the final chapter, University of British Columbia Professor Park Kyung-Ae explores North Korea's approach to participation in international intellectual exchanges under Kim Jong-un and describes North Korea's motivations to engage in collaborative activities with foreign partners. Park describes North Korean willingness to participate in a Visiting Scholar program at the University of British Columbia in Vancouver. In addition, the KPP organized several international conferences in North Korea on SEZs, sustainable development, and the characteristics and state of business education, which included the participation of more than twenty foreign specialists and UN representatives. Park states that through the KPP, North Korea has sought to resuscitate its economy by building human capital, supporting economic development through the establishment of SEZs, earning hard currency and defying of sanctions through tourism development, overcoming food shortages and malnutrition, and achieving Sustainable Development Goals. North Korea's participation in and strong support for the KPP may serve as a bellwether for gauging the scope of leadership interest in participation in aspects of the global economy under Kim Jong-un.

CONCLUSION: NORTH KOREA'S INTERNAL ASSESSMENT OF KIM'S FOREIGN POLICY ACCOMPLISHMENTS

This volume analyzes Kim Jong-un's leadership objectives and their impact on North Korea's foreign policy during the first decade of his rule. Toward this end, it is important to consider North Korea's internal assessment of its foreign policy performance during Kim's leadership. At North Korea's May 2016 Seventh Party Congress and January 2021 Eighth Party Congress, Kim Jong-un provided his assessment of global conditions and North Korea's response to these conditions. These two self-assessments elucidate Kim's own view of the challenges faced and accomplishments made by North Korea under his rule.

The Seventh Party Congress primarily assessed North Korea's domestic economic and political objectives, with little reference to foreign policy. Kim described the pursuit of the *byungjin* policy as a "dynamic struggle" that would "finally conclude[e] the confrontation with the imperialists and the U.S. and accelerating the final victory of our cause."[1] Kim pledged that "as a responsible nuclear state," North Korea would not proliferate and would instead work toward global denuclearization. In a hint of his openness to a transformed relationship with past enemies, Kim also pledged that "the WPK and the DPRK government will improve and normalize relations with those countries which respect the sovereignty of the DPRK and are friendly towards it, though they had been hostile in the past." Kim's statement envisioned that a "responsible" nuclear North Korea would succeed in winning international acceptance and that from that vantage point North Korea could attain acquiescence, acceptance, and accommodation based on its nuclear status.[2] Kim anticipated that he would succeed in attaining both his economic and military objectives and that North Korea's position, prestige, and power in the international community would be enhanced based on those accomplishments.

Following Kim's intensive summitry and failure to achieve either sanctions relaxation or détente with the United States five years later, Kim assessed at the Eighth Party Congress that "the external environment for the DPRK was harshest in its history since its founding, due to the desperate offensive by the US and its followers characterized by frantic manoeuvres to pressurize and blockade the country."[3] Kim emphasized the firmness of North Korea's commitment to independence and willingness to defend its sovereignty in the face of such pressure. The report highlighted the advancement of "friendly relations with China," "fresh development of the traditional DPRK-Russia relations," socialist solidarity through summits with Cuba and Vietnam, and "a dramatic turn in the balance of power between the DPRK and the US during the period under review, thereby wonderfully demonstrating the dignity and prestige of our state."[4] This favorable view of North Korea's international relations implicitly attributed North Korea's progress to Kim's summitry

The report attributed Trump-Kim summitry as an opening for the establishment of new relations between the United States and North Korea that "demonstrated to the world the strategic position of the DPRK, which defends its independent interests and peace and justice against the superpower." But North Korea's pledge to work toward "complete denuclearization" was omitted from Kim Jong-un's report to the Eighth Workers' Party Congress. Instead, Kim made an extensive commitment to a laundry list of military modernization objectives, including the development of tactical nuclear weapons, "supersized" missile capable of delivering multiple nuclear weapons by precision strike to fifteen thousand kilometers, solid-fueled intercontinental ballistic missiles (ICBMs) and submarine-launched ballistic missiles (SLBMs), and military reconnaissance satellites.[5]

In his first decade in power, Kim Jong-un has strengthened North Korea through military development at a severe cost to his ability to bring economic prosperity to his people. Kim's turn to summitry to buy time and space for North Korea to escape this dilemma marked a bold attempt to break out of international sanctions and earn international legitimacy. But Kim's failure to fully achieve his economic and military development goals or follow through on his promises in international summitry has also generated new obstacles and imposed higher costs in the form of opposition to what most international observers characterize as North Korea's illegal nuclear development. The impact of UN sanctions and North Korea's self-quarantine in response to the pandemic has perpetuated and seemingly deepened the dilemma North Korea has long faced between security-first isolation and regime-threatening economic reforms. In sum, Kim Jong-un has ambitiously taken audacious risks to strengthen and preserve his own rule, but in doing so has generated significant international backlash that has obstructed his aims. After a decade in power, the final assessment of the impact of Kim Jong-un's leadership on North Korea's foreign policy is still out, and it will likely continue to unfold as Kim continues to forge North Korean foreign policy in a hostile world. The chapters that follow explore in detail the influence of Kim Jong-un's leadership on North Korean foreign policy and the international community's response.

NOTES

1. "Kim Jong Un Makes Report on Work of WPK Central Committee at Its 7th Congress," Korea Central News Agency, May 7, 2016, https://www.ncnk.org/sites/default/files/content/resources/publications/KJU_Speeches_7th_Congress.pdf.

2. "Kim Jong Un Makes Report."

3. "On Report Made by Supreme Leader Kim Jong Un at Eighth Party Congress of WPK," Korea Central News Agency, January 9, 2021, https://www.ncnk.org/resources/publications/kju_8th_party_congress_speech_summary.pdf/file_view.

4. On Report Made by Supreme Leader Kim Jong Un."

5. On Report Made by Supreme Leader Kim Jong Un."

Part I: Understanding North Korea's Foreign Policy under Kim Jong-un

Chapter 1

Making Sense of the *Byungjin* Policy: Goals, Hopes, and Limitations

Andrei Lankov

North Korea has an established reputation as a country run by an "unpredict-able" and "irrational" regime, even though several observers have tried to rebuke this perception. Indeed, a better look at the history and the current state of North Korean foreign and domestic politics demonstrates beyond reasonable doubt that the North Korean decision makers might have many shortcomings, but a deficit of judgment is clearly not one of their failures. The *byungjin* policy, which Kim Jong-un's government implemented between 2012 and 2017, is further proof of North Korean decision makers' ability to find political solutions that help them attain their goals in a highly unfavor-able environment.

A DANGEROUS NEIGHBOR

For decades, the North Korean elite have existed in a situation that is quite unique in the present world, where wholesale conquest by a neighboring state has otherwise long ceased to be a feared scenario. Unlike ruling classes in most currently existent states, the North Korean elite face a real threat of state/regime collapse and subsequent absorption by their triumphant south-ern neighbor.

North Korea has a spectacularly successful doppelgänger. When Korea was divided in 1945–1948, North Korea was arguably one of the most industrially advanced countries in East Asia outside Japan, while South

Korea was an agrarian backwater. By 1940, the would-be provinces of North Korea produced 85 percent of the metals, 88 percent of the chemicals, and 85 percent of all electricity in Korea.[1] As a result, per capita output in the North was recently estimated to be more than one-third higher than that in the South by 1940.[2] These days are long gone. Even if we believe North Korea's likely optimistic government estimates, its per capita GDP in 2019 was $1,316.[3] Meanwhile in 2019, the South boasted a nominal per capita GDP of $31,936.[4] This places North Korea's per capita GDP slightly below that of Zimbabwe, while the same indicator for South Korea roughly equals that of Italy. The per capita GDP ratio between the two Koreas is a yawning 1:25. This constitutes by far the world's largest gap between two countries that share a land border.

Korea's division into two states, seventy-odd years old, has never been formally accepted by either side. The official discourse, both in North and South Korea, is full of lofty statements about the alleged national unity of Korea. They claim to be two parts of one nation, temporarily divided, whose eventual unification should be the goal of every patriotic Korean. Neither government recognizes the existence of its twin, and each claims itself the sole legitimate power on the entire Korean Peninsula.[5]

Since South Korea is so spectacularly rich and successful, but also supposedly part of the same nation, the North Korean elite live in constant fear of what can be called the German scenario: an outbreak of instability inside North Korea followed by the rise of a massive popular movement demanding unification with the rich South on South Korean terms. The per capita GDP ratio between the two German states that arguably sank East Germany was merely 1:2 or 1:3 at the time of German unification—far less than the 1:25 gap we now see between the two Koreas.[6]

Seen from the North Korean elite's point of view, unification by absorption is essentially synonymous with conquest by the triumphant Southerners. For them, such a conquest will have devastating consequences. If it happens, the North Korean elite will have no chance of emulating, for example, the ex-communist leaders of the former Soviet Union or Eastern Europe. In those countries, the members of old nomenklatura successfully reinvented themselves after the collapse of the old system as capitalist entrepreneurs and democratic/nationalist politicians largely stayed in power. The Communist-era apparatchiks survived regime change because in their societies they often had a near-monopoly on education and administrative experience as well as control of state property.[7] In a unified Korea, the North Korean elite will not enjoy such advantages: their experience will be rendered irrelevant by dramatic changes in the economic and social structure, and their political power will largely or completely evaporate. In a unified, Seoul-dominated

Korean state, major positions will be taken by the Southerners whose knowledge and political connections will be far better suited to the demands of the modern world.

Even if North Korean elites are guaranteed security at the time of unification, they have few reasons to believe that such promises will be kept for long. The government of the newly unified country, inescapably dominated by the Southerners, will have every reason to turn former North Korean officials into scapegoats. Doing so will certainly help distract the public from unavoidable post-unification economic problems—as former dissenter and then Bulgarian president Zhelyu Zhelev observed, "Revolutions, even velvet ones, rarely meet the expectations that they raise. Disenchantment and pessimism creep in."[8] Scapegoating will be made easy by one simple fact: the severity and scale of human rights abuses under the Kim family regime indeed have few analogues in recent history. So a large-scale purge of former North Korean officials, especially those with Party and security police backgrounds, will be easy to justify and will at least initially enjoy much popular support.

Therefore, the North Korean government and, broadly speaking, the entire North Korean elite, see themselves as unwilling players in a life-or-death survival game, a very real version of the Squid Game they cannot leave. They are determined to prevent a system collapse, irrespective of where the challenge will come from.

This group is not small. In 2016, Robert Collins estimated that the number of "elite family members" stood at two hundred thousand.[9] However, the number of people with vested interests in maintaining the regime is not limited to the presumed two hundred thousand members of the core elite— actually, it is much larger. It includes secret police officers, party officials, journalists, indoctrinators, as well as many mid- and high-ranking administrative officials and military officers—not to mention the countless police informants and Party "activists." Including their family members, these stakeholders might number as many as one million. These people overwhelmingly see themselves as cornered. And they are probably right.

This threat perception colors all decision-making by the North Korean elite. One reason the policy of the North Korean state is often perceived as "irrational" is the stubborn unwillingness of North Korean decision-makers to embrace measures conducive for economic growth, especially some variant of China's "reforms and openness" policy. However, many such measures, while beneficial economically, also increase threats to the regime's long-term survival. When the stakes are so high, if interests of survival contradict those of the economic growth, the choice is obvious.

As John Mearsheimer has said:

Survival is the number one goal of great powers. . . . In practice, however, states pursue non-security goals as well. For example, great powers invariably seek greater economic prosperity to enhance the welfare of their citizenry. . . . States can pursue them as long as the requisite behavior does not conflict with balance-of-power logic, which is often the case.[10]

In this case, Mearsheimer did not use the word "survival" in its original and brutally literal meaning. As he himself admitted elsewhere, "survival" for most states merely means the ability to maintain "their territorial integrity and the autonomy of their domestic political order."[11] But as we have seen, North Korean leaders do not care about preserving the autonomy of their domestic political order—rather, they care about not being ruined, sent to prison, or lynched. In the North Korean case, the term "survival" should be understood literally. This, of course, is made even more compelling by the logic described by Mearsheimer.

North Korea must address two challenges to survive under Kim Jong-un's leadership, which, as Mearsheimer points out in the above statement, are not of equal importance. First, North Korean leaders must secure their system against the external and internal threats of forced regime removal, ranging from violent regime change scenarios such as an elite coup to a popular uprising to foreign intervention, or any combination thereof. On the other hand, they would like to achieve economic growth—not least because such economic growth, as demonstrated later, will assist them in dealing with the first task.

Kim Jong-un's *byungjin* policy embodies these dual goals. The term, which can be translated as "simultaneous advancement," implies that the North Korean government should advance military (above all, missile and nuclear) capabilities while developing the civilian economy as well. This policy and the name itself have a remarkable historical pedigree since it was widely used in the 1960s.[12] The present-day version of *byungjin* was launched in 2013 as Kim was consolidating his grip on power. The policy was officially launched at a Workers' Party of Korea (WPK) Central Committee meeting in March 2013.[13]

PLAYING SURVIVAL GAMES

As its name implies, the *byungjin* policy consists of two components: the military and civilian, with the former having clear precedence over the latter. The two dimensions of *byungjin* reflect the two major concerns of the North Korean elite described above.

Recent world events provided North Koreans with critical lessons about the value of nuclear weapons. The first such lesson was provided by the collapse of Saddam Hussein's regime in Iraq in 2003. For a while, Saddam was working to develop nuclear weapons, but in 1981 a daring Israeli air raid put an end to Iraq's nascent nuclear program.[14] Thus, Iraq was left only with conventional forces, and when attacked by the United States the Saddam regime collapsed in a few days.

However, one can surmise that the fear of an Iraq-style open foreign invasion is not what North Korean leaders fear most. Another, and probably more relevant, lesson is the sorry fate of Muammar Gaddafi's regime in Libya.

In the 1990s, Gaddafi's regime worked hard to acquire its own nuclear weapons capacity. But in 2003, the Libyan government accepted a deal similar to that which the United States now hopes to get from North Korea. In exchange for international sanctions being lifted, as well as some other economic benefits, Gaddafi agreed to dismantle his half-baked nuclear weapons acquisition program and shipped its key equipment, as well as sixteen kilograms of highly enriched uranium (HEU), overseas.[15] Back then, his decision was applauded by Western observers and often presented as a "lesson" for the North Koreans to emulate. Such an opinion was expressed in 2004 by none other than John Bolton, who played a major role in negotiations with both Gaddafi's regime in the early 2000s and with North Korea as national security advisor during the Trump administration.[16]

When the wave of Arab Spring revolutions flooded the Arab world in 2011, Gaddafi found himself facing a domestic rebellion. While unpopular, he still had some supporters in a deeply divided Libyan society, and his military forces still had decisive superiority in air power and heavy weaponry. These factors would probably have given Gaddafi and his faction a good fighting chance, but Western powers intervened and, citing the "Responsibility to Protect" norm, established no-fly zones that essentially provided revolutionary forces with NATO air cover. Because he was unable to use his primary advantages, Gaddafi was pursued and killed while on the run, plunging Libya into a civil conflict that continues to this day.[17]

North Korean decision-makers have every reason to believe that had Saddam succeeded in attaining nuclear weapons, he would have survived. They are certain that had Gaddafi not accepted the sweet-sounding Western proposals in the early 2000s, even the remote probability that his government possessed nuclear devices and/or a large amount of fissile material would have prevented the NATO intervention. So he probably would have been able to suppress the rebellion by resorting to the usual combination of violence and concessions. Indeed, as Frederic Wehrey admitted in his study of the Libya Revolution, "Without NATO, the ability of the Libyan uprisings to successfully topple Mu'ammar al-Qadhafi was in serious doubt."[18]

While one must usually resort to guesswork to surmise the thoughts of the North Korean elite, in this case the North Koreans made their position crystal clear. On March 22, 2011, the North Korean Foreign Ministry spokesman commented on Gaddafi's downfall:

> The present Libyan crisis teaches the international community a serious lesson. It was fully exposed before the world that "Libya's nuclear dismantlement," much touted by the United States in the past, turned out to be a mode of aggression whereby the latter coaxed the former with such sweet words as "guarantee of security" and "improvement of relations" to disarm itself and then swallowed it up by force. It proved once again the truth of history that peace can be preserved only when one builds up one's strength as long as high-handed and arbitrary practices go on in the world.[19]

One should pay attention to the word "lesson" used in the statement. Indeed, Libya provided North Korea with a good lesson—albeit not the lesson John Bolton and like-minded persons hoped for.

Han S. Park correctly observed when recalling his encounters with North Koreans, most of whom were presumably officials:

> When one asks any North Korean about the reason for the U.S. invasion of Afghanistan and Iraq, one will get one answer only: Those countries were invaded because they did not have the military capability to defend themselves. Every North Korean is also likely to offer the view that the United States would not have attempted either invasion if the target country had had nuclear weapons.[20]

The author has exactly the same impression from unofficial and frank interactions with several North Koreans, some of whom were actually quite skeptical about their government and its policy.

Thus, the nuclear program is a nonnegotiable part of the North Korean strategy. No "security guarantees" are likely to be taken seriously by North Korean leaders, who not only remember Gaddafi's sorry end, but also what happened to the "territorial integrity guarantees" the Ukrainian government received according to the Budapest Protocol of 1994 (in exchange of its willingness to essentially denuclearize itself, surrendering all Soviet-era nuclear weapons to Russia).[21] North Korean leaders understand that if things go terribly wrong and they face domestic discontent of any kind, the United States, South Korea, and, broadly speaking, the West will likely prevent them from using all their military might to crush the rebels—and no security guarantee will apply in such a scenario.

Therefore, Kim Jong-un's government has never had any intention of surrendering its nuclear weapons, even though in 2018–2019 when facing a seemingly unpredictable and irrational US president, they had no choice but to make vague professions to the contrary. Nonetheless, once the Trump emergency was over, they immediately reverted to their old playbook, rejecting even the nebulous promises they grudgingly made in 2018.

The bedrock of North Korea's *byungjin* strategy is the development of nuclear forces. As early as 1981, in his well-known Adelphi paper, Kenneth Waltz listed the reasons states want nuclear weapons. He wrote that a country "will want nuclear weapons all the more if some of its adversaries have them" or "because it lives in fear of its adversaries' present or future conventional strength." He also mentioned that "by building nuclear weapons a country may hope to enhance its international standing."[22]

Each of these three reasons (of the seven listed by Waltz) apply to North Korea. First, North Korean leaders understand that their conventional armed forces are no match for the US military machine—they also stand little chance of winning against the South Korean military alone. Second, their major opponent, the United States, is the largest nuclear power in the world. Third, the existence of nuclear weapons allows North Korea, a small and very poor country, to punch above its weight diplomatically. Nuclear weapons are an important negotiating tool that allows North Korea to attract much attention to itself and, when necessary, to squeeze significant concessions from countries that under other circumstances would dismiss North Korea's existence.

The North Korean nuclear program began in the late 1950s and greatly accelerated in the 1970s. The first North Korean nuclear test took place in 2006 under Kim Jong-il. He managed to conduct another nuclear test in 2009, but the major breakthrough was achieved under his son, Kim Jong-un. Between 2013 and 2017, North Korea conducted four nuclear tests, including one test of a thermonuclear device.[23]

Even more impressive are the recent achievements of North Korean rocket scientists. Under Kim Jong-il, they began working hard to create a prototype intercontinental ballistic missile (ICBM), largely relying on stolen and/or secretly acquired Russian missile technology. However, for a long time they had little success. Contrary to Pyongyang's claims about the alleged "successful launch of the first North Korean satellite" in 1998, it was not until 2012 that a single North Korean ICBM prototype managed to fly according to its designers' intention.[24]

This changed under Kim Jong-un's watch when the world, with a measure of surprise, saw a chain of highly successful missile tests that culminated in the 2017 tests of Hwasong-14 and Hwasong-15 ICBMs, both seemingly capable of hitting targets on the continental United States. Doubts remain about North Korea's ability to master some essential missile technologies, including building a reliable reentry vehicle or weaponizing the nuclear device.[25] However, even if North Korea still does not have a fully deployable ICBM, it is quite close to reaching the Holy Grail of its policy, the sure second-strike capability—as Terence Roehrig predicted in 2012.[26]

The ultimate goal of the *byungjin* policy's military component is clear. North Korea believes a proven capability of striking US cities with a nuclear warhead will serve as both an ideal deterrent and, whenever necessary, an ideal instrument of blackmail (or, if one prefers, "diplomatic pressure") to secure the regime for decades to come. To quote Roehrig, "Most likely, North Korea will rely on nuclear weapons to deter a United States–South Korea invasion and to use for political leverage."[27] It was said in 2012, it remains valid in 2022, and, quite possibly, it will still apply in 2032.

ATTEMPTED ECONOMIC RECOVERY AND REGIME SURVIVAL

Nuclear and missile developments alone might not be enough to ensure long-term regime survival. There is always a fear of a dramatic internal economic crisis, more or less like the "Arduous March" (the euphemistic name of the devastating famine of 1996–1999) that would destabilize the domestic situation. Therefore, the North Korean elite also understand that it is in their interest to ensure that the common North Koreans have a survivable supply of food while the regime's enforcers are sufficiently well fed. Of course, these pragmatic considerations are not the only reasons that North Korean leaders think about economic development. One should not demonize them: all things being equal, they are willing to preside over economic growth and see their subjects growing more prosperous—if, of course, such changes do not seriously threaten their regime's survival. Therefore, the *byungjin* policy includes a second—and secondary—component: that the government will strive to improve the country's dire economic situation.

At first glance this task does not appear that difficult, since the North Korean government has a nearly perfect model to emulate. Back in the late 1970s, just after Mao Zedong's death, China found itself in dire conditions not much different from present-day North Korea. However, the introduction of the market economy by Deng Xiaoping and his successors produced an economic miracle. For three decades, China's economy grew 10 percent on the average year, doubling in size every seven years, such that it rapidly became a middle-income country and the world's second largest economy.[28] This is likely especially impressive to the North Koreans, since older Koreans still vividly remember the days when, in terms of living standards, China lagged behind Kim Il-sung's North Korea.

To further drive this point home one can consider Vietnam, which emulated the Chinese model, albeit with a few years' delay. While marginally less successful than China, Vietnamese growth is still very impressive.

In both China and Vietnam, the adoption of a "developmental authoritarianism" model did not lead to an outbreak of popular discontent. On the contrary, in both countries the authoritarian governments seemingly enjoyed significant support from below. The old elite did not merely stay in power; they were able to transfer some of their wealth and privileges to the following generations.[29] So there exists an apparently attractive model that twice produced results beyond the most optimistic expectations. This model was implemented in countries whose history and politics the North Korean elite are well aware of, and whose experience they often emulated in past. Thus, one may wonder why North Korean leaders are so reluctant to emulate a seemingly irresistible example.

Such reluctance to launch the Pyongyang version of the "reforms and openness" policy is by no means proof of North Korean leaders' irrationality, ideological rigidity, or insufficient understanding of the modern world. On the contrary, North Korean leaders clearly understand how different their strategic situation is from that of China, and why the wholesale emulation of the Chinese/Vietnamese reforms and openness model will put internal stability at grave risk.

The major reason for this reluctance is the tremendous economic success enjoyed by the rival South. Right now, the North Korean populace is unaware of the prosperity enjoyed by their South Korean brethren. Rumors have been spreading inside the country for the last two or three decades, so North Korean commoners know or suspect that South Koreans live well. However, the size of this gap is not fully appreciated by the majority, even though people living close to the border or in major cities usually have had more exposure and hence are better informed about South Korean prosperity.[30]

This ignorance about even basic details of life in South Korea is a result of a deliberate policy that the North Korean authorities have implemented for decades. One needs a formal security clearance to access the internet in North Korea. Legally purchased North Korean mobile phones cannot be used for overseas calls. Radio sets with free tuning are banned, and possession of such a radio constitutes a crime. All nontechnical publications from foreign countries are available only for those who have received proper security clearance from the political police, and unauthorized interaction with a foreigner usually warrants an investigation.[31]

At first glance these measures appear excessive, but this is not really the case. In the peculiar situation of North Korea, keeping the populace ignorant about the outside world is a prerequisite for maintaining stability. This is the cornerstone of the Kim family regime's policy.

In this regard, North Korea is dramatically different from post-Mao China. Chinese leaders can afford the reforms and openness policy exactly because they do not face another large Chinese-speaking state that is rich and free. With China, Taiwan is the closest analogue, but it is too small to make a difference.

The Chinese populace nowadays is aware of the prosperity enjoyed by the developed world, including countries like Japan, the United States, and Germany. Of course, the reforms and openness policy greatly increased the level of this awareness. However, it did not trigger much political discontent in China because the prosperity in question is enjoyed by people who belong to different nations and whose cultures and histories are dramatically different from those of China.

In a reforming and opening North Korea, this will not be the case. The North Koreans, if exposed to knowledge about South Korean prosperity, fabulous by their standards, will be under the impression that unification with the South (if necessary, on South Korean conditions) will bring them living standards roughly like those of the present-day South Korean middle class. The North Korean elite will be held responsible for the sorry state of affairs in the present-day North. It does not help that this elite is semi-hereditary in nature, so even younger elite members, having received and kept their privileged positions as children of the people responsible for earlier policies, will have even greater trouble in denouncing what their fathers have done. As argued above, a sorry fate likely awaits North Korea's rich and powerful in the absence of strict political control. Therefore, there is nothing "paranoid" about their efforts to keep the country's populace as ignorant about the outside world as possible, even if such efforts frequently create obstacles for the country's economic growth.[32]

In August 2016, the *Rodong Sinmun* characteristically fumed: "Under the army-first revolutionary leadership of the great general, we have annihilated the schemes of the imperialists who try to lure us into 'reforms' and 'openness' in order to infect us with the reactionary bourgeoisie liberal ideas."[33] In May 2020, the North Korean government's mouthpiece repeated the warning: "The imperialists' propaganda talk about reforms and openness is aimed at making us change our course and destroy our socialist system."[34] These statements are abundant in the North Korean press.

Nonetheless, as part of the *byungjin* policy formulated and implemented during the 2012–2017 period, Kim Jong-un's government implemented a pro-market reformist policy that gave it some chance of achieving economic growth without seriously jeopardizing political stability. The key to working out this policy was the realization that the Chinese policy of openness and reform actually consists of two interconnected but distinct components, which can therefore be disentangled. China, and for that matter Vietnam, exercised a policy of reforms and openness, but Kim Jong-un and his advisors designed a strategy that can be described as "reforms without openness policy." This policy became part of the *byungjin* line package.

The reforms without openness policy implied the introduction of market-oriented economic reforms remarkably similar to the reforms conducted in China in the 1980s. However, unlike in China, these reforms were not accompanied by the increase of openness to the outside world or any kind of political liberalization in North Korea. If anything, Kim Jong-un's government, while relaxing its control over the economy, was tightening its control over society.

The reforms initiated by Kim Jong-un were not unique: similar attempts were undertaken in 2002–2005 by his father. Nonetheless, Kim chose to continue the policy his father initially tested but subsequently discarded. To a very large extent the reform plan was patterned after China. Not incidentally, in the first years of Kim's rule, groups of North Korean experts were dispatched to major Chinese universities where they quietly studied the experience of the early Chinese reforms.

FOUR COMPONENTS OF KIM JONG-UN'S REFORMS

Agricultural Reform

In 2012, Kim issued a set of instructions that envisioned a transformation of North Korea's agricultural management policies.

According to the new system, farmers were supposed to work in small teams (*punjo*), each consisting of five to six members—a significant departure from the past when similar teams had at least twice as many members. Additionally, work teams were allocated certain fields that they would till for years into the future. Under the new system, farmers were allowed to keep what was left after they surrendered the required "plan" amount to the state. The required allocations to the state were revised downward.[35]

At the time, these measures resembled a disguised switch to the household responsibility system and, indeed, some families reportedly registered themselves as a work team.[36] However, this practice was soon found too radical and banned. Nonetheless, the new system dramatically increased incentives and resulted in a noticeable improvement in the food situation.

Industrial Management Reform

In May 2014, Kim Jong-un at a meeting with his top economic managers officially introduced the new system of industrial management known as the

"5.30 measures." After some delay and local experimentation, the industry began to switch to a new model known as the "socialist enterprise management responsibility system."

As the name implies, the new policy provided industrial managers with a great deal of autonomy. Among other things, they were allowed to purchase raw materials and components at negotiated quasi-market prices—on top of what was still provided by the state. Part of what they produced had to be shipped to the state per the plan, while the rest could be sold at negotiated prices to customers of their choice. The system resembled the "dual price" system China used in the early stages of its reforms.[37]

Managers were also allowed to adjust their workers' pay according to their efficiency and skills. They also gained some freedom of hiring and firing their personnel. Some enterprises saw a dramatic increase in wages.[38]

Foreign Trade Reform

Restrictions on enterprises' foreign trade activities were significantly relaxed. Other efforts aimed to create a network of special economic zones (SEZ). Building on earlier attempts to establish SEZs to attract foreign capital, Kim Jong-un decided to increase the SEZ numbers dramatically; by 2015, the country had twenty-five SEZs.[39] Kim also promoted some major tourist projects in an ill-conceived attempt to transform his country into a major tourist destination.[40]

New Policy Toward Private Economic Activities

The revival and growth of markets and private economic activity have been the single most important factor in the North Korean economy since the mid-1990s. However, the official stance on markets has vacillated between benevolent neglect and suppression.

In the first years of his rule, Kim Jong-un generally held a positive attitude toward markets and private businesses. North Korean market operators and private businesspeople (known as *donju* or "masters of money") were no longer subject to ongoing harassment and were essentially left alone.

Using satellite imagery, Curtis Melvin located 406 permanent markets operational in North Korea by late 2015, whereas in 2010 just before the death of Kim Jong-il, the country had only 200 markets. The number of markets doubled during the first five years of Kim Jong-un's rule. Because markets are major hubs of the private economy, their number serves as a good indicator of the private economy scale.[41]

Cooperation between official government agencies and private market forces was also encouraged, and the revised Enterprise Law (2015) even included an explicit reference to the right of state-owned enterprises to use private funds, euphemistically referred to as "the unused cash of residents."[42] In the construction industry, for example, state agencies were expected to actively search for private investors—then, when houses were sold, money from the sales was used to reward investors who supported the projects.[43]

The reforms, which ended abruptly during the nuclear crisis of 2017–2018, initially produced positive results. Bank of Korea, South Korea's central bank, estimated that North Korea's GDP from 2012 to 2016 fluctuated between 1.0 percent and 3.9 percent growth, even though it shrank in 2015.[44] The Bank of Korea estimates shown in figure 1.1 are often believed to be excessively conservative. Observers and Pyongyang-based diplomats, including economic analysts and officials from key embassies, privately told the author that they suspected the country's actual annual growth rate being at least 3–4 percent or perhaps even higher.

However, as mentioned above, Kim Jong-un's reforms-without-openness policy did not imply that all these changes in the economic strategies would be accompanied by the relaxation of domestic political control. To the contrary, starting from the first years of his rule, the new North Korean leader was working hard to repair the walls that surrounded his domain. This was necessary since Kim Jong-il in his later years did not pay much attention to the mundane affairs of the state.

To start, Kim Jong-un increased control over North Korea's border with China. Starting from the late 1980s, many North Koreans entered the porous

Figure 1.1. North Korean GDP growth between 2011 and 2020. Source: Bank of Korea. Note: Percentage of North Korea's GDP growth per year.

and poorly protected border between North Korea and China in search of food and work. Around 2000, the number of illegal migrants may have reached or even exceeded 100,000.[45] Most were economic migrants who, having crossed the border illegally, spent some time working in China and then returned home, bringing not only Chinese yuan, but also dangerous knowledge about the outside world.[46] From the beginning of his rule, Kim Jong-un was determined to reduce this cross-border movement. Under North Korean pressure, the Chinese authorities built fences and installed CCTV equipment along the entire length of the border between 2011 and 2013.[47] Campaigns targeting illegal North Korean migrants hiding and working in China also increased in frequency and intensity.[48] These efforts resulted in a significant decrease in the number of North Koreans crossing the border.

Simultaneously, Kim Jong-un took measures against the spread of South Korean pop culture inside North Korea. Starting in the early 2000s, North Korea experienced its version of the "Korean wave." Videotapes and DVDs with recordings of foreign—especially South Korean—movies, music clips, and TV dramas were smuggled and widely copied inside North Korea.[49] It was estimated that in 2009 the penetration rate was 21 percent and 5 percent for VCD and DVD players, respectively.[50]

Technically, the sale, purchase, possession, and use of such video materials, as well as foreign publications, constituted a crime under the 2009 Criminal Code's Article 193 ("Importing, Keeping and Distributing Decadent Culture") and Article 195 ("Listening to Hostile Broadcasting and Collecting, Keeping or Distributing Enemy Propaganda").[51] These restrictions, while systematically and efficiently enforced under Kim Il-sung's rule before 1994, came to be enforced quite sporadically under Kim Jong-il, especially in the early 2000s. Kim Jong-un, however, abandoned this lenient attitude. From around 2013–2014, continuous campaigns targeted smugglers, producers, and retailers who dealt in ideologically subversive content. Everything related to South Korea and showing present-day South Korean life was seen as ideologically subversive by default since it easily demonstrated the massively superior living standards enjoyed by the Southerners.[52]

There were also remarkable efforts aimed at establishing control over the local digital landscape. North Korean computers are required to be formally registered and run on a Linux-based Red Star Operating System (OS). This OS includes applications that track users' activity and prevent the opening of media files that do not have an electronic signature issued by authorities. In other words, the Red Star OS computers cannot be used to access foreign movies or texts. Households with registered computers are subject to random checks by the police.[53]

So the *byungjin* policy, as envisioned and implemented by Kim Jong-un and his advisers in 2012–2017, rested on two pillars. The military buildup, with special emphasis on the nuclear and missile program, ensured that any foreign attack and/or foreign intervention would become prohibitively risky and costly for outside players. Attempts to develop the economy without relaxing the surveillance/repression system helped keep the populace happy and reduced chances for domestic discontent.

The *byungjin* policy can be seen as a modest success. As mentioned above, economic growth resumed. The popular mood is much more difficult to judge, but it is remarkable that throughout Kim Jong-un's rule no news about internal riots have reached the outside world—even though such news did occasionally emerge under his father. It should be left to future historians, of course, to judge whether this quietness reflects great satisfaction due to economic improvement, or greater fear due to more efficient surveillance.

THE TRUMP ADMINISTRATION, COVID-19 OUTBREAK, AND RISING SINO-U.S. RIVALRY

A combination of unexpected challenges and opportunities throughout the Trump administration and the outbreak of a global pandemic interrupted the implementation of the *byungjin* policy beginning in 2017. These developments necessitated adjustments to the policy and raised questions about its sustainability.

In 2017 a new round of the nuclear crisis erupted in Korea. For a short time, a military conflict—perhaps, provoked by a US preemptive strike against North Korean nuclear facilities—appeared to be a real possibility. For now, it is impossible to say whether Trump was bluffing or truly planned to resort to the use of force when he made his "fire and fury" comments and other similar pronouncements. At any rate, nothing happened. Diplomatic maneuvers of both the North and South including Kim Jong-un's 2018 summit diplomacy outreach to South Korea, China, the United States, and Russia seemingly prevented a confrontation, but North Korea found itself under heavy UN Security Council (UNSC) sanctions, far exceeding anything Pyongyang had experienced before.

Following a series of successful missile tests and in response to rising international pressure, Kim successfully utilized the offer to participate in the 2018 Pyeongchang Olympics as a platform for a series of summits with Xi Jinping, Moon Jae-in, and Donald Trump during the first half of 2018. Kim's summitry eased prospects for military confrontation, raised Kim's international profile, and sought to ease UN sanctions on the regime.

But Kim's second summit with Trump in Hanoi did not deliver the desired sanctions relief. Instead, it became clear that for the foreseeable future North Korea would remain under the exceptionally harsh UNSC sanctions regime, which prevents almost any kind of regular economic interaction with the outside world.

The outbreak of COVID-19 in early 2020 further contributed to the sense of emergency. Amid the pandemic, the North Korean government introduced several measures that can only be interpreted as attempts to roll back market-oriented reforms. The general trend is centralization, restoration of government control over the economy, and undermining private economic activities. The virtues of mass mobilizations are loudly extolled once more.[54]

It's possible that this backlash will not last. After all, we have seen similar attempts to return the genie of marketization to the bottle—most remarkably in 2005–2007, when North Korea pursued economic retrenchment and recentralization following a period of economic liberalization under Kim Jong-il.[55] All these attempts ended in failure. However, one cannot be sure, since the 2017–2020 period was also marked by another important, and arguably lasting, strategic change—the outbreak of the Sino-U.S. confrontation. It is possible that this external change has marked the end of the *byungjin* line in its 2013 incarnation.

From the North Korean point of view, the impact of the confrontation between China and the United States is mixed. But on balance, Kim Jong-un and his government have good reason to welcome it—at least, in the short run.

The Chinese attitude toward North Korea has always been ambivalent. To quote Zhu Feng and Nathan Beauchamp-Mustafaga, two foremost specialists on the issue, "Although Chinese and North Korean leaders routinely couch their pronouncements on the nature of their bilateral relationship in terms of their long-standing friendship, such rhetoric betrays the reality that China–North Korea relations have always been neither very strong nor even friendly."[56]

The Chinese government has never been happy about North Korea's nuclear ambitions. In the long run, the North Korean nuclear program undermines the exclusive privileges enjoyed by countries recognized officially as nuclear powers by the 1968 Non-Proliferation Treaty. As one such country, China will not welcome actions that undermine its uniquely privileged position and, in the worst-case scenario, might trigger a nuclear arms race in East and Southeast Asia.[57] However, from the Chinese point of view, North Korea also has a large and lasting value as a strategic buffer zone between the Chinese border and the US forces stationed in South Korea and Japan. China might be unhappy about North Korea's domestic and foreign policies and annoyed by its habitual brinksmanship diplomacy, but at the end of the day, it needs stability and, ideally, continued status quo in Korea. China would like to see a nonnuclear North Korea, but it is much more important for China to deal with a stable and divided Korean Peninsula whose northern part is controlled by a government that, however problematic from Beijing's point of view, is not openly hostile to China and does not let its territory be used for stationing the armed forces of China's rivals (the "strategic buffer" view is often debated but largely prevalent inside China).[58] Such an ambivalent attitude to North Korea has persisted in China for decades. But with the beginning of the Sino-US confrontation in 2017–2018, calculations in Beijing seemingly changed. As recently as late 2017, China was still willing to support US efforts to impose maximum economic pressure on North Korea. One should not forget that the tough 2017 UNSC resolutions would never have been passed without support from Chinese diplomats.[59]

However, things changed soon afterward. In the context of an intense and presumably long-lasting confrontation with the United States, China requires a stable buffer zone more than ever. China now has more of a reason to provide North Korea with basic aid, including both food and other supplies, to reduce the chance of a domestic crisis. China will likely not attach too many conditions to such aid and will accept North Korea as it is. One also can be sure that China will ignore the UNSC resolutions if it can do so without attracting too much attention to such infringements.

Chinese aid will not be generous because China has no reason to indirectly subsidize North Korea's nuclear ambitions and is not interested in bringing about a major economic boom in Pyongyang (an economically successful North Korea would be even more difficult to control). However, China has reasons to worry about a possible outbreak of famine in North Korea—not so much due to humanitarian concerns, but largely because such an outbreak might be destabilizing and could lead to chaos or, even worse, dreaded unification by absorption followed by the emergence of a unified Korean state that is democratic, nationalistic, and probably pro-American. This is something China would like to avoid, especially now, during ongoing Sino-US confrontation.

Therefore, in the current situation, the North Korean government is aware that it can count on some subsistence level support from China. From the point of view of the North Korean government, this access to Chinese interstate "welfare benefits" seriously reduces the perceived need to further advance economic reforms. Economic reforms were initially launched to generate some growth and to ensure that no new famine would strike North Korea. However, in the current situation, Chinese aid appears to be a safer option and the UNSC sanctions regime makes economic success impossible anyway.

For China, providing North Korea with such aid is not particularly burdensome. It can be estimated that the total amount of assistance needed to keep North Korea afloat amounts to $1–$2 billion a year. This is a trivial sum for China, especially considering the long-term strategic benefits such an investment will produce.

CONCLUSION

The *byungjin* policy, as conceived by Kim Jong-un and his advisers in the early 2010s, was a rational strategy designed to ensure the continued survival of the North Korean regime. This survival is the main and overriding goal of all North Korean strategies, which have to be judged against this benchmark alone. Survival is, understandably, the top priority.

The *byungjin* policy consisted of two elements: the development of a nuclear deterrent and the development of the economy in ways that do not contribute to an increase in social instability. This policy has worked and brought some results—including the abovementioned economic growth and noticeable improvement of living standards, particularly in larger cities. However, drastic changes in the geopolitical situation in the region that began in 2017 might spell an end for the *byungjin* policy as it has been known in the first decade of Kim Jong-un's rule.

To be more precise, the military component will remain. North Korea's willingness to develop and maintain a nuclear force is the constant, not the variable, in all calculations related to North Korea's policy. No matter how much pressure outside players, including China, exercise on North Korea, the North Korean government will maintain and further improve its nuclear and missile capabilities. Some compromises are possible: bowing to Chinese pressure, North Korea might agree to slow down and/or refrain from open provocations such as nuclear tests and ICBM launches.

North Korean leaders understand that China might be unhappy about missile engineers and rocket scientists working 24/7 in North Korean laboratories. However, in the current situation, China will not see this as a sufficient reason to stop or even significantly reduce its basic support to Pyongyang. Actually, as earlier experience demonstrated, China has only a limited number of tools at its disposal when it comes to influencing North Korea's nuclear and missile policy since, as Nicholas Khoo observed, "Pyongyang is willing to run extreme costs, including incurring Beijing's ire, to ensure that its nuclear weapons program remains viable."[60] At best, China can use its new economic leverage only to restrain Pyongyang from more provocative actions—the Chinese position might be the reason why North Korea will not test nuclear devices for some time.

On the other hand, another part of the *byungjin* package—its "reforms without openness" policy—is now seemingly under great threat. This part of Kim Jong-un's initial policy package has probably outlived its usefulness.

Reforms without openness, despite being cautious, is still inherently risky. Market-oriented reforms make the North Korean populace increasingly independent of the government and, hence, potentially, more difficult to control.

It's probably not what Kim Jong-un would like to see in his ideal world. Until 2017–2018, he saw such a risk as an acceptable cost to ward off far greater risks of instability being provoked by the economic hardship. However, with China now ready to provide North Korea with aid, the need to take politically risky reforms has diminished, so it probably makes sense to try to freeze the situation and return as much as possible to the state-controlled economy of the old Leninist type.

In a sense, the "Cold War 2.0" gives North Korea the chance to return to the situation it enjoyed during the "first" Cold War of 1945–1991. Back then North Korea knew it could rely on a steady flow of aid from overseas, provided with few conditions to, above all, ensure its domestic stability. This Soviet, Chinese, and East European aid allowed Pyongyang to maintain an economically inefficient but stable system that ensured the elite would stay in power for decades to come. It seems that we might be returning to a similar arrangement.

NOTES

1. George McCune, *Korea* (Cambridge, MA: Harvard University Press, 1950), 56–57.

2. Myung Soo Cha and Nak Nyeon Kim, "Korea's First Industrial Revolution, 1911–1940," *Explorations in Economic History* 49, no. 1 (2012): 73.

3. *DPRK Voluntary National Review on the Implementation of the 2030 Agenda for Sustainable Development.* Pyongyang: Government of the DPRK, June 2021, https://sustainabledevelopment.un.org/content/documents/282482021_VNR_Report_DPRK.pdf.

4. "GDP per Capita (Current US$)—Korea, Republic," World Bank Group, https://data.worldbank.org/indicator/NY.GDP.PCAP.CD?locations=KR.

5. Barry Gills, *Korea Versus Korea: A Case of Contested Legitimacy* (London: Routledge, 1996).

6. *The Economic Integration of East Germany*, Halle Institute for Economic Research (IWH), November 2016, 40.

7. Lawrence King and Ivan Szelenyi, "Post-Communist Economic Systems," in *Handbook of Economic Sociology*, ed. Neil Smelser and Richard Swedberg (Princeton, NJ: Princeton University Press, 2005), 205–29.

8. Zhelyu Zhelev, "Is Communism Returning?," in *The Revolutions of 1989*, ed. Vladimir Tismaneanu (London: Routledge, 1999), 254.

9. Robert Collins, *Pyongyang Republic* (Washington, DC: Committee for Human Rights in North Korea, 2016), 4, 31.

10. John Mearsheimer, *The Tragedy of Great Power Politics* (New York: W.W. Norton & Company, 2001), 46.

11. Mearsheimer, 31.

12. Kim Seong-joo, "Analysis on the Contents and Changes in Logical Structure of Line of Simultaneous Economic and Defense Build-ups (Byoungjin Line)" [북한 병진노선의 내용 및 논리구조 변화 분석], *Quarterly Journal of Defense Policy Studies* 32, no. 2 (2016).

13. Jeon Seong-hun, "Kim Jong-un's Byungjin Policy of Simultaneous Nuclear and Economic Development and 'April 1 Declaration of Nuclear Status'" [김정은 정권의 경제핵무력 병진노선과 "4.1 핵보유 법령"], Korea Institute of the National Unification, 2013.

14. Joshua Kirschenbaum, "Operation Opera: An Ambiguous Success," *Journal of Strategic Security* 3, no. 4 (2010): 49–62.

15. International Atomic Energy Agency, "Implementation of the NPT Safeguards Agreement of the Socialist People's Libyan Arab Jamahiriya," GOV/2004/27, https://nuke.fas.org/guide/libya/iaea0504.pdf.

16. John Bolton, "Lessons from Libya and North Korea's Strategic Choice," Speech at Yonsei University, July 21, 2004, https://2001-2009.state.gov/t/us/rm/34675.htm.

17. Ramazan Erdağ, *Libya in the Arab Spring: From Revolution to Insecurity* (New York: Palgrave Macmillan, 2017), 30–32; Frederic Wehrey, "NATO's Intervention," in *The Libyan Revolution and Its Aftermath*, ed. Peter Cole and Brian McQuinn (New York: Oxford University Press, 2015), 105–26.

18. Wehrey, "NATO's Intervention," 105.

19. "Foreign Ministry Spokesman Denounces U.S. Military Attack on Libya," *KCNA Report*, March 22, 2011.

20. Han S. Park, "Military-First Politics (Songun): Understanding Kim Jong-il's North Korea," *Korea Economic Institute Academic Paper Series* 2, no. 7 (2007): 5.

21. David Yost, "The Budapest Memorandum and Russia's Intervention in Ukraine," *International Affairs* 91, no. 3 (2015): 505–38.

22. Kenneth Waltz, "The Spread of Nuclear Weapons: More May Be Better," *Adelphi Papers*, no. 171 (London: International Institute for Strategic Studies, 1981): 7–8.

23. Bruce W. Bennett, Kang Choi, Myong-Hyun Go, Bruce E. Bechtol, Jiyoung Park, Bruce Klingner, and Du-Hyeogn Cha, *Countering the Risks of North Korean Nuclear Weapons* (Santa Monica, CA: RAND Corporation, 2021), 27–28.

24. Matthew McGrath and Daniel Wertz, *North Korea's Ballistic Missile Program* (Washington, DC: The National Committee on North Korea, 2013), 2–4, 9.

25. McGrath and Wertz, 30.

26. Terence Roehrig, "North Korea's Nuclear Weapons Program: Motivations, Strategy, and Doctrine," in *Strategy in the Second Nuclear Age*, ed. Toshi Yoshihara and James Holmes (Washington, DC: Georgetown University Press, 2012). 96.

27. Roehrig, 94.

28. Arthur Kroeber, *China's Economy* (New York: Oxford University Press, 2016), 86.

29. On the generally supportive attitude of the populace to the current policies, see: Matteo Migheli, "Supporting the Free and Competitive Market in China and India: Differences and Evolution Over Time," *Economic Systems* 34, no.1 (2010): 73–90; Matteo Migheli, "Do the Vietnamese Support the Economic Doi Moi?," *Journal of Development Studies* 48, no. 7 (July 2012): 939–68.

30. Kang Dong-wan and Park Jung Ran, *Hallyu: The Wind of Unification* [한.류: 통일의 바람] (Seoul: Myungin Books), 70–71, 173–77.

31. Martyn Williams, *Digital Trenches: North Korea's Information Counter-Offensive*, (Washington, DC: Committee for Human Rights in North Korea, 2019).

32. Nat Kretchun, "The Need for a New US Information Strategy for North Korea," *United States Institute of Peace Special Report* No. 451, June 2019, https://www.usip.org/sites/default/files/2019-07/sr_451-the_need_for_a_new_u.s._information_strategy_for_north_korea.pdf.

33. Hwang Shin-ryul, "The External Exploits of Establishing a Basis for Completing the Great Deed of Juche under the Banner of Songun" [선군의 기치높이 주체혁명위업완성의 근본담보를 마련하신 불멸의 업적], *Rodong Sinmun*, August 25, 2016, http://www.uriminzokkiri.com/index.php?ptype=cgisas&mtype=view&no=1196893.

34. Han Un-il, "Victory of Socialism Lies in Living and Fighting Our Own Way" [우리 식대로 살며 투쟁하는데 사회주의승리가 있다], *Rodong Sinmun*, May 20, 2020, https://kcnawatch.org/newstream/1588625418-960933186/우리-식대로-살며-투쟁하는데-사회주의승리가-있다/.

35. Han Ki-beom, *North Korea's Economic Reform and Bureaucratic Politics* [북한의 경제개혁과 관료정치] (Seoul: North Korea Research Institute, 2019), 251–56.

36. Moon-Soo Yang, *The Economic Reform of North Korea in the Kim Jong-un Era: Status and Evaluation*, KDI Working Paper (Seoul: Korea Development Institute, 2021), 8–9.

37. Han, *North Korea's Economic Reform and Bureaucratic Politics*, 271–79.

38. Jeong Chang-heong, "Wages of North Korean Workers Reportedly Increased by One Hundredfold" [북한 노동자들의 월급이 100배 인상됐다는데], *Tongil News*, December 2, 2013, http://www.tongilnews.com/news/articleView.html?idxno=105155.

39. Yim Eul-chul, "Kim Jung-un Regime's Economic Development Zone Policy: Characteristics, Assessments, and Prospect" [김정은 시대의 경제개발구 정책: 특징, 평가 및 전망], *Journal of Northeast Asian Economic Studies* 27, no. 3 (2015), 211–12.

40. Dean Ouellette, "The Tourism of North Korea in the Kim Jong-un Era: Propaganda, Profitmaking, and Possibilities for Engagement," *Pacific Focus* 31, no. 3 (2016): 421–51.

41. "Markets Burgeon in N. Korea," *Chosun Ilbo*, October 26, 2015, http://english.chosun.com/site/data/html_dir/2015/10/26/2015102601722.html.

42. Peter Ward, "Market Reforms with North Korean Characteristics: Loosening the Grip on State-Owned Enterprises," *38 North*, December 21, 2017, https://www.38north.org/2017/12/pward122117/.

43. Joung Eun-lee, "Analysis on Change of Property and Development in North Korea" [북한 부동산 개발업자의 등장과 함의에 관한 분석], *KDI Review of North Korean Economy*, no. 9 (2016), 80.

44. "Gross Domestic Product Estimates for North Korea in 2016," *Bank of Korea*, July 13, 2017.

45. Andrei Lankov, "North Korean Refugees in Northeast China," *Asian Survey* 44, no. 6 (2004): 859–60.

46. Kang Dong-wan, "The Status of North Koreans' Access to Foreign Culture and Policy Measures from the Standpoint of North Koreans living in China" [중국 체류 북한 주민을 통해서 본 외래문화 접촉실태와 정책방안], *Journal of Political Science and Communication* 24, no. 1 (February 2021), 41–72.

47. Choi Song Min, "China Electrifying Border Fencing," *DailyNK*, October 11, 2012, https://www.dailynk.com/english/china-electrifying-border-fencing; Seulkee Jang, "China Intensifies Security Along Sino-North Korean Border," *DailyNK*, July 19, 2019, https://www.dailynk.com/english/china-intensifies-security-along-sino-north-korean-border.

48. *2019 World Report* (New York: Human Rights Watch, 2019), 441.

49. Kang Dong-wan, "A Study on the Introduction of Foreign Culture into North Korea and Changes to the North Korean Society: With an Interview Survey with North Koreans in a Third Country" [북한으로의 외래문화 유입 현황과 실태: 제3국에서의 북한주민 면접조사를 중심으로], *Institute of Humanities for Unification* 60 (December 2014), 167–202.

50. *International Broadcasting in North Korea: North Korean Refugee/Traveler Survey Report. April–August 2009* (Washington, DC: InterMedia, 2009).

51. Williams, *Digital Trenches*, 3–4.

52. *Connection Denied: Restrictions on Mobile Phones and Outside Information in North Korea*, (London: Amnesty International, 2016).

53. *Connection Denied*, 34–37.

54. Peter Ward, "North Korea Continues to Claw Back Control from the Private Economy," *NK News Pro*, May 17, 2021, https://www.nknews.org/pro/north-korea-continues-to-claw-back-control-from-the-private-economy/; Peter Ward, "Kim Jong Un's Battle with Teen Spirit, Foreign Media and Bureaucracy Goes Public," *NK News Pro*, May 4, 2021, https://www.nknews.org/pro/kim-jong-uns-battle-with-teen-spirit-foreign-media-and-bureaucracy-goes-public/.

55. Andrei Lankov, "Pyongyang Strikes Back: North Korean Policies of 2002–08 and Attempts to Reverse 'De-Stalinization from Below,'" *Asia Policy* 8, no. 1 (2009): 47–72.

56. Zhu Feng and Nathan Beauchamp-Mustafaga, "North Korea's Security Implications for China," in *China and North Korea: Strategic and Policy Perspectives from a Changing China*, ed. Carla P. Freeman (New York: Palgrave Macmillan, 2015), 37–38.

57. Nicholas Khoo, "Retooling Great Power Nonproliferation Theory: Explaining China's North Korea Nuclear Weapons Policy," *Pacific Review* 34, no. 4 (2019): 523–46.

58. Feng and Beauchamp-Mustafaga, "North Korea's Security Implications for China," 44; Xiangfeng Yang, "Disenchanted Entanglement: The North Korean Shades of Grey on the Chinese Mind," *Journal of Contemporary China* 29, no. 123 (2019): 462–67.

59. Khoo, "Retooling Great Power Nonproliferation Theory," 531–32.

60. Khoo, "Retooling Great Power Nonproliferation Theory," 538.

Chapter 2

North Korea's Economic Development Strategy under Kim Jong-un*

Kim Byung-yeon

Just over ten years have passed since Kim Jong-un became the leader of North Korea in his late twenties. Despite initial expectations for possible instability in North Korea, Kim has proved a politically competent leader capable of maintaining a fairly stable regime. Like any authoritarian dictator, his political objective is to maintain long-term power. Strong military and economic power are critical to this end. What strategies has Kim pursued to maximize the longevity of his power? One thing is already clear. Kim wants North Korea to be a nuclear-weapon state formally recognized by other countries including the United States. Nuclear weapons have been perceived as an economical and effective way for the North to not only claim the high ground against South Korea in terms of military strength but also to deter military attacks from countries like the United States. By contrast, Kim's economic development strategy is less clear. His first public speech in April 2012 indicated that he sought to cultivate a rapidly growing socialist economy, promising "people will never have to tighten their belt again." How did Kim plan to do this? Did he consider economic reforms such as China's reform and open-door policy (改革開放)? Or did he plan to take measures to improve North Korea's economic performance under socialist economic principles? Were his remarks instead mere political rhetoric without economic substance? To this day, debate about Kim's economic development strategy continues among scholars and pundits.[1]

Kim Jong-un's economic policies from 2012 to 2018 can be characterized as prioritizing market-led growth within socialism. Maintaining state ownership of the means of production as a principle, these policies sought to take advantage of the capabilities and resources already embedded in North Korean markets. However, the North Korean authorities appear to have stopped this 'pragmatic' socialism after the implementation of economic sanctions adopted by the United Nations Security Council (UNSC) in 2016–2017 in response to North Korea's tests of nuclear weapons and intercontinental ballistic missiles (ICBMs). Moreover, restrictions on market activities, which had been implicitly encouraged by the pragmatic approach, have been tightened during the COVID-19 pandemic. It is not yet clear whether this change represents a retreat or a reversal from such pragmatic socialism. Having said that, the recent evolution in North Korean economic policy appears consistent with Kim's initial aim not to abandon socialism but to improve the economy with some combination of markets and the state. However, the experiences of economic adjustments like market socialism in former socialist economies suggest that such an attempt will not result in better economic performance than the traditional socialism employed by the Soviet Union and the other East European countries.

This chapter analyzes North Korea's economic development strategy under Kim Jong-un. To understand the nature of this strategy, I first evaluate the contents of economic policies implemented in North Korea from 2012 to 2018, comparing them with those from Kim Jong-un's father Kim Jong-il's era and with those of former socialist economies including China, Eastern Europe, and the Soviet Union. I then consider the self-reliant economic policies emphasized more strongly after 2019 and evaluate the goals and effects of banning foreign trade and restricting market activities as a response to the COVID-19 pandemic. Here I address the question of whether this change represented a retreat or a reversal in North Korean economic policy. I use the North Korean newspaper *Rodong Shinmun* and economic journal *Kyungjeyeongu* to identify any changes in media emphasis on economic policies and development strategies. I turn to interviews with North Korean defectors who formerly worked either in the North Korean government or in foreign trade to complement these findings.

KIM JONG-UN'S ECONOMIC POLICIES, PERFORMANCE, AND LIMITATIONS, 2012–2018

As a young leader, Kim Jong-un has put more emphasis on economic development than his father; the lifetime return on economic growth for Kim Jong-un's maintenance of power is naturally much higher than that of Kim Jong-il, who did not come into power until his fifties. When Kim Jong-un assumed the mantle of leadership, he may have recognized that although ideological discipline could suppress public dissatisfaction with the regime in the short run, it would not do so in the long run. He may also have identified poor economic performance as a major cause of public discontent in North Korea. Moreover, Kim observed the backlash to poorly designed currency reform in 2009, which stipulated the exchange of old and new North Korean won but then limited that exchange, forcing market closures. The 2009 currency reform was interpreted as an attempt to reverse marketization, reflecting Kim Jong-il's 2008 statement that markets are "the residing place of anti-socialism and the stronghold of capitalism."[2] However, the reform ended in disaster. Given the resultant economic chaos and outpouring of complaints from the public, firms, and institutions that relied on markets for their survival, the North Korean authorities made a public apology, reopened markets, and shot a high-ranking government official scapegoated as responsible for the currency reform.[3] This defeat of the government by the markets may have left a lasting impression on Kim Jong-un.

Realizing that reversal to a Stalinist economy was infeasible at least for the time being, Kim had three options to choose from. The first option was preservation of the status quo, and passive acceptance of "marketization from below." The second potential strategy was to employ the functions and resources of markets to catalyze economic growth without institutionalizing them. The third possibility was to gradually transform the economic system from socialism to capitalism, taking into account the risks inherent in a shock-therapy approach. Among these three options, preservation of the status quo would likely have failed to improve entrenched economic difficulties and thus not served Kim's political purpose. Transition to a market economy may have undermined Kim Jong-un's power despite prospects for better economic performance. Kim's subsequent economic policies indicate his preference for the second option, the use of markets without institutionalization.

Kim's economic development strategy, "market-led growth within socialism" or "pragmatic socialism," likely emerged from these economic and political considerations.[4] He understood that markets should not be repressed but used to boost the official socialist economy. At the same time, he sidestepped legal recognition of markets in the form of constitutional amendments to avoid interpretation by foreign and domestic audiences of his reforms as a desertion of socialism in favor of a market economy.

Kim Jong-un's Reforms in Agriculture and Enterprises

Kim implemented two significant reforms to exploit the effects of market incentives for the economy. First, he introduced agricultural reforms called the "field responsibility system" in 2013. *Field* (圃田) denoted a small piece of cultivated land, and *responsibility* referred to a system in which households, rather than collective farms, took charge of managing these parcels of land. The sub-team management system, in which a small number of households belonging to a collective farm worked the same field, was an earlier effort to decrease the number of households jointly working land. Although the sub-team management system was first introduced in the 1960s, it was Kim Jong-il in the 1990s who put more emphasis on its importance in boosting agricultural production. The field responsibility system appeared to further reduce the number of households working the same field, although it is unclear whether a single household or a few households currently work together.

Kim also introduced a similarly spirited reform, called "responsibility management system of socialist enterprise," in the enterprise sector in 2014. It was designed to facilitate decentralization and self-accounting of state-owned enterprises (SOEs). The reform apparently aimed to boost the production of SOEs by using incentives driven by markets and financial resources held by the public. There were two main policies in this enterprise reform. First, central planning was loosened.[5] Instead of imposing central planning on SOEs, the North Korean authorities sought to import market dynamism into SOEs by allowing individual contracts between SOEs; they were now allowed to set indicators of production based on this "order contract system" themselves.[6] Following the reforms, SOEs aimed to achieve an indicator comprised of targets set by both enterprises and central planners. The relative importance of these two targets differs according to the types of SOEs: central planning is dominant for larger and strategically important SOEs, while smaller SOEs may put more emphasis on enterprise planning.

Announced on May 30, 2014, these reforms were reflected in the 2015 revised Law on Planning of the National Economy. A comparison of the 2010 revised version of the law with the 2015 version indicates significant differences in the allocation of production. Previously, the law made no mention of enterprise indicators or order contracts, but the 2015 revisions introduced this language in Article 13 and 18, respectively. The backbone of the law, however, remained the same. The principles of state ownership and planned economy were preserved in Article 2: "The economy of Democratic People's Republic of Korea is a planned economy based on socialist ownership of means of production."

Second, the reform attempted to mobilize household financial resources in service of the economy. The revised 2015 Law on State Enterprises granted SOEs permission to receive bank loans and use idle financial resources held by the public to fill resource gaps. North Korea's decision to allow the use of resources held by the public for enterprise management indicates that a shortage of working capital had impeded enterprise production. The North Korean authorities took a practical approach to relax such financial constraints by allowing private capital to flow into SOEs.

These practical agriculture and enterprise reforms likely contributed to some economic growth. North Korea's agricultural production increased from about 4.32 million tons during 2008–2012 to 4.74 million tons during 2013–2016, according to South Korea's Rural Development Administration (as cited by Statistics Korea).[7] Agricultural reforms account in part for this increase in agricultural production. Overall economic conditions had also improved partially due to the enterprise reform. According to Bank of Korea (BOK, South Korea's central bank) estimates, the North Korean economy grew 1.2 percent per year between 2012 and 2016. The annual growth rate during the previous five years, from 2007 to 2011, had instead hovered around 0 percent. However, Byung-Yeon Kim argues that because BOK estimates do not directly include value created in markets, they underestimate North Korean growth during times of market expansion and overestimate it during times of market shrinkage.[8] Using surveys of North Korean defectors settled in South Korea, Kim determined that market economic activities likely increased from 2012 to 2016 and that BOK appeared to have underestimated North Korea's annual growth rate by up to 1.2 percent. In this case, North Korea's annual growth rate from 2012 to 2016 would be 2.4 percent.

Comparison of North Korean Reforms with Those of Other Socialist Economies

North Korea's economic growth from 2012 to 2016 nonetheless is modest in comparison to that of China when it began economic reforms in 1978. During the early period of reform from 1978 to 1985, China's annual growth rate amounted to 10 percent. One of the main reasons for this difference in growth rates between North Korea and China may be the shallowness of North Korean reform. China made fundamental changes in its economic systems ranging from de-collectivization of the agricultural sector to the creation of township village enterprises (TVEs) as non-SOEs and Special Economic Zones. Although reforms were made slowly, they comprehensively addressed nearly all economic sectors and deeply transformed institutions including ownership of property rights and the coordination mechanism from central planning to markets.

By contrast, Kim Jong-un's economic measures were neither comprehensive nor deep. Reform in the Kim Jong-un era was limited in the sense that it was not meant for a transition toward a market economy but a practical compromise between socialist ideals and economic realities, especially considering pervasive marketization in North Korea. The government focused on certain areas such as agriculture and SOEs, and it attempted to enhance economic performance by using market incentives rather than unleashing market forces by institutionalizing them. For example, China institutionally acknowledged TVEs based on non-state ownership, while North Korea only allowed idle capital to flow into SOEs. The former represented a change in property rights from the state to the private sector, while the latter reflected an effort to take advantage of available market resources. The field responsibility system in North Korea sought to divide agricultural production between the state and farmers at a ratio of three to seven. However, the incentives for production activities were much stronger in the Chinese household responsibility system, where farming households were the residual claimants of their remaining products after selling their predetermined volume to the state.[9]

Changes in the Chinese and North Korean constitutions reveal the sharpest contrast in economic development strategies between the two countries. China revised its constitution in 1982 to officially permit private economic activities. Article 11 of China's revised 1982 constitution states that "the individual economy (个体经济) of urban and rural working people, operated within the limits prescribed by law, is a complement to the socialist public economy."[10] In contrast, North Korea's constitution revised in 2019 still does not officially recognize an individual or private economy. Article 24 of North Korea's revised constitution, which relates to individual ownership, limits such ownership to individual consumption, with no provision for the means of production. Unlike China, North Korean authorities still adhere to state and collective ownership without acknowledging private ownership even at the margin.

North Korea's modest reforms appear to reflect the economic objectives of the North Korean authorities. In fact, in major speeches, including the New Year's and Policy speeches since gaining power in late 2011, Kim Jong-un made no mention of markets. In all New Year's speeches since 2013, he instead emphasized the importance of building a self-reliant economy. Even with the change of North Korea's 2013 official policy line from "Nuclear-Economy Parallel Development" to "Concentration on Economic Construction" in April 2018, Kim's 2019 New Year's Speech continued to emphasize self-reliance by calling it a "precious sword for prosperity."[11] The above observation indicates that Kim Jong-un regards markets as an instrument for the self-reliant economy rather than as an intended destination.

Some elements of North Korea's "responsibility management system of socialist enterprise" reforms resemble those of market socialism in Hungary and the Soviet Union. The reform called the New Economic Mechanism (NEM) began in Hungary in 1968, which permitted the socialist sector to coexist with the private sector. For example, an employee working at a bakery was allowed to purchase bread from their official workplace to sell at their private shop in Hungary. Many households held second, mostly private, jobs. Compulsory central planning was abolished in favor of indicative planning meant to guide, rather than instruct, the economy and enterprises. The Soviet Union's New Economic Policy (NEP), instituted from 1921 to 1928, provided an early example of such a mixed economy. Under NEP, small enterprises were privatized, and farmers were allowed to have their own land. In other words, North Korean reforms, along with the market socialism of NEM and NEP, allowed the private sector operating at markets to coexist with the socialist sector. However, there are important distinctions. NEM and NEP abolished central planning and explicitly endorsed private ownership, although it was confined to certain forms such as small firms and individual activities. By contrast, North Korea permitted enterprises to follow some market rules without legalizing privately owned enterprises. In addition, central planning in North Korea was preserved to different degrees depending on the types of enterprises, with requirements for enterprise indicators to be reported to a central planning body with control over the economy. North Korea's economic development strategy of 2012–2018 certainly deviated from the traditional socialism embodied in the Stalinist command economy, but it did not reach the level of market socialism of NEM and NEP.

CHANGES IN ECONOMIC DEVELOPMENT STRATEGY, 2019–2021

Kim Jong-un's strategy of pragmatic socialism faced a serious challenge in the form of sanctions beginning in 2016. In response to his testing of nuclear weapons and ICBMs from 2016 to 2017, the UNSC adopted five resolutions (UNSC Resolutions 2270, 2321, 2371, 2375, and 2379). These new sanctions differed from previous ones (UNSC Resolutions 1718, 1874, 2087, and 2094) in that they aimed to incapacitate the economy, while earlier efforts had focused on preventing the development of weapons of mass destruction. The new resolutions targeted North Korea's foreign trade and activities related to hard currency earnings to economically penalize North Korea's development of nuclear weapons and ICBMs. The United States also enacted laws that provided a legal basis for secondary boycotts against North Korea.

Impact of Sanctions

Sanctions hit the North Korean economy hard. BOK estimates that the annual growth rate of North Korea's economy declined from 3.9 percent in 2016 to -3.5 percent in 2017 and fell to -4.1 percent in 2018.[12] As discussed, these are likely overestimates given the shrinkage of markets after the implementation of the sanctions. Using data from North Korean refugees, Kim

(2020) estimated that the average monthly household income decreased by 25 percent in the post-sanctions period (2017–2019) compared to the pre-sanctions period (2014–2016).[13] Studies using satellite imagery to measure nocturnal luminosity, known to be associated with national income, support this finding. Dawool Kim found that regional nighttime lights in North Korea decreased by 5.4 percent per year, on average, from 2017 to 2019 due to sanctions and that such negative effects were particularly pronounced in regions with more exposure to foreign trade and domestic markets.[14] In another study using nocturnal luminosity data, Jihee Kim et al. claimed that the economic sanctions adopted in 2016–2017 decreased North Korea's manufacturing output by 20 percent.[15]

North Korean authorities initially appeared not to recognize the severity of the sanctions. In his 2017 New Year's Speech, Kim Jong-un maintained that North Korea soared as a nuclear-strong country in East Asia and was set to reach the objectives for national economic development it set in the five-year plan that began in 2016.[16] Although Kim emphasized the localization of materials, energy, and equipment, the tone of his speech was generally optimistic, with Kim claiming victory.[17] However, the tone of Kim's 2018 New Year's Speech was much more sober. Not only did he refer to "self-reliance" more frequently, but Kim also called sanctions "survival-threatening."

Did Kim Jong-un's realization of the effects of the sanctions change his economic development strategy? We used two North Korean sources to investigate whether a shift in economic policy took place between the pre- and the post-sanction period. One is a quarterly North Korean academic journal titled *Economic Research* (*Gyeongje Yeongu*) that contains thirty to forty short articles per issue. The other, *Rodong Shinmun*, is a daily state-run North Korean newspaper published by the Korean Worker's Party. We counted how many titles of articles published by these two sources from 2012 to 2019 referred to self-reliance. The words *localization* (domestic supply of raw materials, equipment, and fuel), *self-reliance, self-empowerment*, and *self-strong* are categorized under the concept of self-reliance.

Figure 2.1 shows a sharp increase in self-reliance language in *Economic Research* and *Rodong Shinmun* during the sanction period. Words related to self-reliance appeared once or twice in the titles of *Economic Research* articles published from 2012 to 2015, four times in 2016, and fourteen times in 2019. A similar trend is observed in *Rodong Shinmun*, with the number of titles on self-reliance rapidly increasing from 2016 and peaking in 2019. This stronger emphasis on self-reliance in 2019 is likely a consequence of the failed Hanoi Summit between US president Donald Trump and Kim Jong-un that took place in February 2019. Realizing that sanctions relief was unlikely for the foreseeable future, Kim Jong-un might have tried to muddle through and thus reiterated the importance of the self-reliant economy.

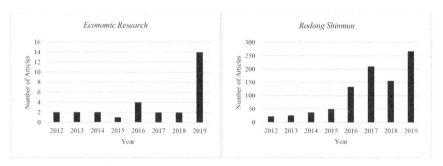

Figure 2.1. Trend of "self-reliant economy" keywords. Source: *Economic Research* **and** *Rodong Shinmun*

Sanctions significantly undermined the feasibility of Kim's market-led growth strategy, as foreign economic activities and domestic markets are closely intertwined. Earnings from exports and workers dispatched to foreign countries produce the demand for goods and services transacted in domestic markets. Imports of raw materials, intermediate goods, and capital equipment are used for domestic production. Similarly, imports of food and consumer goods supply domestic markets. Hence, the negative shock on foreign economic activities produced by economic sanctions likely reduced market activities.[18] This observation corroborates with Byung-Yeon Kim's and Dawool Kim's empirical findings that market activities substantially weakened due to sanctions. Although North Korea had strengthened its military power by testing nuclear weapons and ICBMs, these activities impaired its development strategy using markets as a leverage for growth. Kim's policy of accepting and using markets as sources of incentives and resources weakened in effectiveness due to the economic sanctions, forcing the shift to a focus on self-reliance.

Impact of the COVID-19 Pandemic

The COVID-19 pandemic dealt a further blow to Kim's pragmatic socialism using markets as leverage for economic growth. With North Korea's blockage of foreign trade to prevent the spread of COVID-19 starting in January 2020, its foreign trade—including smuggling—was drastically reduced. Market activities further weakened as a result. Moreover, North Korean authorities forbade travel between regions, causing increasing regional disparities in prices and exchange rates at markets. In some regions, people were ordered to stay at home to prevent the spread of COVID-19, making market activities virtually impossible.

During 2020 and 2021, authorities reportedly intervened in markets directly by banning unregistered individual economic activities and installing state retail shops selling grain.[19] These measures might be used to control infectious disease by reducing human contact at markets. Yet, at the same time, these interventions might have originated with Kim Jong-un's emphasis on the restoration of socialist commerce. Especially, repressing market activities, which can be justified as a COVID-19 prevention measure, provided a good opportunity to strengthen the system of state-led commerce. In a speech at the Eighth Party Congress in January 2021, Kim said that "an important task our commerce needs to solve in this period is to restore the leading and controlling role of the state in all areas of commercial services and to activate the nature of socialist commerce to serve the people." These talking points fall in line with Kim's broader policy orientation toward preserving unified state control over the economy. This shift from pragmatic socialism between 2012 and 2018 to repressing markets between 2019 and the present may be related with his weakened reputation as a competent leader due to the failure to reach an agreement at the Hanoi Summit in 2019. In other words, Kim Jong-un might have felt a need to strengthen the state control over the economy as well as the society to prevent his leadership from being further challenged by increasing marketization.

RETREAT OR REVERSAL?

Kim's emphasis on the self-reliant economy and restriction of market activities from 2019 onward can be interpreted in two ways. First, these efforts can be seen as a temporary retreat from Kim Jong-un's pragmatic socialism from 2012 to 2018. According to this view, sanctions and COVID-19 severely restricted Kim's maneuvering room. Given his objective of maintaining power, Kim sought to consolidate state control over the economy and to concentrate economic resources into the state sector. In addition, he emphasized socialist ideology to prime North Koreans to endure serious economic hardship. In this regard, self-reliance was viewed as a way to instill discipline in North Koreans and signal that Kim would not yield to US pressure. Nevertheless, this view sees the emphasis on self-reliance as an interim strategy to ensure Kim's political survival. If the pandemic disappears and foreign trade resumes, Kim will revert to the previous pragmatic socialism. A recently available North Korean legal document on the Development of Cities and Counties states that the "field responsibility system should be accurately implemented . . . (and) production effort of farmers should not be destroyed by applying egalitarianism." It also says that "the people's committee of a city or a county should strongly establish a production base for export." This document indicates that reforms relying on economic incentives will likely resume in due course.

An alternative view is that Kim Jong-un sought to take advantage of the current situation to achieve his ultimate goal, restoration of government control over the economy. According to this view, pragmatic socialism was a temporary compromise in a situation where growth was impossible without reliance on markets. Once the official socialist economy recovered thanks to the development strategy using markets, Kim Jong-un would have returned to socialism without markets. Such a path would have echoed the establishment of the Stalinist economy in the Soviet Union following NEP from 1921 to 1928. In 1921, former leader of the Soviet Union Vladimir Lenin abruptly halted efforts to rapidly establish the socialist economic system due to an economic crisis and public uprisings. Lenin accepted NEP as a temporary solution that mixed socialism with markets, viewing it as strategic expedience or "one step backward to take two steps forward later on." After Lenin's death in 1924, however, Joseph Stalin abandoned NEP to establish a full-fledged socialist economy.

Which view more closely resembles Kim Jong-un's genuine intentions? It is possible that nobody knows for sure. Kim Jong-un himself may not have made up his mind on which path to take. Given that Kim cannot fully control external circumstances such as the COVID-19 pandemic, economic sanctions, and Sino-US relations, he may simply put off a decision on his economic development strategy and concentrate on the current political and economic problems he faces. After the resumption of foreign trade, Kim may take stock of the situation and decide which strategy to pursue.

Having said that, Kim Jong-un's recent speeches reveal his near-term goal. In a speech at the Plenary Session of Workers' Party at the end of 2020, he argued that "our priority task is to make a rational order of the system of economic works" and thus that the "transitory and provisional style of work does not have to continue." In addition, at the Eighth Party Congress in January 2021, Kim emphasized the development of state-led commerce and the invigoration of socialism in the service sector. These remarks indicate that Kim wants to strengthen the role of the government in the service sector, particularly in retail. This tracks with recent North Korean policies that established state retail shops for the sale of food.

North Korean Won

The restoration of the system of state commerce may explain the mysterious appreciation of the North Korean won against hard currencies that started in October 2020. For over a decade, a majority of North Koreans have held savings in hard currencies and used dollars and yuan for daily transactions at markets.[20] In other words, markets activities are intertwined with the "dollarization" and "yuanization" of the economy. From the North Korean government's perspective, de-dollarization and de-yuanization—increasing the use of won instead of dollars and yuan—contribute not only to restoring the system of state commerce but also to strengthening the overall state control of the economy. Increased use of won allows the government to monitor money supply, use discretionary monetary policy, and supply working capital to enterprises through state banks, which receive deposits from state retail shops. To achieve these objectives, won must regain dominance over dollars and yuan. The blockage of foreign trade may present a unique opportunity to quietly implement policies that appreciate the won, inducing a public preference for holding the won over dollars and yuan.

The worth of North Korean currency against US dollars and Chinese yuan was stable from 2013 until September 2020. During this period, one dollar and one yuan were exchanged for 8,000 and 1,200 North Korean won, respectively, according to the exchange rates at informal markets. However, exchange rates suddenly began to drop in late 2020, and further plunged in summer 2021 to 5,000 and 600, respectively.[21] According to South Korean intelligence, Kim Jong-un ascribed the won's sudden appreciation to a major player in informal currency exchange markets and ordered his/her execution.[22] Yet it is unlikely that the won sharply appreciated because of an intervention by currency dealers. If this allegation were true, exchange rates would have returned to the previous decade's equilibrium after the currency dealer's execution. The fact that the exchange rates for one dollar and one yuan still stand at 5,000 and 600 won, respectively, after a year suggests that the government intervened to maintain these rates. What kind of intervention the North Korean authorities made is uncertain. Some reports suggest the repression of the use of foreign currencies at markets.[23] As far as we are aware, however, no decree, law, or explicit policy prevents the use of foreign currencies at markets. The traumatic experience of currency reform in 2009 may explain this "quiet" government intervention. If North Koreans saw the government as behind this disruption in exchange rates, public anger and frustration would likely deepen. North Korean authorities would want to avoid an aftermath similar to that of the 2009 currency reform efforts because such an outcome would destabilize Kim's rule. This may explain why no explicit government policy has clamped down on the use of foreign currencies at markets.

The issuance of cash coupons in the latter half of 2021, which provide a way for the government to cheaply purchase hard currencies, rounds out this picture of quiet efforts to increase the use of the won.[24] These coupons help the state supplement foreign currency reserves held by the government, which have likely rapidly decreased since the implementation of sanctions. In addition, they help mitigate the credit crunch experienced by state institutions and enterprises that suffered from a shortage of working capital.[25] The sole use of won at markets would end up with a decrease in total money stock expressed in won if it is combined with appreciation against dollars and yuan. Hence, issuing more domestic currency would not necessarily result in inflation.[26] Furthermore, the government's economic power increases when it holds more hard currencies than the public. In this way, the combined effects of the appreciation of won and its dominance in use at markets were expected to improve the capability of the government in monetary and commercial policy.

Kim Jong-un's Intention and Actual Outcome

How does Kim Jong-un view markets? Does he see them as a rich stranger to be befriended only for the time being? Or as a companion who can peacefully accompany socialism? How far policies that seek to restore the system of state commerce go will indicate his genuine intention. The former is true if state retail shops remain open and employ individual retailers as paid workers while repressing private markets. By contrast, the latter is a more accurate description if state retail shops coexist with private retailers at markets that need only to be registered with the state and pay taxes.

Kim Jong-un's intention may differ from the actual outcome. Given the extent of marketization in North Korea, the nationalization of the retail sector is unlikely to be successful.[27] In particular, the goal of state monopoly over commerce will be difficult to achieve when foreign trade, including smuggling, resumes. Demand for hard currencies will likely increase, causing the won to depreciate, and private retailers will sell imported goods at domestic markets. Repression and restriction of both foreign trade and individuals' market activities will be extremely unpopular. This view is shared by defectors who used to work in the North Korean government. One defector argued that individual retailers are likely to bribe officials and managers of SOEs in order to carry on market activities privately, and thus repressing markets would be unsuccessful. Another defector who formerly worked as a high-ranking official in the North Korean cabinet said that the maximum Kim Jong-un can hope to achieve is an expansion of universal markets where individual retailers sell goods to customers but pay taxes to the government. Hence, it will be an uphill battle for Kim Jong-un to regain the state's dominance over commerce so long as bribery aligns the economic interests of government officials and market participants. As a result, even if Kim Jong-un takes a hardline approach to markets, he may be forced to accept a reality that requires a compromise with markets.[28]

SUMMARY AND IMPLICATIONS
FOR FOREIGN POLICY

Kim Jong-un's approach to markets from 2012 to 2018 differs from that of his father. Unlike his father's zigzagging and cautious approach vis-à-vis markets, Kim Jong-un has sought to more consistently and actively use incentives and resources embedded in markets. Both the "field-responsibility system" in agriculture and the "responsibility management system of socialist enterprise" exemplify this approach. Moreover, although Kim did not repress market activities, most of which are carried out by individuals, his economic policies have fallen short of institutionalizing private ownership of the means of production. Kim has also failed to abolish central planning, unlike what was done in market socialism in Hungary's NEM and the Soviet Union's NEP. In this sense, his economic development strategy can be seen as pragmatic socialism, using markets as a leverage for growth.

Kim Jong-un appeared to reverse these policies in 2019, a change that intensified after the outbreak of the COVID-19 pandemic. His speeches put a much stronger emphasis on self-reliance and state control over the economy than before. Since late 2020, currency markets have been disrupted by the substantial appreciation of the North Korean won against the US dollar and Chinese yuan. This phenomenon appears unnatural for a country experiencing an economic crisis. In addition, North Korean authorities reportedly recently issued cash coupons. This policy likely aims to absorb hard currencies held by the public into the government at a low price. Hence, Kim's economic development strategy changed from market-led growth to market-weakening self-reliance. Having said that, it is unclear whether this U-turn represents a temporary retreat from pragmatic socialism or an ultimate reversal to socialism without markets. Whatever his intention is, experts on the North Korean economy tend to agree that a reversal to old socialism will face strong resistance not only from the North Korean public but also from a majority of government officials.

One implication for foreign policy is that Kim Jong-un will take economic conditions into consideration when making decisions about nuclear-related issues. The trade-off between the development of nuclear weapons and the economy, created by economic sanctions, brought him to the negotiating table at the Hanoi Summit. Given the constraints imposed by economic sanctions, Kim believed that he could maximize the possibility of maintaining his power by exchanging partial denuclearization for the lifting of all economic sanctions. When Kim's attempt to make this exchange failed at Hanoi, he turned to an economic policy of self-reliance. In one sense, this evolution is inevitable because Kim had to endure economic hardship caused by both sanctions and COVID-19. In another sense, it represented a signal that he would not yield to US pressure.

What will happen in the future with US–North Korea negotiations? Changes in economic conditions may provide some clues. If the economic crisis deepens and the strategy of self-reliance turns out to be grossly self-punishing, Kim may be ready to return to negotiations under conditions more favorable to the United States. On the contrary, if the economy recovers after the COVID-19 pandemic, bolstered by redoubled Chinese political and economic support, Kim will likely claim that he holds the upper hand in negotiations with the United States and thus take a tougher position on denuclearization. This is why understanding North Korea's economy is so important for ensuring its denuclearization.

NOTES

* This work was supported by the Seoul National University Research Grant in 2021.

1. Especially during the period of summitry in 2018, there were high expectations in South Korea that Kim Jong-un would become a reformer like Deng Xiaoping. An editorial column that appeared in *Kyunghyang Shinmun*, a liberal South Korean newspaper, and an interview with Lee Jong-seok, former minister of unification in the Roh Moo-hyun administration, provide two examples. Yong-chae Park, "Kim Jong-un Becomes Deng Xiaoping and Wonsan Does Shanghai," *Kyunghyang Shinmun*, June 19, 2018, https://m.khan.co.kr/opinion/column/article/201806182030015 #c2b; Jong-seok Lee, "Kim Jong-un Wants Reform and Open-Up as Deng Xiaoping Did for China," Yonhap News Agency, November 28, 2019, https://www.yna.co.kr/view/AKR20191128141100504.

2. This was known to be part of Kim Jong-il's speech on June 18, 2008, addressed to officials in charge of economic affairs. *Understanding North Korea* (Seoul: National Institute for Unification Education, 2021).

3. According to a survey of 133 North Korean defectors who escaped from North Korea after the currency reform and settled in South Korea in 2010, 94.7 percent of respondents agreed that currency reform was an incorrect policy. And 61 percent of respondents replied that they lost money due to currency reform. Refer to the following for survey results: Byung-Yeon Kim, *Unveiling the North Korean Economy* (Oxford: Cambridge University Press, 2017), 91–99.

4. This analysis is in line with Kim and Sohn's investigation of whether and how economic policies under the Kim Jong-un's regime are different from those of the previous regimes. Soohyon Kim and Wook Sohn, "Economic Policy Changes in North Korea: A Text Mining Approach to Economic Research," BOK Economic Research working paper, 2020. They use articles published from 2012 to 2018 in *Economic Research*, a North Korean academic journal on economics, to assess changes in article keywords since Kim Jong-un's time as leader. Kim and Sohn argue that during

the Kim Jong-un era, keywords such as *production, knowledge, technology, strong nation, information,* and *science* are more frequently observed, while the frequency of articles critical of capitalism drastically decreases. They suggest that these changes represent a policy shift toward a more pragmatic approach to economic growth under Kim Jong-un.

5. This policy is regarded as an attempt to formalize unofficial contracts between SOEs prevailing in practice. In addition, central planning has stopped applying to small regional SOEs already from the 1990s.

6. The order contract system indicates the authorities' recognition that an enterprise voluntarily makes a deal with another enterprise without being dictated by central planning. Accordingly, production target, which is the most important indicator in centrally planned economies, cannot be totally controlled by central planners.

7. See South Korea's National Statistics Office portal on statistics related to North Korea for more details: https://kosis.kr/bukhan/.

8. Byung-Yeon Kim, "North Korean Economy in Kim Jong-un's Era," in *Today's North Korea*, ed. Youngkwan Yoon (Seoul: Neulpoom Plus, 2019).

9. A North Korean defector with extensive knowledge of collective farms told the author that the field responsibility system resulted in only modest output growth partially due to the egalitarianism that is still pervasive in collective farms. Households that substantially increased production bore the burden of subsidizing those that failed to satisfy minimum output amounts for state procurement.

10. China's Constitution revised in 1982 can be found at USC-China Institute, Constitution of the People's Republic of China, 1982. Accessed January 17, 2022. https://china.usc.edu/constitution-peoples-republic-china-1982#chap1.

11. The word *self-reliance* appeared in Kim Jong-un's New Year Speech eight and nine times in 2018 and 2019, respectively. This represents a significant increase from the period from 2013 to 2017, when self-reliance was mentioned one or two times yearly. This may have related to the harsh impact of economic sanctions on the North Korean economy.

12. UNSC sanctions did not appear to reduce economic growth in North Korea until 2017, likely because China did not implement sanctions seriously until after its Ministry of Commerce announced a suspension of China's imports of coal from North Korea in February 2017.

13. Byung-Yeon Kim, "Marketization during Kim Jong-un's Era: Policies and the Sanctions," The Korea Development Institute working paper, February 24, 2022.

14. Dawool Kim, "Determinants of Regional Economic Performance in North Korea: Evidence from Satellite Nighttime Lights" (PhD dissertation Seoul National University, 2021).

15. Jihee Kim, Kyoochul Kim, Sangyoon Park, and Chang Sun, "The Economics Costs of Trade Sanctions: Evidence from North Korea," *Social Science Research Network*, November 15, 2021.

16. According to a Japanese newspaper that cited a North Korean official document, Kim aimed to achieve an 8 percent annual growth rate from 2016 to 2020. "Docs Shed Light on Scope of N. Korean Development Strategy through 2020," *Mainichi*, April 20, 2019, https://mainichi.jp/english/articles/20190420/p2a/00m/0in

/018000c. In this document, North Korea suggested three ways to achieve this target: diversification of foreign trade, technological development, and the full-scale introduction of New Economic Management Measures.

17. Some columnists in South Korean newspapers also claimed that the sanctions were not effective at all. Refer to Jong-suk Lee, "The Sanctions Are Not a Universal Talisman," *Hankyoreh*, July 16, 2017, https://www.hani.co.kr/arti/opinion /column/803026.html; Il-young Lee, "To What Extent Are the Sanctions Effective," *Kyunghayng Shinmun*, February 7, 2018, https://m.khan.co.kr/opinion/column/article /201802072057015#c2b.

18. Some goods intended for export can be supplied to domestic markets in the short run, but over time a decrease in production will likely result in reduced supply for domestic markets. One main reason for lower production is price differences between exported goods and domestically-supplied ones.

19. For example, *Daily NK* reported in early 2020 that the government was controlling market prices and activities, and Asia Press reported that North Korea began a strong anti-market policy in April 2021. "The Direct Control of the State over Permission of Market Prices and Economic Activities." *DailyNK*, February 6, 2020, https: //www.dailynk.com/□□-□□-□-□□□□-□□-□□□-□□-□□-□-□/; "Strong Control on Individual Commercial Activities Started Eventually. Is It Part of Kim Jong-un's Anti-Market Policies?" Asia Press, April 26, 2021, https://www.asiapress.org/korean /2021/04/society-human-rights/people-life/tousei/.

20. In a 2016 survey of North Korean defectors carried out by the Korea Development Institute (KDI), 93 percent of the 1,010 respondents replied they used won for daily transactions prior to 2002. However, this share decreased to 43 percent after 2013: 53 percent and 4 percent of respondents answered that they used yuan and dollars, respectively. "Dollarization of North Korean Economy: Causes and Effects," *Korea Development Institute North Korea Economy Review*, November 2019.

21. Prices of rice and corn also sharply increased in June and July 2021. Prices of imported goods reportedly skyrocketed during this period as well. Goods became much more expensive in terms of dollars and yuan due to the combined effects of their depreciation and increased prices expressed in won.

22. South Korea's National Intelligence Service reported to congressmen that North Korean authorities irrationally responded to a situation of soaring prices and decreasing rate of capacity utilization of industries by executing a major figure in currency exchange markets. "According to National Intelligence Service, Kim Jong-un Executed a Major Player in Currency Markets," Yonhap News Agency, November 27, 2020, https://www.yna.co.kr/view/AKR20201127072351001.

23. Several media outlets have reported incidences of repression of the use of hard currencies at markets. See "The Value of Dollars Drops by 20% for Two Weeks Because of Ban of Use of Foreign Currencies," *Hankyung*, November 28, 2020, https: //www.hankyung.com/economy/article/2020112814387; "North Korean Authorities Ban Use of Foreign Currencies in Domestic Markets," *Maeil Kyungje*, December 29, 2020, https://www.mk.co.kr/news/economy/view/2020/12/1329539/.

24. The media reported that North Korea issued cash coupons in early September 2021. "North Korea Resumes Foreign Currency Control," *The Freedom and Life*,

September 6, 2021 https://thefreedomandlife.com/2021/09/06/%ef%bb%bf%eb%8b
%a8%eb%8f%85-%eb%b6%81%ed%95%9c-%ec%99%b8%ed%99%94-%ed%86
%b5%ec%a0%9c-%eb%8b%a4%ec%8b%9c-%eb%82%98%ec%84%b0%eb%8b
%a4/. A Japanese newspaper article claims that these cash coupons were issued due
to a shortage of the papers and ink required to print banknotes. "North Korea Is Not
Able to Print Money," *DailyWill*, October 5, 2021, https://web-willmagazine.com/
international/fUQAi. However, this provides a technical reason for the issuance but
fails to provide convincing economic logic for issuing cash in any form.

25. There are two reasons why these organizations experienced the credit crunch.
First, they have been unable to generate a sufficient amount of hard currency for their
operations due to economic sanctions and COVID-19. Second, the government's
ability to print more money to assist them was limited by its desire to avoid inflation
and further dollarization.

26. One remaining problem is pressure on exchange rates: a larger supply of won
will likely cause its depreciation against hard currencies at markets, facilitating dollarization. The North Korean authorities may not have any effective plan to counter
this, but they may hope that "quiet" restrictions on hard currency use at markets work.

27. This is in line with views of economists working on North Korean economy.
"De-dollarization of North Korean Economy: Realities, Implications and Prospects,"
Korea Development Institute North Korea Economy Review, November 2021.

28. A defector who engaged in foreign trade in North Korea shared this view,
claiming that individual retailers would not join the system of state commerce
because they were concerned about the disclosure of their wealth to the authorities.

Chapter 3

North Korea's Nuclear Strategy and Global Security

Virginie Grzelczyk

The 2012 Twelfth Supreme People's Assembly was one of the most remarkable moments in recent North Korean history. It was the first time Kim Jong-un represented the Democratic People's Republic of Korea (DPRK), or North Korea, as its sole leader after the passing of his father Kim Jong-il on December 17, 2011. But more important, it was an opportunity for North Korea to revise its constitution, something done only sporadically since its establishment in 1948. While Kim Jong-un's elevation to First Chairman of the National Defense Committee was a necessary political step to solidify the regime transition, the preamble to North Korea's constitution also stated that North Korea was now a nuclear-armed state.[1] This new status marked the culmination of a long and arduous quest for a state like North Korea.

In roughly five decades, North Korea had developed as an independent state, born out of the ashes of the decolonized Kingdom of Korea. It had engaged in a war with its Southern counterpart and committed most of its economy to the fight. It had developed its own brand of socialism, the *juche* ideology. It had survived the end of the Cold War and the loss of the Union of Soviet Socialist Republics (USSR) and People's Republic of China (PRC) as its main protectors. Its leadership had survived two hereditary political successions, and despite its failed economy and limited external engagement with the globalized world, it had succeeded in conducting six nuclear tests between 2006 and 2017. More telling for this volume's subject is that four of those tests took place during Kim Jong-un's leadership. What does this mean in the context of North Korea's very public commitments and efforts toward denuclearization, and for a return to a non-militarized Korean Peninsula?

Kim Jong-un's North Korea is different from that of his father and grand-father. His grandfather Kim Il-sung's task was to create a system that would ensure citizens' commitment to the state, while at the same time navigating the treacherous waters of Cold War relationships and security uncertainties. His father, Kim Jong-il, sought to ensure North Korea's survival and to capture the hearts and minds of a population raised within the cult of personality of his father, while dealing with the post–Cold War environment and the turn of close allies, particularly China, to global trade. Kim Jong-un's task is to manage the nuclear program he inherited and to jumpstart North Korea's economic development now that its security is assured by its nuclear capability and the shared understanding of mutual assured destruction.

Kim Jong-un is the only North Korean leader who has benefited from not just one, but three summit meetings with a sitting US president. To understand Kim Jong-un's position and potential policies, it is important to consider (1) what North Korea's nuclear strategy means, (2) why Kim Jong-un decided to promote North Korea's status as a nuclear state and (3) the costs and potential benefits of such nuclear policy in light of both North Korea's foreign relations and its present and future economic development. To do so, this chapter adopts Scott Sagan's understanding of why states pursue nuclear weapons: to increase their own security in light of a specific threat; to speak to a country's internal politics; and to project modernity and prestige beyond its borders.[2] In the case of North Korea, all three orientations matter: they are underpinned by a characterization of North Korea as a rational actor that is, in the purest Waltzian term, looking to survive.[3]

NORTH KOREA'S ROAD TO NUCLEAR STATUS

North Korea's Nuclear Development

Pyongyang's quest for nuclear energy and nuclear weapons began during the Kim Il-sung era. In 1952, North Korea established an atomic energy research institute as a part of its Academy of Science, and the North Korea Committee for Atomic Energy often sought help within the communist bloc to develop its programs.[4] The United States deployed tactical nuclear weapons in South Korea in 1958, and by 1964, the Soviet Union, United Kingdom, France, and China had all joined the United States in developing and testing nuclear weapons.[5] An atomic energy research center was then established in Yongbyon in 1964 with the help of Soviet-trained specialists, but Soviet support was slowly waning, as it was entangled in its own security concerns and often denied North Korea's requests for assistance to enhance its security and defense.[6] North Korea was certainly not alone in its quest to develop nuclear energy, as several smaller states, such as South Africa and Israel, were attempting to do the same. More important to North Korea, South Korea's president Park Chung-hee was also pursuing a nuclear capability.[7] In 1974, South Korea's defense spending caught up with that of the North, before exceeding it for good.[8] By 1982, South Korea had opened its first nuclear power reactor, the Kori-1, in partnership with US Westinghouse Electric Cooperation, which provided the reactor.[9] Pyongyang joined the Non-Proliferation Treaty (NPT) in 1985 and continued its attempt to convince Moscow to aid it in developing its own peaceful nuclear energy.[10] That same year, Moscow finally agreed to build a reactor on North Korean soil.[11] Plans were drafted and Soviet nuclear experts visited North Korea, but no decision could be made on location. By 1988, the agreement had fallen through.[12]

With the end of the Cold War and the dissolution of the Soviet Union, the card deck was largely reshuffled, and North Korea needed to look beyond Russia for military and economic support and for trading partners. For many years, it was unclear how North Korea managed to get their hands on the gas centrifuges that would allow the production of weapons-grade uranium on North Korean soil.[13] Ultimately, it emerged that Pakistan's top nuclear scientist Abdul Qadeer Khan had supplied North Korea with the initial nuclear technology: a North Korean official letter to Pakistan's Chief of Army Staff in 1998 disclosed important details regarding a North Korean multimillion-dollar payment made in exchange for technical help.[14] During the 1990s, North Korea was heavily involved in multilateral diplomacy via the Korean Peninsula Economic Development Organization and the 1994 Agreed Framework program. Under the deal, North Korea would renounce the development of its own nuclear energy and in return receive two peaceful-use Light-Water nuclear reactors sponsored by an international consortium led by the United States.[15] The agreement had many starts and stops, with parties reneging on several of their promises. North Korea exacerbated trust issues further by carrying out a missile testing program in the late 1990s. The Agreed Framework became moot, Pyongyang withdrew from the NPT in 2003, and North Koreans talked about their nuclear weapons program for the first time that year at late April trilateral talks in Beijing with the Chinese and Americans.[16] Following several rounds, the Six Party Talks succeeded in establishing a mutually agreed denuclearization framework in the September 19, 2005, Joint Statement, but the talks on implementation broke off shortly thereafter. North Korea tested its first nuclear weapon on October 9, 2006.[17] An additional test under Kim Jong-il would follow on May 25, 2009, with four more tests taking place under Kim Jong-un's leadership between 2013 and 2017. (see table 3.1)

Table 3.1. North Korean Nuclear Tests

Date	Magnitude[a]	Yield[b]
October 9, 2006	4.2	1
May 25, 2009	4.7	5
February 12, 2013	5	10
January 6, 2016	4.9	<10
September 9, 2016	5.2	20
September 3, 2017	5.8	120

Source: Adapted from US Geological Survey, Norsar Norway, Republic of Korea Ministry of National Defense, and United States intelligence community. [a] Richter Scale. [b] Kiloton.

North Korea's Nuclear Development Rationale

Since the inception of its nuclear program, North Korea has never stopped its pursuit of both a conventional and military approach to the use of nuclear energy. On the one hand, North Korea has seen nuclear energy as necessary to support its economy and industry, especially considering the perceived US "hostile policies" underpinning economic and military sanctions. On the other hand, North Korea has seen nuclear weapons as a viable way for it to overcome the security asymmetry resulting from the US alliance with and involvement in South Korea. Given the difference in size of the North Korean and US economies, it would never have been feasible for North Korea to match the US level of military commitment, readiness, and equipment on the peninsula.

Nuclear weapons development, however, presented a potential great equalizer that would guarantee North Korea's safety from a US first strike. In 1962, in the aftermath of the Cuban missile crisis and Park Chung-hee's seizure of power in South Korea, Kim Il-sung adopted the *byungjin* policy. *Byungjin* meant that North Korea's strategic direction would involve the pursuit of both economic development and national defense as equally important top priorities. Kim Il-sung's *byungjin* line would see North Korea concentrate on building its own security as well as its economy, therefore focusing on self-sufficiency in both aspects. This foundation meant that North Korea would be less dependent on the Soviet Union and China for its own defense and security, which was crucial at a time when the Soviet Union and China were starting to drift away from one another. Upon his father's death in 1994, Kim Jong-il sought to carry out the same line, though external conditions in the 1990s had drastically changed from those of the 1960s, and North Korea was already experiencing serious economic difficulties.[18] For Kim Jong-il, it was imperative to secure North Korea's survival amid a reconfiguration of most of the world in the post–Cold War era.

In addition to the *byungjin* line, Kim Jong-il revived *songun*, or the military-first policy. *Songun* policy involved a prioritization of the military and an increase in its influence within the North Korean governing system.[19] More than a simple allocation of wealth to fund military activities, *songun* sought to ensure the primacy of the Korean People's Army (KPA) in the affairs of the state and military power guiding the North Korean economy, diplomacy, and domestic politics.[20] *Songun* was directed at two internal audiences, the North Korean people and the North Korean political leadership. A power shift from the Workers' Party of Korea (WPK) to the KPA occurred as a result of *songun*, which in part aimed to prevent any military move to threaten Kim Jong-il's leadership position.[21] There also were a number of purges and executions of key military figures in the elite group who had organized around Kim Jong-il and were then tasked with "looking after" the younger son, Kim Jong-un.[22]

The development of a nuclear program under Kim Jong-il and especially visible activities like nuclear tests were also designed to showcase to a domestic audience the regime's ability and strength as well as its legitimacy. This was important for Kim Jong-il, who lacked the authentic legitimacy his father had gained from his rise to power as a guerrilla fighter and five decades as North Korea's first leader. The presence of American military forces on the Korean Peninsula also provided fodder for fear and for *songun*.

Although the United States decided to remove all its tactical nuclear weapons from South Korea in 1991, it maintained many troops in South Korea, continued to carry out military exercises on the peninsula, and, most important, retained a large number of strategic nuclear weapons around North Korea.[23] The United States has always maintained the position that its nuclear weapons could be used against North Korea. The United States' role in the death of former Iraqi leader Saddam Hussein in 2006 and of former Libyan leader Muammar Gaddafi in 2011 bring credibility to American resolve to tackle leaders that are perceived as dangerous.[24] Given that North Korea could not expand its conventional arms build-up to balance US troops or develop alliances that would allow for the balancing of US influence, the acquisition of a nuclear deterrent was logical and comparatively inexpensive

Table 3.2. Cost Estimate for North Korea's Nuclear Program under Kim Jong-il

	Expenditure[a]
Nuclear weapons development	1
Nuclear weapons testing	0.4–0.5
Long-range missiles	1.65
Total	3.05–3.15

Source: Adapted from *Chosun Ilbo*, March 20, 2012.

[a] Billion USD

(see table 3.2). Estimates place the proportion of North Korean core expenditures on nuclear weapons and missiles at the end of the Kim Jong-il era at only around 6 to 8 percent of North Korea's total military spending.[25]

The fragility of North Korea's economy meant that its impetus to support the military was limited if Pyongyang were to use only its own resources. To carry out its *songun* policy, therefore, North Korea's strategy incorporated the use of its nuclear and missile programs as negotiating tools to extract security and economic guarantees from the United States, South Korea, and China to a certain extent.[26] North Korea started to develop its nuclear program in parallel to being involved in several diplomatic processes, including discussions about moving beyond the Korean armistice (Four-Party Talks), the denuclearization of the peninsula (Six-Party Talks), and missile launches (Bilateral Talks). Though North Korea's nuclear status remained unclear until it tested its first nuclear weapon in 2006, it is now apparent that Pyongyang used delays and deception tactics during the 1980s and 1990s. These tactics involved pulling out of specific talks, demanding compensation, withdrawing from treaties, and negotiating financial compensation in return for their participation at multilateral events.[27]

North Korea does not pursue nuclear capabilities only as a means to balance and deter against the United States: its strategy fits into a more complex set of goals that integrates the search for security guarantees with bureaucratic pursuits and symbolic signaling at the international level, as outlined by Sagan in his work on modeling nuclear behaviors.[28] Though North Korea is often labeled as crazy by the international media and by political figures, analysts of Korean affairs largely understand North Korea as operating rationally to ensure its survival.[29] The nuclear path pursued by North Korea makes this abundantly clear: while Pyongyang's early endeavors focused on acquiring nuclear energy, it ultimately managed to both develop and successfully test a nuclear weapon, acquiring for all intents and purposes a nuclear deterrent. Under Kim Jong-un, recent endeavors have focused on the delivery of capabilities and especially the development of miniature nuclear warheads that could propel North Korea's nuclear strategy beyond self-defense.[30]

KIM JONG-UN: DEPARTURE FROM THE NORM?

Codifying North Korea's Nuclear Status

Kim Jong-un's ascent to power was considerably shorter than that of his father, Kim Jong-il. Kim Jong-il was slowly installed over the course of twenty-six years, from his role as the deputy chief of the Propaganda and Agitation Department in the WPK to his role as supreme commander of the KPA and chairman of the National Defense Commission in 1993.[31] He came into power amid two large crises: a severe domestic economic crisis accelerated by the end of the Cold War and the loss of support from former socialist allies, and a dangerous nuclear crisis that threatened North Korea's security, as it had not yet achieved a nuclear deterrent to balance against the United States.[32] In contrast, Kim Jong-un inherited a nuclear program that was well underway and an economic situation already reliant on marketization from below but with a growth model clearly constrained by international sanctions.[33] Moreover, as a new leader with little military experience and no formal military title at the time he assumed power, it was delicate for Kim Jong-un to propose a drastic increase in military powers.

The North Korean leadership had to determine how to offer people not just security but also economic benefits.[34] The younger Kim would be guided by a close entourage of advisers, including his uncle Jang Song-thaek, to perpetuate the seemingly monolithic political system that would place Kim Jong-un at the heart of every process.[35] Kim Jong-un's power began to formally crystalize in 2012 through a series of moves that charted his current political course. The first such move was Kim Jong-un's election as first secretary and de facto leader of the WPK in April 2012.[36] The second was Kim's modification of North Korea's constitution and proclamation of North Korea as a nuclear state.[37] Kim Jong-un sought to take up the mantle of his father and grandfather's legacy and did so with his first public speech on April 15, 2012, which marked Kim Il-sung's 100th birthday. In the speech, Kim Jong-un committed to following both Kim Il-sung's *juche* ideology and Kim Jong-il's military-first policy.[38] In only a few months after his father's death, Kim Jong-un and his entourage managed to consolidate power and to keep order within the society despite the political change.[39] Diplomacy continued behind the scenes, but talks between US Special Envoy Glyn Davies and North Korean Envoy Kim Kye-gwan on February 25, 2012, confirmed that North Korea would not become more inclined to denuclearize under its new leadership.[40]

Consolidating North Korea's Nuclear Strategy

A year later, it started to become clear that Kim Jong-un's regime was different from that of his father. By May 2013, more than two-thirds of senior North Korean generals had been removed from government or moved to new nonmilitary positions.[41] Kim's strategy was less to divide competing interests than it was to unify them under a new structure. In doing so, Kim attempted to centralize North Korean politics and policy making under his own leadership and to transcend infighting over power between the KPA and WPK. Observers of internal North Korean politics saw Kim's reliance on Party conferences as a way for him to expand his power and charisma. As a fairly new leader, he decided to host a WPK Congress in 2016, which is significant, as there had been no such event for the past thirty-six years.[42] Kim Jong-un also aimed to reduce the KPA's power in everyday North Korean affairs: under Kim Jong-il, the military had intervened in many large projects to gain economic benefits. Kim Jong-un's own *byungjin* line, the parallel development of the economy and nuclear weapons, echoed that of Kim Il-sung's in the sense that North Korea was once again focusing on building a self-defense capability in the form of nuclear weapons.[43] It also required more freedom and autonomy to develop flexible new economic policies that tackled North Korea's sinking economy. Some of those policies included a shift to households as the responsible unit of production, therefore relying on inner competition and the need to improve productivity.[44] Resources were also shifted away from the military to support civilian programs, such as the conversion of a North Hamgyong airfield into a farming area or a Gangwon military drill ground into a tourist resort.[45] A comparison of each of Kim Jong-un's New Year's addresses between 2013 and 2021 shows three trends: a decline over time in perfunctory mentions of *songun*, Kim Il-sung, and Kim Jong-il; persistent mentions of the WKP but fading of mentions of the KPA; and increased references to the economy and the nuclear weapons program (see table 3.3). These public addresses illuminate the erosion of the *songun* military-first policy and the primacy of the KPA to the *byungjin* simultaneous economic and nuclear weapons development policy.

By 2017, it was clear that Kim Jong-un had achieved his power succession process, had managed to consolidate his leadership arrangements, and

Table 3.3. Mentions in Kim Jong-un's New Year Addresses

	Songun	Workers' Party of Korea	Korean People's Army	Kim Il-sung	Kim Jong-il	Nuclear	Economy
2013	6	1	10	6	7	0	8
2014	3	4	10	5	1	6	12
2015	0	2	11	1	2	4	3
2016	2	8	10	3	4	2	9
2017	1	7	6	4	3	5	9
2018	0	5	5	3	2	24	12
2019	0	2	7	0	0	1	16
2020[a]	/	/	/	/	/	/	/
2021[b]	0	1	2	2	2	11	18

Source: Adapted from Kim Jong-un's New Year Addresses, made available by the National Committee on North Korea

[a] No address due to COVID-19

[b] Report of the Fifth Plenary Meeting of the Seventh Central Committee of the WPK (Replacing Kim Jong-un's New Year Address)

had succeeded in North Korea becoming a nuclear power.[46] Kim Jong-un now seeks to develop the ability to launch both pre-emptive and retaliatory strikes.[47] To do so, North Korea needs to develop a vehicle with a reliable reentry rate into the atmosphere after launching and a nuclear warhead small enough to travel on an intercontinental ballistic missile (ICBM). Kim Jong-un's first nuclear test was conducted on February 12, 2013: the Comprehensive Test Ban Treaty Organization (CTBTO) Executive Secretary Tibor Toth confirmed in its aftermath that the seismic activity the CTBTO had detected was indeed nuclear-like and located in areas previously used by North Korea for its 2006 and 2009 nuclear test.[48] Kim Jong-un is not pursuing a policy of denuclearization in exchange for security and economic guarantees to ensure the regime's survival.[49] Instead, Kim Jong-un has chartered North Korea's course as a nuclear weapons state unbound by any overarching principles, since it withdrew from the Treaty on the Non-Proliferation of Nuclear Weapons (NPT) in 2003. Nuclear tests and short-range, long-range, and intercontinental ballistic missile tests all indicate that Kim Jong-un's North Korea may achieve a potentially credible nuclear warfighting and deterrent capability soon.[50] These capabilities are also enhanced by a rapid increase in testing. While 15 missiles were launched under Kim Il-sung during his fifty-four years at the head of North Korea and 16 were launched under Kim Jong-il during his seventeen years in leadership, Kim Jong-un has already overseen over 151 tests during the past ten years.[51] North Korea has shown both consistency in testing and a focus on longer-range missiles since Kim Jong-un's rise to power (see table 3.4). Kim Jong-un has also repeatedly stated his desire to be a responsible nuclear weapons state: for Kim, this means adhering to a no-first-use policy, and North Korean nuclear weapons would then only be used if threatened by a nuclear weapon. This stance is therefore not incompatible with the current ramped-up missile launches, which would support North Korea's own military capabilities should it be threatened and attacked first.

Korean Missile Tests

A conventional missile with a conventional warhead is no equalizer for the United States' own nuclear arsenal, and an intercontinental missile would be intercepted before landing on US soil. But a missile capped with a thermonuclear warhead, a hydrogen H-bomb (which requires considerably less uranium and plutonium than a traditional atomic weapon), or an A-bomb could be the game-changer North Korea has been after, according to nuclear deterrence theory.[52] North Korea is also developing a new range of ballistic missile submarines to enhance its capabilities and shift from defense only to both defensive and preemptive postures.[53] In April 2018, Kim Jong-un

Table 3.4. North Korean Missiles and Tests (Known)

Name	Range	km	Launches / Number
KN-02	Short	150	2013 (6), 2014 (4), 2015 (10)
Hwasong-6; Scud C	Short	500	1990 (1), 1991 (1), 1993 (3), 2006 (2), 2009 (5), 2014 (9), 2015 (2), 2016 (4),
KN-23	Short	500	2019 (8)
KN-24	Short	300	2019 (4), 2020 (2)
KN-25	Short	500	2019 (20), 2020 (7)
Hwasong-7; Scud D; Nodong	Medium	800-1,500	1990 (1), 1992 (2), 1993 (1), 2006 (4), 2009 (2), 2014 (2), 2016 (5)
Hwasong-9; Scud ER	Medium	1,000	2016 (3), 2017 (5)
KN-11; Pukguksong-1	Submarine	1,200	2015 (3), 2016 (3)
KN-15; Pukguksong-2	Medium	1,200	2017 (2)
KN-26; Pukguksong-3	Short	1,900	2019 (1)
Musudan BM-25; Hwasong-10	Intermediate	4,000	2016 (8)
KN-17; Hwasong-12	Intermediate	4,500	2017 (6)
KN-20 / Hwasong-14	Intercontinental	10,000+	2017 (2)
KN-22 / Hwasong-15	Intercontinental	13,000+	2017 (1)

Source: Center for Strategic and International Studies, Missile Defense Project

stated during the Third Plenary Meeting of the Seventh Central Committee of the WPK that North Korea no longer needed to test nuclear weapons or intermediate and intercontinental ballistic missiles since it had achieved its goal of developing a working nuclear weapons suite.[54] This status has clear implications for North Korea's foreign policy, both regionally and globally, as it could potentially imply that it has developed the range of weapons it needs to achieve deterrence. There is a potential tension between Kim's will to defend his country by deterring an American attack in the first place and one that would see Kim using nuclear weapons to start a conflict. While the latter would eradicate any attempt made by North Korea to frame itself as a responsible nuclear weapons state, the former would imply reaching a de-escalation level that does not seem possible if US military forces stay on the Korean Peninsula.

The rise of nuclear activities under Kim Jong-un raises important questions about the future of the Korean state. First, while the investment in nuclear weapons has led to North Korea achieving a de facto nuclear state status outside of the confines of the Non-Proliferation Treaty, a development like that of Pakistan in the 1990s, its nuclear program has led to a tightening of sanctions. Second, Kim Jong-un's first ten years in power have not led to any substantial economic strengthening despite some internal reforms that allowed for more private investments. Third, the North Korean economy has greatly suffered from international alienation and natural disaster, as well as the global pandemic, and Kim Jong-un's nuclear success might not be sufficient to mobilize a population behind their leader when the promise of a better economic landscape has not realized itself. Kim Jong-un's pursuit of more favorable economic circumstances abroad, via a renewal of dialogue with both South Korea and the United States from 2018 until 2020 has also not succeeded. Kim Jong-un appears to be aware that he has reached the limits of an autarkic economic system: to generate more economic opportunities, North Korea has to consider the fact that improved inter-Korean relations might not occur if it remains a nuclear power.

WHAT PLACE FOR A NUCLEAR NORTH IN THE INTERNATIONAL SYSTEM?

North Korea's Strategic Development

North Korea's evolution from a post-colonial power to a state seeking nuclear parity with the United States has taken only about six decades and is unprecedented given North Korea's modest size and economic difficulties. North Korea's strategy and objectives have regularly been articulated at Party congresses by all three Kims. The 1946 First Party Congress consolidated North Korea's political elite and crafted a place for Kim Il-sung as the country's leader following his years of political work and military combat against Japanese occupation. The 1948 Second Party Congress that took place as the two Koreas voted for independent governments focused on establishing North Korea as a discrete political state. The 1956 Third Party Congress focused on political ideology post–Korean War and pre-Sino-Soviet split and revealed North Korea's commitment to socialism as a political force to contend with the West and imperialism. After the 1961 Fourth Party Congress, North Korea started to focus on its domestic economy, while the 1970 Fifth Party Congress proclaimed Kim Il-sung's *juche* as a departure from the Marxist-Leninist model, given the growing estrangement between North Korea and the Soviet Union: *juche* emphasized nationalism and relied on the Korean experience of trauma through colonialization and euphoria through Kim il-sung's image as a guerrilla hero fighting against imperial Japan, and brought a deep nationalistic focus. Kim Il-sung's last 1980 Sixth Party Congress centered on modernizing North Korea technologically and ideologically. This was especially important as waning support from China and the Soviet Union and intense economic competition with South Korea had clearly challenged the notion that North Korea could develop in autarky. Kim Jong-un's 2016 Seventh Party Congress renewed focus on the *byungjin* policy adopted in 2013 and in a marked departure from the past, Kim Jong-un posited North Korea as a nuclear power both internally and externally. Kim Jong-il had a less contentious grip on power because he benefited from a longer transition period into power, and the nuclear tests he oversaw were designed to convince an international audience of North Korea's might. For Kim Jong-un, who had much shorter political transition, economic development is currently paramount, yet nuclear tests have also been used to create buy-in from the people and elite.[55] But Kim Jong-un's nuclear focus has resulted in a continued strain imposed by sanctions on daily North Korean life (see table 3.5).

While sanctions under UN Security Council Resolutions 1718 and 1874 predate Kim Jong-un's accession to power, many bilateral and multilateral sanctions have resulted directly from his missile and nuclear testing. But sanctions have failed to change North Korea's stance on nuclear development, even though they have exerted economic pressure on many within the country and forced the regime to contend with managing people's expectations and economic behaviors. Overall, sanctions have led to two main developments. Domestically, North Korea has developed a pseudo market economy that has arisen from black market patterns. Internationally, the sanction regime has induced many countries to turn away from their trade relationships with North Korea: Angola, Uganda, and Tanzania had extensive trade relationships with North Korea in the field of police and military training as well as North Korean construction activities.[56] The more involved North Korea becomes in illicit trading with fringe countries, however, the less effectively it can project the image of a responsible nuclear power that wants only to further develop its economy. Sanctions therefore impose high political costs, as they harm North Korea's image and impede its ability to join alliances, participate in multilateral diplomacy, or provide credible steps toward denuclearization.

The Crafting of a Nuclear Policy

North Korea's understanding of international relations centers on the notion of power, which is achieved through military strength, and nuclear power is a large part of it.[57] Negotiations in the 2000s thus often centered on the question of nuclear weapons. What to do with them and North Korea have been constant in both rejecting preconditions to earn a seat at a negotiating table as well as renouncing nuclear weapons first before receiving a reward.[58] Kim Jong-un has taken a similar approach, with regard to both negotiations and taking the first step toward denuclearization.[59] The reason for such rejection is simple: North Korea shares a bitter past with both the United States and South

Table 3.5. Sanctions against North Korea

Unilateral	Period	Designation
Australia	2017–	Autonomous Sanctions Amendment: Prohibits service and business with North Korea
Canada	2011–	Special Economic Measures Act: Bans on export, investment, technical data, transit
China	2013–	Bank of China shuts down the accounts of North Korea's Foreign Trade Bank
Japan	2013–	Ban on interactions with North Korea's Foreign Trade Bank
	2016–	Remittance freeze, North Korean people travel ban, North Korean scientists travel ban
South Korea	2010–	Ban on North Korean ships in territorial waters and suspension of inter-Korea trade
United States	1988–2008 2017–	Declares North Korea a State Sponsor of Terrorism
	2011–	Iran, North Korea, and Syria Nonproliferation Act (INKSNA)
	2016–	North Korea Sanctions and Policy Enhancement Act (Human rights and illegal activities)
	2017–	Ban on US travel to North Korea
	2017–	Countering America's Adversaries through Sanctions Act
European Union	2009–	Export ban on dual-use goods
	2016–	Autonomous Sanctions (Import ban, transfer fund block, transport block)
	2017–	Autonomous Sanctions (Ban on EU investment, remittance, work authorization for North Koreans)
UN	2006–	United Nations Security Council Resolution 1718: Stop nuclear testing and prohibit military and luxury goods
	2009–	United Nations Security Council Resolution 1874: Gives right to inspect cargo
	2013–	United Nations Security Council Resolution 2087: Gives right to seize cargo
	2013–	United Nations Security Council Resolution 2094: Stops money transfers
	2016–	United Nations Security Council Resolution 2270: Bans raw material exports
	2016–	United Nations Security Council Resolution 2321: Caps coal exports
	2017–	United Nations Security Council Resolution 2371: Bans North Korean foreign workers increase
	2017–	United Nations Security Council Resolution 2375: Bans joint ventures, exports, and all North Korean foreign workers abroad

Source: Compiled by author using public domain, governmental, and news resources

Korea. North Korea has little reason to trust that the United States would not conduct a strike to terminate the regime if it gave up its nuclear weapons first. Indeed, North Korea witnessed Saddam Hussein's fall in Iraq in 2003 and Muammar Gaddafi's death in 2011, even though Libya was touted in the early 2000s as a prime example of how a "dangerous" regime could be reintegrated.[60]

First, nuclear weapons are North Korea's best asset to ensure its survival and deter a preemptive strike. This rationale likely features highly in North Korea's cost-benefit calculations and has proven solid given the lack of military moves against North Korea. This has held true even during moments of crisis, including missile tests and American university student Otto Warmbier's incarceration.

Second, the prestige associated with the development of a nuclear program provides North Korean citizens with a reason to be proud of the sacrifices they have made because of the country's nuclear development and assuages discontent. Internationally, this prestige allows North Korea to position itself as a potential leader of a group of countries opposing the established Western international order.

Third, the nuclear program is a revenue-making opportunity, despite the cost of sanctions. As indicated by the sanction regime's failure to curb North Korea's nuclear development, North Korea has managed to find ways to avoid collapse and cope with ever-tightening restrictions. North Korea can generate revenue by negotiating its participation in various bilateral and multilateral events by asking for concessions, payments, and shipments of goods, for example. North Korea can also generate revenue through nuclear technology sales. Because North Korea's main security contention is with the United States, it has little concern over relative access of third-party states to nuclear weapons, South Korea excluded. Given that North Korea itself purchased nuclear blueprints and expertise from Pakistan, it has little reason not to make some of its nuclear materials available to other states attempting to acquire a nuclear deterrent.[61] Committing again to denuclearization is then problematic, since North Korea has agreed to it before (September 19, 2005, Six Party Joint Statement and February 13, 2007, Six Party Implementing Agreement to dismantle its nuclear facilities[62]). Given Kim Jong-un's declaration that North Korea is a nuclear state, there is little doubt that North Korea reneged on some of its commitments even as it made them.

Kim Jong-un has also succeeded where both his father and grandfather had failed when it comes to securing direct talks with the United States: first at the May 2018 Singapore Summit and again at the February 2019 Hanoi Summit. Trump and Kim agreed on the denuclearization of the Korean Peninsula in Singapore, but the vaguely worded agreement provided little basis for actual progress. The Hanoi Summit broke down early because of

North Korea's attempts to negotiate its way out of sanctions. Given North Korea's commitment to its nuclear status, denuclearization talks cannot begin with the assumption that North Korea would eliminate its programs and current weapon stocks.

CONCLUSION: WHAT WAY FORWARD?

Under Kim Jong-un, North Korea has accelerated its nuclear development, increased its missile range technology, shifted its power base from the KPA to the WPK, and expanded to include a market element in its domestic economy. It declared itself a nuclear weapons state and twice secured direct talks with a sitting US president, all while experiencing tightly restrictive international sanctions. North Korea may be unwilling to denuclearize given that nuclear weapons provide a security guarantee it perceives as essential for its survival and development. If so, one way forward might be to encourage North Korea in becoming a responsible nuclear power holder and foreboding nuclear tests. However, this might mean that the international community and United States would have to recognize North Korea as a nuclear state, which would essentially nullify years of engagement and prodding of North Korea toward denuclearization. This also has implications for the sanctions regime: sanctions increasingly lose their effectiveness as a result of North Korean evasion and international failures of enforcement: at this point, they do little more than express moral objections to North Korea's nuclear acquisition. In the current setup, it appears likely that North Korea's nuclear program is here to stay, regardless of Kim Jong-un's own political future: North Korea has striven for the past half a century to defend itself against a potential US military action, and though self-defense is now articulated via a nuclear deterrent, the need to defend itself, originated under Kim Il-sung, is a pervasive stance that all North Koreans can rally behind regardless of who the leader of the country is.

NOTES

1. "Socialist Constitution of the Democratic People's Republic of Korea," The Committee for Human Rights in North Korea, Accessed October 8, 2021, https://www.hrnk.org/uploads/pdfs/4047.pdf.

2. Scott D. Sagan, "Why Do States Build Nuclear Weapons? Three Models in Search of a Bomb," *International Security* 21, no.3 (1996): 54–86.

3. E. W. Tan, and G. Govindasamy, "From Kim Jong Il to Kim Jong Un: Nuclear Impasse or Diplomatic Opportunity?," *Asia Europe Journal* 10, no. 4 (2012): 301–16; Youngwon Cho, "Method to the Madness of Chairman Kim: The Instrumental

Rationality of North Korea's Pursuit of Nuclear Weapons," *International Journal* 69, no. 1 (2014): 5–25; Edward Kwon, "Policies of Last Resort for Dealing with North Korea's Nuclear Weapons Programme," *Asian Affairs* 49, no. 3 (2018): 402–32; Kenneth Waltz, *Man, the State, and War* (New York: Columbia University Press, 1959).

4. "북한네트-백과: 과학기술 연구기관" [DPRK Net—Encyclopedia: Science Technology Research Institutions], *Joongang Ilbo*, http://nk.joins.com. See also Romanian Ministry of Foreign Affairs, "Telegram from Pyongyang to Bucharest, No.76.121, TOP SECRET, April 8, 1967," History and Public Policy Program Digital Archive, Archive of the Romanian Ministry of Foreign Affairs, April 8, 1967. Obtained and translated for NKIDP by Eliza Gheorghe.

5. Hans M. Kristensen, and Robert S. Norris, "A History of US Nuclear Weapons in South Korea," *Bulletin of the Atomic Scientists* 73, no. 6 (2017): 349–57.

6. "시사백과: 북핵/일지" [North Korea Diary], *Chosun Ilbo*, October 2006, Accessed October 14, 2021, http://nkchosun.com; Yong Soo Park, "Policies and Ideologies of the Kim Jong-un Regime in North Korea: Theoretical Implications," *Asian Studies Review* 38, no. 1 (2014): 1–14.

7. "After Tests in the North, Conservatives in South Korea Call for a Nuclear Program," *New York Times*, February 19, 2016.

8. Cho, "Method to the Madness of Chairman Kim.

9. "Kori Nuclear Power Complex," Nuclear Threat Initiative, Accessed October 8, 2021, https://www.nti.org/learn/facilities/5/.

10. Timothy S. Rich, "Deciphering North Korea's Nuclear Rhetoric: An Automated Content Analysis of KCNA News," *Asian Affairs* 39, no. 2 (2012): 73–89.

11. *Report, Embassy of Hungary in North Korea to the Hungarian Foreign Ministry*, History and Public Policy Program Digital Archive, Wilson Center, March 9, 1985, Accessed October 8, 2021, https://digitalarchive.wilsoncenter.org/document /110142. Obtained and translated for NKIDP by Balazs Szalontai.

12. *Report, Embassy of Hungary in North Korea to the Hungarian Foreign Ministry*.

13. "Pakistan Supplied North Korea with Nuclear Weapons Technology: Daily," Agence France Presse, October 18, 2002.

14. "Pakistan Denies it was Bribed by North Korea," Defenseweb, July 8, 2011.

15. "US and North Korea sign historic nuclear accord," Agence France Presse, October 2, 1994.

16. "Chronology of U.S.–North Korean Nuclear and Missile Diplomacy," Arms Control Association, Accessed January 25, 2022, https://www.armscontrol.org/factsheets/dprkchron.

17. That test catalyzed the revival of the Six Party Talks and the forging of an implementation agreement in February of 2007, but the process foundered in late 2008 over differences regarding verification of North Korea's nuclear programs.

18. Young-chul Chung, Yong-hyun Kim, and Kyungyon Moon, "State Strategy in the Kim Jong-Un Era: The 'Byongjin' Policy of Pursuing Economic and Nuclear Development," *Korea Observer* 47, no. 1 (2016): 1–34.

19. Chung et al., "State Strategy in the Kim Jong-Un Era"; Bomi Kim, "North Korea's Siege Mentality: A Sociopolitical Analysis of the Kim Jong-un Regime's Foreign Policies," *Asian Perspective* 40, no. 2 (2016): 223–43.

20. Seong-Yong Park, "North Korea's Military Policy under the Kim Jong-Un Regime," *Journal of Asian Public Policy* 9, no. 1 (2016): 57–74; Stephan Haggard, and Marcus Noland, "Sanctioning North Korea: The Political Economy of Denuclearization and Proliferation," *Asian Survey* 50, no. 3 (2010): 539–68.

21. Seongji Woo, "Pyongyang and the World: North Korean Perspectives on International Relations under Kim Jong-il," *Pacific Focus* 26, no. 2 (2011): 188–205.

22. Yong Soo Park, "Policies and Ideologies of the Kim Jong-un Regime in North Korea."

23. Youngwon Cho, "Method to the Madness of Chairman Kim."

24. Jung Hoon Choi, "Advancement of North Korea's Nuclear Weapons and Survivability under the Kim Jong Un Regime: An Assessment Based on Nuclear Deterrence Theory," *Journal of the Asia-Japan Research Institute of Ritsumeikan University* (2019).

25. Youngwon Cho, "Method to the Madness of Chairman Kim."

26. Chung et al., "State Strategy in the Kim Jong-Un Era."

27. Ralph Hassig, and Oh Kongdan, "Kim Jong-un Inherits the Bomb," *International Journal of Korean Unification Studies* 20, no. 1 (2011): 31–54.

28. Sagan, "Why Do States Build Nuclear Weapons?"

29. Victor Cha, "Hawk Engagement and Preventive Defense on the Korean Peninsula," *International Security* 27, no. 1 (2002): 40–78; Patrick McEachern, "Centralizing North Korean Policymaking under Kim Jong Un," *Asian Perspective* 43, no. 1 (2019): 35–67; Hans M. Kristensen, and Robert S. Norris, "North Korean Nuclear Capabilities, 2018," *Bulletin of the Atomic Scientists* 74, no. 1 (2018): 41–51; Cho, "Method to the Madness of Chairman Kim"; Virginie Grzelczyk, "Going at It Alone? North Korea's Adaptability as a Small Power in a Changing World," *Third World Thematics* 1, no. 1 (2016): 63–78.

30. Haggard, and Noland, "Sanctioning North Korea."

31. Yongho Kim, "North Korea's Threat Perception and Provocation under Kim Jong-un: The Security Dilemma and the Obsession with Political Survival," *North Korean Review* 9, no. 1 (2013): 6–19.

32. McEachern, "Centralizing North Korean Policymaking under Kim Jong Un."

33. Haggard, and Noland, "Sanctioning North Korea."

34. Hong Yung Lee, "North Korea in 2012," *Asian Survey* 53, no. 1 (2013): 176–83.

35. Tan, and Govindasamy, "From Kim Jong Il to Kim Jong Un"; Park, "Policies and Ideologies of the Kim Jong-un Regime in North Korea."

36. Choi, "Advancement of North Korea's Nuclear Weapons and Survivability under the Kim Jong Un Regime."

37. Kwon, "Policies of Last Resort."

38. Park, "Policies and Ideologies of the Kim Jong-un Regime in North Korea."

39. Peter Hayes and R. Cavazos, "North Korea in 2015," *Asian Survey* 56, no. 3 (2016): 68–77.

40. Tan, and Govindasamy, "From Kim Jong Il to Kim Jong Un."

41. Park, "North Korea's Military Policy under the Kim Jong-Un Regime."

42. Hayes and Cavazos, "North Korea in 2015."

43. Park, "North Korea's Military Policy under the Kim Jong-Un Regime."

44. "Game-Changing Agricultural Policies for North Korea?," *38North*, February 26, 2014, https://www.38north.org/2014/02/rireson022414/.

45. "Dear Leader Kim Jong Un Did Field Guidance at Onpo Greenhouse Factory in Kyungsung County, North Hamgyong Province," *Rodong Sinmun*, August 8, 2018; "Dear Leader Kim Jong Un Did Field Guidance at Yangduk Spa Tourist District," *Rodong Sinmun*, August 31, 2019.

46. Kristensen and Norris, "North Korean Nuclear Capabilities, 2018."

47. Kwon, "Policies of Last Resort."

48. "Chronology of U.S.-North Korean Nuclear and Missile Diplomacy."

49. McEachern, "Centralizing North Korean Policymaking under Kim Jong Un."

50. Mary Beth Dunham Nikitin and Samuel D. Ryder, "North Koreas Nuclear Weapons and Missile Programs," Congressional Research Service, January 5, 2021.

51. "Missiles of North Korea," Center for Strategic and International Studies, accessed September 6, 2022, https://missilethreat.csis.org/country/dprk/.

52. Choi, "Advancement of North Korea's Nuclear Weapons and Survivability under the Kim Jong Un Regime."

53. "North Korea Submarine Capabilities," Nuclear Threat Initiative, Accessed October 14, 2021, https://www.nti.org/analysis/articles/north-korea-submarine-capabilities/.

54. *DPRK Report on the Third Plenary Meeting of the Seventh Central Committee*, The National Committee on North Korea, April 21, 2018, https://www.ncnk.org/resources/publications/dprk_report_third_plenary_meeting_of_seventh_central_committee_of_wpk.pdf.

55. Taehee Whang, Michael Lammbrau, and Hyung-min Joo, "Talking to Whom? The Changing Audience of North Korean Nuclear Tests," *Social Science Quarterly* 98, no. 3 (2017): 976–92.

56. Virginie Grzelczyk, "From Balancing to Bandwagoning: Evaluating the Impact of the Sanction Regime on North Korea–Africa Relationships," *North Korean Review* 15, no. 1 (2019): 9–33; Haggard and Noland, "Sanctioning North Korea."

57. Seongji Woo, "Pyongyang and the World: North Korean Perspectives on International Relations under Kim Jong-il," *Pacific Focus* 26, no. 2 (2011): 188–205.

58. Joel S. Wit, Daniel B. Poneman, and Robert L. Gallucci, *Going Critical: The First North Korean Nuclear Crisis* (Washington, DC: Brookings Institution Press, 2004); Scott Snyder, *Negotiating on the Edge: North Korean Negotiating Behavior* (Washington, DC: United States Insitute of Peace Press, 1999); C. Kenneth Quinones, "The Six Party Talks: Going in Circles," *World & I* (April 2006); Virginie Grzelczyk, "Six-Party Talks and Negotiation Strategy: When Do We Get There?," *International Negotiation* 14, no.1 (2009): 95–119.

59. Tan and Govindasamy, "From Kim Jong Il to Kim Jong Un."

60. Yahia H. Zoubir, "Libya in US Foreign Policy: From Rogue State to Good Fellow?," *Third World Quarterly* 23, no. 1 (2002): 31–53; Youngwon Cho, "Method to the Madness of Chairman Kim."

61. Kwon, "Policies of Last Resort."
62. Tan and Govindasamy, "From Kim Jong Il to Kim Jong Un."

PART II: North Korea's Summit Diplomacy under Kim Jong-un

Chapter 4

Inter-Korean Path to Peace: Jump-Started but Stalled

Haksoon Paik

In 2018, South Korea (also known as the Republic of Korea, or ROK) and North Korea (also known as the Democratic People's Republic of Korea, or DPRK) held three inter-Korean summits, produced two joint declarations, and signed one comprehensive military agreement. These included the inter-Korean "Panmunjom Declaration on Peace, Prosperity and Reunification of the Korean Peninsula" on April 27, 2018, the inter-Korean "Pyongyang Joint Declaration of September 2018," and as an annex to it the "Agreement on the Implementation of the Historic Panmunjom Declaration in the Military Domain" (hereafter referred to as the CMA, or "comprehensive military agreement") signed in Pyongyang on September 19, 2018, by the defense ministers of both Koreas.

This chapter explores the role of summitry in inter-Korean relations; analyzes the motives and goals influencing North Korean leader Kim Jong-un's choice to engage in summitry with South Korean president Moon Jae-in and vice versa; assesses the progress made toward these objectives; interrogates the impact of inter-Korean summitry on inter-Korean, US–North Korean, and US–South Korean relations; and addresses implications and prospects for the future of inter-Korean relations.

THREAT OF NUCLEAR WAR ON THE KOREAN PENINSULA IN 2017

North Korea increased its defense preparedness by developing and upgrading its weapons and equipment due to the "threat of nuclear war" it experienced in the second half of 2017. At that time, the world witnessed an egregious escalation in the threat of nuclear war on the Korean Peninsula. North Korea test-fired at a high angle a series of intercontinental ballistic missiles (ICBMs) that potentially had the US continent within range and tested a hydrogen bomb. North Korea celebrated the success of both tests as the "completion of national nuclear forces."[1] Seriously concerned by the potential North Korean ICBM threat to the United States, the incumbent Donald Trump administration prepared multiple military options including "Bloody Nose." The Bloody Nose attack plan included preemptive strikes on the North Korean leadership and key military bases and facilities with nuclear weapons if necessary.[2]

The US Bloody Nose attack plan emerged during the second major period of heightened nuclear risk following a previous escalation in March–April 2013 during the US–South Korea joint military exercises. In the spring of 2013, the United States and North Korea publicly exchanged threats of nuclear war for the first time in the history of US–South Korea joint military drills against North Korea.[3] Repeated threats of nuclear war on the Korean Peninsula between the United States and North Korea gave the incorrect impression that nuclear weapons were "usable," raising concerns about a possible nuclear war on the Korean Peninsula.

Moreover, during the first two days of 2018, Kim Jong-un and then US president Donald Trump traded verbal attacks, both mentioning the "nuclear buttons" on their office desks.[4] The treatment of nuclear weapons like toys by political leaders during a period of heightened tension shocked and frustrated many Koreans living on the Korean Peninsula, who proclaimed "Enough is enough," "Never again," and "Let us cure the root cause of the Korean Problem once and for all."[5]

Summit diplomacy between both Koreas and the United States began against this backdrop in 2018. Two considerations loomed large: the three countries' determination to end the crisis and avert the threat of nuclear war, and Kim Jong-un's peace initiative based on North Korea's newly attained nuclear deterrent. Kim was well aware that the nuclear deterrent enabled him to negotiate with the United States for a peace deal from a position of strength.

THE ROLE OF SUMMITRY IN
INTER-KOREAN RELATIONS

The inter-Korean summits, declarations, and military agreement ushered in a great transition to peace on the Korean Peninsula in 2018 that contrasted sharply with the extremely treacherous threat of nuclear war in 2017. Inter-Korean summitry led to a drastic reduction in military tension on the

Korean Peninsula and catalyzed the first-ever US–North Korea summit in June 2018 in Singapore, which produced the historic "Joint Statement of President Donald J. Trump of the United States of America and Chairman Kim Jong Un of the Democratic People's Republic of Korea at the Singapore Summit."[6]

Inter-Korean summitry in 2018 resurrected the spirit and legacy of four prior inter-Korean agreements. These include the "North-South Joint Statement," the "Agreement on Reconciliation, Non-Aggression, and Exchanges and Cooperation between North and South Korea" (also known as the "Basic Agreement"), the "North-South Joint Declaration," and the "Declaration for Advancing Inter-Korean Relations and Peace and Prosperity."[7]

These inter-Korean agreements were the results of choices made by the leaders of both Koreas at critical junctures in world history—that is, the détente in the early 1970s, the Soviet demise in early 1990s, and the post–Cold War transition period until the emergence of a US-China world order—and the victory of revisionist forces against the status quo in South Korea to reconcile and cooperate with the North during the aforementioned critical junctures for geostrategic, military-security, and economic reasons.

Within the broader context of strategic choices made by the Korean leaders at critical junctures in history and the power struggle between status quo and revisionist forces regarding inter-Korean relations, the summitry in 2018 could be interpreted as a continuation of the revisionist tradition toward peace. Summitry helped reconciliation and peace take precedence over hostility and war between the two Koreas.

THE PANMUNJOM DECLARATION, PYONGYANG JOINT DECLARATION, AND CMA

The two inter-Korean declarations and the 2018 CMA reduced military tensions and promoted peace and denuclearization on the Korean Peninsula.

Panmunjom Declaration, April 27, 2018

The Panmunjom Declaration asserts that "there will be no more war and a new era of peace has begun on the Korean peninsula." In the declaration, both Korean leaders agreed "to completely cease all hostile acts against each other in every domain including land, sea and air that are the root cause of military tension and conflicts." Second, they agreed to "reconnect the blood relations of the nation and bring forward the future of co-prosperity and independent reunification led by Koreans," affirming "the principle of national independence which specifies that the destiny of our nation is determined on their own accord." Third, they agreed to "actively cooperate to build a permanent and stable peace regime on the Korean peninsula" and reaffirmed "the non-aggression agreement that precludes the use of force in any form against each other and agreed to strictly abide by it." Fourth, they agreed "to declare the end of war" in 2018 and "actively promote the holding of trilateral meetings involving the two sides and the United States, or quadrilateral meetings involving the two sides, the United States and China with a view to replacing the Armistice Agreement with a peace agreement and establishing a permanent and solid peace regime." Finally, they "confirmed the common goal of realizing, through complete denuclearization, a nuclear-free Korean peninsula."[8]

It is noteworthy that the Panmunjom Declaration went beyond the historic June 15, 2000, "North-South Joint Declaration" and the October 4, 2007, "Declaration for Advancing Inter-Korean Relations and Peace and Prosperity" in terms of improving inter-Korean relations, reducing military tension, and promoting peace and denuclearization on the Korean Peninsula. The accomplishments of the Panmunjom Declaration included agreements on opening an inter-Korean joint liaison office at the Kaesong Industrial Complex, the comprehensive military agreement, the transformation of the demilitarized zone (DMZ) into a peace zone, disarmament in a phased manner, an end-of-war declaration within the year, the pursuit of three-party or four-party talks for transforming the Armistice Agreement into a permanent and solid peace regime, and the confirmation of complete denuclearization and a nuclear-free Korean Peninsula.

Pyongyang Joint Declaration, September 19, 2018

The "Pyongyang Joint Declaration of September 2018" emphatically "reaffirmed the principle of independence and self-determination of the Korean nation" and stated that both Korean leaders "agreed to expand the cessation of military hostilities in regions of confrontation such as the DMZ to the substantial removal of the danger of war across the entire Korean Peninsula and a fundamental resolution of the hostile relations."[9]

Two agreements loom large in the Pyongyang Joint Declaration: the adoption of the CMA signed by the North and South Korean defense ministers, and Kim Jong-un's explicit intention to permanently dismantle the Yongbyon nuclear facility in exchange for corresponding US measures in accordance with the spirit of the US-DPRK Joint Statement in Singapore.

First, both Korean leaders adopted and agreed to "fully abide by and faithfully implement" the CMA and to "actively take practical measures to transform the Korean Peninsula into a zone of permanent peace."[10]

Second, the two sides "shared the view that the Korean Peninsula must be turned into a land of peace free from nuclear weapons and nuclear threats." In particular, it was agreed that North Korea would "permanently dismantle the Dongchang-ri missile engine test site and launch platform under the observation of experts from relevant countries" and "continue to take additional measures, such as the permanent dismantlement of the nuclear facilities in Yongbyon, as the United States takes corresponding measures in accordance with the spirit of the June 12 U.S.-DPRK Joint Statement."[11]

It is important to note that this was the first time in the history of inter-Korean relations that an inter-Korean agreement contained specific measures that North Korea pledged to take toward the permanent dismantlement of its nuclear and missile facilities. Though conditional, Kim Jong-un's offer of permanent and total dismantlement of the Dongchang-ri missile engine test site and launch platform and Yongbyon nuclear facility represented a bold offer that aimed to secure the success of the U.S.-North Korea Hanoi summit.

The CMA, September 19, 2018

The CMA, adopted as an annex to the Pyongyang Joint Declaration, was designed to implement Article 2 of the Panmunjom Declaration in the military domain and cease all hostile acts that stoked tension between the two Koreas.

To that effect, the two Koreas agreed to implement several military confidence-building measures (CBMs) and early-stage arms control measures. First, the two sides agreed "to completely cease all hostile acts against each other in every domain including land, sea and air that are the root cause of military tension and conflicts." Second, they agreed to transform the DMZ into a peace zone. Third, they agreed to transform the Northern Limit Line (NLL) into a maritime peace zone. Fourth, they agreed on military assurance measures including the East and West transportation corridors and East/West railways and roads. Fifth, they agreed on military CBMs including direct communication lines and an inter-Korean joint military committee.[12]

The CMA constitutes the most detailed agreement on the prevention of accidental clashes between the two Koreas and early stages of arms control on the Korean Peninsula. The CMA includes five annexes: "Withdrawal of Guard Posts (GP) within the DMZ," "Demilitarization of the 'Joint Security Area in Panmunjom,'" "Pilot Inter-Korean Joint Remains Recovery Project within DMZ, Preventing Accidental Military Clashes, Establishing a Maritime Peace Zone and Ensuring Safe Fishing Activities in the West Sea," and "Military Assurance for the Joint Use of Han (Imjin) River Estuary."[13]

MOTIVES AND OBJECTIVES OF
INTER-KOREAN SUMMITRY

Chairman Kim Jong-un of North Korea and President Moon Jae-in of South Korea had their own motives and objectives toward inter-Korean summitry. Some motives and objectives—such as the stabilization of inter-Korean relations, reduction of military tension, and promotion of peace on the Korean Peninsula—were jointly shared by both leaders, while others were not.

Kim Jong-un's Motives and Objectives

Three major motives and objectives appear to have influenced Kim Jong-un to engage Moon Jae-in through summitry: to stabilize inter-Korean relations to set the stage for a peace initiative bolstered by his newly acquired nuclear deterrent; to "go to Washington through Seoul" for direct dialogue and negotiations with the United States to resolve U.S.-North Korea problems; and more fundamentally, to implement North Korea's long-held "strategy of survival and development for the 21st century" by engaging the United States.[14]

First, Kim initiated summitry with Moon to stabilize inter-Korean relations with a view to establishing a "peaceful environment" for preventing a nuclear war and to begin dialogue and summitry with Trump.[15] Believing that his acquisition of a nuclear deterrent reduced the threat of war on the Korean Peninsula, Kim made clear that he wanted peace, not war. He appeared to believe that he could deal with the United States from a position of strength, even though Central Intelligence Agency (CIA) Director Mike Pompeo publicly stated that the United States was dealing with North Korea "from a position of enormous strength with sanctions that are unrivaled against the North Korean regime."[16]

Second, by "going to Washington through Seoul" Kim apparently sought an opportunity to directly negotiate with the United States to resolve pending issues and establish peace on the Korean Peninsula. North Korea has long wanted to do so, but the United States has been generally unreceptive to North Korean demands for a negotiated end-of-war declaration and peace agreement. The United States has tended to be more focused on rivalry and confrontation with the Soviet Union and China, which helped ignore the demands from North Korea, an ally of both countries. North Korean demands for dialogue and negotiations with the United States became more necessary and urgent following the collapse of the Soviet Union in 1991 and with dramatically growing Chinese influence over North Korea in the absence of the Soviet Union.

Third, Kim decided to commence his leadership by implementing North Korea's long-held "strategy of survival and development for the 21st century" that was formulated at the time of Soviet demise in 1991. The strategy aimed to achieve two objectives. One was to posit the United States as a counter-force to China in the Soviet Union's absence in Northeast Asia to secure more North Korean independence in international politics. The other was to negotiate a peace regime and end-of-war declaration, normalization of rela-tions, and economic cooperation with the United States in exchange for North Korea's denuclearization and "informal" tolerance of the US forces stationed in South Korea. North Korea needed the United States to carry out its survival strategy and develop in the highly amorphous international political environ-ment of the post–Cold War era.[17]

Kim's effort to carry out the aforementioned strategy represents the sixth such attempt in the history of US–North Korea relations since 1991: first, the January 1992 Arnold Kanter–Kim Yong-sun meeting at the US Mission to the United Nations in New York City; second, the outbreak of the first North Korean nuclear crisis in 1993 and negotiations with the United States that led to the Agreed Framework in Geneva in 1994; third, North Korean Vice Marshal Cho Myong-rok's visit to Washington, D.C., and the October 12, 2000, US-DPRK Joint Communique and Secretary of State Madeline Albright's return visit to Pyongyang that month; fourth, the outbreak of the second North Korean nuclear crisis and US–North Korea negotiations amid the Six Party Talks that led to the September 19, 2005, Joint Statement; fifth, North Korea's June 16, 2013, proposal for high-level talks with the United States that hinted at a nuclear-weapon-free zone on the Korean Peninsula fol-lowing escalating tensions after the US–South Korea joint military exercise in spring of 2013; and sixth, Kim Jong-un's peace initiative after obtaining a nuclear deterrent in 2017 that led to the first-ever US–North Korea summit in Singapore and the US-DPRK Joint Statement in June 2018.[18]

Moon Jae-in's Motives and Objectives

Moon Jae-in's motives and objectives in engaging Kim Jong-un in summitry were threefold: to make the February 2018 Pyeongchang Winter Olympics a success with North Korea's participation and leverage the momentum toward peace; to stabilize inter-Korean relations to reduce military tensions and move inter-Korean reconciliation and cooperation forward; and to denuclear-ize and establish a peace regime on the Korean Peninsula.

First, Moon was eager to make the February 2018 Pyeongchang Winter Olympics a "Peace Olympics" with North Korea's participation. In fact, Moon invited Kim to the Pyeongchang Olympics about seven months ear-lier in his "Peace Design of the New Government of South Korea" speech delivered in Berlin, Germany, on July 6, 2017—just two days after North Korea test-launched the Hwasong-14 ICBM.[19] Kim responded to Moon's invitation by confirming North Korea's participation in the Winter Olympics during his 2018 New Year's Speech.[20]

Negotiations over North Korea's participation in the Winter Olympics and Moon-Kim summit talks began almost immediately. Kim Yo-jong, Kim Jong-un's special envoy and only sister, came to South Korea with Kim Yong-nam, chairman of the Standing Committee of the Supreme People's Assembly, to attend the Pyeongchang Winter Olympics opening ceremony. She delivered Kim Jong-un's message to Moon Jae-in at the Blue House that Kim wanted to invite Moon to Pyongyang for a summit and begin dialogue with the United States.

Concurrently, a deputy head of the United Front Department of the Workers' Party of Korea (WPK), which manages intelligence work on South Korea and the United States, accompanied the North Korean athletes and began dialogue with his South Korean counterpart and the head of the CIA's Korea Mission Center.[21] South Korea now had a golden opportunity to arrange a summit by leveraging the momentum toward peace created by the Pyeongchang Winter Olympics. Bilateral and trilateral dialogue among representatives from the two Koreas and the United States gave birth to the inter-Korean Panmunjom summit and the U.S-North Korea Singapore summit.

Second, Moon was desperate to stabilize inter-Korean relations to reduce military tensions and move national reconciliation and cooperation forward. After experiencing the threat of nuclear war in the second half of 2017, Moon, like other Koreans, saw military tension reduction on the Korean Peninsula as his top priority. Moon sought to promote inter-Korean reconciliation and cooperation as a way to initiate a peace process. Moon's aspirations for promoting peace were faithfully reflected in the Panmunjom Declaration, Pyongyang Joint Declaration, and the CMA.

Third, Moon strived to establish a peace regime and denuclearize the Korean Peninsula, as expressed in his "Peace Design of the New Government of South Korea" speech in Berlin. Moon's "Peace Process" policy was designed to uproot the "root cause" of military tension and threat of nuclear war on the Korean Peninsula by transforming the Korean Armistice Agreement into a permanent and solid peace regime. However, without the denuclearization of North Korea, a permanent peace regime could not be established. And without a peace settlement, Koreans would be unable to break the seven-decade-long vicious cycle of hostilities and war on their land.

ASSESSMENT ONE: A MIXED
OUTCOME FOR BOTH LEADERS

Two basic criteria for policy assessment are whether the policy has achieved its declared objectives and what kind of impact the policy has had on the issues it addressed.[22] The scoresheets of summitry for both Kim Jong-un and Moon Jae-in show that both leaders attained mixed results in their objectives: initial success, followed by failure. The assessment of the impact of summitry on inter-Korean relations and on U.S.-North Korea and U.S.-South Korea relations will be dealt with in the following two sections.

Kim Jong-un's Scoresheet

For Kim Jong-un, inter-Korean summitry brought about mixed results: initial success, followed by failure.

On the success side, the Panmunjom Declaration, Pyongyang Joint Declaration, and CMA resulted in an unprecedented reduction of military tension on the Korean Peninsula. They also provided the peaceful environment required for both Koreas to promote reconciliation, cooperation, and progress toward an end-of-war declaration, peace regime, normalization in relations, etcetera—all issues Kim wanted to address in his summits with Trump.

Early in 2018, Kim Jong-un was perceived as very forward-leaning and proactive in his interactions with Moon during dialogue and summitry. It is noteworthy that Kim Jong-un assigned Kim Yo-jong, none other than his own sibling and his most trusted aide, the task of making significant breakthroughs in North Korea's relationships with South Korea and the United States. She visited South Korea as Kim Jong-un's special envoy to deliver a message to Moon that paved the way for an inter-Korean summit, participated with her brother in important meetings with US delegations, and issued a series of official statements on inter-Korean and US–North Korea affairs.

Furthermore, summitry with South Korean and US leaders provided Kim Jong-un with a rare opportunity to carry out North Korea's long-overdue implementation of the "strategy of survival and development for the 21st century." As discussed, Kim's summitry in 2018–2019 with Moon and Trump constitutes North Korea's sixth attempt to carry out the strategy and open a bright new era for North Korea and Kim Jong-un himself.

Again, it is important to note that Kim dealt with South Korean and US leaders from a position of strength based on his newly obtained nuclear deterrent, which brought about at least a partial correction of the "asymmetry" in military power and capabilities between the United States and North Korea.

However, Kim Jong-un's disillusionment with South Korea loomed large. He was frustrated with the failure of the following to materialize: South Korea's much-advocated argument of "South Korea in the driver's seat," which indicated its determination to seek more autonomy and independence from the United States in dealing with Korean Peninsula–related issues; South Korea's promised implementation of the Panmunjom Declaration and Pyongyang Joint Declaration; and South Korea's alleged influence on the United States in coordinating their North Korea policies to ensure faithful implementation of the inter-Korean summit declarations and the US-DPRK Joint Statement in Singapore.[23]

Kim's disillusionment with South Korea derived mainly from its perceived lack of independence in constructing its North Korea policy and failure to defy US influence. The Panmunjom Declaration stated that "the two sides affirmed the principle of national independence which specifies that the destiny of our nation is determined on their own accord."[24] And the Pyongyang Joint Declaration "reaffirmed the principle of independence and self-determination of the Korean nation."[25] North Korea repeatedly reminded South Korea of its duty to carry out the inter-Korean summit declarations faithfully as a signatory to the declaration.[26]

Kim was dissatisfied with the degree to which South Korea implemented the Panmunjom Declaration and Pyongyang Joint Declaration. It is important to note that the Panmunjom Declaration promised that "for the present, they agreed to stop all the hostile acts including the loudspeaker broadcasting and scattering of leaflets in the areas along the Military Demarcation Line (MDL) from May 1, to dismantle their means, and further to transform the DMZ into a peace zone in a genuine sense."[27]

Kim's displeasure with Moon's performance in implementing the inter-Korean summit declarations was apparent in Kim Yo-jong's statements on June 4, 13, and 17, 2020.[28] Her June 17 statement issued just after North Korea blew up the inter-Korean joint liaison office at the Kaesong Industrial Complex in particular illustrated Kim Jong-un's frustration with the South.[29] In her statement, Kim Yo-jong slammed South Korea and Moon for not preventing North Korean defectors from "publicly" flying "anti-Kim Jong-un" propaganda leaflets over the border on May 31, 2020.[30] As a matter of fact, flying leaflets over the border was a violation of Article 2, Section 1 of the Panmunjom Declaration.

Kim Yo-jong blamed South Korea for compromising the mutual respect and trust foundational for inter-Korean relations. She criticized Moon for ascribing his inability to faithfully implement the Panmunjom Declaration and Pyongyang Joint Declaration to internal and external factors like US pressure, rather than to his personal failure and lack of responsibility. And she castigated Moon for his "toadyism" and "subservience" to the United States, asserting that South Korea would pay dearly for its betrayal of "trust."[31]

More important, however, Kim Jong-un appears to have regarded the flying of anti-Kim propaganda leaflets as part of a greater scheme designed to undermine and collapse his regime, in line with renewed "US provocations" after Kim's absence from an April 15, 2020, memorial service for his late grandfather, Kim Il-sung. Following the service, news reports swirled with rumors of Kim Jong-un's death and loss of power, Kim Yo-jong's succession to leadership, and so on.[32] During this period, the US Department of Defense increased aerial reconnaissance into the Korean theater, which Kim apparently perceived as US provocations.[33]

Finally, Kim Jong-un's disillusionment with the Moon government had much to do with South Korea's limited ability to persuade the Trump administration to take further steps to act in accordance with the spirit of the Singapore Joint Statement—an end-of-war declaration to close the Korean War, normalization of US–North Korea relations, the removal of sanctions against North Korea, etcetera.

In preparing for the September 2018 summit in Pyongyang, Moon Jae-in vigorously persuaded Kim Jong-un to totally and irreversibly dismantle the Dongchang-ri missile engine test site and launch platform and the Yongbyon nuclear facility. Kim Jong-un accommodated Moon's persuasion, trusting South Korea's ability to influence US policy toward the North to ensure the success of the upcoming Hanoi deal. North Korea agreed beforehand with South Korea that it would make these concessions in exchange for "corresponding measures" by the United States.[34] Kim notified Trump of his intention to give up all nuclear facilities in Yongbyon and even "more" in his letter to Trump of September 6, 2018.[35]

South Korean persuasion, however, missed the mark in Hanoi. Trump and his hardliner aides rejected Kim's proposal to totally dismantle and abandon the Yongbyon nuclear facility and Dongchang-ri missile engine test site and launch platform in exchange for the "partial" removal of UN Security Council sanctions against North Korea.[36]

At the Hanoi summit, Kim repeatedly explained to Trump how significant North Korea's total destruction of the Yongbyon nuclear complex would be for the denuclearization of the Korean Peninsula, but Trump and his aides did not buy it and "walked away."[37]

Kim appears to have blamed Moon for Kim's failure to carry out North Korea's "strategy of survival and development for the 21st century" and the resulting disgrace Kim suffered. North Korea completely halted inter-Korean cooperation after the Hanoi summit.

Moon Jae-in's Scoresheet

Moon experienced a mixed outcome from inter-Korean summitry paralleling that of Kim Jong-un: initial success, followed by failure.

Moon Jae-in celebrated an enormous success in 2018 thanks to North Korea's participation in the Pyeongchang Winter Olympics and the historic Panmunjom Declaration, Pyongyang Joint Declaration of September 2018, and the CMA for military tension reduction and promotion of peace on the Korean Peninsula.

Concretely, the Pyeongchang Winter Olympics left a rich legacy of promoting peace on the Korean Peninsula: North Korea's participation made it the "Peace Olympics," and Kim Yo-jong visited the Blue House and delivered her brother's intention to have summitry with South Korea. The Panmunjom Declaration promised a complete cessation of all hostile acts against each other in every domain including land, sea, and air. The CMA was a detailed agreement of its implementation. The Pyongyang Joint Declaration succeeded for the first time in having Kim Jong-un agree to a permanent dismantlement of the Dongchang-ri missile engine test site and launch platform, and also of the nuclear facilities in Yongbyon on condition that the United States take corresponding measures in accordance with the spirit of the June 12, 2018, Joint Statement.

However, Trump's last-minute reversal of his well-intended preparations for a successful Hanoi deal with Kim Jong-un negated whatever successes Moon had enjoyed with the North until that time. The US–North Korea Hanoi summit failure, combined with Kim Jong-un's disillusionment with South Korea's ability to influence US policy toward North Korea, halted the implementation of the inter-Korean summit declarations and CMA.

In November 2019, Kim Jong-un visited a frontline military unit at Changrindo Island near South Korea's Baengnyeongdo Island and ordered the unit to fire artillery toward South Korean waters. Even more grave, Kim continued to advance North Korea's weapons technology in the areas of super-large multiple rocket launchers (MRLs), North Korean versions of the Russian *Iskander* and US Army Tactical Missile System (ATACMS), cruise missiles, submarine-launched ballistic missiles (SLBMs), and supersonic missiles. All this means that Kim was determined to solidify North Korea's missile capabilities as a war deterrent against South Korea and the United States.

Most recently, on January 12, 2022, the Biden administration imposed its first sanctions over North Korea's aforementioned missile test-firings, particularly after the supersonic missiles.[38] In response, the politburo meeting of the WPK held on January 19, 2022, resulted in a decision to bolster North Korea's defenses against the United States and reconsider the resumption of "all temporarily suspended activities"—North Korea's self-imposed morato-rium on nuclear and long-range missile tests intended as CBMs in the lead-up to the April 27, 2018, Panmunjom Declaration and June 12, 2018, US–DPRK Joint Statement.[39] In accordance with the decision, North Korea resumed test-firings of Hwasong-12 intermediate-range ballistic missiles (IRBMs) on January 30 and Hwasong-17 ICBMs on March 16 (failed) and March 24, all at high angles.[40]

Kim Jong-un also punished the South in the nonmilitary realm: he visited the South Korea–developed Mt. Gumgang tourism resort in October 2019 and ordered the demolition of "unpleasant-looking" South Korean facilities; he blew up the inter-Korean joint liaison office at the Kaesong Industrial Complex in June 2020; and North Korea killed and incinerated "as an anti-coronavirus measure" an official from South Korea's Ministry of Oceans and Fisheries who disappeared from a patrol boat near the border and was later found in the North's waters.[41]

In other words, Moon suffered greatly in his effort to promote peace on the Korean Peninsula due to the failure of the US–North Korea summit in Hanoi and resulting decrease in North Korea's trust in South Korea as a partner for the transition to peace on the Korean Peninsula.

ASSESSMENT TWO: IMPACT OF INTER-KOREAN SUMMITRY ON INTER-KOREAN, US–NORTH KOREA, AND US–SOUTH KOREA RELATIONS

Another criterion for policy assessment revolves around the impact of the policy on the issues it was intended to solve.[42] Inter-Korean summitry had significant impacts on inter-Korean, US–North Korea, and US–South Korea relations. They included: inter-Korean rapprochement and increased peace, prevention of military clashes, and hope for denuclearization; South Korea's mediating role between the United States and North Korea, and Pyongyang's use of Seoul as a bridge between Pyongyang and Washington; and US–North Korea direct dialogue and negotiations sidelining South Korea.

Impact of Inter-Korean Summitry on Inter-Korean Relations

Inter-Korean summitry had a threefold impact on inter-Korean relations: inter-Korean rapprochement and increased peace, prevention of military clashes, and hope for denuclearization.

First, in the history of inter-Korean relations, all summits and joint declara-tions have marked epoch-making events or turning points for rapprochement and peace. Inter-Korean summitry in 2018 was no exception: it constituted a departure from the egregiously heightened threat of nuclear war on the Korean Peninsula in 2017 and powerfully promoted a transition to peace on the Korean Peninsula.

The summitry cultivated a "peaceful environment" absent during the tenures of former South Korean presidents Lee Myung-bak and Park Geun-hye, elevating prospects for peace and prosperity on the Korean Peninsula, as well as for national reconciliation and cooperation. The Panmunjom Declaration and Pyongyang Joint Declaration agreed on a comprehensive list of areas of cooperation between the two Koreas—politico-diplomatic, military-security, socioeconomic, cultural, humanitarian, tourism, environmental, medical, sports, etcetera.

Second, following inter-Korean summitry, the two Koreas have not engaged in any notable military clashes since 2018. This compares favorably with past North Korean military provocations, which have included: two naval clashes in the West Sea (Yellow Sea) in 1999 and 2002 during the Kim Dae-jung government; a naval clash in the West Sea in 2009, the sinking of the South Korean navy corvette *Cheonan* in the West Sea in 2010, and North Korea's bombardment of South Korea's Yeonpyeong Island in 2010 during the Lee Myung-bak government; and a mine blast at the DMZ in 2015 and the North Korean army's shooting of loud speakers at South Korea's western front in 2015 during the Park Geun-hye government.

Third, inter-Korean summitry also gave rise to hope for the denuclearization of the Korean Peninsula, as agreed upon in the Panmunjom Declaration and Pyongyang Joint Declaration. Unfortunately, as the Hanoi failure revealed, the Panmunjom Declaration and Pyongyang Joint Declaration were limited in their ability to impact bilateral US–North Korea negotiations conducted with South Korea sidelined. This clearly demonstrated the closely intertwined nature of inter-Korean relations and US–North Korea relations and the resultant necessity of US support for the two Koreas to progress toward a nuclear-free, peaceful, and prosperous Korean Peninsula.

Impact of Inter-Korean Summitry on U.S.-North Korea Relations

The impact of inter-Korean summitry on US–North Korea relations is mainly apparent in South Korea's mediating role between the United States and North Korea, and Pyongyang's use of Seoul as a bridge between Pyongyang and Washington, as discussed above.

First, both the United States and North Korea requested that South Korea play a mediating role when they experienced difficulties in making progress in bilateral negotiations.

When Trump, on May 24, 2018, canceled the US–North Korea summit scheduled for June 12, 2018, in Singapore "based on the tremendous anger and open hostility displayed" in statements by senior North Korean Foreign Ministry officials, North Korea requested South Korea's help on May 25.[43] An inter-Korean summit took place at Panmunjom the very next day, on May 26, and South Korea successfully brought both the United States and North Korea together. Trump confirmed on June 1 that he would meet Kim Jong-un in Singapore as scheduled.[44]

The United States and North Korea also sought South Korean mediation when they faced a series of obstacles during high-level and working-level negotiations over concrete steps to carry out the Singapore Joint Statement, which were to be approved at the Hanoi summit. Even after the Hanoi summit stalled, Trump called Moon to request mediation.[45]

Second, Pyongyang used Seoul as a stepping-stone to Washington so that Kim could negotiate directly with Trump for an end-of-war declaration, peace regime, normalization of relations, and economic cooperation including sanctions relief for North Korea. On March 9, 2018, Moon dispatched a special envoy delegation, which met with Kim in Pyongyang on March 5, to Trump to convey Kim's message that he wanted to have a summit talk with Trump. Trump agreed to a summit with Kim during the South Korean special envoy delegation's briefing and publicized the summit right away outside the West Wing of the White House.[46] However, as will be discussed below, Pyongyang's utilization of Seoul was quite effective at first, particularly until the US–North Korea summit in Singapore, but not afterward.

Impact of Inter-Korean Summitry on US–South Korea Relations

Inter-Korean summitry has had a twofold impact on US—South Korea relations: South Korea took on a leading mediator's role "in the driver's seat" during the first half of 2018, when the United States sought dialogue with North Korea, and then was sidelined afterward when the United States put the brakes on inter-Korean cooperation and conducted direct dialogue and negotiations with North Korea.

South Korea's leading, intermediary role at the initial phase of the transition to peace on the Korean Peninsula was possible because the United States and North Korea were not in direct contact but sought dialogue and negotiation and required a third-party mediator to make this happen. Once the US–North Korea summit took place in Singapore in June 2018, however, South Korea's sidelining by the United States was most strikingly demonstrated: Trump promised Kim at the Singapore summit, without any prior consultation with South Korea, that he would stop the US–South Korea "war games," or joint military exercises.[47]

South Korea's practical exclusion from negotiations, particularly on the "war and peace" issues of the Korean Peninsula, had much to do with the fact that South Korea has not yet taken over wartime operational control (OPCON) of its military forces from the US–South Korea Combined Forces Command (CFC), the commander of which is a four-star US general.

Once a direct US–North Korea negotiation channel was opened, the United States also sought to reduce the speed and scope of inter-Korean cooperation. The United States wanted to have South Korea be "on the same page" in their policies toward North Korea.[48] To that end, the United States established a US–South Korea working group in November 2018 to coordinate their policies in the areas of denuclearization, sanctions, etcetera. The strong US grip on South Korea in coordinating approaches to North Korea was explicitly expressed in the May 21, 2021, US–South Korea summit joint statement, in which both agreed to coordinate their approaches to North Korea "in lockstep."[49]

It was also noteworthy that the United States wanted South Korea to play a role in resolving the North Korean nuclear problem, but to not overly limit the scope of US options. For instance, the United States "urged" South Korea to "avoid discussing denuclearization" with North Korea at the April 2018 Panmunjom summit.[50]

IMPLICATIONS AND PROSPECTS FOR THE FUTURE OF INTER-KOREAN RELATIONS

Finally, inter-Korean summitry influenced the future of inter-Korean relations around three central questions: how to secure more autonomy from the United States for inter-Korean relations; how to increase South Korea's influence on the North, lest North Korea ignore South Korea's push for inter-Korean development and peace settlement on the Korean Peninsula; and how to build trust among the countries involved in Korean affairs.

US policy toward the Korean Peninsula has heavily influenced inter-Korean relations, as abundantly evidenced by the impact of the failure of the Hanoi summit on inter-Korean relations. The question of how both Koreas can secure more autonomy in inter-Korean relations from the United States applies particularly to South Korea. South Korea has to cooperate with the United States, an asymmetrical ally in military power, in particular, in dealing with the North, while North Korea as an enemy does not necessarily need to coordinate with or be controlled by the United States on its policies toward the South.

As discussed above, South Korea's dependence on the United States regarding North Korea policy in part stems from South Korea's current lack of wartime OPCON over its own military forces. More seriously, Operation Plan (OPLAN) 5015, employed by US–South Korea joint military exercises, is essentially the operation plan of the US Indo-Pacific Command, which "calls for a prompt response to a North Korean attack with a preventive strike on the North's core military facilities and weapons as well as its top leaders."[51] In other words, OPLAN 5015 includes the so-called decapitation of North Korean leader Kim Jong-un, which, South Koreans worry, could trigger a full-scale war on the Korean Peninsula.

South Korea has made efforts to take OPCON back from the United States, but its ability to qualify for "conditions-based" OPCON transfer is still being tested through assessment of whether the future CFC's capabilities meet required conditions in areas including operations, intelligence, logistics, and communication. Considering that "conditions-based" OPCON transfer can only take place once hundreds of complex and multilevel conditions are met, OPCON transfer is in effect postponed indefinitely.

However, if South Korea had taken over wartime OPCON before 2018, the United States and North Korea would have been unable to sideline South Korea from negotiations on "war and peace" issues of the Korean Peninsula. South Korea would also have secured more autonomy for inter-Korean relations from the United States in 2018 and onward.

Despite South Korea seeking to increase its influence over North Korea, the North's ignoring or sidelining of South Korea, intentional or unintentional, likely relates to three issues: North Korea's view of South Korea as a rival or competitor to North Korea in the pursuit of national unification; North Korea's strategy of "going to Washington directly" for bilateral dialogue and negotiation; and South Korea's lack of wartime OPCON of its military.

The second and third factors are addressed above; the first item, however, is also important to consider. South Korea poses a competitive threat to the North Korean regime in that the more prosperous and democratic South could present an alternative regime for North Koreans who suffer tremendously from an ever-worsening economy in autocratic North Korea. North Korea's government and leaders have therefore been defensive and incremental in their policies toward the South, more often than not.

All in all, the independence of North Korea's South Korea policy from its US policy appears to depend ultimately on the extent to which South Korea expands autonomy in its North Korea policy from the United States; whether and how soon South Korea gains wartime OPCON of its military from the United States; and the extent to which US–South Korea alliance cooperation contributes to solving the long-overdue Korean problem and settling peace through a comprehensive give-and-take deal with North Korea.

Last but not least, trust-building among the countries involved in Korean affairs is a matter of grave concern for the transition to peace on the Korean Peninsula. The US-DPRK Joint Statement in Singapore made clear that both Trump and Kim "recogniz[ed] that mutual confidence building can promote the denuclearization of the Korean Peninsula."[52] Despite both leaders' understanding of the importance of trust building between their countries for the implementation of the joint statement, the whole period from June 2018 to February 2019 was spent on wrestling with the question of how to do so. The United States was focused on "denuclearization first, others later," but North Korea focused on "trust-building first, denuclearization later." The failure to build trust between the United States and North Korea until the last moment in February 2019 led to the failure of the Hanoi summit.

The conditions for resuming dialogue and negotiation between the two Koreas and also between the United States and North Korea have deteriorated substantially since the failure in Hanoi. We are in a time of disillusionment among the parties involved. But North Korea says it will do to the United States and South Korea what the United States and South Korea do to North Korea: "force for force, goodwill for goodwill."[53] In other words, trust-building will realistically depend on which path the United States and South Korea will take. That is why we need to resume dialogue and negotiations to build trust, albeit incrementally, if we want to resolve pending issues and move forward the great transition to peace on the Korean Peninsula that began in 2018.

NOTES

1. "Statement of the DPRK: On the Success of Test-Firing of New Type of ICBM," Korean Central Television, November 29, 2019 https://kcnawatch.org /newstream/1575000035-956784991/supreme-leader-kim-jong-un-inspects-test-fire -of-super-large-multiple-launch-rocket-system%e2%80%8b/; Kim Jong-un, "New Year's Address," Korea Central News Agency, January 1, 2018 https://kcnawatch.org /newstream/284839/kim-jong-un-makes-new-year-address/.

2. Bob Woodward, *Rage* (New York: Simon & Schuster, 2020), 71–82.

3. Cheryl Pellerin, "Carter Reaffirms U.S. Commitment to South Korea," American Forces Press Service, March 18, 2013, http://www.defense.gov/news/newsarticle .aspx?id=119556; Jim Garamone, "Bombers Show U.S. Resolve to Defend South Korea, Spokesman Says," American Forces Press Service, March 18, 2013, http:// www.defense.gov/news/newsarticle.aspx?id=119555; "Statement of the Spokesperson of the Foreign Ministry of the DPRK," Korean Central News Agency, March 7, 2013.

4. Kim Jong-un, "New Year's Address," January 1, 2018; Donald J. Trump (@ realDonaldTrump), "I too have a Nuclear Button, but it is a much bigger & more

powerful one than his," Twitter, January 2, 2018, https://twitter.com/nbcnews/status/948357374162726913.

5. "The Korean Problem" describes a comprehensive set of problems that need to be resolved with regard to the Korean Peninsula, which includes: consolidated division of the Korean Peninsula, no termination of the Korean War, existence and deterioration of the Korean armistice, North Korean nuclear and missile problems, threat of nuclear war between the United States and North Korea, conflict between inter-Korean cooperation and US–South Korea alliance cooperation, etcetera.

6. "Joint Statement of President Donald J. Trump of the United States of America and Chairman Kim Jong Un of the Democratic People's Republic of Korea at the Singapore Summit," June 12, 2018, https://trumpwhitehouse.archives.gov/briefings-statements/joint-statement-president-donald-j-trump-united-states-america-chairman-kim-jong-un-democratic-peoples-republic-korea-singapore-summit/.

7. "North-South Joint Statement," UN Peacemaker, July 4, 1971, https://peacemaker.un.org/korea-4july-communique72; "Agreement on Reconciliation, Non-Aggression, and Exchanges and Cooperation between North and South Korea," UN Peacemaker, December 13, 1991, https://peacemaker.un.org/korea-reconciliation-nonaggression91; "North-South Joint Declaration," UN Peacemaker, June 15, 2000, https://peacemaker.un.org/koreadprk-southnorthdeclaration; "Declaration for Advancing Inter-Korean Relations and Peace and Prosperity," National Committee on Korea, October 4, 2007, https://www.ncnk.org/resources/publications/North-South%20Declaration.doc.

8. "Panmunjom Declaration on Peace, Prosperity and Reunification of the Korean Peninsula," Inter-Korea Summit, April 27, 2018, https://koreasummit.kr/Summit2018/Performance.

9. "Pyongyang Joint Declaration of September 2018," National Committee on North Korea, September 19, 2018, https://www.ncnk.org/node/1633.

10. "Pyongyang Joint Declaration of September 2018."

11. "Pyongyang Joint Declaration of September 2018."

12. "Agreement on the Implementation of the Historic Panmunjom Declaration in the Military Domain," National Committee on North Korea, September 19, 2018, https://www.ncnk.org/resources/publications/agreement-implementation-historic-panmunjom-declaration-military-domain.pdf.

13. "Agreement on the Implementation."

14. Haksoon Paik, "North Korea's Choices for Survival and Prosperity since 1990s: Interplay between Politics and Economics," *Sejong Policy Studies* 3, no. 2 (2007): 250–77; Haksoon Paik, "Changes and Continuities in Inter-Korean Relations," in *North Korea in Transition*, ed. Kyung-Ae Park and Scott Snyder (Lanham, MD: Rowman and Littlefield, 2013), 245–46.

15. Kim Jong-un, "New Year's Address," Korea Central News Agency, January 1, 2018. https://kcnawatch.org/newstream/284839/kim-jong-un-makes-new-year-address/.

16. CBS News, "Transcript: CIA Director Mike Pompeo on *Face the Nation*, March 11, 2018," https://www.cbsnews.com/news/transcript-cia-director-mike-pompeo-on-face-the-nation-march-11-2018/.

17. The author dubbed North Korea's strategic design formulated at the time of the 1991 collapse of the Soviet Union as North Korea's "strategy of survival and development for the 21st century."

18. Don Oberdorfer and Robert Carlin, *The Two Koreas: A Contemporary History* (New York: Basic Books, 2001), 266–67; "U.S. and North Korea Meet for First Cabinet-Level Talks," *New York Times*, January 23, 1992; "Agreed Framework between the United States of America and the Democratic People's Republic of Korea," Geneva, October 21, 1994; "U.S.-DPRK Joint Communique," October 12, 2000; "Secretary of State Madeleine K. Albright Press Conference, Koryo Hotel," U.S. Department of State, October 24, 2000, https://1997-2001.state.gov/statements /2000/001024b.html; "Joint Statement of the Fourth Round of the Six-Party Talks," U.S. Department of State Archive, September 19, 2005, https://2001-2009.state.gov /r/pa/prs/ps/2005/53490.htm; "National Defense Commission Proposes to Hold a High-Level Meeting between the DPRK and the United States," Korean Central News Agency, June 16, 2013.

19. Moon Jae-in, "Address at the Körber Foundation, Germany," Office of the President, July 6, 2017, https://www1.presideant.go.kr/articles/57.

20. Kim Jong-un, "Kim Jong-un's 2018 New Year's Address," January 1, 2018.

21. Kim Ji-eun, "'National Intelligence Service—United Front Department' Emerged as Informal Channel for Communication," Hankyoreh, February 22, 2018, https://www.hani.co.kr/arti/politics/defense/833329.html; Elizabeth Shim, "CIA Korea Head Paved Way for Kim Jong Un, Mike Pompeo Meeting," UPI, May 15, 2018, https://www.upi.com/Top_News/World-News/2018/05/15/CIA-Korea-head -paved-way-for-Kim-Jong-Un-Mike-Pompeo-meeting/2421526400224/.

22. Charles O. Jones, *An Introduction to the Study of Public Policy* (Monterey, CA: Brooks/Cole Publishing Co., 1984), 198–201.

23. Kim Yo-jong, "Honeyed Words of Impudent Man Are Disgusting: Statement of the First Vice Department Director of WPK Central Committee," Korean Central News Agency, June 17, 2020.

24. "Panmunjom Declaration," Inter-Korea Summit, April 27, 2018. https:// koreasummit.kr/Summit2018/Performance.

25. "Pyongyang Joint Declaration of September 2018." National Committee on North Korea, September 19, 2018, https://www.ncnk.org/node/1633.

26. "Kim Yo-jong Rebukes S. Korean Authorities for Conniving at Anti-DPRK Hostile Act of 'Defectors from North,'" Korean Central News Agency, June 4, 2020.

27. "Panmunjom Declaration."

28. "Kim Yo Jong Rebukes S. Korean Authorities"; Kim Yo-jong, "First Vice Department Director of WPK Central Committee Issues Statement," Korean Central News Agency, June 13, 2020; Kim Yo-jong, "Honeyed Words of Impudent Man Are Disgusting: Statement of the First Vice Department Director of WPK Central Committee," Korean Central News Agency, June 17, 2020.

29. Kim Yo-jong, "Honeyed Words of Impudent Man."

30. "Kim Yo Jong Rebukes S. Korean Authorities."

31. Kim Yo-jong, "Honeyed Words of Impudent Man."

32. For instance, Jim Sciutto, Joshua Berlinger, Yoonjung Seo, Kylie Atwood and Zachary Cohen, "US Monitoring Intelligence That North Korean Leader Is in Grave Danger after Surgery," CNN, April 21, 2020; Choe Sang-Hun, "Kim Jong-un's Absence and North Korea's Silence Keep Rumor Mill Churning," *New York Times*, April 26, 2020.

33. Chris Pleasance and Tim Stickings, "South Korean Ministers Say They KNOW Kim Jong Un's Location and the Dictator Is Laying Low, Not Because He Is Ill, but to Avoid Coronavirus, amid Rumours He Had Died," *Daily Mail*, April 28, 2020, https://www.dailymail.co.uk/news/article-8263905/S-Korea-says-North-Koreas-Kim-trying-avoid-coronavirus.html.

34. "Pyongyang Joint Declaration of September 2018," National Committee on North Korea, September 19, 2018, https://www.ncnk.org/node/1633

35. "Transcript: Kim Jong Un's Letters to President Trump." CNN, September 9, 2020, https://www.cnn.com/2020/09/09/politics/transcripts-kim-jong-un-letters-trump/index.html; Robert L. Carlin, "The Real Lessons of the Trump-Kim Love Letters," *Foreign Policy*, August 13, 2021, https://foreignpolicy.com/2021/08/13/north-korea-trump-kim-jong-un-love-letters-diplomacy-nuclear-talks/.

36. DPRK Minister of Foreign Affairs Ri Yong-ho, Press Conference, March 1, 2019; "Remarks by Ri-Yong-ho and Choe Sun-hee at Late-Night Press Conference," Yonhap News Agency, March 1, 2019, https://www.yna.co.kr/view/AKR20190301006451504; "North Korea to Decide Soon Whether to Continue Denuclearization Negotiations with US," *BBC News*, March 16, 2019, https://www.bbc.com/korean/news-47579198; Lesley Wroughton and David Brunnstrom, "Exclusive: With a Piece of Paper, Trump Called on Kim to Hand Over Nuclear Weapons," Reuters, March 30, 2019, https://www.reuters.com/article/us-northkorea-usa-document-exclusive-idUSKCN1RA2NR.

37. John Bolton, *The Room Where It Happened: A White House Memoir* (New York: Simon & Schuster, 2020), 321, 322, 325–26, 328–30.

38. David Brunnstrom and Chris Gallagher, "Biden Imposes First Sanctions over North Korea's Missiles Program after Missile Tests," Reuters, January 13, 2022, https://www.reuters.com/world/asia-pacific/us-imposes-sanctions-north-koreans-russian-after-missile-tests-2022-01-12/.

39. "The 6th Politburo Meeting of the 8th Central Committee of the WPK in Progress," *Rodong Sinmun*, January 20, 2022.

40. "Striking Demonstration of Great Military Muscle of Juche Korea: Successful Test-Launch of New-Type ICBM Respected Comrade Kim Jong Un Guides Test Launch of ICBM Hwasongpho-17," *Rodong Sinmun*, March 25, 2022. Note that there were disagreements with North Korea's announced claim in terms of whether the missile was actually the Hwasong-17, the smaller Hwasong-15, or a modified version of it. See Michelle Ye Hee Lee, "North Korea's Latest Missile Test May Not Have Been What It Claimed," *Washington Post*, March 28, 2022, https://www.washingtonpost.com/world/2022/03/28/north-korea-missile-hwasong; Timothy W. Martin, Dasl Yoon, and Nancy A. Youssef, "North Korea's ICBM Intrigue: Is Latest Missile New or Old Technology?," *Wall Street Journal*, April 1, 2022, https://www.wsj.com/articles/north-koreas-icbm-intrigue-is-latest-missile-new-or-old-technology

-11648819821; and Vann H. Van Diepen, "North Korea's March 24 ICMB Launch: What If It Was the Hwasong-17?," *38 North*, April 7, 2022, https://www.38north.org/2022/04/north-koreas-march-24-icbm-launch-what-if-it-was-the-hwasong-17/#_ftn1.

41. "Dear Supreme Leader Comrade Kim Jong-un Conducted an On-the-Spot Guidance to Mt. Kumgang Tourism District," *Rodong Sinmun*, October 23, 2019; "North Korea Blows Up Joint Liaison Office with South in Kaesong," BBC, June 16, 2020, https://www.bbc.com/news/world-asia-53060620; Choe Sang-Hun, "North Korea Accused of Shooting and Burning South Korean Defector," *New York Times*, September 24, 2020, https://www.nytimes.com/2020/09/24/world/asia/korea-defector-covid-19.html.

42. Charles O. Jones, *An Introduction to the Study of Public Policy*, 198–201.

43. "Trump's Letter to Kim Jong-un," *Korea Times*, May 24, 2018, https://www.koreatimes.co.kr/www/nation/2022/02/103_249571.html; "Full text of Statement by Kim Kye-gwan on 'the Possibility of Reconsidering the North Korea–US Summit,'" *Hankyung*, May 16, 2018, https://www.hankyung.com/politics/article/201805160032Y; "North Korea's Choe Son-hui 'Pence is a dumb idiot,'" BBC, May 24, 2018, https://www.bbc.com/korean/news-44235459; Moon Jae-in, "Report to the People on the Result of the Second North-South Summit of 2018," May 27, 2018, https://koreasummit.kr/Newsroom/News/138.

44. Kevin Liptak, "Trump Says Singapore Summit with Kim Is Back On," CNN, June 1, 2018, https://edition.cnn.com/2018/06/01/politics/trump-north-korea-letter/index.html.

45. Seong Yeon-cheol, "Moon Encourages Trump to Continue Making 'Bold Decisions' for Peace on the Korean Peninsula," *Hankyoreh*, March 1, 2019, https://www.hani.co.kr/arti/PRINT/884169.html.

46. Woodward, *Rage*, 90–91.

47. "Press Conference by President Trump," National Committee on North Korea, June 12, 2018, https://www.ncnk.org/resources/publications/singapore_summit_press_conference.pdf/file_view; Woodward, *Rage*, 108–9.

48. Christy Lee, "US, South Korea to Launch Joint Working Group on North Korea," *Voice of America*, November 3, 2018.

49. "U.S.-ROK Leaders' Joint Statement," May 21, 2021.

50. Bolton, *The Room Where It Happened*, 78.

51. "OPLAN 5015 Operation Plans," *Global Security*, accessed December 20, 2021, https://www.globalsecurity.org/military/ops/oplan-5015.htm.

52. Donald J. Trump and Chairman Kim Jong Un, "Joint Statement of President Donald J. Trump of the United States of America and Chairman Kim Jong Un of the Democratic People's Republic of Korea at the Singapore Summit," Trump White House, June 12, 2018. https://trumpwhitehouse.archives.gov/briefings-statements/joint-statement-president-donald-j-trump-united-states-america-chairman-kim-jong-un-democratic-peoples-republic-korea-singapore-summit/

53. "The Great Combat Platform Leading Our-Style Socialist Construction to a New Victory: On Dear Comrade Kim Jong-un's Report Delivered at the Eighth Congress of the WPK," *Rodong Sinmun*, January 9, 2021.

Chapter 5

The Restoration of Special Sino–North Korean Relations and Xi Jinping–Kim Jong-un Summitry

Yun Sun

Sino–North Korean leadership summits were suspended for seven years after Kim Jong-un assumed power in 2011. It was not until the spring of 2018 that summit diplomacy was resumed. During this period, relations between China and North Korea deteriorated severely due to Chinese perceptions of uncertainty inside North Korea as well as China's warming ties with South Korea. As such, no Sino–North Korean leadership summits took place between May 2011 and March 2018.

Leadership summits are an important instrument in Sino–North Korean bilateral relations. At various historical junctures, both nations have used summits to demonstrate solidarity, coordinate positions, and express support for each other's domestic and foreign agendas. In some cases, they are examples of North Korean manipulation of Chinese positions and preferences, usually through leveraging diplomacy and engagement with another great power to provoke China's sense of anxiety. Chinese president Xi Jinping and Kim Jong-un have engaged in five summits since 2018, and these meetings are no exception. Kim successfully leveraged his engagement with US president Donald Trump to coax China into reengaging with North Korea in the first Xi-Kim summit of March 2018. Kim's approach served three aims: improvement of relations with China, improvement of Kim's negotiation position vis-à-vis the United States, and improvement of Kim's domestic political image as a world leader on par with Trump and Xi. The successful March 2018 summit preceded four additional Xi-Kim meetings that focused on the coordination of positions before and after the Singapore and Hanoi summits with the United States.

This chapter opens with a discussion of the historical record of leadership summits between China and North Korea, followed by an analysis of the context surrounding the 2018 and 2019 Xi-Kim summits. It examines the five summit meetings in detail and assesses the strategic importance of summitry for China–North Korea relations as well as for China–North Korea relations vis-à-vis the United States.

LEADERSHIP SUMMITRY IN CHINA–NORTH KOREA RELATIONS

Historically, Sino–North Korean leadership summitry has served three roles: to advance and strengthen strategic relations; to sustain and enhance personal ties between leaders; and to provide mutual support to counterbalance against external threats in the event of a crisis. Summits are a matter of formality, but they also infuse substance into the strategic relationship between the two countries, as well as into their individual national security strategies. Summits symbolize both mutual support and strategic leverage, especially in their respective relationships with the United States. (See table 5.1 for a list of Sino–North Korean senior leader summits.)

Leadership Summitry as an Instrument to Advance and Strengthen Bilateral Relations

Sino–North Korean leadership summitry demonstrates bilateral solidarity and strengthens strategic relations. In the Chinese official narrative, China–North Korea relations are described as close as "between lips and teeth" based on traditional friendly cooperation forged through "blood and fire" during the Korean War.[1] The historical memory of the war and the joint fighting against the United States are constantly referred to as one of the foundations of the special relationship between the two nations. However, a brief historical review reveals that summitry has been subject to fluctuations in China–North Korea relations at different historical stages. The frequency of leadership summits correlates with the health of bilateral relations.

The first meeting between Chairman Mao Zedong and Chairman Kim Il-sung took place in the context of Kim's preparation for the Korean War as Kim sought support from both Moscow and Beijing for his war plan. Upon obtaining General Secretary Joseph Stalin's endorsement for his plan to invade South Korea, Kim Il-sung traveled to Beijing on May 13, 1950, to inform Mao of the agreement he and Stalin had reached.[2] The Korean War

Table 5.1. Leadership Summits between China and North Korea (1950–Now)

Time	Visit
May 1950	Chairman Kim Il-sung visit to China
June 1951	Kim Il-sung visit to China
September 1954	Kim Il-sung visit to China
February 1958	Chinese Premier Zhou Enlai visit to North Korea
November 1958	Kim Il-sung visit to China
July 1961	Kim Il-sung visit to China and the signing of the Sino–North Korean Mutual Aid and Cooperation Friendship Treaty
April 1975	Kim Il-sung visit to China
May 1978	CCP General Secretary and Chinese Premier Hua Guofeng visit to North Korea
April 1981	Kim Il-sung visit to China
April 1982	CCP General Secretary Hu Yaobang and Deng Xiaoping joint visit to North Korea
September 1982	Kim Il-sung visit to China
June 1983	Kim Jong-il visit to China
November 1989	Kim Il-sung visit to China
March 1990	Chinese President Jiang Zemin visit of North Korea
October 1990	Kim Il-sung visit to China
May 2000	Chairman Kim Jong-il's visit to China
January 2001	Kim Jong-il's visit to China
September 2001	Chinese President Jiang Zemin visit to North Korea
October 2003	Chairman of National People's Congress Wu Bangguo visit to North Korea
April 2004	Kim Jong-il visit to China
October 2005	Chinese President Hu Jintao visit to North Korea
January 2006	Kim Jong-il visit to China
June 2008	Chinese Vice President Xi Jinping visit to North Korea
October 2009	Chinese Premier Wen Jiabao visit to North Korea
May 2010	Kim Jong-il visit to China
August 2010	Kim Jong-il visit to China
May 2011	Kim Jong-il visit to China
March 2018	Chairman Kim Jong-un visit to China
May 2018	Kim Jong-un visit to China
June 2018	Kim Jong-un visit to China
January 2019	Kim Jong-un visit to China
June 2019	Chinese President Xi Jinping visit to North Korea

Source: Zhihua Shen, "Chaoxian zhanzheng: Chaoxian wenti zhudongquan zhuanyi (1949–1953) [Korean War: Shift of agency in the Korea question]," in *Zuihou de tianchao: Mao Zedong, jin richeng yu zhongchao guanxi* [The Last Celestial Empire: Mao Zedong, Kim Il-Sung and Sino-North Korean relations], expanded, 189–276, Hong Kong: The Chinese University of Hong Kong, 205, https://www.marxists.org /chinese/pdf/history_of_international/china/20200622l.pdf; Junsheng Wang, "Zhongchao 'teshuguanxi' de luoji,"5; Embassy of the People's Republic of China in the Democratic People's Republic of Korea, "Zhongguo tong chaoxian de guanxi (Jiezhi 2021nian 2yue)" [China's relationship with North Korea (up until February 2021)], accessed October 16, 2021, http://kp.chineseembassy.org/chn/zcgx/zcgxgk/; Foreign Ministry of the People's Republic of China, "Shuangbian guanxi" [Bilateral relations], accessed October 16, 2021, https://www.fmprc.gov.cn/web/gjhdq_676201/gj_676203/yz_676205/1206_676404/ sbgx_676408/.

is the defining event in the establishment of special relations between China and North Korea.[3] After the Korean War, leadership summits between Kim Il-sung and the first generation of Chinese leaders occurred frequently, with Kim Il-sung visiting China in 1954 and 1958, and in 1961 for the signing of the Sino–North Korean Treaty of Friendship, Cooperation, and Mutual Assistance. The treaty is automatically renewed every twenty years. Article II of the treaty calls on the two nations to immediately adopt all necessary measures to oppose any country or coalition of countries that might attack either nation.[4]

During the Cultural Revolution, domestic turmoil in China and ideological differences between Beijing and Pyongyang, first due to the Sino-Soviet split, followed by China's rapprochement with the United States (which raised questions about the purity of China's revolutionary path), led to a hiatus of senior leader summits from 1961 to 1975.[5] After Deng Xiaoping assumed power in China, the two countries witnessed a resurgent high tide of bilateral summits, including five visits by Kim Il-sung to China and three visits by top Chinese leaders to North Korea between 1978 and 1991.[6] However, the establishment of diplomatic relations between China and South Korea in 1992 drove China–North Korea relations to its nadir. Following Kim Il-sung's death, no leader summit happened for nine years between Kim Il-sung's final visit to China in October 1991 and his son Kim Jong-il's first visit to China in May 2000.

Kim Jong-il's reign witnessed another decade of high-frequency leadership summitry between North Korea and China, with seven visits by Kim to China and five visits by top Chinese leaders to North Korea. Under Kim Jong-il's leadership, North Korea conducted its first two nuclear tests in 2006 and 2009 and successfully crossed the threshold to become a nuclear-weapon state. Given the positive correlation between the health of bilateral relations and the frequency of leadership summits, the high regularity of leadership summits in the 2000s, eleven meetings during the decade, would suggest that Kim's nuclear testing did not initially fundamentally damage the Sino-North Korean relationship given China's opposition to the nuclear tests. Such opposition to the tests was much less significant compared to that from China's establishment of relations with South Korea, or from the ideological division between China and North Korea during the Cultural Revolution. Although sustained leadership summits seem counterintuitive in the face of North Korea's repeated weapons testing, China's leadership attempted to act as a liaison between the rogue state and the international community. The Hu Jintao-Wen Jiabao leadership sought to stabilize North Korea with a two-pronged approach of economic and diplomatic engagement on the one hand, and support for international denuclearization efforts through a sanctions regime on the other.[7]

China–North Korea relations experienced a period of grave deterioration after Kim Jong-un took power in 2011. No meetings occurred between Kim and Xi from 2011 to 2018. Many factors contributed to the deterioration, including domestic politics in both countries and China's currying favors with South Korea. China was not sure about Kim Jong-un's ability to manage the political transition and China's new leader Xi Jinping was not in favor of Kim Jong-un's defiance against China on his nuclear tests. In comparison, Xi pursued an improvement of ties with South Korean president Park Geun-hye. The Xi-Kim summit hiatus did coincide with four nuclear tests conducted by North Korea under Kim Jong-un in February 2013, January and September 2016, and September 2017. Given the sustained leadership summits under Kim Jong-il even after two nuclear tests, the state of the Sino–North Korean relationship seems to be leadership dependent, rather than dependent on whether North Korea engages in nuclear tests. Another factor that aggravated the downward trend was China's warming ties with South Korea under then president Park Geun-hye. These dynamics will be examined in the following sections.

Summitry as a Vehicle for Advancing National and Personal Leadership Ties

Senior leadership summits provide an opportunity for Chinese and North Korean leaders to familiarize themselves with each other's visions, strategies, and policies. Through frequent visits and policy consultations, top leaders discuss key bilateral issues and share views on regional and global affairs. For example, during Kim Il-sung's 1975 visit to Beijing, Deng Xiaoping and Kim exchanged views about relations between the two countries, the two ruling parties, the situation on the peninsula, and the possibility of peaceful unification of the Korean Peninsula, as well as Sino-U.S. and Sino-Japanese relations.[8]

Leadership summits also provide opportunities for future North Korean and Chinese leaders to build personal relationships to carry on the historical legacy of the "blood alliance." The leaders of both countries have developed a tradition of introducing designated successors to the other side. As early as 1984, when Kim Il-sung was still alive, Kim Jong-il visited China unofficially as a member of the Workers' Party of Korea (WPK) Politburo Standing Committee.[9] Jiang Zemin was present at multiple meetings between Deng Xiaoping and Kim Il-sung, and Kim Il-sung brought Kim Jong-il to meet with Chinese leaders on multiple occasions.[10] Before assuming the role of general secretary of the Chinese Communist Party (CCP), both Hu Jintao and Xi Jinping conducted official visits to North Korea.[11] Hu visited Pyongyang in July 1993 as a member of the Politburo Standing Committee and Secretary of the Secretariat of the CCP; Xi visited North Korea in June 2008 as vice president of China.[12]

Leadership Summits to Demonstrate Mutual Support in the Face of External Threats

Leadership summits provide China and North Korea with an important opportunity to coordinate positions and demonstrate mutual support for each other's agendas in times of crisis. For example, after the Tiananmen Incident in June 1989, Beijing came under severe international criticism and experienced diplomatic isolation, including sanctions due to its human rights violation. Kim Il-sung was the first foreign state leader to visit China post-Tiananmen in November 1989.[13] Similarly, after North Korea conducted its second nuclear test in May 2009, then Chinese Premier Wen Jiabao visited North Korea in October 2009. Although China sought to neutralize the impact on Sino–North Korean relations of its support for UN Security Council Resolution 1874, which toughened sanctions against North Korea, Wen's visit also demonstrated support for the Kim Jong-il regime at a time of broad international condemnation of North Korea.[14] After Wen's visit, Kim Jong-il conducted three formal visits to China in May and August 2010 and in May 2011, just a few months before his death. Aware that his health was deteriorating and concerned for North Korea's domestic stability, Kim Jong-il hoped his visits would secure Chinese support as North Korea prepared for the looming leadership transition.[15] Little did he know, however, that the next bilateral summit would not occur for another seven years.

CONTEXT FOR SUMMITRY BETWEEN XI JINPING AND KIM JONG-UN

By early 2018, China's relationship with the Korean Peninsula had undergone a striking reversal. Beijing's ties with Seoul had warmed and relations with Pyongyang had deteriorated. While China's frustration with North Korea's nuclear program was nothing new, Kim Jong-un's defiant stance drove Chinese antagonism to a new level. Angered by Beijing's pro-Seoul policy shift, Pyongyang repeatedly defied Beijing's calls for restraints and conducted three nuclear tests between 2013 and 2016. China rejected North Korea's membership to the Asian Infrastructure Investment Bank in 2015, and Kim reportedly rejected China's invitation to attend its Victory Day Parade.[16] After Kim Jong-un's first nuclear test in 2013, China's Ministry of Foreign Affairs publicly characterized the Sino–North Korean relationship as a "normal state-to-state relationship," openly denying the security commitment outlined in the Sino–North Korean Friendship, Cooperation, and Mutual Assistance Treaty.[17]

The clash of personalities between Kim Jong-un and Xi Jinping may also explain the deterioration of China-North Korea relations. No Chinese leader since Deng Xiaoping has commanded such absolute authority in Chinese domestic politics and foreign policy making as Xi today. From the anti-corruption campaign and deepening domestic reform to the Belt and Road Initiative and assertive policy in the South China Sea, Xi's preferences and decisions have dominated China's policy courses. The same can be said about Kim Jong-un, who is also a princeling and bears an ownership mentality toward his country. Xi and Kim have adopted assertive and domineering attitudes at home and have insisted on respect from other countries abroad. Both are unlikely to make concessions or compromise. Xi's disdain for Kim's perceived defiance and Kim's contempt for Xi's perceived condescension were perhaps important factors in the deterioration of bilateral relations.

When Kim Jong-un first rose to power, the North Korean leadership had wanted Xi to visit North Korea first in a show of support for the young and inexperienced North Korean leader.[18] However, the Chinese government thought Kim should visit China first, given the seniority of both China and Xi in bilateral relations. Neither trip materialized. The relationship deteriorated further following Xi's rapprochement with South Korea, North Korea's continued nuclear and missile testing, and China's cooperation with the United States on trade sanctions, which collectively rendered a top-level summit infeasible.

Under Xi, China's most acute foreign policy priorities have included strengthening its domestic security, minimizing the US threat on its periphery, and establishing a power equilibrium with the United States as its peer in the Asia-Pacific region. Because China views the US security umbrella and US–South Korea alliance, which are necessitated by North Korean nuclear threats, as fundamentally undermining China's security, it aims to contain the North Korean threat to alter South Korea's strategic alignment choices.

However, events following North Korea's fourth nuclear test in January 2016 derailed China's strategy. Beijing overestimated its influence over Seoul and failed to adequately address Seoul's security concerns. South Korea subsequently decided to deploy the Terminal High Altitude Aerial Defense (THAAD) system, which China perceived as a threat to strategic stability with the United States and as an obstacle to achieving its desired regional influence. The year 2016 witnessed a significant evolution in Chinese policy toward the Korean Peninsula—not because of North Korea's unprecedented nuclear and missile tests or South Korea's decision to deploy the THAAD system in response. Rather, the decision provided an important wake-up call to China, which realized that it could not fundamentally improve ties with

South Korea or undermine the US–South Korea alliance without first putting North Korean provocation under control.

After Trump took office in 2017, Chinese concern about the future of North Korean nuclear development and the security arrangement on the Korean Peninsula skyrocketed. US–North Korea tensions peaked in mid-2017 with Trump's threats of "fire and fury," leading China to assess that some level of military conflict was imminent and to plan for a North Korea contingency.[19] When tensions subsided after the North Korean charm offensive in 2018 and US–North Korea diplomatic engagement leading up to the Singapore Summit, China grew concerned not about contingencies but that it would be excluded from the dialogue.

Summits between Xi Jinping and Kim Jong-un

First Summit, March 2018

More than six years after his ascension to power, Kim Jong-un paid his first visit to China on March 25, 2018. The visit came as the world still reeled from the shocking announcement of an upcoming summit between Kim and Trump, the first sitting US president to agree to such a meeting. Kim's meeting with Xi revived Sino–North Korean relations, which had deteriorated since Kim became supreme leader in 2011. North Korea took advantage of the opportunity to exploit Chinese anxieties about being excluded, using the meeting to enhance its position in upcoming summits and negotiations with the United States and South Korea.

The March 8, 2018, announcement of a Trump-Kim summit catalyzed the first Xi-Kim summit. China appeared to have been excluded from center stage due to the bilateral US–North Korea negotiations on nuclear and peninsular issues resulting from a historic meeting between American and North Korean leaders. China's anxiety to reassert its role in negotiations and influence over the Korean Peninsula's future prompted the invitation of Kim Jong-un to Beijing. The Chinese official media portrayed Kim as a junior partner visiting the imperial capital to brief his senior, quoting Kim as saying that he felt he "should come to China to brief Xi in person."[20] In reality, North Korea threatened China with exclusion from US–North Korea dialogue and forced China to extend an invitation that it otherwise would not have granted.

In engineering this first meeting, Kim Jong-un exploited the competition between the United States and China to maximize North Korea's strategic options and reap benefits in a striking parallel to his grandfather's manipulation of Beijing and Moscow in the 1960s. When the Sino-Soviet split deepened in 1960, North Korea leveraged its status in the Communist Bloc, alternating its support of Beijing and Moscow in their doctrinal divergence, in return for political and economic benefits from both sides. In May 1960, disappointed with the Soviets' refusal to provide additional economic assistance and the postponement of Khrushchev's trip to North Korea, Kim Il-sung paid a secret visit to China, during which he sang high praises of China's domestic and foreign policies. As competition escalated, Moscow forgave 900 million rubles in debt owed by North Korea, which in turn prompted China to grant North Korea 420 million rubles in assistance between 1961 to 1964 despite China's domestic famine and economic difficulties. Kim Il-sung alternated between pro-China and pro-Soviet statements and positions, prompting both to sweeten their trade and economic assistance, as well as their alliance treaties with North Korea to curry his favor. Experts such as Shen Zhihua also argue that North Korea leveraged the Sino-Soviet split against China, forcing China into major concessions in border demarcation. Kim Il-sung's leaning on China motivated Russia to invite him to Moscow twenty days after his trip to China, just like the announcement of Kim Jong-un's meeting with Trump prompted an invitation by China seventeen days later.[21]

The strategy of playing off Washington and Beijing against each other also worked for Kim Jong-un. Although Kim reiterated his commitment to denuclearization during his visit to China, preconditions remained. Strengthening ties with China bolstered North Korea's position in negotiations with the United States. The more options North Korea has and the less isolated it is, the less susceptible it is to US pressure.

Second and Third Summits, May and June 2018

The second Xi-Kim summit from May 7 to 8, 2018, in Dalian, China, and the third Xi-Kim summit from June 19 to 20, 2018, in Beijing bookended the Trump-Kim Singapore Summit. The second meeting provided a forum for preparatory consultation and the third meeting an opportunity to debrief after Singapore. Both summits allowed China and North Korea to share information, coordinate positions, and align strategies. The summits also served to reassure each nation that they were on the same page and had no secret agenda. For China, this was particularly important to ensure there was no surprise for China.

When the May summit was arranged in April, Kim Jong-un had just participated in an inter-Korean summit with South Korean president Moon Jae-in at Panmunjom, where the two sides jointly issued the Panmunjom Declaration. The upcoming Trump-Kim Singapore Summit had also been confirmed. Like the first summit, Kim's arrival in Dalian caught the world by surprise, with the *New York Times* referring to the Dalian summit as a "second surprise visit."[22]

At the Dalian meeting, Xi described the outcome of his first summit with Kim Jong-un in March 2018, listing four points of consensus: the precious nature of Sino–North Korean relations; the strategic importance of the bilateral relationship for both nations; work to increase trust and communications; and work to strengthen friendly people-to-people ties. Xi also expressed his support for the US-North Korea summit and committed to China's continued involvement in the resolution of the peninsula question.[23] The official Chinese statement emphasized Kim Jong-un's reiteration of his commitment to the denuclearization of the Korean Peninsula and North Korea's willingness to denuclearize once hostile policies and security threats against North Korea are eliminated.[24] Both sides also discussed the North Korean economy. As Kim prepared for negotiations with the United States, he sought reassurance that China would have his back by continuing to support North Korea economically.

Based on the Chinese official statement, Kim's primary goal in Dalian was to secure China's buy-in, input, and advice ahead of his summit with Trump. The subsequent summit showed Kim's intention to repair fraught relations with China. Given that China is North Korea's top trading partner, Kim sought to bring North Korea's economy into the conversation because of the negative impacts of sanctions and the need for Chinese aid.

China certainly had deep stakes vested in Kim's meeting with Trump as well. By meeting with Kim, China positioned itself to gain more leverage vis-à-vis the United States. The meeting allowed China to exert influence over the outcome of the upcoming Trump-Kim meeting by expressing its preferences and concerns. Xi's meeting with Kim Jong-un twice in two months demonstrated China's central role and critical influence over North Korea at a time of evolution in the US-North Korea relationship. China proved once more to the international community that all roads to Pyongyang go through Beijing.

The second summit helped further repair China–North Korea relations at the top level, which suited both Kim and Xi's objectives. Four days after the summit on May 12, 2018, the *People's Daily* reported that North Korea decommissioned its northern nuclear test site.[25] Although the decommissioning was aimed at paving the way for the Singapore Summit more than anything else, China nevertheless appeared to have played an important role in ushering North Korea toward denuclearization.

The third Xi-Kim summit took place from June 19 to 20, 2018, roughly one week after the Singapore Summit. The Singapore Summit rendered a four-point agreement between the United States and North Korea that: the two nations will establish new relations; both will work to build a peace regime on the Korean Peninsula; North Korea will work toward "complete denuclearization of the Korean Peninsula" and reaffirm the 2018 Panmunjom

Declaration; and both will commit to the recovery and repatriation of the remains of American prisoners of war and soldiers missing in action in North Korea. The third Xi-Kim Summit served as a concluding consultation about the Singapore Summit, where Xi and Kim discussed takeaways and follow-up measures in their relations with the United States regarding Korean Peninsular issues.

Xi articulated the importance of the Singapore Summit during his third meeting with Kim. According to the *People's Daily*, Xi first affirmed the strength of Sino–North Korean relations, considering the three visits in less than three months. He then praised Kim's high regard for strategic communication with China given the timing of the meeting after the Singapore Summit, and then committed to support North Korea's socioeconomic development.[26] Then, Xi praised the outcome of the Singapore Summit and expressed China's willingness to continue to play a role in the denuclearization and peace process. As a response, Kim also committed to building a "lasting and stable peace regime on the Korean Peninsula with China and other relevant parties."[27]

Meanwhile, official Chinese media took note of the differences in the diplomatic protocol and reception between the first two summits and the third summit, underscoring its significance in reconsolidating Sino–North Korean ties. Most noticeably, a *People's Daily* photograph of the third summit showed a grand welcoming ceremony in Beijing with military and young students present, a scale unseen in the previous two summits.[28] It was also noteworthy that while information of the first two summits was only released after Kim left China, the third summit was publicized during Kim's visit.[29]

Both Xi and Kim saw value in a third summit. For them to meet both before and after the Singapore Summit demonstrated the special tie between China and North Korea. For North Korea, the third summit added to Kim Jong-un's foreign policy credentials and provided further leverage in his relations with both China and the United States. For China, the summit exemplified the unique influence China still enjoys over North Korea, which translates into Chinese leverage vis-à-vis the United States. Given the widespread speculation before the Singapore Summit about whether a joint declaration of an end to the Korean War would happen without China's participation, the second and the third summits provided a clear answer—that no solution to the Korean War, or the North Korean nuclear issue, could be reached without China's input. The third Xi-Kim summit provided a diplomatic boost for both sides, strengthened their bilateral relationship, and allowed each to extract more diplomatic leverage, not against each other but against the United States.

Fourth Summit, January 2019

Like Kim Jong-un's second trip to China to discuss the upcoming Singapore Summit, his fourth visit to China, January 7–9, 2019, took place right before the planned Hanoi Summit. The fourth summit received the least media coverage, especially in comparison to the grand welcome Kim experienced during the third summit in 2018. On January 8, one day after Kim's arrival, China's International Liaison Department announced that Kim would visit China from January 7 to 10.[30] There was no further official coverage during the visit. The visit was only confirmed by international media after a sighting of Kim's distinctive train arriving at a Beijing railway station.[31] The Chinese Foreign Ministry was equally austere about the details of the trip. Spokesperson Lu Kang told reporters that the summit would focus on "deepening the bilateral relations between the two parties and countries and exchanging views on international and regional issues."[32] South Korean news outlet *Yonhap* reported that the two leaders discussed a potential second US–North Korea summit.[33]

By the time of the fourth summit, the stalemate between the United States and North Korea had persisted for six months after the Singapore Summit. US and North Korean bureaucrats reportedly met a number of times but failed to reach a compromise on the steps North Korea would take toward denuclearization in return for what benefits from the United States. North Korea was eager to meet Trump again regardless of whether a deal would materialize—it is widely assumed by foreign observers that Kim Jong-un was using diplomatic engagement with Trump to strengthen his domestic authority and international prestige, hence his legitimacy. Kim expressed in his New Year's address that he was ready "whenever" to meet again with Trump.[34] North Korea expert Harry Kazianis told the BBC that the Xi-Kim summit was Kim's reminder to Trump that he had "diplomatic and economic options besides what Washington and Seoul can offer."[35] To that end, North Korea aimed to not only discuss with China its roadmap to a deal with Trump, but also to solicit Chinese support to help achieve that goal.

Beijing was equally eager to discern the Trump administration's "final price" for moving forward with the North Korea nuclear issue. By January 2019, the trade war between the United States and China had persisted for six months, and China was eager to exploit any issue to gain leverage over the United States. The linkage was clear—China was more than willing to "help" the United States with North Korea if the United States adopted a more lenient trade policy toward China.

This fourth summit served to preserve the goodwill between China and North Korea that had accumulated over the previous year and to pave the way for Xi's June 2019 visit to North Korea. Trump and Kim ultimately met in Hanoi in late February 2019, although no breakthrough was achieved.

Fifth Summit in June 2019

After many years of speculation about a Xi Jinping visit to North Korea, the Chinese leader finally paid a two-day state visit to Pyongyang in June 2019. The last time was in 2009 when Chinese Premier Wen Jiabao visited Pyongyang. The trip took place at the peak of the Sino-US trade war, one week before an expected Trump-Xi showdown over trade at the G20 Summit in Osaka, Japan. When the trip was announced, many assumed that Beijing would use it to leverage Pyongyang in its trade war with Washington. But judging from Chinese statements during and after the trip, Xi's agenda went beyond whatever immediate tactical gains he hoped to achieve on the trade issue.[36] In fact, Xi primarily sought to use his visit to reinforce China's pivotal role in negotiations on North Korea's denuclearization and security arrangements on the Korean Peninsula in order to stabilize increasingly turbulent Sino-US relations.

China's ability to use North Korea as trade bait depends on its capacity to induce good or bad behavior from North Korea; China's capacity in this regard is low. History shows that China is unable to deter or prevent confrontational North Korean behavior (including six nuclear tests in defiance of China's warnings), deliver North Korea to the negotiating table, or instigate provocative North Korean acts, primarily because Pyongyang has its own strategic considerations and China is strongly averse to instability. Considering Pyongyang's current preoccupation with security and sanctions relief to promote economic development, it is unclear what incentive China would have to encourage North Korean intransigence.

Indeed, the deliverables from Xi's trip were mostly symbolic and rhetorical, and this would disappoint the North Koreans. China vowed solidarity with North Korea and reiterated its support for Kim Jong-un and his new priority of economic development. However, Xi made no specific commitments on economic cooperation despite widespread speculation prior to the trip that China would offer increased agricultural and development assistance and new economic deals.[37] Xi clearly signaled the importance he places on diplomacy and a political process to address Korean Peninsular issues, which China sees as the precondition to denuclearization of the peninsula. By vowing to support North Korea's "reasonable concerns," Xi made a thinly veiled reference to a potential Chinese security guarantee for North Korea.[38]

But the most important message from Xi's visit is that China seeks a central role in solving the North Korean nuclear problem and aims to settle Korean Peninsula issues through a multilateral mechanism instead of bilateral negotiations. From China's perspective, the Hanoi Summit failure dramatized the infeasibility of a US–North Korea bilateral solution. The deep distrust between the United States and North Korea and serious risk that both sides will renege on their commitments makes a multilateral framework essential, according to China, to ensuring North Korea's complete denuclearization and its security during and after the process. Consequently, China's path forward envisions a multilateral solution with China as a key guarantor of a future multilateral peace and security mechanism.

Xi Jinping's visit to Pyongyang is the most recent testament to China's determination to ensure its role as an indispensable participant in any future security arrangements on the Korean Peninsula—ranging from a declaration of intent to end the Korean War and the conclusion of a peace treaty to the reconciliation of the two Koreas and international assistance for North Korea's economic development. In China's eyes, Pyongyang's dependence on Beijing for political, economic, and, most important, security support entitles China to a special seat at the negotiating table that cannot be replaced by any other country.

These calculations about ensuring China's central role are deeply embedded in Beijing's hope for the G20 meeting in Osaka to pursue cooperation with Washington, the future of Sino-US competition, and the priority Xi attaches to stability and cooperation between the United States and China. In Xi's view, Sino-US competition need not poison cooperation on issues where the two countries have shared interests. China's relationship with North Korea might not offer leverage in trade negotiations with the United States. But by visiting Pyongyang and asserting China's essential role in a future political solution for the Korean Peninsula, Xi signaled to Trump that China would not be marginalized in its own backyard and that the United States should seek China's assistance in addressing an issue it cannot solve independently. Xi has big plans: to restore cooperation between the United States and China in solving the North Korean problem and to leverage this success to stabilize turbulent Sino-US bilateral relations. His first visit to Pyongyang is just the start.

ASSESSMENT OF THE REVIVAL OF
SINO–NORTH KOREAN SUMMITRY

It is worth discussing the causal effect between leadership summits and Sino–North Korean relations. Given the tremendous deterioration in bilateral relations over the seven years preceding the first Xi-Kim summit, the meetings appear to have gone far in improving the fraught relationship between the two allies. However, the first Xi-Kim leadership summit did not emerge from any substantive progress in the Sino–North Korean relationship but, instead, as a response to an external factor—specifically, the announced Trump-Kim summit.

The first Xi-Kim meeting was motivated by China's anxiety over being excluded from US–North Korean engagement, and by North Korea's desire to leverage diplomatic engagement with the United States to improve ties with China and to use that relationship to strengthen its position in negotiations with the United States. Despite questions surrounding the origins, motivations, and authenticity of the improvement in Sino–North Korean ties, both sides left the first summit pleased with the tactical gains they made.

The five summits undeniably played a critical role in reinvigorating, reshaping, and remapping China-North Korea relations. They provided key opportunities for both nations to strategically demonstrate their friendship and solidarity. Summit consultations not only helped to alleviate differences, but also to build consensus between the two countries regarding issues ranging from denuclearization to peace and stability on the Korean Peninsula to North Korea's economic development. Moreover, they sent a clear message that the United States cannot exploit differences between China and North Korea because Xi and Kim share, coordinate, and mutually agree upon their strategic positions.

Both Kim and Xi also extracted important benefits from these summits to serve their domestic purposes. Projecting himself as Xi's peer by hosting leader-to-leader summits greatly boosted Kim Jong-un's domestic political standing. Kim gained the international recognition that neither his father nor his grandfather was able to achieve, neutralizing most, if not all, domestic challenges to his legitimacy. Xi was able to project China's seniority over North Korea by positioning himself as an elder advisor to Kim Jong-un. This not only helped China recoup its credibility with regard to its ability to exert positive influence over North Korea, but also resolved criticisms Xi had received from some corners in China for the damage his pursuit of rapprochement with South Korea did to China-North Korea relations.[39]

The Xi-Kim summits additionally played a central role in enabling Sino–North Korean consultation and coordination of positions before and after North Korea's engagement with the United States. Kim sought Xi's advice and endorsement of his negotiating positions during Kim's first, second, and fourth trips to China before the Singapore and Hanoi Trump-Kim summits, and during his third trip to China Kim debriefed with Xi directly after the Singapore Summit. Kim relied heavily on China for his travel plans to Singapore and Hanoi. China provided an airplane from state-owned Air China to fly Kim to Singapore. Kim's special train traveled through China to the China-Vietnam border for the Hanoi summit. These logistics were reportedly agreed upon during the Xi-Kim summits and without them, the trips would not have been feasible. Through logistical support, China once again demonstrated its indispensable role. Despite the improvement of bilateral ties, however, questions remain regarding the foundation and sustainability of Sino–North Korean relations. Unless North Korea genuinely commits to denuclearization and takes actions to pursue it (of which outside observers are not yet convinced), the essential disagreement between China and North Korea will persist. Similarly, unless China makes its peace with Kim Jong-un's defiance, manipulation, and adventurism, distrust will continue to run deep between the two. China and North Korea might coordinate and cooperate tactically out of selfish calculations, but scars remain.

CONCLUSION

Historically, leadership summits have played a significant role in maintaining and advancing the close relationship between China and North Korea. The two countries have used leadership summits to coordinate positions, express mutual support, and demonstrate solidarity to the world. Especially during periods of intense crisis or external challenges, leadership summits have alleviated both countries' external isolation and mitigated the effects of international criticism. Given Pyongyang's nuclear development in defiance of international pressure, China has played this role more frequently, but North Korea has also provided such support to China, including after the Tiananmen incident in 1989.

The Xi-Kim summits followed a seven-year hiatus in leadership meetings that resulted from deteriorating China-North Korea relations after the 2011 leadership transition in North Korea. The first summit in March 2018 was not a genuine manifestation of improved relations, but instead a reaction to US–North Korea engagement and an antidote to China's exclusion anxiety. It exemplified classic North Korean manipulation of Chinese perceptions, positions, and strategies. Still, the meeting opened a new chapter in China–North Korea relations, a revival of the frozen relationship between the two since Kim Jong-un took power, and it paved the way for four additional leadership summits that facilitated coordination of positions and diplomatic maneuvering between China and North Korea, especially in their respective interactions with the United States.

Leadership summits are a clear indicator of the health of China–North Korea relations. As the dynamics surrounding the North Korean nuclear issue and unification of the Korean Peninsula evolve, external observers can closely monitor leadership summits between Beijing and Pyongyang to discern shifting priorities, differences in their preferred approach to North Korean security, and consensus-building between the two countries.

NOTES

1. Foreign Ministry of the People's Republic of China, "Shuangbian guanxi: Zhonghua renmin gongheguo waijiaobu" [Bilateral relations: The Ministry of Foreign Affairs of the People's Republic of China], accessed October 16, 2021, https://www.fmprc.gov.cn/web/gjhdq_676201/gj_676203/yz_676205/1206_676404/sbgx_676408/.

2. Alan Cooperman, "Stalin Approved Start of Korean War, Documents Show," AP News, January 13, 1993, https://apnews.com/article/adf271706570fbe753e6783955675e60.

3. Junsheng Wang, "Zhongchao 'teshuguanxi' de luoji: Fuza zhanlve pingheng de chanwu" [The logic of the Sino-DPRK Special Relationship: The complex product of strategic balancing], *Dongbeiya Luntan* [*Northeast Asia Forum*], no. 1 (2016): 51–65, https://doi.org/10.13654/j.cnki.naf.2016.01.005.

4. "Treaty of Friendship, Co-Operation and Mutual Assistance between the People's Republic of China and the Democratic People's Republic of Korea," Marxist.org, accessed October 16, 2021, https://www.marxists.org/subject/china/documents/china_dprk.htm.

5. Zhihua Shen, "Features and Future of Sino-DPRK Alliance," Chahar Institute, June 29, 2017, http://www.charhar.org.cn/newsinfo.aspx?newsid=11892.

6. Hongjun Yu, "Lengzhan suiyue de zhongchao guanxi (1976–1991)" [Sino-DPRK relations during the Cold War (1976–1991)], *US-China Perception Monitor*, June 25, 2019, https://www.uscnpm.com/model_item.html?action=view&table=article&id=18828.

7. Carla Freeman, "Developments in China's North Korea Policy and Contingency Planning," Testimony before the US-China Economic and Security Review Commission, Washington, DC, April 12, 2018, 6, accessed on January 20, 2019, https://www.uscc.gov/sites/default/files/Freeman%20Testimony_China-North%20Korea%20Contingencies%20Roundtable_20180412.pdf.

8. Yu, "Lengzhan suiyue."

9. Embassy of the People's Republic of China in the Democratic People's Republic of Korea, "Chaoxian dangzhongyang juxing jinian jin zhengri fanghua 25 zhounian zhaodaihui" [North Korean Central Party leadership hosts reception on 25th anniversary of Kim Jong-Il's visit to China], June 11, 2008, http://kp.china-embassy.org/chn/zcgx/gchf/08sbgx/t464213.htm.

10. "Chaoxian lingdaoren de zhongguo zuji: Jin richeng zhuxi shengqian 40duoci fanghu" [Footprints in China by North Korean leaders], *Huanqiu Renwu* [*Global Figure*], March 31, 2018, http://news.sina.com.cn/c/nd/2018-03-31/doc-ifysuikp4628977.shtml.

11. Junsheng Wang, "Zhongchao 'teshuguanxi' de luoji," 8.

12. Wang, 8.

13. Wang, 8.

14. Wang, 8.

15. Interview with Chinese analysts, Beijing, July 2010.

16. Elizabeth Shim, "China Rejects North Korea Request to Join Asian Infrastructure Investment Bank," United Press International, March 31, 2015, https://www.upi.com/Top_News/World-News/2015/03/31/China-rejects-North-Korea-request-to-join-Asian-Infrastructure-Investment-Bank/4481427814172/.

17. "China-North Korea Normal State Relationship," *Daily NK*, May 27, 2013, https://www.dailynk.com/english/chinanorth-korea-a-normal-state-re/.

18. Interview with Chinese experts, Beijing, July 2014.

19. Peter Baker and Choe Sang-Hun, "Trump Threatens Fire and Fury with North Korea If It Endangers U.S.," *New York Times*, August 8, 2017, https://www.nytimes.com/2017/08/08/world/asia/north-korea-un-sanctions-nuclear-missile-united-nations.html; Adam Mount, "How China Sees North Korea," *The Atlantic*, August 29, 2017, https://www.theatlantic.com/international/archive/2017/08/china-military-strength-north-korea-crisis/538344/.

20. "Xi Jinping tong jin zhengen juxing huitan" [Xi Jinping holds talks with Kim Jong-un], *Xinhua*, March 28, 2018, http://www.xinhuanet.com/politics/2018-03/28/c_1122600292.htm.

21. Zhihua Shen, *Zuihou de "tianchao: Mao zedong, jin richeng yu zhongchao guanxi [The final dynasty: Mao Zedong, Kim Il-sung, and Sino-North Korean relations]* (Hong Kong: Chinese University of Hong Kong, 2017), https://www.marxists.org/chinese/pdf/history_of_international/china/20200622l.pdf.

22. Jane Perlez, "Kim's Second Surprise Visit to China Heightens Diplomatic Drama," *New York Times*, May 8, 2018, https://www.nytimes.com/2018/05/08/world/asia/kim-jong-un-xi-jinping-china-north-korea.html.

23. "Xi Jinping tong chaoxian laodongdang weiyuanzhang jin zhengen zaidalian juxing huiwu" [Xi Jinping holds meeting in Dalian with North Korean Worker's Party Commissioner Kim Jong-Un], Xinhua News Agency, May 8, 2018, http://www.xinhuanet.com/politics/leaders/2018-05/08/c_1122802575.htm.

24. "Xi Jinping tong chaoxian laodongdang weiyuanzhang jin zhengen zaidalian juxing huiwu."

25. "Chaoxian jiangyu 23 ri zhi 25 ri zeqi feiqi beibu he shiyanchang" [North Korea to abandon norther nuclear testing site between 23rd and 25th], *People's Daily*, May 12, 2018, https://world.huanqiu.com/article/9CaKrnK8qO0.

26. "Xi Jinping tong chaoxian laodongdang weiyuanzhang jin zhengen juxing huitan" [Xi Jinping holds talks with North Korean Worker's Party Commissioner Kim Jong-Un], *People's Daily*, June 20, 2018, http://politics.people.com.cn/n1/2018/0620/c1001-30067148.html.

27. "Xi Jinping tong chaoxian laodongdang weiyuanzhang jin zhengen juxing huitan."

28. "Xi Jinping tong chaoxian laodongdang weiyuanzhang jin zhengen juxing huitan."

29. "Jin Zhengen 7ri kaishi dui zhongguo jinxing fangwen" [Kim Jong-Un Begins China visit on the 7th], Guancha.cn, January 8, 2019. https://www.guancha.cn/internation/2019_01_08_485993.shtml?s=zwyxgtjbt.

30. "Jin Zhengen dui zhongguo jinxing fangwen" [Kim Jong-un visits China], *People's Daily*, January 8, 2019, http://world.people.com.cn/n1/2019/0108/c1002-30508702.html.

31. "North Korea's Kim Jong-Un Visits China's Xi Jinping," BBC News, January 8, 2019, https://www.bbc.com/news/world-asia-46789925.

32. Foreign Ministry of the People's Republic of China, "2019nian 1yue 8ri waijiaobu fayanren lu kang zhuchi lixing jizhehui" [January 8, 2019 Foreign Ministry spokesperson Lu Kang Hosts press conference], January 8, 2019, https://www.fmprc.gov.cn/web/fyrbt_673021/t1627853.shtml.

33. "North Korea's Kim Jong-Un Visits China's Xi Jinping."

34. "Jin Zhengen 7ri kaishi dui zhongguo jinxing fangwen."

35. "North Korea's Kim Jong-Un Visits China's Xi Jinping."

36. "Xi Jinping dui chaoxian jinxing guoshifangwen," Xinhua News Agency, June 10, 2019, http://www.xinhuanet.com/world/cnleaders/xijinping/xjpcfcx1906/index.htm.

37. Interviews with Chinese experts, Beijing, October 2019.

38. "Xi Jinping tong chaoxian laodongdang weiyuanzhang guowu weiyuanhui weiyuanzhang jin zhengen juxing huitan."

39. Interview with Chinese analysts in Beijing, October 2019.

Chapter 6

Historic Showmanship between Trump and Kim Jong-un: The Possible Normalization of US–North Korean Summitry

Ramon Pacheco Pardo

On June 12, 2018, US president Donald J. Trump and North Korean leader Kim Jong-un made history. In the city-state of Singapore, the two leaders held the first ever US–North Korea summit. This would be followed by a second summit in Hanoi on February 28, 2019, and a third summit including South Korean president Moon Jae-in at the demilitarized zone (DMZ) separating the two Koreas on June 30 of the same year. During the latter, Trump once again made history by becoming the first sitting US president to set foot in North Korean territory.

This flurry of activity in the space of merely a year did not resolve the fundamental disagreements between Washington and Pyongyang, including on North Korea's nuclear program, the normalization of bilateral diplomatic relations, or the Kim regime's poor human rights record. But it introduced a new element to the complex relationship between Washington and Pyongyang: high-level summitry.

Indeed, Trump broke a taboo. Though North Korea had for decades sought summits at the highest level with the United States, successive US presidents had refused to seriously contemplate this option. Trump's decision to meet with Kim opened the door for bilateral US-North Korea summitry to resume in the future, after the Trump-Kim talks ceased with no real outcome. Whether this summitry takes place at the start of a bilateral dialogue process, as was the case with Trump, or at the end, as would be the case under more normal diplomatic processes, US presidents will be able to point to the precedent that Trump set in Singapore.

This chapter analyzes US–North Korea relations through the lens of bilateral summitry between Trump and Kim. The chapter investigates why Washington and Pyongyang engaged in this summitry, the outcome of the three summits between Trump and Kim, and the potential impact of their meetings on future relations between the two countries.

To this end, the chapter proceeds as follows. The first section focuses on North Korea's decades-old objective of holding a bilateral summit with the United States. The next focuses on Kim Jong-un's decision to hold summits with Trump. The third section analyzes the goals and outcomes of the Trump-Kim summits and is followed by a discussion that links the summits to broader relations between Washington and Pyongyang. The fifth section discusses the future of US–North Korea summitry. A concluding section summarizes the key points developed in the chapter.

SUMMITRY WITH THE UNITED STATES
AS A NORTH KOREAN OBJECTIVE

In March 1974, North Korea's Fifth Supreme People's Assembly sent a letter to the US Congress to request the normalization of bilateral diplomatic relations between the two countries.[1] Considering the assembly's rubber-stamp role, the message was clear: Kim Il-sung—the leader of North Korea—wanted Pyongyang to normalize relations with Washington.

From a North Korean perspective, this request seemed logical. In February 1972, US president Richard Nixon had visited China, met with Chinese leader Mao Zedong, and agreed to diplomatic normalization between Washington and Beijing.[2] Five months later, the two Koreas had held their first ever summit and issued the July 4th Joint Statement whereby they agreed to seek an independent, peaceful, and national unity-based solution.[3] The statement had helped to ease tensions between the two Koreas, even if only limited steps were taken toward its implementation. By the time the People's Assembly had sent its letter to the US Congress, Washington and Beijing on the one hand and the two Koreas on the other were taking steps to lower tensions. In this context, Kim appears to have felt emboldened to seek normalized relations with the United States.

Kim continued to insist on this idea, even after his early attempt proved unsuccessful. In September 1978, he called for diplomatic normalization with Washington during a speech to commemorate the thirtieth anniversary of the founding of North Korea.[4] Normalization would likely have necessitated a summit at the highest level, as had been the case between Nixon and Mao and later US president Jimmy Carter and Chinese leader Deng Xiaoping in the context of formal diplomatic normalization. In March 1987 in the context of the US-Soviet détente, US president Ronald Reagan allowed US diplomats to meet with North Korean diplomats during social occasions.[5] Restrictions on diplomatic contact were further lifted as South Korean president Roh Tae-woo's *Nordpolitik* encouraged the United States to meet with North Korean officials.[6] With this policy, Roh was promoting rapprochement between the United States and Japan on the one hand and North Korea on the other, as a means to support better inter-Korean relations. In January 1992, a meeting in New York at the undersecretary of state level marked the highest-level meeting ever between representatives from the United States and North Korea.[7] In an April 1992 interview with the *Washington Times*, Kim stated that he wanted a US Embassy in Pyongyang.[8] And in June 1994, Jimmy Carter became the first former US president both to visit North Korea and to meet with Kim.[9] With this crisis, Pyongyang was arguably seeking to grab Washington's attention, normalize relations, and ensure regime survival at a time when communist regimes elsewhere were collapsing. Kim probably thought that Carter's visit would help to achieve these goals. Carter, meanwhile, was trying to defuse tensions between Washington and Pyongyang. Yet US president Bill Clinton was not pleased with Carter's visit, which to an extent undermined his own administration's policy toward North Korea. The visit, in any case, helped put an end to the nuclear crisis that had prompted Carter's visit. However, Kim passed away a few weeks later without fulfilling his long-term goal of holding a summit with a sitting US president.

North Korea's push for a top-level bilateral summit with the United States emerged from its diplomatic competition with South Korea. By the mid-1980s, Seoul had the upper hand as Central and Eastern European states sought South Korean investment.[10] By then, it was clear that South Korea had a bigger and more modern economy than North Korea. Thus, Central and Eastern European states wanted to benefit from Seoul's economic strength compared to Pyongyang. China and the Soviet Union then attended the 1988 Seoul Olympic Games despite Pyongyang's calls for a boycott. Following the US-led Western boycott of Moscow 1980 and the Soviet-led Communist retaliation of Los Angeles 1984, Pyongyang saw a boycott of Seoul 1988 as a way to undermine what was shaping up to be South Korea's coming-out party on the global stage. But North Korea's failure to lead a boycott set the stage for better relations between Seoul and Communist countries. In June 1990, South Korean president Roh Tae-woo met with his Soviet counterpart, Mikhail Gorbachev.[11] And in September 1992, Roh traveled to China to meet with his Chinese counterpart, Yang Shangkun.[12] Seoul also normalized diplomatic relations with Moscow and Beijing in 1990 and 1992, respectively. Simply put, Kim needed a summit with his US counterpart to match South

Korea's achievements and potentially establish diplomatic relations with Washington.

A summit between Kim and a US president followed by diplomatic normalization would also have benefited North Korea economically, most notably by opening the door for Pyongyang to access the International Monetary Fund (IMF) and the World Bank.[13] North Korea would have been able to tap into the resources and expertise of both institutions, much like China had done since the 1980s. Considering the poor state of the North Korean economy even in the 1980s, the prospect of this material benefit probably also drove North Korea's decision to pursue a summit with the United States. Yet, it should be noted, diplomatic normalization would have required US congressional approval. Therefore, a leaders' summit would only be the first step toward eventual normalization.

After taking power in 1994, Kim Jong-il continued his father's policy of trying to hold a top-level summit with the United States and normalize diplomatic relations. In fact, Kim came very close to achieving success where his father had failed. Washington and Pyongyang signed the Agreed Framework in October 1994, which put an end to the first North Korean nuclear crisis and included a commitment to the establishment of bilateral diplomatic relations.[14] Application of the agreement stalled initially, as North Korea suffered a severe economic crisis that concentrated all its efforts, and the US Congress withheld the necessary funds for the Clinton administration to fully implement its side of the agreement. It was revived, however, in 1999–2000 after South Korean president Kim Dae-jung launched his Sunshine Policy calling for North and South Korea to boost their bilateral links.[15] Meanwhile, North Korea's 1998 missile launch over the East Sea and Japan showed that the United States had failed in its attempt to rein in North Korea's behavior.[16] As Clinton neared the end of his time in office, he ordered a review of Washington's North Korea policy. Thus, a combination of South Korean policy preferences, North Korean provocations, and US domestic politics gave the necessary impetus for Washington to review its policy toward Pyongyang. This resulted in the Perry Process, whereby the Clinton administration sought to engage in diplomacy with Pyongyang from 1999. In June 2000, Kim Dae-jung and Kim Jong-il held the first ever leader-level inter-Korean summit.[17] In October, Secretary of State Madeline Albright visited Pyongyang and met with Kim.[18] She was the highest-level US official to ever meet with a North Korean leader. Clinton entertained the idea of meeting with Kim himself, but his time in office ran out before the meeting could take place.[19]

Almost ten years later, however, Clinton finally visited North Korea. In August 2009, he traveled to Pyongyang on a mission to free two US journalists arrested by the Kim regime. During his visit, Clinton met with Kim himself.[20] But the Obama administration had limited the scope of Clinton's trip to hostage retrieval, and North Korea was unsuccessful in its attempts to discuss broader bilateral matters. One year later—in August 2010—Carter visited Pyongyang for a second time, also on a mission to repatriate a US citizen arrested by the Kim regime.[21] Kim would pass away in December 2011, having met with two former US presidents in the span of two years. But he had failed to secure a summit with a sitting US president.

Kim Jong-il probably had the same reasons as his father for trying to secure a summit at the highest level with Washington. A summit would have served Pyongyang in its diplomatic competition with Seoul, even if by the 2000s the two Koreas inhabited completely different places on the world stage. By then, South Korea was rich, democratic, and increasingly active in the United Nations and as a global player. In contrast, North Korea was poor, authoritarian, and repressive, and a secondary actor beyond the Korean Peninsula at best. A summit would have also supported North Korea's long-standing goal of diplomatic normalization with the United States. Finally, if followed by normalization of relations between Washington and Pyongyang, a summit could have brought much-needed economic benefits to Pyongyang—including potential membership of the IMF and World Bank.

KIM JONG-UN'S SUMMITRY WITH DONALD TRUMP

Kim Jong-un became North Korea's leader in December 2011 just after his father's death. In March 2013, Kim presented his *byungjin*, or "Parallel Development" line, which called for the parallel development of North Korea's nuclear weapons program and economy.[22] And indeed, Pyongyang sought to develop both over the next few years. However, North Korea's record number of nuclear and missile tests under Kim Jong-un led the UN Security Council to impose a record number of sanctions on Pyongyang in return.[23] Furthermore, North Korea's test program forestalled any possible summit between US president Barack Obama and Kim. This despite Obama announcing that he would be willing to meet with his North Korean counterpart, if necessary, during the 2008 US presidential election campaign.[24]

After Trump took office in January 2017, the new US president and Kim engaged in a war of insults and showmanship. Kim ramped up North Korea's nuclear and missile testing program, including its sixth nuclear test in September as well as Pyongyang's first two intercontinental ballistic missile (ICBM) tests ever.[25] In November 2017, Kim declared that North Korea had become a nuclear power.[26] Tensions between Washington and Pyongyang had never been so high.

Yet, the situation changed dramatically in 2018. A North Korean delegation visited South Korea for the 2018 Pyeongchang Winter Olympic Games.[27]

South Korean president Moon Jae-in, who had been inaugurated in May 2017, was pursuing a policy that prioritized engagement with North Korea. And he reaped the benefits with the visit by the North Korean delegation, led by Kim Yo-jong—none other than Kim Jong-un's sister. A flurry of diplomacy followed. In April 2018, Moon and Kim held the first inter-Korean summit since 2007.[28] This was followed by a second, unannounced meeting in May.[29] Trump and Kim then held the first ever summit between a sitting US president and North Korean leader in June.[30] Moon and Kim followed suit with their third summit in the space of six months since their first meeting in September.[31] In February 2019, Trump and Kim held their second summit.[32] And in June of the same year, Trump and Kim met with Moon at the DMZ, where Trump briefly crossed over into North Korea.[33]

What explains Kim's decision to engage in summitry, especially with Trump? After all, Trump and Kim traded insults throughout 2017, and US–North Korea relations were at a low point by the end of the year. There are several reasons behind this choice, some structural and others more specific to the time period when engagement took place. Among the structural reasons, three stand out: the needs for recognition, for diplomatic normalization, and for economic development. Among the time-specific reasons, two matter most: the election of an unorthodox president in the United States and the election of a pro-engagement president in South Korea.

With regard to the need for recognition, Pyongyang continues to believe that the two Koreas are in competition to become the recognized representative of the whole of Korea.[34] However, North Korea cannot claim to be the "true" representative of Korea so long as Seoul continues to grow in economic, political, and military clout, while Pyongyang remains unable to hold a summit between its leader and the US president. The summit with Trump thus allowed Kim to be seen as a "normal" political leader capable of holding a meeting with the leader of a twenty-first-century superpower. This recognition matters to Pyongyang. Kim himself made this clear when he lauded his meetings with Trump as "an event of the greatest significance in the history or world politics," during the Eighth Party Congress of the Workers' Party of Korea held in January 2021.[35]

Furthermore, summitry between Trump and Kim allowed the North Korean leader to press the case for diplomatic normalization between his country and the United States. And indeed, the Singapore Summit joint statement called for the normalization of bilateral diplomatic relations.[36] Kim Jong-un has not abandoned this goal dating back to the 1970s. Throughout his tenure, North Korean officials and official media outlets have called for Washington to establish diplomatic relations with Pyongyang on multiple occasions.[37] This will likely remain North Korean policy into the future and until—or if—normalization occurs.

Economic development is another structural reason for Kim's pursuit of summitry with Trump. As long as relations between Washington and Pyongyang remain strained, the comprehensive array of economic sanctions on North Korea will stay in place, preventing Kim from pursuing his *byungjin* policy and promoting further economic development. Even if Kim was willing to fully implement *byungjin*—and there is a lively debate about this—he would not be able to access the necessary investment, goods and technologies, and foreign markets for reform to be successful. By meeting with Trump, Kim increased the chances that the United States would acquiesce to removal of some sanctions—which could have resulted in trade and investment flowing into North Korea.[38] Even though sanctions removal did not ultimately happen, Kim's meeting with Trump did increase the chances that this would have happened. After all, neither a US president nor US Congress will see the need to remove sanctions unless they are closer to achieving their goals vis-à-vis North Korea. Summits are a way for Pyongyang to portray the image that it is considering denuclearization, which would make the United States more willing to consider sanction removal.

The time-specific election of Trump as the new US president also led Kim to engage in summitry. As a candidate in the 2016 US presidential elections, Trump stated that he would meet with Kim if necessary. Once in office, he argued that he would be able to solve the North Korean nuclear issue if he met with Kim.[39] And he exchanged multiple letters with the North Korean leader.[40] Trump's belief in personal diplomacy opened the door for a summit with Kim, and the North Korean leader eagerly crossed that threshold.

Trump's inauguration was shortly followed by Moon's in South Korea. The new South Korean president pushed for engagement with Pyongyang, since in his view diplomacy had stalled under the two previous conservative South Korean presidents. For Kim, engagement with Seoul facilitated diplomacy with Washington, since Moon offered himself and his government as a channel of communication between Trump and Kim.[41] North Korea thus faced both a pro-engagement president in South Korea and a US president who believed in personal diplomacy. This combination made it easier for Kim to reach out to the United States via summitry.

GOALS AND OUTCOMES OF THE
TRUMP-KIM SUMMITS

Trump and Kim attended the summits in Singapore, Hanoi, and the DMZ with different goals in mind. And although the joint statement issued by the two leaders after their Singapore Summit went unimplemented—considering that the Hanoi and DMZ summits did not result in similar documents—other less obvious goals were achieved.

On the US side, Trump agreed to a summit with Kim mainly out of the expectation that he might make North Korea agree to denuclearize. The denuclearization of North Korea has been a long-term US goal, dating back to before the first North Korean nuclear crisis and reinforced since the onset of the second nuclear crisis in 2002.[42] Trump thought his personal diplomacy could convince Kim to give up Pyongyang's nuclear weapons program. Although North Korea took no steps toward denuclearization, Trump declared after the Singapore Summit that he had defused the North Korean nuclear threat.[43] He apparently believed that the North Korean leader had indeed agreed to denuclearize when he signed the Singapore joint statement.[44] As of February 2022, North Korea has not conducted any nuclear or ICBM test since the 2018 summit. Even if Pyongyang has indicated that it does not feel bound by the moratorium, it has not breached it three and a half years after agreeing to it.[45] It may be that Trump simply sought to reduce the potential threat coming from North Korea, rather than denuclearization per se.

Another important reason behind Trump's summit with Kim was showmanship. Understandably, summitry between Trump and Kim drew the attention of the world media—especially the first summit in Singapore.[46] And from what has transpired during his time in office, frequent tweets, and bombastic claims, the US president craves the attention of the media and public opinion. Plus, Trump's engagement in summitry helped him cultivate his image as a leader dedicated to peace. In fact, Japan nominated Trump for the 2018 Nobel Peace Prize.[47] From this perspective, the summits with Kim satisfied Trump's desire to be in the spotlight for his work fostering peace on the Korean Peninsula.

On the North Korean side, sanctions relief was arguably the foremost goal for summitry with Trump. This was an important demand from the North Korean delegation during the Singapore Summit.[48] And it was Kim's main request during the Hanoi Summit. Indeed, North Korean Foreign Minister Ri Yong-ho gave a hastily arranged press conference a few hours after Trump abruptly left the Hanoi Summit to explain that North Korea had requested the removal of UN Security Council sanctions imposed in 2016–2017.[49] In this way, Pyongyang acknowledged sanctions removal as a crucial goal that it wanted to achieve from US–North Korea summitry. This objective aligns with Kim's push to improve the North Korean economy, which will only succeed if sanctions limiting trade and investment between North Korea and the outside world are removed.

Kim also sought recognition as a "normal" leader through his summit with Trump. From 2017 to 2019, he met with the leaders of China, Russia, Singapore, South Korea, and Vietnam, setting foot in each country.[50]

Compared to his father, Kim had a much more active international agenda. His meeting with Trump, however, topped all the other meetings from a North Korean perspective. In a sense, it put Pyongyang on equal footing with the Seoul of 1990–1992, when South Korea held summits with China and the Soviet Union and normalized relations with both. The summits with Trump finally implied US recognition of North Korea as a valid interlocutor.

In addition, and closely related to the above, Pyongyang wanted to normalize diplomatic relations with Washington through summitry. The meeting between Nixon and Mao in 1972 paved the way for Sino–US normalization. In the same way, the summits between Trump and Kim could have led to normalization between the United States and North Korea. And indeed, the Singapore joint statement committed to normalization as explained above.[51] Kim could reasonably have expected that meeting with Trump would have helped him to achieve this goal.

Despite Trump's and Kim's failure to achieve their preferred goals, arguably the most important outcome was the "normalization" of top-level summitry between Washington and Pyongyang. Questions had long persisted in the United States about the benefits and drawbacks of holding such a summit with Pyongyang. Ultimately, those who believed that summitry implied "recognition" of North Korea as is—that is, a nuclear-armed dictatorship—and would be a "concession" to the Kim regime had won the argument.[52] The Trump-Kim summit, however, showed that the leaders of the two countries could meet without fundamentally altering the nature of the US–North Korea relationship. In other words, a US leader can meet their North Korean counterpart as part of the policy toolkit to address Pyongyang's nuclear program.

At a more practical level, a second key outcome of the summits between Washington and Pyongyang was the Singapore joint statement, which enshrined the goals that both countries hope to achieve for their relationship: diplomatic normalization, a peace regime on the Korean Peninsula, and the denuclearization of North Korea. These goals have not fundamentally changed since the signing of the Agreed Framework in 1994.[53] But the Singapore Summit reinforced them for the first time at the leader level.

SUMMITRY AND US–NORTH KOREA RELATIONS

The two key outcomes of US–North Korea summitry explained above changed the relationship between the two countries. With the taboo of top-level meetings a thing of the past, future US leaders can meet with their North Korean counterparts without fear of breaking new ground that may have held past presidents back. On the North Korean side, Kim or any other future leader can point to the precedents of Singapore, Hanoi, and the DMZ as proof that relations between Washington and Pyongyang can involve top-level meetings.

Having said that, the summitry between Trump and Kim showed that the issues impeding a better relationship between the United States and North Korea are structural, rather than a product of the leadership on either side. The relationship between Washington and Pyongyang continues to be unchanged more than two years after the last of the three meetings between Trump and Kim. From this perspective, Trump's summitry did not result in a significantly different outcome from the refusal of Clinton, Bush, and Obama to meet with their North Korean counterpart.

What structural problems obstruct improvement in US–North Korea relations? To begin with, Washington and Pyongyang have different priorities. The United States prioritizes the denuclearization of North Korea; Pyongyang focuses above all else on economic benefits and diplomatic normalization. Although the Singapore Summit joint statement identified these goals as priorities for both, in reality, because of this structural constraint the statement was not implemented. Indeed, working-level meetings between the United States and North Korea broke down due to a difference in opinion over what should come first.[54] A summit cannot bridge such fundamental differences in priority.

Furthermore, another central stumbling block is US displeasure with North Korean behavior, especially with its nuclear and missile tests, but also with its poor human rights record. Congress, in particular, would need to be satisfied that the human rights situation in North Korea has improved to the point that it would support diplomatic normalization. The Trump administration certainly deprioritized the latter compared to the Bush and Obama administrations.[55] But North Korea resumed its missile tests in May 2019, a few weeks after the failure of the Hanoi Summit.[56] Relations between Trump and Kim did not recover even after their meeting at the DMZ. Summits were thus limited in their ability to rein in North Korea's actions. Thus, Washington's displeasure with North Korea's overall behavior is another structural impediment to better US–North Korea relations that cannot be addressed via summitry alone.

An additional, related structural block to better relations between Washington and Pyongyang is the latter's unwillingness to make concessions to improve relations with the former. North Korea sees its nuclear deterrent as its means to guarantee survival, particularly since Afghanistan, Iraq, or Libya arguably witnessed regime change because they lacked weapons of mass destruction (WMD) to deter US intervention. And indeed, Pyongyang regularly points to these three countries' experiences as reasons not to give up its own WMD capability.[57] Trump thought that top-level meetings with Kim would change North Korea's strategic calculus. But this was not the case.

After all, there is a fundamental distrust between Washington and Pyongyang that cannot be solved via summits alone.

A final, important structural obstacle to improved US–North Korea relations is Washington's apparent contentment with the status quo. Certainly, the United States ideally would like for North Korea to relinquish its nuclear weapons program. But North Korea's nuclear weapons development has not triggered a nuclear arms race as some have feared. Meanwhile, the sanctions regime on Pyongyang, with other tools, such as the Proliferation Security Initiative, seem to have reduced nuclear technology and WMD transfers from North Korea to third parties.[58] This has been an important objective for successive US governments, given Washington's focus on preventing proliferation of these technologies. Though top-level summitry has failed to change Kim's calculus, Washington may be satisfied with the status quo insofar as it can still achieve other goals related to its nonproliferation policy, even in the absence of a denuclearization agreement with Pyongyang.

THE FUTURE OF US–NORTH KOREA SUMMITRY

With the Trump-Kim meetings a thing of the past, questions remain surrounding the future of US–North Korea summitry. Will the three Trump-Kim summits prove a one-off? Or has Trump-Kim summitry opened the doors for future meetings at the highest level between the United States and North Korea? While it is not possible to predict the future of US–North Korea summitry, there are some clues as to whether future summits will take place.

First of all, it is reasonable to assume that Pyongyang will continue to request summits between its leader and the US president. This has been a long-standing North Korean policy, dating back to the Kim Il-sung era and especially from the 1970s onward. North Korea has no reason to back down from this decades-old policy, particularly since it resulted in success. And Kim seems willing to travel for meetings with foreign leaders, unlike his father. After all, Kim Jong-il only ever traveled to China and Russia during his time as North Korean leader. Kim Jong-un has ventured farther abroad. Kim may feel that further meetings with a US president could have benefits beyond the possibility of an agreement leading to economic benefits and diplomatic normalization. Some analysts believe Kim lost face with the no-deal Hanoi Summit, which may make him reluctant to take part in future summits.[59] But the potential benefits certainly outweigh the costs, particularly since the authoritarian nature of the North Korean regime means that Kim cannot be challenged on his policy choices.

Furthermore, the Singapore joint statement could provide the basis for future summits, making it more likely that Pyongyang will press for them.

Indeed, the Joe Biden administration has indicated that this statement will serve as the basis for future engagement with North Korea.[60] The statement closely resembles those signed by Clinton and Bush and is similar to the Leap Day agreement that the United States and North Korea issued in 2012, during the Obama presidency and shortly after Kim took office.[61] Since the parameters for future US–North Korea discussions seem clear, Pyongyang has an incentive to ask for top-level summits in the future. This is because North Korea knows—or should know—what the United States expects; after all, US expectations date back to the Clinton years and have survived Democratic and Republican presidencies—including Trump's populist foreign policy.

On the US side, although Trump was the first president to actually hold a summit with a North Korean leader, he was not the first president to entertain such an idea. Clinton and Obama did as well. And Biden has also indicated his willingness to meet with Kim if useful and necessary.[62] So the question seems to be not whether such a meeting will take place, but under what conditions a US president would meet with a North Korean leader in the future. For the Biden administration and more mainstream presidents, it seems, summitry for its own sake does not make sense. But summitry to seal a political deal after a bottom-up diplomatic process would be possible. The question is whether such a process could survive administrations, or whether the election of a new US president signals a "new beginning" in US–North Korea communications—which would only slow down diplomacy and potential summits. Yet, with an unorthodox president in the White House, a "personalist" approach to foreign policy could lead to a new summit without much advance preparation. After all, Trump may not be the only president to believe their power of persuasion is sufficient to solve a decades-old foreign policy conundrum.

With a more orthodox president in office, however, a top-level summit would likely only be possible following working-level negotiations between the United States and North Korea. Clinton only entertained the idea of a summit with Kim Jong-il toward the end of his tenure and once implementation of the Agreed Framework signed years before had resumed. Obama backed away from his campaign promise to meet with the North Korean leader because there was no diplomatic process between Washington and Pyongyang to build on.[63] Biden, for his part, has asserted that he will only meet with Kim at the end of a diplomatic process between their respective governments.[64] US presidents are, largely speaking, more willing to meet with North Korean leaders at the end of a bottom-up process in which working-level negotiations result in an agreement that leaders then ratify in person.

Still, the international community broadly supported Trump's decision to hold a bilateral summit with Kim. Moon encouraged the meetings, which he thought would lower tensions on the Korean Peninsula. China, Japan, and Russia did so as well.[65] Any future US–North Korea summit will likely also receive the support of the international community. After all, any summit is more likely than no summit to lead to mutual understanding, lowered tensions, and potentially the development of a peace process on the Korean Peninsula. Most of the international community does not share the reluctance of some analysts regarding US–North Korea bilateral leader-to-leader summitry. Most notably, the summits between Trump and Kim were welcomed by South Korea, China, Russia, and most countries in Europe and Southeast Asia. From the perspective of many foreign policy makers and analysts, US–North Korea summits help to defuse tensions and create mutual understanding, which is why they are welcome even if the Trump-Kim summits did not produce long-lasting results.

CONCLUSION

There is no doubt that the three summits between Trump and Kim were truly historic. The Singapore Summit was the first in history between a US and North Korean leader. The second in Hanoi helped normalize such meetings. The third at the DMZ marked the first time that a sitting US president stepped inside North Korea.

A mixture of structural factors and unique, time-specific circumstances led Trump and Kim to hold the three summits. On the structural side, North Korea's decades-long fixation with holding a top-level summit with the United States helped the process along. Furthermore, Pyongyang wanted to achieve an enduring set of goals—most notably, economic development and diplomatic normalization with the United States. On the US side, its goal of North Korean denuclearization drove Trump's agreement to hold a bilateral summit with Kim.

As for more time-specific reasons, Trump was an unorthodox leader who believed in the power of personal diplomacy. He saw the value of a summit with Kim for himself personally, both in driving the media agenda and in spreading his image as a peace-loving leader. Kim in turn faced US and South Korean leaders bent on engagement for the first time since his ascent as North Korea's leader. Furthermore, North Korea had completed its nuclear weapons program according to Kim's own statements and thus shifted its attention to the other component of its *byungjin* policy: economic development. These time-specific factors provided the necessary impetus for Trump-Kim summitry.

Moving forward, more US–North Korea top-level summitry will likely take place. After all, Trump has opened the door for future US presidents to meet with their North Korean counterparts. And Pyongyang will continue to insist on holding summits with Washington. However, more orthodox US leaders will probably only agree to hold meetings with North Korean leaders after a diplomatic process involving lengthy negotiations. In other words, summits will likely serve to finalize a diplomatic process rather than to kick-start it.

The value of US–North Korea summits, however, remains uncertain. As of 2022, Washington and Pyongyang are no closer to solving their bilateral problems than they were prior to the Trump-Kim summits. Their positions continue to diverge, and each thinks the other should make concessions so they can engage in a process that will result in a positive outcome for both sides. But the United States and North Korea have sought to mend their differences at various points dating back to the early 1990s. This suggests a willingness to at least consider how to improve their relationship. In this context, summits between Washington and Pyongyang have a role to play as part of a broader process that could result in North Korea taking steps toward denuclearization, normalization of diplomatic relations between Washington and Pyongyang, economic support for North Korea, and peace on the Korean Peninsula. In short, US–North Korea summitry is part of the toolkit that both countries can use to address their differences. It is not, however, a magic bullet that will eliminate decades of hostility between Washington and Pyongyang.

NOTES

1. Supreme People's Assembly of the Democratic People's Republic of Korea, "The Letter to the Congress of the United States of America," March 25, 1974.

2. Max Frankel, "Nixon Arrives in Peking to Begin an 8-Day Visit; Met by Chou at Airport," *New York Times*, February 21, 1972.

3. Democratic People's Republic of Korea and Republic of Korea, "The July 4 South-North Communiqué," July 4, 1972.

4. "A Chronology of U.S. Relations with North Korea, 1970–February 1985," *Korea and World Affairs* 9, no. 1 (1985): 153.

5. "Questions and Answers on New U.S. Guidelines Governing Contact between U.S. and North Korean Diplomats, during Briefing by U.S. State Department Spokesman Charles Redman Washington, March 9, 1987," *Korea and World Affairs* 11, no. 1 (1987): 173.

6. Ming Lee, "Seoul's Searching for '*Nordpolitik*': Evolution and Perspective," *Asian Perspective* 13, no. 2 (1989): 158.

7. Don Oberdorfer, "North Korean Leader Promotes Son," *Washington Post*, January 24, 1992.

8. Josette Shiner, "Kim Il-sung Asks for a Thaw in Ties with the U.S.," *Washington Times*, April 15, 1992.

9. David Sanger, "Carter Visit to North Korea: Whose Trip Was It Really?," *New York Times*, June 18, 1994.

10. Lee, "Seoul's Searching for '*Nordpolitik*': Evolution and Perspective," 164–65.

11. "The Gorbachev-Roh Breakthrough," *Washington Post*, June 6, 1990.

12. James Sterngold, "Seoul Gets Some Diplomatic Backing in China," *New York Times*, September 30, 1992.

13. Ramon Pacheco Pardo, *North Korea–US Relations from Kim Jong Il to Kim Jong Un* (London: Routledge, 2019), 82, 126.

14. United States of America and Democratic People's Republic of Korea, "Agreed Framework between the United States of America and Democratic People's Republic of Korea 1994," October 21, 1994.

15. Kim Dae-jung, *Conscience in Action: The Autobiography of Kim Dae-jung*, trans. Jeon Seung-hee (London: Palgrave Macmillan, 2018).

16. Sheryl Wuddun, "North Korea Fires Missile over Japanese Territory," *New York Times*, September 1, 1998.

17. "Inter-Korean Summit," KBS, June 15, 2000.

18. Steven Mufson, "Albright, N. Korea's Kim Meet for Historic Talks," *Washington Post*, October 24, 2000.

19. Bill Clinton, *My Life* (London: Arrow Books, 2005), 938.

20. Jack Kim, "Bill Clinton in North Korea, Meets Kim Jong-il," Reuters, August 4, 2009.

21. Sang-Hun Choe and Sharon LaFraniere, "Carter Wins Release of American in North Korea," *New York Times*, August 27, 2010.

22. Tak Sung Han and Jeon Kyung Joo, "Can North Korea Catch Two Rabbits at Once? Nuke and Economy. One Year of the Byungjin Line in North Korea and Its Future," *Korean Journal of Defense Analysis* 26, no. 2 (2014): 133.

23. United Nations Security Council, "Security Council Committee Established Pursuant to Resolution 1718 (2006)," Accessed November 10, 2021, https://www.un .org/securitycouncil/sanctions/1718.

24. The Commission on Presidential Debates, "September 26, 2008 Debate Transcript," Accessed November 10, 2021, https://www.debates.org/voter-education/ debate-transcripts/2008-debate-transcript/.

25. Ramon Pacheco Pardo, "Pyongyang's Failure: Explaining North Korea's Inability to Normalize Diplomatic Relations with the United States," *Asia Policy* 16, no. 1 (2021): 99.

26. "DPRK Gov't on Successful Test-Fire of New-Type ICBM," KCNA, November 29, 2017.

27. "N. Korean Leader's Visit Highlights 'Charm Offensive,'" Yonhap News Agency, February 9, 2018.

28. Andrew Jeong, "One Small Step for Moon, One Large Stride for Korean Harmony," *Wall Street Journal*, April 27, 2018.

29. Jonathan Cheng and Andrew Jeong, "Kim Reaffirms Korean Denuclearization Push, Looks Forward to Trump Meeting, Moon Says," *Wall Street Journal*, May 27, 2018.

30. Michael R. Gordon, Jonathan Cheng, and Michael C. Bender, "Trump, Kim Begin New Phase of Diplomacy," *Wall Street Journal*, June 15, 2018.

31. "Moon to Stay in Paekhwawon Guest House Known for Hosting VIPs," Yonhap News Agency, September 18, 2018.

32. Michael R. Gordon, Jonathan Cheng, and Vivian Salama, "U.S., North Korea Trade Blame for Failed Summit," *Wall Street Journal*, February 28, 2019.

33. Roberta Rampton, and Hyonhee Shin, "After Surprise Trump-Kim Meeting, U.S. and North Korea to Reopen Talks," Reuters, June 30, 2019.

34. Pacheco Pardo, *North Korea-US Relations from Kim Jong Il to Kim Jong Un*, 28–29.

35. "On Report Made by Supreme Leader Kim Jong Un at Eighth Party Congress of WPK," KCNA, January 9, 2021.

36. Donald J. Trump and Kim Jong-un, "Joint Statement of President Donald J. Trump of the United States of America and Chairman Kim Jon Un of the Democratic People's Republic of Korea at the Singapore Summit," June 12, 2018, Accessed November 15, 2021. https://trumpwhitehouse.archives.gov/briefings-statements/joint -statement-president-donald-j-trump-united-states-america-chairman-kim-jong-un -democratic-peoples-republic-korea-singapore-summit/.

37. Pacheco Pardo, *North Korea–US Relations from Kim Jong Il to Kim Jong Un*.

38. Gi-Wook Shin and Rennie J. Moon, "North Korea in 2018: Kim's Summit Diplomacy," *Asian Survey* 59, no. 1 (2019): 35–43.

39. Pacheco Pardo, *North Korea–US Relations from Kim Jong Il to Kim Jong Un*.

40. Bob Woodward, *Rage* (New York: Simon & Schuster, 2020).

41. Pacheco Pardo, *North Korea–US Relations from Kim Jong Il to Kim Jong Un*.

42. Pacheco Pardo.

43. Woodward, "Rage," 171–73.

44. Woodward, 171–73.

45. "N. Korea Hints at Lifting Moratorium on ICBM, Nuclear Tests, Citing U.S. 'Hostile Policy,'" Yonhap News Agency, January 20, 2022.

46. Woodward, *Rage*, 192.

47. Alex Johnson and Arata Yamamoto, "Japan Nominated Trump for Nobel Peace Prize after White House Asked, Newspaper Reports," NBC, February 18, 2019.

48. Woodward, *Rage*, 171–73.

49. "N. Korea Says It Wants Partial Sanctions Relief," Yonhap News Agency, March 1, 2019.

50. Pacheco Pardo, *North Korea–US Relations from Kim Jong Il to Kim Jong Un*.

51. Trump and Kim, "Joint Statement."

52. Leif-Eric Easley, "Trump and Kim Jong Un: Climbing the Diplomatic Ladder," *North Korean Review* 16, no. 1 (2020): 105.

53. Pacheco Pardo, *North Korea–US Relations from Kim Jong Il to Kim Jong Un*.

54. Johan Ahlander and Philip O'Connor, "North Korea Breaks Off Nuclear Talks with U.S. in Sweden," Reuters, October 5, 2019.

55. Pacheco Pardo, *North Korea–US Relations from Kim Jong Il to Kim Jong Un*.

56. Tim Martin and Andrew Jeong, "North Korea Fires Unidentified Short-Range Weapon," *Wall Street Journal*, May 4, 2019.

57. Pacheco Pardo, *North Korea–US Relations from Kim Jong Il to Kim Jong Un*.

58. Andrea Berger, *Target Markets: North Korea's Military Customers in the Sanctions Era* (London: Routledge, 2017).

59. Patricia Kim, "Failure in Hanoi Doesn't Mean Peace Is Dead," *Foreign Policy*, March 1, 2019.

60. "U.S.-ROK Leaders' Joint Statement," *White House*, May 21, 2021.

61. Victoria Nuland, "U.S.-DPRK Bilateral Discussions," US Department of State, February 29, 2012.

62. "Biden Says Will Meet N.K. Leader If He Agrees to Draw Down Nuclear Capacity," Yonhap News Agency, October 23, 2020.

63. Pacheco Pardo, *North Korea–US Relations from Kim Jong Il to Kim Jong Un*.

64. "Biden Says Will Meet N.K. Leader If He Agrees to Draw Down Nuclear Capacity."

65. Pacheco Pardo, *North Korea-US Relations from Kim Jong Il to Kim Jong Un*.

Chapter 7

Moscow-Pyongyang Summitry: From Stalin and Kim Il-sung to Putin and Kim Jong-un

Artyom Lukin

Russia and North Korea have a rich history of bilateral summitry. Since the late 1940s, seventeen or so leader-to-leader meetings have taken place between the two countries. While rulers in Moscow came and went, the Kim dynasty stayed on, accumulating experience in dealing with the Kremlin. Since 2000, Russia, not unlike North Korea, has known just one paramount leader—Vladimir Putin. He has already met with two of the Kims, gaining some useful, albeit not necessarily satisfying, experience in the process. This chapter provides an overview of North Korea-Soviet/Russia summitry, with an emphasis on the leader-level meetings that have taken place since 2000.

KIM IL-SUNG'S SUMMIT DIPLOMACY WITH THE SOVIETS: FROM AN OBEDIENT UNDERLING TO A RECALCITRANT QUASI-ALLY

In 1945, Soviet army captain Kim Il-sung was handpicked by the Soviet military command in Korea for a leadership role in the North Korean civilian administration, subsequently receiving confirmation from Joseph Stalin. In March 1949, Kim Il-sung made his first official visit to Moscow as North Korea's prime minister, where he was received by Stalin. The negotiations resulted in the signing of the Agreement on Economic and Cultural Cooperation between North Korea and the Soviet Union that established a framework for Soviet economic assistance to the North.[1] Kim secretly made a second visit to Moscow in April 1950 to request Stalin's permission to invade South Korea. Kim's last meeting with the Soviet dictator also took place in secret: in September 1952, Stalin chaired a China–North Korea–Soviet Union conference in Moscow where he and Kim discussed the conduct of the Korean War.[2]

In the early period of the North Korea–Soviet Union relationship, there was no doubt as to who was the overlord and who was the subordinate. Official photographs clearly reveal this dynamic. For example, a group picture from Kim's 1949 Moscow visit had Soviet officials at the center while the North Korean leader and other members of his delegation stood beside them.[3] In a conversation with the Soviet ambassador in January 1950, Kim was quoted as saying that "the directions of comrade Stalin have the force of law for me."[4]

Kim's first post-Stalin visit to the Soviet Union took place in September 1953, where he was received by Georgy Malenkov, the Soviet premier who topped the Soviet state hierarchy at that time. When Kim next visited the Soviet Union in the summer of 1956, Nikita Khrushchev was the Soviet leader. Earlier that year, at the Twentieth Congress of the Communist Party of the Soviet Union (CPSU), Khrushchev had launched the process of de-Stalinization. At his talks with Kim Il-sung, Khrushchev criticized the manifestations "of Stalinism and the personality cult of Kim Il-sung in the DPRK" and urged Kim "to take appropriate measures" to redress the situation, a request that certainly did not sit well with Kim.[5]

The second half of the 1950s marked the end of the period of North Korea's subordination to the Kremlin. Kim Il-sung's personal ambition and nationalism, coupled with his increased leadership experience and self-confidence, led Pyongyang to gradually distance itself from Moscow to achieve full political autonomy. Moscow's split with Beijing, which began to develop in the late 1950s, aided Pyongyang's quest for independence. Kim Il-sung could now play both ends against the middle, avoiding excessive dependence on Beijing and Moscow while extracting benefits from both major powers.

In 1959, Kim visited Moscow to attend the Twenty-First Congress of the CPSU accompanied by his teenage son, and future successor, Kim Jong-il. Kim's next visit to the Soviet Union, in 1960, took place in secret.

In 1961, Kim visited Moscow twice. In the summer of 1961, he came to the Soviet capital to sign the Treaty of Friendship, Cooperation and Mutual Assistance, a de facto alliance treaty that committed North Korea and the Soviet Union to immediately provide military assistance to the other if either experienced "an armed attack from a state or a coalition of states."[6] In October that year, Kim returned to Moscow to attend the Twenty-Second Congress of the CPSU, where he gave a speech praising North Korea-Soviet relations. However, as a deep split developed between the Soviet Union and China in the first half of the 1960s, Moscow's relationship with Pyongyang rapidly degraded too, with Kim Il-sung tilting toward Beijing and away from Moscow. Due to the cooling of the political relationship, a planned first visit by Khrushchev to Pyongyang never materialized.[7]

At the same time, neither Moscow nor Pyongyang was interested in a complete rupture. In 1966, North Korean–Soviet summitry resumed, with General Secretary Leonid Brezhnev and Kim Il-sung holding two secret meetings that year. The agenda and other details of these summits have never been officially disclosed. However, subjects for discussion most likely included the war in Vietnam and the Cultural Revolution in China. Pyongyang remained friendly with China, but Kim felt increasingly uncomfortable with Maoist extremes. Obtaining some insurance by moving a bit closer to the Soviet Union likely seemed a prudent policy. The first of the 1966 Brezhnev-Kim meetings reportedly took place in May in Vladivostok, while the other was apparently held later that year in Moscow. Despite the lack of official documentation, there are some witness accounts about the Vladivostok rendezvous. The main talks were held at sea off Vladivostok, aboard the Soviet Pacific Fleet's flagship missile cruiser *Varyag*, one of the newest and most powerful warships in the Soviet Navy. Moscow obviously wanted to impress the North Korean leader with a display of Soviet military might. To top it off, *Varyag* carried out an anti-ship cruise missile launch with Kim on board as a spectator.[8] To add a human touch to the summit, a day before the main negotiations Brezhnev took Kim by plane to the village of Vyatskoye near Khabarovsk, where Kim Il-sung had spent several years as an officer of the Soviet army and where his first son was born.[9]

The 1966 meetings resulted in agreements whereby the Soviet Union provided significant economic aid to North Korea in exchange for Pyongyang's neutrality in the Beijing-Moscow conflict.[10] In particular, the Soviet Union agreed to host thousands of North Korean laborers who worked as loggers in the Soviet Far East, with much of the proceeds going to Pyongyang's coffers.[11] But the North Korea-Soviet rapprochement had its limits. This became clear during the 1968 *Pueblo* crisis.[12] Moscow was concerned that North Korea's provocative behavior could lead to a major war in the Far East. Kim Il-sung was invited to Moscow for consultations. Kim declined to go, sending instead his minister of defense. At the consultations in Moscow, the Soviets made it clear that the 1961 treaty was strictly for defensive purposes and meant as an "instrument of peace in the Far East."[13] Hence it did not apply in situations in which North Korea acted provocatively.

Throughout the 1970s and 1980s, relations between North Korea and the Soviet Union remained outwardly friendly, but Moscow did not treat Pyongyang as a real ally and Pyongyang kept its distance from the Kremlin. Top Soviet leaders, including defense ministers and economic officials, did not visit Pyongyang.[14] In his foreign policy, Kim Il-sung deftly maneuvered between Moscow and Beijing in order to keep getting benefits from both rival patrons. For example, in 1978 he condemned the invasion of Cambodia by the Soviet ally Vietnam, whereas a year later Pyongyang endorsed Soviet intervention in Afghanistan.[15]

After a long pause in bilateral summitry, the Great Leader's last visits to the Soviet Union occurred in 1984 and 1986, when he met, respectively, with General Secretary Konstantin Chernenko and his successor Mikhail Gorbachev. Following a well-established pattern, Kim sought to secure Soviet economic, technological, and military assistance, selling North Korea as a reliable bastion against the US–Japan–South Korea bloc and trying to extract the maximum price for maintaining Pyongyang's neutrality in the Sino-Soviet rivalry. As a result of Kim's negotiations in Moscow in 1984 and 1986, the Soviet Union agreed to supply North Korea, free of charge, with modern Mig-23 and Mig-29 fighter jets and long-range radar equipment. Moscow also promised Pyongyang financial assistance and agreed to assist in the construction of a nuclear power plant in North Korea.[16]

Despite these pledges, the 1986 meeting in Moscow provoked suspicion and apprehension among the North Korean leadership. Kim Il-sung did not support Gorbachev's reformist initiatives of "perestroika" and "new thinking" and worried about a possible decline in bilateral relations because of the new priorities of Gorbachev's policy. The North Korean leader understood that the Soviet Union was focused on the normalization of relations with the West. The rapid development of Soviet–South Korea ties made North Korea especially uneasy.

In June 1990, Gorbachev met with South Korean president Roh Tae-woo in San Francisco, which resulted in the establishment of diplomatic relations between the two countries the same year. Predictably, there was an angry reaction in Pyongyang. Kim Il-sung refused to meet with Shevardnadze when the Soviet foreign minister arrived in Pyongyang in September 1990.

In 1991, the Soviet Union, which was facing spiraling domestic economic and political crises, essentially halted all assistance to North Korea and switched from subsidized trade via the so-called clearing mechanism to settlements in hard currency, which significantly worsened the terms of trade for North Korea. The disintegration of the Soviet Union in 1991 and the emergence in Moscow of Boris Yeltsin's administration, which avowed principles of liberal democracy and saw Russia as a close partner of the West, dealt the final blow to the Moscow-Pyongyang alliance. The Yeltsin administration saw North Korea as a totalitarian pariah state with no future. During the Korean Peninsula nuclear crisis of 1993–1994, Russia mostly was a passive observer, effectively siding with the United States and even supporting the US threat of imposing UN sanctions against North Korea.[17] In 1995, Moscow formally notified Pyongyang that the alliance treaty of 1961 had become obsolete and needed to be replaced with a new treaty not containing a mutual defense clause.[18]

Kim Jong-il's Summitry with Russia: Restoring the Relationship

By the second half of the 1990s, concerns were increasingly raised in Moscow that the heavy tilt toward Seoul at the expense of Pyongyang had only served to undermine Russia's position in Northeast Asia without generating any tangible benefits. Moscow was growing unhappy with its exclusion from the emerging four-party group, consisting of China, North Korea, South Korea, and the United States, that had become the main mechanism for dealing with Korean Peninsula issues. Moscow also felt that Seoul showed less interest in Russia after it scaled down its ties with the North.

With Vladimir Putin coming to power in 2000 and Russia's recovery from the chaos of the 1990s, Moscow had more resources—and more political will—to pursue proactive and independent foreign policies. By the late 1990s, the divergence of views on some key issues between Russia and the West had also become obvious. Russia felt much less obliged to defer to the West—and Seoul—on Korean Peninsula questions. At the same time, predictions of the imminent fall of the North Korean regime, which were prevalent in the 1990s, had proven wrong. It became clear to Moscow that North Korea was not destined for an inevitable implosion and could endure for quite a long time. Furthermore, with the economic situation in Russia rapidly improving, Moscow no longer needed South Korea's largesse, especially considering the disappointing fact that large anticipated South Korean investments failed to materialize in the 1990s.[19]

Moscow saw an opportunity to heighten Russia's international influence and prestige by reinserting itself into Korean Peninsula politics through restoring links with North Korea. In February 2000, Foreign Minister Igor Ivanov visited Pyongyang for the first high-level talks since Shevardnadze's 1990 visit to North Korea. During Ivanov's visit, the new Treaty of Friendship, Good Neighborliness, and Cooperation was signed with his North Korean counterpart. The document serves as the main legal framework for the North Korea–Russia relationship to this day. Unlike the 1961 North Korea–Soviet pact, the 2000 treaty contained no obligations of mutual military assistance. Instead, it only contained a clause that Moscow and Pyongyang should consult with each other in case there is a danger of aggression against one of the parties.[20]

As a result of further talks in April 2000 between North Korean and Russian diplomats, President Putin received an official signed invitation from Kim Jong-il to visit North Korea. Putin traveled to North Korea in July

2000, spending two days in Pyongyang and becoming the first Russian head of state to visit North Korea. It was also one of Putin's first foreign trips as Russian president.

Kim's invitation to Putin was part of a broader diplomatic offensive North Korea launched in 2000. In May 2000, Kim Jong-il went to China, holding his first summit with the Chinese leadership. In June that year, Kim hosted South Korean president Kim Dae-jung in Pyongyang for the first inter-Korean summit. In October, one of Kim's deputies was dispatched to Washington, D.C., where he had a White House meeting with President Bill Clinton, while Secretary of State Madeleine Albright became the highest US official to visit Pyongyang. A US presidential visit to North Korea was to become the culmination of Kim's diplomatic game, but it did not materialize.

The most significant outcome of Putin's visit to Pyongyang was a joint declaration issued by the two leaders. According to some assessments, North Koreans still see this political declaration, rather than the legal treaty concluded a few months earlier, as the main document guiding bilateral relations.[21] Unlike the treaty signed by foreign ministers, the declaration was issued directly by the top leaders, Kim Jong-il and Vladimir Putin. In a not-so-subtle rebuke to US unipolarity, the core part of the declaration was dedicated to North Korea and Russia's shared approaches to international order and strategic stability. Putin and Kim pledged support for the "central role" of the UN in "world affairs." The declaration emphasized "the sovereign right of each state to choose its own ways of political, economic and social development" and opposed "interference in internal affairs of other states, including under the pretext of humanitarian intervention."[22]

Reflecting primarily Russian concerns, the declaration paid much attention to strategic arms control issues, stating support for US-Russia strategic arms reduction treaties (START II and START III). It also stated the need to preserve the US-Russia 1972 Anti-Ballistic Missile (ABM) Treaty as a "cornerstone of strategic stability." The declaration contained a North Korean assurance that "its rocket program does not threaten anyone and is exclusively peaceful," with an implication that US references to a "missile threat" from North Korea were "completely unjustified." North Korea and Russia also stated that the deployment of theater missile defense systems in the Asia-Pacific could result in a "serious disruption of the regional stability and security."

The declaration expressed the intention "to actively develop bilateral trade, economic, scientific and technological links." During the talks, Putin and Kim also discussed possible infrastructure megaprojects, including the connection of a Trans-Korean railway network with Russia's Trans-Siberian that would provide a direct route between Europe and the Korean Peninsula.[23] Speaking to the press in Pyongyang after his talks with Kim, Putin sensationally revealed that the North Korean leader was "ready to use exclusively rockets of other states . . . for the peaceful exploration of space."[24] According to Putin, Kim Jong-il was seemingly ready to abandon North Korea's long-range missile program that was causing so much concern in the United States and other countries. A few days later, Putin shared Kim's message with the G8 leaders gathered for a summit in Okinawa.[25] However, a few weeks later, Kim Jong-il in a meeting with South Korean media representatives said that his remarks to Putin were merely "a joke."[26] This embarrassing incident no doubt influenced Putin's subsequent attitude to North Korean diplomacy and taught him something about the peculiarities of dealing with North Korean rulers.

From July 26 to August 18, 2001, Kim Jong-il's return visit to Russia took place. Following in the footsteps, or rather railroad tracks, of his father, Kim used his personal train to travel all the way from the North Korean border to Moscow and back, making sightseeing stops along the route. His second summit with Putin was held in the Kremlin, with the two sides issuing the Moscow Declaration. The declaration built upon the previous joint statement from Putin's visit to Pyongyang while introducing some new topics. It pronounced that each state has the right to an "equal degree of security," taking an implicit jab at Washington's supposed pursuit of absolute security at the expense of others.[27]

One especially interesting item in the Moscow Declaration concerned the problem of the US military presence in the South. North Korea "clarified its position that the removal of American troops from South Korea" is an "urgent" issue that needs to be resolved "in the interests of peace and security on the Korean Peninsula and in Northeast Asia." The Russian side refrained from endorsing this position, limiting itself to expressing an "understanding" of North Korea's stance on the issue.

At the Moscow summit, Putin and Kim continued to discuss potential areas for economic cooperation. In addition to railway projects and the reconstruction of Soviet-built industrial facilities, the Kremlin readout highlighted "joint extraction of minerals, particularly magnesium."[28]

Kim's next visit to Russia was unofficial. In August 2002, the North Korean supreme leader took a five-day train trip to the Russian Far East, with stops in Khabarovsk, Komsomolsk-on-Amur, and Vladivostok. In Vladivostok, Kim held what turned out to be his last meeting with Putin. After the talks in Vladivostok, Putin made a brief statement to the press. According to the Russian president, the two leaders mainly discussed economic cooperation, particularly the possible linking of the Trans-Siberian Railway with the Trans-Korean Railway. Korean Peninsula security was also on the agenda, with Putin expressing optimism that "there are some positive signs," as well as pointing out that North Korea's "good will is there."[29]

The three Putin-Kim summits restored the North Korea-Russia relationship that had remained broken since the late 1980s, although in its new reincarnation it became a relationship of official friendship and good-neighborliness, rather than that of an alliance. The summits with Kim also helped Moscow secure a seat at the Six-Party talks that began in August 2003. The United States was not initially going to invite Russia to participate in multilateral talks on North Korea, and even China, Moscow's "strategic partner," was not at first eager to see Russia as a player in the negotiation process on Korean affairs. According to some sources, it was Kim Jong-il who insisted on Russia being part of the talks.[30]

There was a long pause in North Korea–Russia summitry until 2011, when Kim Jong-il traveled to Russia by train to meet with then president Dmitry Medvedev in the Eastern Siberian city of Ulan Ude. In the second half of the 2000s, North Korea-Russia relations had somewhat cooled, mainly due to Moscow's disapproval of Pyongyang's nuclear and missile testing. An additional factor was the advent in 2008 of a conservative administration in South Korea led by Lee Myung-bak. Lee developed rapport with Medvedev, meeting him several times and promising support for Russia's modernization effort and even expressing the desire to become Russia's "strategic partner."[31] Given Lee's hardline stance on the North, the Kremlin's friendship with him caused irritation in Pyongyang. To show his displeasure with Moscow, Kim Jong-il refused to meet with the visiting Foreign Minister Sergey Lavrov in April 2009 and then, in November 2009, with Federation Council (the upper chamber of Russia's parliament) Chairman Sergey Mironov. However, even under such circumstances, both Moscow and Pyongyang were interested in preserving the relationship, which led to Kim's summit with Medvedev.[32] Incidentally, ahead of the summit, Russia decided to provide the North with fifty thousand tons of wheat as food assistance.

During the Ulan Ude talks, Kim apparently "expressed willingness to return to the Six Party Talks without preliminary preconditions." According to Medvedev's press secretary, Kim was even ready "in the process of negotiations, to introduce a moratorium on fissile materials production and tests."[33] It is hard to say how much the Kremlin trusted the assurances Kim reportedly made when meeting with Medvedev.

The meeting focused on economic issues, especially on the project of constructing a natural gas pipeline from Russia to South Korea via the North. During the talks, Kim gave his consent to the trilateral project, the funding for which was supposed to come from South Korea.[34] Kim and Medvedev also reached an agreement on the long-standing issue of Pyongyang's Soviet-era debt estimated at $11 billion. Following the summit, Moscow essentially wrote off the sum. Befitting Kim's official status as chairman of the State Defense Commission, and apparently accommodating his personal taste for military matters, after the talks Medvedev and Kim watched drills of elite Russian paratroopers demonstrating their martial skills.

North Korea-Russia Summitry in the Era of Kim Jong-un: A Quasi-Friendship?

Kim Jong-il's death in December 2011 did not initially affect Russia's approach to North Korea. There was little doubt in Moscow that his heir, Kim Jong-un, would be able to retain power and assert himself as North Korea's supreme leader. However, the junior Kim's acceleration of the North's nuclear and missile program caused concerns in Moscow. Following North Korea's nuclear test in February 2013, the Russian Foreign Ministry issued an unprecedentedly harsh statement that accused Pyongyang of committing "another violation of the norms of international law, demonstrating the defiance of the United Nations Security Council decisions."[35] Putin himself made no public comments on North Korea's nuclear test, but the Kremlin certainly authorized the Foreign Ministry's position.

The Ukraine crisis, which started to unfold in the autumn of 2013 and culminated in 2014, resulted in a dramatic deterioration of Moscow's relations with the West and profoundly impacted Russia's foreign policy.

Both ostracized by the West and subject to sanctions, North Korea and Russia began to feel more empathy and solidarity with each other. Sensing an opportunity, North Korea quickly expressed support for Russia, becoming one of the few nations to endorse Moscow's actions regarding Crimea. In turn, Moscow defended North Korea at the UN Security Council (UNSC) when it voted, along with China, against the inclusion of the issue of human rights in North Korea on the UNSC agenda.[36]

The shared anti-US stance was not the only reason for the rapprochement between Moscow and Pyongyang. Pyongyang's desire to reduce its dependence on China was another motivation. After coming to power, Kim Jong-un purged the pro-China faction from North Korea's elite, executing its leader (and his uncle-in-law) Jang Song-thaek. Kim's policy to assert his independence from Beijing led to tensions in China–North Korea relations. In its standoff with China, Pyongyang tried to play the Moscow card.

During 2014 and 2015, North Korea-Russia diplomatic relations grew remarkably in intensity. A flurry of high-level visit exchanges took place. In February 2014, North Korea's ceremonial head of state Kim Young-nam attended the opening ceremony of the Sochi Winter Olympics, even in the absence of North Korean athletes, and had a meeting, albeit a short one, with Putin. This contrasted with South Korea's decision to send a mere minister of sports and culture to Sochi.[37] In the course of 2014 and 2015, Minister of Foreign Trade Lee Ryong-Nam, Foreign Minister Lee Soo-young, Kim

Jong-un's special envoy Choe Ryong-hae, Supreme People's Assembly Chairman Choi Thae-baek, and other senior officials visited Russia.[38] Russia reciprocated by sending multiple delegations to Pyongyang, including Deputy Prime Minister Yuri Trutnev and Minister for Russian Far East Development Alexander Galushka. The year 2015 was designated as the Russia-North Korea Year of Friendship. In November 2015, Moscow and Pyongyang signed an agreement on "preventing dangerous military activity."[39] The document, concluded at the level of the two countries' general staffs, was an indication of increased military contact between North Korea and Russia. Moscow and Pyongyang took a number of steps to boost economic exchange, with more than a dozen agreements signed. Russia also extended food aid to North Korea through the World Food Program.[40]

Kim Jong-un's visit to Moscow in May 2015 for a celebration of the seventieth anniversary of victory over Nazi Germany was to become the culmination of the newfound Russia–North Korea diplomatic closeness. There was a tentative agreement that Kim would attend the Victory Day parade in Moscow, but Kim's decision to stay home caused some disappointment in Moscow. Pyongyang was instead represented by the DPRK Supreme People's Assembly Presidium Chairman Kim Yong-nam. North Korea never explained Kim's absence. Some speculated that Kim's decision not to go might have stemmed from domestic politics in Pyongyang or the Kremlin's reluctance to guarantee Kim the exclusive guest-of-honor treatment, considering the large number of other foreign dignitaries coming to Moscow. However, in hindsight, another explanation seems more convincing: Kim did not go to Russia in 2015 because he had reserved his first foreign visit for China, North Korea's main ally and benefactor. Even amid Sino–North Korean acrimony, Kim likely believed that the quarrel with Beijing would not last long, and he intended to use his first foreign visit strategically, which he eventually did in March 2018 when he traveled to Beijing for a summit with Xi Jinping.

Increasingly harsh international sanctions imposed on Pyongyang in 2016 and 2017 in response to its nuclear and missile spree took a toll on North Korea-Russia relations. Bilateral trade shrank, while most commercial projects that had been negotiated before 2016 were put on hold. Russia also curtailed high-level political contact with North Korea. Despite the rapprochement that had developed between Moscow and Pyongyang in 2014 and 2015, Russia did essentially nothing to shield Pyongyang from punishing sanctions. In particular, Moscow did not exercise its leverage as a permanent, veto-holding member of the UNSC. Instead, Russia let the United States and China bilaterally craft sanctions resolutions against North Korea and then voted in support of them. Moscow took this position for two main reasons. First, the Kremlin was angered by the rapid expansion of North Korea's nuclear and missile capabilities that culminated in intercontinental ballistic missile (ICBM) launches and what appeared to be a thermonuclear explosion in 2017. Kim Jong-un's nuclear and missile drive was gravely undermining the global non-proliferation regime, of which Russia was a main stakeholder. Second, due to its deepening entente with China, Moscow chose to defer to Beijing on the North Korea issue, implicitly recognizing the Korean Peninsula as falling under Beijing's sphere of influence. If, as was the case in 2016 and 2017, China decided to collaborate with the United States to punish North Korea, the Kremlin was not going to intervene.

During the "fire and fury" months of 2017, when tensions around North Korea were peaking and Donald Trump and Kim were exchanging threats, Putin made a number of remarks on the unfolding crisis. He asserted that the North Korean nuclear problem was a direct consequence of the ongoing systemic crisis of international order where universal rules were disregarded and "might has become right," alluding to the pernicious effects of preponderant US power, including Washington's perceived propensity to unilaterally use military force when dealing with foreign opponents and tendency to withdraw from previously negotiated agreements:

> Small nations see no other way to protect their independence, security and sovereignty than possession of nuclear weapons. This is what the abuse of power leads to.[41]

> They (North Koreans) know full well how the situation developed, for example, in Iraq when, under the pretext—which is now obvious to everyone—under the specious pretext of searching for weapons of mass destruction a country and its leadership were destroyed, and even the family members and children were shot dead. They are aware of all this and they see possession of nuclear weapons and missiles as the only way to defend themselves.[42]

> Yes, we unequivocally condemn the nuclear tests conducted by the DPRK and fully comply with the UN Security Council resolutions concerning North Korea. . . . However, this problem can, of course, only be resolved through dialogue. We should not drive North Korea into a corner, threaten force, stoop to unabashed rudeness or invective. Whether someone likes or dislikes the North Korean regime, we must not forget that the Democratic People's Republic of Korea is a sovereign state. All disputes must be resolved in a civilised manner. Russia has always favoured such an approach. We are firmly convinced that even the most complex knots—be it the crisis in Syria or Libya, the Korean Peninsula or, say, Ukraine—must be disentangled rather than cut. . . . Talking about a preventive disarming strike . . . is dangerous. . . . Who knows where and what the North Koreans have stashed away, and whether they will be able to destroy everything at once with one strike. I doubt it. I am almost sure that this is impossible. . . . So, there is only one way, which is to reach an agreement and to treat that country with respect.[43]

Putin obviously understood that these statements would be heard in Pyongyang. They were partly intended as a form of strategic communication with Kim. But Putin's messaging to Kim was ambivalent. The Russian leader expressed some understanding and even empathy with North Korea, putting blame on the imperious United States. However, as Putin delivered his statements, Russia's representatives at the UNSC voted for sectoral sanctions designed to cripple North Korea's economy, which, of course, they could not have done without approval from the Russian president.

Following its time-tested playbook of switching from belligerency to a charm offensive, Pyongyang kicked off a vigorous diplomatic campaign with the North Korean leader's sister Kim Yo-jong's attendance of the February 2018 Pyeongchang Winter Olympics. In 2018, Kim Jong-un held a series of meetings with China's Xi Jinping, South Korea's Moon Jae-in, and the United States' Donald Trump. Russian Foreign Minister Sergey Lavrov visited Pyongyang in late May 2018, getting an audience with Kim and becoming the first Russian official to hold direct talks with the young North Korean leader. Addressing the Russian foreign minister in the presence of cameras, Kim praised Lavrov's boss, Vladimir Putin, for "standing up to US hegemony."[44]

Lavrov passed an invitation to Kim to visit Russia, sparking rumors that a Kim-Putin summit might be in the offing.[45] However, Moscow and Pyongyang did not seem in a hurry to organize the meeting. In 2018, the only other direct contact between Russian officials and Kim took place when Chairwoman of the Federation Council Valentina Matvienko visited Pyongyang. She represented Russia at the celebration of North Korea's seventieth anniversary and received an audience with Kim Jong-un. Matvienko passed Putin's letter to Kim, with Kim reportedly confirming his intention to visit Russia "in the near future." According to Matvienko's account of the conversation, Kim was "very hopeful that Russia, too, will be making efforts to ease the sanctions (against North Korea)."[46] Matvienko's remark probably revealed Kim's top priority at that moment—removing the sanctions regime—and his expectation that Russia could help in achieving that goal.

Throughout Kim's diplomatic offensive in 2018 and up until the unsuccessful Hanoi Summit with Trump in late February 2019, Pyongyang was clearly focused on the United States and South Korea, while seeking Chinese backing in the process. Other players, including Russia, were relatively peripheral to that effort, which likely explains why it took Kim a while to make his promised visit to Russia.

Post-Hanoi, the diplomatic process with Washington and Seoul stalled and Kim had already traveled to China four times. So, Russia looked like the most logical choice for Kim's next visit. He could expect a warm reception in Russia that would boost his international and domestic prestige and demonstrate that Pyongyang had close friends beyond China or Cuba.

Furthermore, Kim apparently hoped to obtain political and economic support from Moscow, especially considering that prospects for ending the US-led economic isolation of North Korea had significantly dimmed after Hanoi. As for Putin, a summit with the North Korean leader was mainly important for international prestige. The summit would symbolically reaffirm Russia's traditional great-power role as a major player on the Korean Peninsula.[47]

Kim's official visit to Russia finally occurred from April 24 to 26, 2019, with a Kim-Putin summit taking place in Vladivostok on April 25. The choice of Vladivostok, the capital of the Russian Far East, as the summit venue seemed convenient for both sides: it was a short ride by train for Kim from North Korea, while Putin crossed the nearby Chinese border to meet Xi Jinping in Beijing after holding talks with Kim. However, the fact that Kim's first official visit to Russia was not to Moscow raised questions over whether it was a downgraded summit. By contrast, Kim's first official visit to China in March 2018 took place in Beijing.

The Kim-Putin summit held on the premises of the Far Eastern Federal University campus on Russky Island off Vladivostok was brief. Still, it had all the trappings of an official visit, complete with the Kremlin's honor guard flown in from Moscow. The two leaders first had a one-on-one conversation, after which they were joined by their delegations. The talks lasted three and a half hours.[48] The summit ended with an official dinner. On the same day, Putin departed for China, where he would spend three days attending Xi Jinping's Belt and Road Forum, leaving his North Korean guest to enjoy the Russian Far East.

During the summit, interactions between the two leaders appeared polite, albeit somewhat stiff. Some observers characterized the rendezvous as "an old style Soviet meeting, with a bit of a formal chill to it."[49] In their public statements, both Kim and Putin emphasized "the traditional and long-standing ties of friendship between the DPRK and Russia."[50] Nevertheless, few if any concrete agreements or decisions were made at the summit. No joint statement followed the meeting. In his remarks to the press after the talks, Putin sounded rather anodyne and noncommittal regarding political, diplomatic, and economic steps Russia would be willing to take to assist North Korea. Kim apparently failed to get Putin to commit to any substantial aid to the North, either in the form of major relaxation of sanctions regime enforcement or provision of a direct economic lifeline to North Korea. Putin may have made it clear to Kim that he should not expect too much generosity from Russia.[51] One indirect indication that Kim was not quite happy with the summit's outcome was his decision to cut short his stay in Russia: on the last day of his visit, he departed Vladivostok seven hours earlier than initially planned.[52]

However, Kim did not leave Vladivostok entirely empty-handed. Speaking to the press after the summit, Putin mentioned that the issue of North Korean guest workers in Russia was discussed. Under UNSC resolutions, all North Korean guest workers were to leave host countries by December 2019. Putin commented that there were "several different options" and "non-confrontational solutions" to deal with the issue.[53] Incidentally, a few weeks prior to Kim and Putin's Vladivostok rendezvous, the Russian minister of internal affairs visited Pyongyang accompanied by his deputy in charge of regulating foreign migration in Russia.[54] The issue of "temporary foreign workers" was discussed during that visit.[55] Based on the consultations of their officials, Kim and Putin might have authorized an arrangement for North Korean nationals in Russia. The summit might have also contributed to Russia's decision to provide fifty thousand tons of wheat in humanitarian aid to North Korea. The grain was delivered in 2020.[56]

Concerning the problem of denuclearization, the summit produced little. Kim did not bring to Vladivostok any proposals that Pyongyang had not already made before. After the talks, Putin hinted that the North Korean leader was not in the mood for concessions: "He (Kim) is determined to defend his country's national interests and to maintain its security."[57] Putin spoke about the need for "international guarantees" for North Korea but did not clarify what those guarantees could be. During and after the summit, the Russian president showed no desire for a possible mediation role between Pyongyang and Washington.

At the post-summit press conference, Putin took a jab at South Korea. When commenting on the lack of progress in trilateral North Korea–Russia–South Korea economic projects, Putin suggested it was due to Seoul's "shortage of sovereignty" related to South Korea's "allied obligations before the United States."[58] Putin's somewhat derogatory remark may have been partly intended to contrast Seoul's status as a junior and subordinate ally of Washington with Pyongyang's full sovereignty and political independence.

Ironically, the next significant development in North Korea-Russia relations following the Kim-Putin summit in Vladivostok was a mini-crisis caused by a surge in North Korean poaching in Russia's exclusive economic zone and territorial waters in the East Sea/Sea of Japan.[59] In the summer and fall of 2019, thousands of North Korean schooners and motorboats entered Russian waters to illegally catch fish, mostly squid. To make matters worse, North Korean flotillas used destructive fishing methods like drift nets, which severely harm the marine environment. For a while, Moscow turned a blind eye to North Korean poaching, but finally Russian authorities ran out of patience and resorted to tougher measures, which resulted in several skirmishes between poachers and Russian coast guard vessels, leaving one North Korean fisherman dead and several wounded.[60]

CONCLUSION

North Korea-Russia summitry has progressed through several distinct stages that reflect the general evolution of political relations between Moscow and Pyongyang. The first period, lasting from the late 1940s to the mid-1950s, was marked by the North's subordination to the Soviet Union, with Stalin essentially acting as an overlord to Kim Il-sung.

In the second half of the 1950s, Pyongyang managed to gain full agency, becoming an independent player. North Korea's relationship with the Soviet Union became politically equal. A formal alliance treaty existed, but the Soviet–North Korean relationship was a less than full alignment, with Pyongyang keeping its distance from Moscow. There were long pauses in summitry, with Kim Il-sung not meeting Soviet general secretaries for eighteen years between 1966 and 1984. When summits did take place, Kim mainly sought to secure maximum amounts of Soviet economic and military aid. The Great Leader was more or less successful in these efforts. The Soviet Union, which during the Cold War faced the hostile bloc of the United States, Japan, and South Korea on its Far Eastern borders, needed a friendly North Korea. Pyongyang also skillfully manipulated Soviet fears of China, with which the Soviet Union was in a state of confrontation from the 1960s until the mid-1980s.

The end of the Cold War and the collapse of the Soviet Union effectively ended Moscow's relationship with Pyongyang. The Russian leadership believed it no longer needed North Korea. A long break in high-level political contacts lasted until 2000 when Putin made a visit to Pyongyang, the first by any Russian leader. Putin's three summits with Kim Jong-il in 2000, 2001, and 2002 signified a resurrection of North Korea-Russia relations and the beginning of a new chapter in their relations, which continues to this day. The bilateral relationship of this current period is officially characterized as "friendship" and "good-neighborliness" and is based on the joint declarations adopted by Putin and Kim Jong-il during their 2000 and 2001 summits. So far, these documents remain the only joint statements issued by leaders of North Korea and the Russian Federation.

After 2002, North Korea and Russia held only two additional summits, with Medvedev meeting Kim Jong-il in 2011 and Putin meeting Kim Jong-un in 2019. This lack of meetings somewhat contradicts the official designation of the bilateral relationship as "friendly," "cooperative," and "good-neighborly." The paucity in top-level North Korea-Russia interactions has resulted from several factors.

First and foremost, the Kremlin has little interest in North Korea. In the early 2000s, when starting his summitry with Kim Jong-il, Putin may have harbored high expectations, as well as perhaps some curiosity about the hermit Juche dynasty. But it did not take long for him to realize what a difficult partner North Korea is. The North Korean nuclear and missile problem was only getting worse, while commercial opportunities with the North proved either impossible or fraught with major risks.

Strategically, the North has marginal value for modern Russia. Even an absorption of North Korea by South Korea, with the North's subsequent incorporation into the US-led alliance network, would not substantially impact Russia's security. For Moscow, North Korea's importance does not even remotely approach that of Belarus or Ukraine, whose geopolitical fates are seen by Moscow as an existential question and whose potential integration into Western institutions is a red line for the Kremlin.

The dramatic deterioration of Russia's relations with the West in the wake of the 2014 Ukraine crisis boosted North Korea-Russia ties. Since the mid-2010s, exploitation of the theme of supposed shared resistance to the US hegemonic empire has become a fixture of North Korean diplomacy toward Moscow. In a typical example of such rhetoric, in August 2021 North Korea's ambassador to Moscow stated that North Korea and Russia "will be enhancing their interaction in order to counter the US, which is a common threat."[61] However, Pyongyang largely failed to convert Russia's newfound hostility toward the United States into material benefits for itself. Moscow proved unwilling to return to the Soviet model of subsidizing North Korea in exchange for Pyongyang's role as a self-styled bastion against American imperialism.

Russia's foreign policy under Putin is extremely pragmatic and calculating. Moscow is only prepared to provide economic assistance to a limited number of countries, mostly in the post-Soviet space, whom it considers vital for Russia's security and over whose policies the Kremlin can exercise a considerable degree of influence. Pyongyang's realization that Putin's Russia would not be another Soviet Union in terms of economic and military aid undoubtedly dampened North Korea's appetite for summitry with Moscow. Pyongyang has always used its summits with great powers strategically, seeking to extract as many material benefits as possible. This explains why Kim Jong-il has had five summits with Xi Jinping and only one meeting with Vladimir Putin.

Russia's increasingly close strategic ties with China also explain Moscow's limited top-level engagement with the North. The Kremlin seems to have tacitly recognized the Korean Peninsula as Beijing's sphere of influence. Russia mostly follows Beijing's line on North Korea. Furthermore, having been around in world politics for more than two decades, Putin probably understands better than anyone the rigid and intractable nature of the structural problems on the peninsula. One might even speculate that Putin is simply bored of the repetitive geopolitics on the Korean Peninsula, which is also a region where Russia has relatively limited leverage. By contrast, he is far more excited about dynamic political developments in places like Europe, the Middle East, and more recently Africa, where Russia can often play crucial roles.

As the leader of an autocratic and historically insecure state, Putin may feel some empathy for the motives driving North Korea's pursuit of nuclear and missile weapons. Still, the North's expanding and increasingly sophisticated nuclear arsenal causes serious concern for Russia. Although Pyongyang's nuclear weapons do not directly threaten Russia, Moscow cannot ignore North Korea's defiance of the global nonproliferation regime, of which Russia is a major stakeholder and beneficiary. An arsenal of thermonuclear weapons capable of destroying the world's only superpower has been post-Soviet Russia's Holy Grail and one of the pillars of its claim to great-power status. If a small, poor country like North Korea can obtain an ICBM capability, it would inevitably devalue Russia's own, eroding Moscow's international prestige and influence.[62] This helps explain why Moscow, despite its avowed friendship with the North, has supported international sanctions against North Korea and, unlike China, continues to be generally faithful in their enforcement.

Putin does not believe that sanctions will succeed in forcing North Korea to abandon its hard-won nuclear weapons. But he might well concur with the US national intelligence officer for North Korea, who opined that the true objective of the sanctions against Pyongyang now may lie in deterring other potential nuclear aspirants.[63] It is not surprising that the North Korean nuclear problem is one of the few areas where Moscow and Washington's interests align.[64]

Moscow and Pyongyang have a rich history of summitry between themselves. But it is unlikely the camaraderie between the Russian and North Korean top leaders will resume any time soon. The isolation induced by COVID-19 is partly to blame. However, Moscow's relative lack of interest in North Korea is the bigger reason. When Kim Jong-il met with Putin in Moscow in August 2001, he invited the Russian president to "again visit the DPRK at his convenience."[65] The invitation was "accepted with gratitude." Two decades have passed, but Putin has yet to use Kim's invite. It is almost certain that he never will.

NOTES

1. "USSR–North Korea Agreement on Economic and Cultural Cooperation," Encyclopedia of Korean Culture, http://encykorea.aks.ac.kr/Contents/Item/E0070145.

2. Beijing was represented by Peng Dehuai. Leonid Maksimenkov, "A Korean Tango of Three," *Kommersant*, September 9, 2017, https://www.kommersant.ru/doc/3414521 (in Russian).

3. The photo is available in the report: "The History of the Visits by the Leaders of the DPRK to the USSR and Russia," TASS, April 24, 2019. https://tass.ru/info/6370930 (in Russian).

4. Artem Krechetnikov, "The Korean War: Another Mystery of Stalin," BBC, July 26, 2013, https://www.bbc.com/russian/russia/2013/07/130727_korean_war_stalin (in Russian).

5. "The History of the Visits by the Leaders of the DPRK to the USSR and Russia."

6. "Treaty of Friendship, Cooperation and Mutual Assistance between the USSR and the DPRK," July 6, 1961, https://www.documentcloud.org/documents/3005971-1961-Treaty-of-Friendship-Cooperation-and-Mutual.

7. "Society and Power in the Russian Far East in 1960–1991," in *History of the Russian Far East. Vol. 3. Book 5*, ed. Victor Larin and Angelina Vashchuk, Vladivostok: Institute of History, Archaeology and Ethnography of the Peoples of the Russian Far East of the Far Eastern Branch of the Russian Academy of Sciences, 2016, 144. http://ihaefe.org/files/publications/full/dv-history-2016.pdf (in Russian).

8. Mikhail Voznesensky, "The Secret Summit of Brezhnev and Kim Il-sung," https://pub.wikireading.ru/ha5ETGb0nv (in Russian).

9. Alexey Volynets, "Number-One Persons Visiting the Far Eastern Border," *DV. Land*, November 23, 2020, https://dv.land/history/pervye-litca-na-dalnevostochnoi-granitce-3 (in Russian).

10. Igor Bezik, "The Participation of DPRK Nationals in the Economic Development of the Soviet Far East (1950s–early 1960s)," *Oriental Institute Journal*, no. 1 (2011), 74. (in Russian)

11. Andrei Lankov, "North Korean Workers in the USSR and Russia," *Polit.ru*, May 21, 2021, https://polit.ru/article/2021/05/10/lankovrabochie/ (in Russian).

12. In January 1968, the US Navy surveillance ship *Pueblo*, which operated in international waters, was attacked and seized by North Koreans, leading to a tense standoff between the United States and North Korea.

13. Ella Bikmurzina, "The North Korean Attack on Oceanographers," *Vokrug Sveta*, November 30, 2010, https://www.vokrugsveta.ru/telegraph/history/1285/ (in Russian).

14. "Society and Power in the Russian Far East in 1960–1991," 149–50.

15. Andrey Mozzhuhin, "The Foundling Dictator," *Lenta.ru*, December 25, 2018, https://lenta.ru/articles/2018/12/25/kndr/ (in Russian).

16. "The History of the Visits by the Leaders of the DPRK to the USSR and Russia."

17. Georgy Toloraya, "Korean Peninsula and Russia: The Problems of Interaction," *Mezhdunarodnaya Zhizn* [International Affairs], November 2002, http://world.lib.ru/k/kim_o_i/a9616.shtml (in Russian).

18. "Final Report on the Project 'Russia-Korea Relations in the Architecture of Northeast Asia and the Asia-Pacific,'" Gorbachev Foundation, February 2003, http://www.gorby.ru/activity/conference/show_70/view_13120/ (in Russian).

19. Artyom Lukin, Georgy Toloraya, Ilya Dyachkov, et al. "Nuclear Weapons and Russian–North Korean Relations," *Foreign Policy Research Institute*, November 2017, https://www.fpri.org/article/2017/11/nuclear-weapons-russian-north-korean -relations/.

20. Treaty of Friendship, Good Neighborliness, and Cooperation between the Russian Federation and the DPRK, February 9, 2000, http://oldsite.nautilus.org /DPRKBriefingBook/agreements/CanKor_VTK_2000_07_19_dprk_russia_joint _declaration.pdf.

21. Georgy Toloraya and Lyubov Yakovleva, "Russia and North Korea: Ups and Downs in Relations," Asian Politics and Policy 13, no. 2 (2021): 370

22. "Joint Russian-Korean Declaration," Kremlin, July 19, 2000, http://kremlin.ru /supplement/3183 (in Russian).

23. Vladimir Putin, "Replies to Russian Journalists' Questions about Talks with Kim Jong-il, Chairman of the Defence Committee of the Democratic People's Republic of Korea," Kremlin, July 19, 2000, http://en.kremlin.ru/events/president/ transcripts/24172.

24. Putin.

25. "Vladimir Putin Took Part in a Meeting of G8 Heads of State and Government," Kremlin.ru, July 22, 2000, http://en.kremlin.ru/events/president/news/38481.

26. "Kim Jong Il Says Missile Remarks 'Laughing Matter,'" Kyodo News International, August 14, 2000, https://www.thefreelibrary.com/Kim+Jong+Il+says+missile +remarks+%27laughing+matter%27-a064528189.

27. "Moscow Declaration of the Russian Federation and the DPRK," Kremlin, August 4, 2001, http://kremlin.ru/supplement/3410 (in Russian).

28. "Russian President Vladimir Putin Held Talks with His Visiting North Korean Counterpart, Kim Jong Il," Kremlin.ru, August 4, 2001, http://en.kremlin.ru/events/ president/news/41779.

29. Vladimir Putin, "Statement to the press after the talks with the Chairman of the State Defence Committee of the DPRK Kim Jong Il," Kremlin, August 23, 2002, http://en.kremlin.ru/events/president/transcripts/21688.

30. Georgy Toloraya and Lyubov Yakovleva, 371.

31. Alexander Gabuev, "Dmitry Medvedev Is Building a Bridge from Seoul to Skolkovo," *Kommersant*, November 11, 2010, https://www.kommersant.ru/doc /1536317 (in Russian).

32. Kim's rendezvous with Medvedev in August 2011 turned out to be his last meeting with a foreign leader.

33. "Dmitry Medvedev and Kim Jong-il Resolved the Problem of DPRK's Debt to Russia," *Rossiyskaya Gazeta*, August 24, 2011, https://rg.ru/2011/08/24/dolg2-anons .html (in Russian).

34. "Meeting with Journalists Following Talks with Chairman of the State Defence Commission of the Democratic People's Republic of Korea Kim Jong Il," Kremlin. ru, August 24, 2011, http://en.kremlin.ru/events/president/news/12432.

35. "World Leaders React to North Korea's Nuclear Test," CNN, February 12, 2013, https://www.cnn.com/2013/02/12/world/north-korea-nuclear-reax/index.html.

36. Ankit Panda, "North Korean Human Rights Abuses on the Agenda at UN Security Council," *The Diplomat*, December 23, 2014, http://thediplomat.com/2014/12/north-korean-human-rights-abuses-on-the-agenda-at-un-security-council/.

37. Oleg Kiryanov, "South Korea Has Missed a Chance for Diplomacy in Sochi," *Rossiyskaya Gazeta*, February 8, 2014, https://rg.ru/2014/02/08/koreya-site-anons .html (in Russian).

38. Pavel Cherkashin, "Current Russian-North Korean Relations and Prospects of Their Development," Russian International Affairs Council, August 24, 2015, https://russiancouncil.ru/en/blogs/dvfu-en/32874/.

39. Leo Byrne, "N. Korea, Russia Sign Military Agreement," *NK News*, November 13, 2015, http://www.nknews.org/2015/11/n-korea-russia-sign-military-agreement.

40. Lukin, et al., Nuclear Weapons and Russian–North Korean Relations."

41. Vladimir Putin, "Remarks at Saint Petersburg Economic Forum," Kremlin, June 2, 2017, http://kremlin.ru/events/president/news/54667 (in Russian).

42. Vladimir Putin, "Remarks at Eastern Economic Forum, Vladivostok," Kremlin, September 7, 2017, http://kremlin.ru/events/president/news/55552 (in Russian).

43. Vladimir Putin, "Remarks at the Meeting of the Valdai International Discussion Club," Kremlin, October 19, 2017, http://en.kremlin.ru/events/president/news/55882.

44. "The DPRK Leader Kim Jong-un Will Come to Russia at the End of April," Radio Liberty, Svoboda, April 18, 2019, https://www.svoboda.org/a/29889549.html (in Russian).

45. Mikhail Korostikov, "Sergey Lavrov Made a Visit to Pyongyang," *Kommersant*, May 31, 2018, https://www.kommersant.ru/doc/3645195.

46. "Matvienko: Kim Jong-un Hopes That the Russian Federation Could Assist in Easing the Sanctions Imposed on the DPRK," TASS, September 10, 2018, https://tass .ru/politika/5545605 (in Russian).

47. Artyom Lukin, "The Putin and Kim Rendezvous in Vladivostok: A Drive-By Summit," *38North*, May 2, 2019, https://www.38north.org/2019/05/alukin050219/.

48. "The First Summit of Putin and Kim Jong-un Lasts Three and a Half Hours," *RIA Novosti*, April 25, 2019, https://ria.ru/20190425/1553033104.html (in Russian).

49. Eric Talmadge, "Deciphering the Body Language at the Kim-Putin Summit, from Hearty Handshakes to Manspreading," *National Post*, April 25, 2019, https://nationalpost.com/news/world/at-kim-putin-summit-hearty-handshakes-and -manspreading.

50. "Beginning of Conversation with DPRK State Affairs Commission Chairman Kim Jong-un," Kremlin.ru, April 25, 2019, http://en.kremlin.ru/events/president/ transcripts/60366.

51. Artyom Lukin, "The Putin and Kim Rendezvous in Vladivostok: A Drive-By Summit."

52. "Kim Jong-un Left Russia Seven Hours Earlier Than Initially Planned," BBC, April 26, 2019, https://www.bbc.com/russian/news-48062871 (in Russian).

53. Vladimir Putin, "News Conference Following Russian-North Korean Talks," Kremlin, April 25, 2019, http://en.kremlin.ru/events/president/news/60370.

54. "Russia and the DPRK Step Up the Contacts of Law-Enforcement Agencies," *Izvestiya*, April 2, 2019, https://iz.ru/863353/2019-04-02/rossiia-i-kndr-aktivizirovali -kontakty-pravookhranitelnykh-organov (in Russian).

55. Ministry of Internal Affairs, April 3, 2019, https://xn--b1aew.xn--p1ai/mvd/ structure1/Glavnie_upravlenija/guvm/news/item/16411249 (in Russian).

56. "Russia Supplied 50,000 Tons of Wheat as Humanitarian Aid to the DPRK," *Interfax*, September 12, 2020, https://www.interfax.ru/russia/726627 (in Russian).

57. Putin, "News Conference Following Russian-North Korean Talks."

58. Putin.

59. Artyom Lukin, "Will North Korea's Squid Poaching Strain Its Ties with Russia?," *World Politics Review*, October 8, 2019, https://www.worldpoliticsreview.com/ trend-lines/28249/will-north-korea-s-squid-poaching-strain-its-close-ties-with-russia.

60. Artyom Lukin, "Russia's Policy Toward North Korea: Following China's Lead," *38North*, December 23, 2019, https://www.38north.org/2019/12/alukin122319 /.

61. "The DPRK Ambassador Says Peace on the Korean Peninsula Is Impossible without the Withdrawal of US Troops," TASS, August 12, 2021, https://tass.ru/ mezhdunarodnaya-panorama/12109215 (in Russian).

62. Artyom Lukin, "North Korea Stuck Between a Rock and a Hard Place: One Year After the Hanoi Summit," *Foreign Policy Research Institute*, March 10. 2020, https://www.fpri.org/article/2020/03/north-korea-stuck-between-a-rock-and-a-hard -place-one-year-after-the-hanoi-summit/.

63. "US Will Not Accept Nuclear North Korea Despite North Korean Ambitions: US Official," *Korea Times*, August 4, 2021, https://www.koreatimes.co.kr/www/ nation/2021/08/103_313330.html?tw.

64. Anton Troianovski and David Sanger, "Rivals on World Stage, Russia and U.S. Quietly Seek Areas of Accord," *New York Times*, October 31, 2021, https://www .nytimes.com/2021/10/31/world/europe/biden-putin-russia-united-states.html.

65. "Moscow Declaration of the Russian Federation and the DPRK," August 4, 2001, http://kremlin.ru/supplement/3410 (in Russian).

Part III: North Korean Diplomacy toward the World

Chapter 8

United Nations Sanctions and North Korean Diplomatic Engagement with the International Community

Justin V. Hastings

An understanding of North Korea's foreign policy under Kim Jong-un is incomplete without a discussion of the effect of United Nations (UN) sanctions. North Korea is arguably the most sanctioned country in the world. Not only has it been subject to a range of unilateral sanctions by the United States, the European Union, Australia, and others, but North Korea has also been the subject of many UN Security Council (UNSC) sanctions resolutions that are theoretically binding on all member states (including North Korea). Moreover, the vast majority of sanctions passed against North Korea have been passed during Kim Jong-un's rule, meaning that North Korea now finds itself in a significantly more hostile political and economic environment compared to what it faced upon Kim Jong-il's death.

In this chapter, I argue that while the course of North Korea's foreign policy has itself led to the imposition and intensification of UN sanctions, the sanctions themselves have also impacted North Korea's engagement with the international community. North Korea's foreign policy objectives have largely served its overarching goal, the regime's continuing survival on its own terms. In pursuing this goal, North Korea has developed strategies that allow it to withstand outside pressure, both politically and economically, including via sanctions. However, these strategies, such as the development and repeated testing of nuclear weapons and missile delivery systems, have also led to external pressures on North Korea.

The upshot of this is that many of North Korea's foreign policy goals, such as minimizing China's influence over the country while maintaining a steady flow of trade with the outside world, operate at cross-purposes and are made even more difficult to achieve under sanctions. To a large extent, the immediate goals of North Korea's foreign policy have become seeing sanctions formally rolled back or, barring that, minimizing the enforcement of those sanctions or evading sanctions entirely. While this logic explains much of North Korea's high-profile summitry since 2018, North Korea's foreign policy profile and the primary way in which it interacts with the rest of the world have generally become economic in nature. In practice, North Korea uses a series of strategies to evade sanctions, including deploying its diplomatic personnel and outposts as business actors, engaging in obfuscation, picking and choosing the countries with which it interacts to arbitrage sanctions enforcement, and smuggling. While these strategies have enabled North Korea to decrease the direct effects of sanctions, they have had other effects on North Korea's foreign policy profile: much of North Korea's foreign activity has moved from the public government sphere to the private business sphere. The actions of North Korean actors necessary to operate the networks that are evading sanctions irritate the countries that are (often unwillingly) hosting them. Furthermore, North Korea has become dependent on a handful of countries that are unable or unwilling to enforce sanctions, narrowing its diplomatic horizons.

THE IMPACT OF UN SANCTIONS ON NORTH KOREAN FOREIGN POLICY OBJECTIVES

North Korea's Foreign Policy Objectives

The overarching goal of North Korea in its domestic and foreign policies is the survival of the Kim Jong-un regime on its own terms. North Korea has pinned its regime survival on its possession of nuclear weapons and the means of using them to attack countries that can threaten its existence, namely the United States. This means that North Korea's foreign policy objectives are in large part meant to allow for the continued possession of nuclear weapons and to mitigate the economic and political consequences of that continued possession. As a result, North Korea seeks to secure recognition, or at least tacit acceptance, of its nuclear weapons status from the international community. North Korea's objective likely includes the decoupling of denuclearization from normalization of relations with Japan and the United States. More realistically, North Korea seeks to secure the elimination, or at least the diminution of enforcement, of the sanctions imposed upon it. Finally, North Korea seeks to eliminate challenges to Kim Jong-un's leadership that might emanate from outside North Korea.

In economic terms, North Korea's survival entails bringing in necessary hard currency through both licit and illicit economic activity. North Korea's foreign policy objectives involve encouraging legal trade with other countries and bringing in hard currency through a variety of means that break sanctions, including exports of banned items such as coal, seafood, and textiles. North Korea also seeks to engage in economic activities always considered illegal in other countries, including cybercrime, insurance fraud, drug trafficking, and illegal, unreported, and unregulated (IUU) fishing outside its territorial waters.[1] Finally, North Korea seeks to use its hard currency reserves and barter to bring in the goods and technology needed to support not only its weapons program, but also the functioning of its economy.

Inherent in the North Korean state's understanding of regime survival is the maintenance of North Korean military, party, and political elite support for Kim Jong-un's rule as he plays the interests of different groups of elites off of each other.[2] North Korean leaders have traditionally paid off elites with luxury goods. However, the straitened circumstances that North Korea has faced since the early 1990s has made North Korean provision of goods to elites difficult. Instead, to a large extent, the state came to expect elite-run state organizations, whether revenue-raising entities or not, to provide for themselves financially and to give a cut of the profits to the central state.[3] Embedded in this reconfiguration of the relationship between the Kim regime and elites is the need for the regime to minimize the hindrances for political-business elites to make money. As a result, North Korea seeks to minimize the impact of sanctions on these elites, through (ideally) sanctions removal or (failing that) a lack of enforcement of sanctions and a prioritization of elites for business opportunities not impacted by sanctions or that can be conducted through sanctions evasion measures.

North Korea's goal of survival on its own terms also implies an ability to withstand economic and political pressure from other countries. Sanctions, and variable sanctions enforcement, have cut North Korea off from extensive economic ties with many potential trading partners. North Korea has therefore become increasingly dependent on trade with China, which has accounted for over 90 percent of North Korea's reported trade in the past five years, although formal Chinese trade with North Korea collapsed with the imposition of tighter sanctions in 2016 and 2017 and then with North Korea's COVID-19-related closure of its border in 2020 (see figure 8.1). This outsized trade dependence strongly incentivizes North Korea to diversify its trading partners so as to lessen China's ability to damage the North Korean economy by cutting off trade or harshly enforcing sanctions.

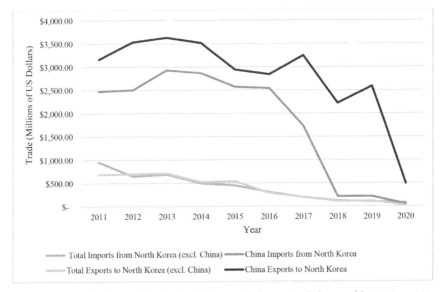

Figure 8.1. North Korean Trade with China and the rest of the world (2011–2020). *Source*: United Nations Comtrade, "UN Comtrade Database," United Nations, New York, 2022. https://comtrade.un.org/data/. *Note*: Because North Korea does not report trade data, the trade figures are reported by other countries in their trade with North Korea.

The Course of North Korean Foreign Policy under Kim Jong-un

For several years after he came to power upon the death of Kim Jong-il in December 2011, Kim Jong-un focused inward as he concentrated on consolidating power by replacing his father's elite supporters with his own, culminating in the execution of his uncle Jang Song-thaek in December 2013.[4]

Toward the end of this transition period in December 2012, North Korea launched an intercontinental ballistic missile (ICBM), setting off a series of tit-for-tat actions involving North Korea, South Korea, the United States, China, and the UN. This cycle roughly followed a standard pattern: North Korea would stage a provocation, generally either a nuclear or missile test, and otherwise ramp up tensions. This would provoke a reaction by the UNSC—generally a resolution tightening and expanding sanctions—and North Korea would then escalate with another provocation (see table 8.1). Eventually, the cycle would burn itself out and North Korea would return to a less confrontational stance. In response to North Korea's January 2013 missile test, for example, the UNSC imposed further economic sanctions, after which North Korea conducted a nuclear weapons test the following month and ramped up tensions through increasingly provocative rhetoric. Eventually, North Korea

Table 8.1. North Korean Provocations and UN Sanctions (2012–2017)

Date of Provocation	North Korean Provocation	UN Sanctions in Response
December 12, 2012	ICBM test	Resolution 2087
February 12, 2013	Nuclear test	Resolution 2094
January 6, 2016	Nuclear test	Resolution 2270
February 7, 2016	Missile test	
September 9, 2016	Nuclear test	Resolution 2321
February 11, 2017	Missile test	
July 3–28, 2017	ICBM tests	Resolution 2371
September 3, 2017	Nuclear test	Resolution 2375
November 28, 2017	ICBM test	Resolution 2397

essentially closed the Kaesong Industrial Zone by withdrawing its workers in April, with the zone only reopening in September 2013.[5]

Several years later, North Korea began a new tit-for-tat cycle with a new nuclear weapons test in January 2016, which was followed by another round of sanctions. North Korea again tested a nuclear device in September 2016, which led to a new UN sanctions resolution in November 2016. After US president Donald Trump came into office in January 2017, North Korea and the United States exchanged rhetorical barbs while tensions increased, although never to the point of actual provocations along the demilitarized zone dividing North and South Korea. Throughout this period, North Korea ramped up its missile testing frequency, culminating in ICBM tests in July 2017, which led to another round of sanctions. In September 2017, North Korea staged a sixth nuclear weapons test, triggering yet more sanctions, and finished off with an ICBM launch on November 28, 2017, which was followed up with the most recent round of UN sanctions that December.[6]

Interspersed with these periods of tension were attempts by North Korea to pursue its foreign policy objectives in less confrontational ways, particularly with regard to minimizing both the effects of sanctions (and sanctions enforcement) and its economic and political dependence on China. Periods of quiet—a lack of missile tests, nuclear tests, or saber-rattling—coincided with relatively lax Chinese enforcement of sanctions (or more specifically, no slowdown of trade movement at the border) and thus an improved North Korean ability to trade both legally and illegally across the border. They also coincided with North Korean outreach to other countries. During the period of quiet between the opening of Kaesong in September 2013 and the third nuclear test in January 2016, North Korea reached out to several countries, including backdoor discussions with Japan and business deals with Russia.[7]

Similarly, after the "final" ICBM test, Kim Jong-un proclaimed a new era in North Korean foreign policy in January 2018 and moved toward conciliation with South Korea and the United States.[8] North Korea sent a joint team with South Korea to the Pyeongchang Winter Olympics in 2018, and Kim Jong-un eventually held three summits each with Trump and South Korean president Moon Jae-in. While the summitry eventually produced the Singapore Declaration (with the United States) and the somewhat more detailed Panmunjom Declaration (with South Korea), they did not give North Korea what it ultimately sought: a removal of at least some sanctions.[9] While North Korea was clearly frustrated by the failure of the Hanoi summit with the United States, for at least the next three years it refrained from engaging in provocations (defined as a nuclear test or a long-range missile test) that would attract additional sanctions or harsher enforcement of existing sanctions.[10]

This relative quiescence came about because North Korea, by its own admission, had succeeded in at least part of its quest for security. In the midst of the 2013 Korean Peninsula crisis, Kim Jong-un had announced the *byungjin* policy, in which the North Korean state would simultaneously pursue both nuclear weapons development and economic development.[11] Given that every nuclear weapons test was met with increased UN and unilateral sanctions (and at least temporarily increased sanctions enforcement), the two planks of the *byungjin* policy seemed to operate at cross-purposes. In 2018, Kim Jong-un proclaimed that North Korea had succeeded in its task to create a nuclear deterrent (presumably meaning it believed it had developed a nuclear warhead sufficiently small to be mounted on top of a reliable ICBM) and would switch to focusing on economic development.[12] Absent any move to give up its nuclear weapons, however, sanctions remained in place.

North Korea continued this pattern in the first months of Joe Biden's presidency in the United States, particularly after the conclusion of the Biden administration's North Korea policy review. While North Korea did not resort to provocative long-range missile or nuclear weapons tests, it has increased shorter-range missile testing. North Korea has also engaged in on-again, off-again attempts to rekindle relations with South Korea, and will likely continue to do so with future South Korean successors sympathetic to engagement with North Korea. This is in line with North Korea's policy of attempting to use improved relations with one country as leverage over another (in this case the United States), or as a way to mitigate the negative impact of one country's policy on North Korea. Given the relative lack both of major North Korean provocations since 2018 and of progress on denuclearization or even negotiations, China and Russia have both urged that UN sanctions be relaxed to get North Korea to come to the table. China has also undercut the ability of the UN Panel of Experts to investigate sanctions violations.[13]

UNITED NATIONS SANCTIONS AS AN OBSTACLE TO THE CONDUCT OF NORTH KOREAN FOREIGN POLICY

While the sanctions themselves are intended to accomplish a political objective—North Korean nuclear disarmament—they seek to accomplish this through inflicting economic pain on the North Korean regime. More specifically, sanctions in theory aim to deny North Korean officials the ability to move around and do business, trade revenue from state-owned companies, as well as physical equipment and materials that could be used for weapons programs. This, combined with North Korea's political isolation resulting from sanctions and its attempts to evade sanctions, means that North Korea's everyday foreign policy in practice can primarily be seen in economic terms. Even the political aspects of its foreign policy can be framed as pushing its economic goals.

Impact on North Korea's Economy and Diplomatic Strategy

In economic terms, UN sanctions curb North Korea's efforts to attract foreign investment. Despite North Korea's reputation for economic autarky, at least before the COVID-19 pandemic, North Korea under Kim Jong-un engaged in a fair amount of effort to attract foreign investors. Such efforts included passing a law to create new special economic zones, streamlining the joint venture law with tax incentives for foreign investors, introducing eased access for Chinese tourists, and striking deals (mostly unfinished) with China and Russia for infrastructure construction.[14] UN sanctions resolutions gradually put pressure on the ability of foreign companies to do business in North Korea, progressively banning foreign company branches in the country as well as joint ventures, and making financial flows in and out of the country considerably more difficult.

Sanctions have meant that North Korea is forced to trade with foreign companies and countries that are, for completely legal transactions, willing to bear the costs of complying with sanctions and the hassles of dealing with a hobbled international payments system. Outside of China, there are few such companies or countries. North Korea has thus had to focus its foreign trade in both goods and services on countries and companies that are either seeking to evade sanctions of their own or are ignorant of sanctions (or at least plead ignorance). North Korea shipped missile parts to Egypt, missile technology to Iran, and military equipment to Syria after the imposition of at least some UN sanctions.[15] Much of North Korea's trade with African countries, in terms of exports of weapons or maintenance and training contracts for their militaries, essentially comes from finding countries that need low-cost military goods with no questions asked and that are willing to plead ignorance (or actually are ignorant) of UN sanctions.[16]

North Korea's diplomatic strategy of pivoting to improve relations, at least temporarily, with countries outside of China in a bid to minimize the leverage China might exercise over North Korea is limited by the political reality that sanctions constrain what other countries can feasibly do. During the period of optimism about improving North-South relations in 2018, South Korea sent officials to survey the potential for improvement of North Korea's rail infrastructure, and South Korean companies began expressing enthusiasm about investing in North Korea.[17] However, they were warned by the United States not to break sanctions. While there was some pressure from South Korean companies to relax the enforcement of sanctions for South Korean companies in the name of peace and reconciliation, this never eventuated. Likewise, though North Korea made overtures to Japan in 2014, no Japanese aid ever appeared, nor did Japan relax its ban on trade with North Korea.[18] Likewise, during the warming in U.S.-North Korea relations in 2018 and early 2019, the United States proved unwilling to relax its unilateral sanctions (in April 2018, the United States temporarily sanctioned the Chinese telecommunications corporation ZTE for illegally trading with North Korea).[19] While an equilibrium developed where the United States agreed not to impose more sanctions as long as North Korea did not engage in any provocations (defined implicitly as a nuclear weapon test or a long-range missile test), this simply maintained a status quo unacceptable to North Korea.

China's Role in United Nations Sanctions

Despite North Korea's pivot toward the United States and South Korea in 2018, North Korea's main political economic relationship is not with South Korea or the United States, but with China. China has its own foreign policy objectives vis-à-vis North Korea: to preserve North Korea's existence, but also to minimize the instability and insecurity North Korea produces on its border. Ideally, from China's perspective, this means a North Korean path toward economic "reform and opening up" that would ensure it can feed itself without Chinese aid and encourage less provocative behavior, including eventual denuclearization. In practice what this means in terms of China's regulation of trade across the Sino–North Korean border is complex. China encourages cross-border trade with North Korea as a means of sustaining the North Korean economy and gives some unreported direct aid to North Korea.[20] It has also encouraged private Chinese investment in North Korea and allowed North Korean workers to work in China. This policy comes coupled with a largely lackadaisical enforcement of sanctions against North

Korea and a tolerance for some smuggling across the Sino–North Korean border, up to and including the illegal importation of substantial quantities of coal and oil.[21]

By definition, all UN sanctions are passed with China's vote, or at least abstention, in the UNSC. China has often used sanctions and sanctions enforcement as a means of signaling its displeasure at North Korean provocations. Immediately after sanctions are passed, China has regularly, if only temporarily, stepped up enforcement of those sanctions. It has at times limited the throughput of all goods entering and leaving North Korea, ostensibly to check for prohibited items, and informed smugglers that they were not to engage in smuggling during periods of heightened sanctions enforcement. The effect is increased staple prices in North Korea (despite food not being sanctioned) and economic pain for North Korea, sending a signal of China's disapproval.[22]

With each new round of sanctions, and the accompanying period of Chinese government sanctions enforcement, there is a ratchet effect in North Korea's experience of sanctions: conditions do not go back to what they were before the sanctions. While sanctions enforcement inevitably decreases once China's signal has been sent, new industries may be off-limits to Chinese companies, and more Chinese companies may, with every new round of sanctions, cease to do any business in North Korea. This in part stems from compliance and corruption costs of trading with North Korea that remain regardless of sanctions enforcement. This also occurs because sanctions' selective shutting down of trade sector by sector has knock-on effects beyond individual sectors. Chinese companies engaged in trade or even investment with North Korea are often engaged in multiple sectors, either to diversify their risk, because trade in certain items helps them build relationships with North Korean officials, or because certain trade goods are loss leaders for more profitable trade goods. When sanctions render trade in certain items unlawful, the traders who traded in those items may decide to smuggle them or pull out of North Korea entirely rather than continue to trade in the unprofitable items. A number of Chinese food traders, for instance, stopped shipping food to North Korea in 2017 not because of any restrictions on food exports to North Korea (which have never been sanctioned), but because their main businesses were banned in sectoral sanctions in 2017.[23] Unsanctioned North Korean business sectors thus suffer during sanctions enforcement and continue to suffer even afterward.

Even if sanctions are not enforced rigorously by the Chinese government, UN sanctions render many aspects of cross-border business difficult or impossible. Companies are unable or unwilling to engage in business with North Korea that requires long-term investment or expenditure on capital projects inside of North Korea, not only because of worries about North

Korean state expropriation, but also because there is no mechanism for resolution of business disputes or contract enforcement.[24] Furthermore, creating such mechanisms is difficult given that sanctions mean investments often skirt the edge of legality outside North Korea.

Easing of Chinese sanctions enforcement also has little effect on the difficulties North Korea has in engaging in sanctioned financial transactions. At best, the Chinese government may look the other way when North Korean businesses engage in bulk cash transfers into and out of China, or when North Koreans establish accounts in Chinese banks. But any Chinese bank connected to the international financial system and handling US dollars will likely be wary of handling North Korean accounts, as was the case after the United States blacklisted Banco Delta Asia (BDA) in Macau in 2005, when many banks were unwilling to transfer the money in North Korea's BDA accounts back to North Korea.[25]

Impact of Non-UN Sanctions

As the BDA episode suggests, in addition to UN sanctions, North Korea has also had to navigate unilateral sanctions by a number of countries, particularly the United States, Japan, Australia, and to a lesser extent the European Union. These sanctions generally prohibit or significantly restrict trade between that country, its citizens, and North Korea, and often precede or are in addition to UN sanctions—Japan cut off *all* non-humanitarian trade with North Korea in 2009, for example. Many of the unilateral sanctions laws themselves are rarely actively enforced—as of 2022, for instance, Australia has successfully prosecuted just one person for North Korean sanctions violations.[26] Rather, their main effect is arguably to deter firms and individuals within or that do business with the sanctioning country from doing business with the target country.

While unilateral trade sanctions in isolation do not necessarily impinge on a country's overall trade, given that the target country can shift trade to a third country that does not have (and certainly does not enforce) unilateral sanctions, the shift in trade ties to non-sanctioning countries is itself an effect of unilateral sanctions.[27] North Korea's increasing dependence on trade with China in the face of the progressive curtailment of trade with Japan from 2006 to 2009 is a case in point.

Given its position in the global economy, and the status of the US dollar as a reserve currency, US sanctions have a disproportionate effect on North Korea relative to other countries' unilateral sanctions—the ability of the Office of Foreign Assets Control within the US Department of the Treasury to cut off certain firms and individuals from access to the US banking system means that many non-American firms that might otherwise be willing to do business with North Korea are deterred due to the possibility of losing access to the US-led global financial system.[28] The United States has reinforced this deterrent effect through the occasional resort to secondary sanctions—measures against third-country firms that do business with North Korea, as when between 2016 and 2018 the United States temporarily banned the Chinese telecommunications ZTE from doing business with American suppliers for its alleged role in violating North Korean and Iranian sanctions.[29]

The North Korea Sanctions and Policy Enhancement Act of 2016 goes further than UN sanctions and requires the US president to sanction individuals and firms found to have engaged in a variety of activities with North Korea, including not only weapons of mass destruction proliferation (the main target of UN sanctions) but also human rights abuses and cybersecurity activities. It also allows the U.S. president to impose secondary sanctions on firms and individuals who support UN-sanctioned entities.[30]

In response to these efforts, North Korea's foreign policy objectives thus include not only the minimization of the effects of United Nations sanctions, but also the circumvention of unilateral countermeasures by adversary states, particularly the United States.

HOW SANCTIONS EVASION MEASURES HAVE INFLUENCED NORTH KOREA'S FOREIGN POLICY PROFILE

Given that North Korea's foreign policy objectives involve minimizing the effect of sanctions, particularly the economic effects on elites and their businesses and the logistical and supply effects on its weapons programs, North Korea has developed a range of sanctions evasion strategies. While these strategies do, to an extent, further North Korea's sanctions-minimizing foreign policy objectives, the measures North Korea takes to evade sanctions also tend to work at cross-purposes with North Korea's other foreign policy objectives.

Sanctions Evasion Strategies

Because the activities and goods sanctioned under UN resolutions are not generally illegal absent a connection to North Korea, enforcement of sanctions by other countries means both correctly identifying the activity or good being traded and identifying the connection to North Korea, whether North Korean nationals are involved or North Korea is an origin or destination for the goods. This has led North Korea to pursue several strategies for evading sanctions.

First, North Korea *makes use of its state prerogatives and resources* to evade sanctions. While the sanctions themselves directly prohibit the use of North Korean diplomatic personnel and outposts to engage in business or more generally evade sanctions, obviously North Korea still uses its primary state presence overseas. In general, state resources serve three functions. State-owned ships and airplanes can be used to transport sanctioned items under less scrutiny than private, third-party transports, although they are also easier to target for inspection. Diplomatic outposts can be used as the locations of front companies and other businesses, and diplomatic pouches can be used to transport goods. Diplomats themselves, particularly those who enjoy diplomatic immunity, can also serve as brokers for illicit transactions, either by transporting the goods themselves or by arranging for the sale to or from North Korea of sanctioned goods and services.

Second, North Korea *obfuscates* its sanctioned trade. It can obfuscate sanctioned items themselves, through mislabeling shipped items or through hiding sanctioned items within more legitimate shipments. It may also, through falsified customs documents, false end users, and extra links in supply chains, attempt to hide the origin of the goods being sold by North Korea or the destination of goods intended for North Korea. Given that sanctions adhere to North Korean nationals, North Korea may also take steps to obfuscate the involvement of North Koreans in the networks, such as through front companies domiciled in less suspicious countries, use of third-country nationals as brokers, or through false identity documents.

Third, North Korea engages in *arbitrage*, choosing to engage with countries that will allow it to maximize the success of attempts to bypass sanctions. Countries vary in their ability and willingness to enforce sanctions, and even in their awareness of sanctions and the difference between North Korea and South Korea. Many countries may have potential suppliers for North Korea's programs but also be on high alert for North Korean sanctions evasion and have an ability to block North Korea from accessing their markets. At the other end of the spectrum, many countries have low awareness of North Korean sanctions and an inability to enforce sanctions, but also offer North Korea little in the way of supplies or a market for North Korean goods and services. Other countries provide a sweet spot for North Korean sanctions evasion, inasmuch as they may be sufficiently geographically proximate to enable illicit movement to and from North Korea and are technologically sophisticated or economically developed enough to serve as potential supplier or broker countries.

Fourth, North Korea *strategically structures* the trade networks stretching between North Korea and the rest of the world to minimize the presence of North Koreans inside the networks, and to maximize the proportion of the networks that appear to be legitimate to outside observers. This means that, in combination with arbitrage and obfuscation strategies, North Korea attempts to make transactions appear actually legitimate up until the point the goods enter or leave North Korea. In practice, North Korea's trade networks are thus mostly not North Korean—many of the brokers, buyers, and sellers outside of North Korea are genuine third-country nationals and firms, and they themselves deal (often unsuspectingly) with other third-country nationals and firms.

Finally, North Korea engages in *informal trade*—essentially smuggling and trafficking—to bypass sanctions enforcement, which largely focuses on matching goods and people with customs and immigration documents at standard air, sea, and land ports of entry. Skipping cross-border checkpoints allows North Korea to avoid scrutiny entirely and shifts the problem of sanctions enforcement from customs and immigrations to border forces. Such a strategy is geographically limited. Moving goods informally by land or sea, and particularly smuggling that does not make extensive use of North Korean state resources, takes places only in countries near to or adjacent to North Korean territory. Goods can only be smuggled to or from North Korea by land via China or Russia given the relative impassibility of the border with South Korea, and goods smuggled by sea are likely to move to and from China, Japan, Russia, South Korea, or Taiwan.[31]

Sanctions Evasion and the Effect on the Practice of North Korea's Foreign Policy

Sanctions minimization has in practice become North Korea's foreign policy profile. Much of North Korea's diplomatic apparatus has been turned to either attempt to reduce formal sanctions such as through improving relations with the United States, reduce the effects of sanctions through appeasing China, or evade sanctions.

In practice, North Korean diplomats stationed outside of North Korea use diplomatic immunity of personnel, diplomatic pouches, and facilities to become businesspeople, bringing in income to support themselves and the regime and arranging for the shipment of goods to and from North Korea, even if they themselves never touch the goods. In the 2013 sale of Scud missile parts to Egypt, for example, the Ryongsong Trading Co. operated out of the North Korean embassy in Beijing. It arranged for the missile parts to be shipped from another possibly related trading company in Pyongyang via Air Koryo to Beijing, and then on a commercial cargo to a front company for the Egyptian military in Cairo.[32]

North Korea's diplomatic profile has retreated under sanctions in that there are fewer official North Korean diplomats around the world, but it has also evolved toward ostensibly private individuals doing business through pur-portedly private companies by a mix of commercial and diplomatic means. For instance, when selling goods to Syria in violation of sanctions and mov-ing people between North Korea and Syria, North Korea has generally used commercial routes and methods but also used its diplomatic assets where necessary.[33] In October 2016, a North Korean representative of the Korea Mining Development Trading Corporation (KOMID), the state-owned com-pany that sells many of North Korea's weapons, was denied transit in Dubai on a commercial airline on the way from Damascus to Moscow and eventu-ally Pyongyang. He managed to acquire a new North Korean passport with an alias and flew to Pyongyang through Moscow.[34] When shipping items to Syria, North Korea used a combination of diplomatic assets and commercial transport. In one instance, a theoretically Chinese company in Pyongyang—China Delixi Group Pyongyang Office—shipped items to the North Korean embassy in Damascus in a diplomatic pouch, thus minimizing scrutiny.[35]

The movement of North Korea's state-owned transportation assets has been severely circumscribed by sanctions. North Korean planes are denied jet fuel and North Korean-owned or -flagged ships are denied entry to, servicing, or supply in foreign ports and registration in ships' registries. Compared to more extensive private shipping networks, North Korea's state-owned assets are also easier for sanctions enforcers to track. These state-owned assets have been forced to engage in obfuscation, smuggling, and arbitrage strategies of their own to continue operating and minimize the effects of sanctions.

The UN Panel of Experts has noted repeated attempts by North Korean ships to export coal, in an example of arbitrage, by traveling directly to ports in Northeast and Southeast Asia that may not exercise high levels of scrutiny over the activities of North Korean ships, including ports in China, Russia, and some Southeast Asian countries including Vietnam and Indonesia.[36]

As they move, the ships themselves engage in obfuscation—flying false flags, intermittently turning off their Automated Identification System (AIS) trackers to obscure their location, filing false declarations of cargo on board and destination ports, and changing the stated draft of their hull to hide whether they are carrying cargo—all to hide their cargo, location, and identity.[37]

Because of the difficulty of using state prerogatives and assets to evade sanctions, the shift in focus of North Korea's foreign profile toward sanctions minimization and evasion has also meant that the center of gravity for North Korean foreign policy enactment has moved from the public state-based sphere to the private business sphere. The state officials serving as brokers often serve as directors of privately held front companies registered in third countries. Perhaps more importantly, they behave as private businesspeo-ple—making contracts with other businesses, transferring money between commercial bank accounts (or using cash), and using commercial firms for supply, logistics, and transport.

Both before and since the onset of sanctions, the broker and supply roles within North Korea's illicit and ostensibly commercial trade networks have shifted geographically as North Korea has searched for countries with the right combination of logistical connections to the outside world, technological sophistication, and political inattentiveness or incapacity. Japan was actually one of North Korea's main trading partners in the 1990s before trade, generally facilitated by Korean residents in Japan who identified as North Koreans, slowed down and then stopped as the Japanese government created unilateral sanctions in response to the revelation of North Korea's kidnapping of Japanese citizens and North Korean missile tests.[38] China then took pride of place from 2004 onward as North Korea's main trading partner. While Taiwanese businesses were never a major trading partner of North Korea, it served a broker role between North Korea and the rest of world from the early 2000s, in part because Taiwan is *not* part of the UN.[39] North Korea continues to use both China and Taiwan as broker countries under Kim Jong-un and under sanctions.

This geographical arbitrage of North Korea's sanctions evasion efforts can be seen in the manner in which North Korea imports oil in violation of UN sanctions. Indeed, North Korea's oil deals exemplify how the combination of sanctions evasion strategies results in a geographically shifted and ostensibly privatized foreign policy profile for North Korea. Unable to enter foreign ports, North Korean ships leave North Korean ports and meet third-country tankers in international waters to receive oil in ship-to-ship transfers. The commercial tankers are generally owned, operated, or commissioned by third-country firms that contract with third-country brokerages operating on North Korea's behalf. These brokerage firms are often staffed by third-country nationals or North Koreans operating under business cover.

In one such incident in September 2017, three interconnected companies owned by the same Taiwanese businessman, Chen Shih-hsien, approached a Singaporean broker company to charter a ship, the *Lighthouse Winmore*, and instructed it to deliver oil from South Korea to Taiwan. *Lighthouse Winmore* was owned and operated by a network of Hong Kong–registered companies run by a Chinese national in Guangzhou, but, in reality, it was likely owned by the Taiwanese businessman who originated the order.

The oil was purchased by two linked Hong Kong-registered, Singapore-based companies from the Singaporean branch of a Netherlands oil supply company. They subsequently sold the oil to the original Taiwanese company. The *Lighthouse Winmore* then set sail from Yeosu, South Korea. Using its AIS intermittently, the ship rendezvoused in the East China Sea with a North

Korea–flagged vessel that had left port in North Korea, transferred the oil, and returned to Yeosu without going on to Taiwan.[40]

The transaction involved all of North Korea's sanctions evasion strategies. First, North Korea used state assets—North Korean-owned and -flagged vessels to receive the oil—and bypassed the scrutiny that would have come from a private vessel entering North Korean waters. Second, the obfuscation of the trading network was extensive. Chen Shih-hsien claimed he had been approached for the sale of the oil by a Chinese broker, indicating that North Korea may have gone through several brokers in a chain before buying the oil.[41] The companies involved in purchasing the oil and chartering the tanker used several front companies and the final destination of the oil was obviously mis-declared. Third, North Korea arbitraged the countries it used for obtaining oil: several of the brokers and front companies operated from China, which had an ambivalent record in enforcing sanctions and a strong trade record with North Korea. And the main brokering firm was based in Taiwan, a country without UN membership but with strong trade ties with other Asian countries and relative geographic proximity to North Korea. Notably, the oil physically came from South Korea, which is even more geographically proximate to North Korea, for a delivery ostensibly destined to Taiwan.

Finally, the actual supply chain demonstrated both strategic structuring and informal trade. The network consisted of brokers and suppliers in Singapore, Hong Kong, China, and Taiwan, all of whom were involved in what appeared to be a legitimate oil supply operation up until the oil was transferred at sea. The only obvious smuggling in the supply chain was the movement of the oil from the ship-to-ship transfer back to North Korea.

The oil deal, which was similar in structure to many other sanctions-evading oil deals, shows how North Korea's foreign policy profile has changed under sanctions. North Korea's ability to use its diplomatic personnel and outposts has been constrained, and state-owned resources such as ships and planes are no longer able to operate in much of the world. Instead, North Korean state assets operate closer to North Korea to avoid sanctions enforcement measures.[42] At the same time, North Korea's foreign profile has not disappeared. Instead, it has been driven underground into areas of the world with less wherewithal or interest in enforcing sanctions, and North Korea uses commercial interests and methods rather than overt diplomatic prerogatives to achieve its goals.

The Impact of Sanctions Evasion Measures on North Korea's Foreign Relations

The measures North Korea has taken to evade sanctions have hindered its relations with some countries. For example, UN sanctions have prohibited the export of seafood products from North Korea since 2017.[43] In a bid to continue to profit from seafood exports, North Korean exporters have continued to smuggle seafood into China for processing and sale. North Korea has also continued to sell fishing licenses in its own territorial waters to foreign fishing vessels, primarily Chinese, but also South Korean and Japanese vessels.[44] The sale of licenses to Chinese squid-fishing vessels off the eastern coast of North Korea has had knock-on effects in North Korea's foreign relations. Because Chinese vessels take the squid early in their migration routes (as they pass through North Korean waters en route to South Korean and Japanese waters), Japanese and South Korean fishing vessels have lower catches, resulting in international irritation.[45] The larger Chinese fishing vessels also outcompete smaller North Korean fishing vessels, forcing North Koreans outward from the coast in search of catches. North Korean fishing vessels have thus illegally appeared in Japanese and Russian waters, causing diplomatic problems for North Korea.[46] On North Korea's western coast, Chinese fishing vessels searching for blue crab in waters claimed by North Korea have similarly clashed with South Korean naval and coast guard vessels, exacerbating international tensions.[47] In this sense, North Korea's sanctions evasion measures, particularly those designed to allow North Korea to continue to bring in hard currency, have indirectly stoked tensions with its neighbors.

Given North Korea's traditional approach to international relations, poor relations with other countries are not necessarily a problem. Indeed, North Korea's foreign policy to a certain extent requires occasional tensions with South Korea, Japan, and the United States, at the very least. But poor relations with other countries paradoxically may, over time, impinge on North Korea's ability to achieve its foreign policy objective of minimizing the effect of sanctions.

The assassination of Kim Jong-un's brother Kim Jong-nam in Malaysia in February 2017 showed how North Korea's other foreign policy goals often operate at cross-purposes with its sanctions-evasion measures. In the case of Kim Jong-nam's death, the assassination presumably aimed to remove a potential challenger to Kim Jong-un and preserve the Kim (Jong-un) regime. The location of the attack in the Kuala Lumpur International Airport meant that North Korean agents did not have to attempt to attack Kim Jong-nam in China or Macau (which would cause problems with China) but effectively sacrificed North Korea's relations with Malaysia in the process. In the aftermath of the killing, Malaysia and North Korea cut off diplomatic relations, and both refused to let the other country's citizens leave.[48]

In the process of harming relations with Malaysia by using its territory for an assassination, North Korea also lost a number of benefits that Malaysia had provided for sanctions evasion. First, North Korean operatives, both diplomats and people operating as businessmen, had used diplomatic outposts and businesses registered in Malaysia as front companies and in brokerage roles for selling goods and services to other countries. As with North Korea's use of state resources to evade sanctions, the North Koreans in Malaysia who were involved in the assassination were a mix of diplomats and businesspeople at the North Korean state-owned Air Koryo.[49] Similarly, in July 2016, Eritrea received a shipment of radio equipment from China that had been arranged by the Singaporean and Malaysian subsidiaries of a Pyongyang-based front company, Pan Systems Pyongyang.[50] The Singaporean branch was affiliated with another North Korean front company, Glocom, which was based but not registered in Malaysia, and was affiliated with North Korea's primary spy agency, the Reconnaissance General Bureau.[51] Two ostensibly Malaysian companies—International Golden Services Sdn Bhd and International Global System—run by North Koreans operating as businesspeople in Malaysia illegally sold radio equipment under the Glocom brand at arms shows hosted by the Malaysian military.[52]

Second, North Korea had earned money by sending labor to Malaysia and subsequently lost that revenue: by September 2017, Malaysia had also expelled three hundred North Korean workers from a mine in Sarawak.[53]

Third, unlike many other countries, Malaysia maintained normal diplomatic relations with North Korea and was one of the few countries before the assassination to allow North Korean passport holders visa-free entry. The North Korean plotters presumably used this to their advantage in planning the assassination, as they moved around Southeast Asia practicing the attack with the apparently unwitting Indonesian and Vietnamese women who actually ended up poisoning Kim Jong-nam.[54]

Malaysia and North Korea worked toward reestablishing ties in the wake of North Korea's 2018 diplomatic offensive, and Malaysia announced in 2020 that it would reopen its embassy in Pyongyang. However, North Korea severed diplomatic relations with Malaysia in March 2021 after a Malaysian court approved an extradition to the United States of a North Korean charged with money laundering in Singapore on the grounds that sanctions evasion was also a crime in Malaysia.[55] Singapore halted all commercial trade with North Korea in November 2017 and began prosecuting Singaporean businesspeople who violated sanctions to supply luxury goods and other items, generally through China, to North Korean stores.[56] The Singaporean companies prosecuted were run by Singaporean citizens who contracted with North

Korean brokers to deliver the items to North Korea.[57] Thus, North Korea's pursuit of its broader foreign policy objectives in Southeast Asia to a certain extent relied on methods similar to those used to avoid sanctions, but also ended up stunting the country's diplomatic profile in the region, and harming its ability to use Southeast Asian countries to evade sanctions.

CONCLUSION

North Korea's foreign policy profile has often been defined in the public consciousness by its confrontational behavior, illustrated most pointedly by nuclear weapons tests, isolation, and defiance of international norms. However, sanctions themselves define North Korea's mundane foreign policy objectives and shape the ways in which North Korea engages with the rest of the world. Given that it seeks to maintain its weapons programs and minimize its dependence on any other country, North Korea's foreign policy objectives have come to focus on removing sanctions, or at least minimizing their effects. This has resulted in a diplomatic profile around the world that has adapted to sanctions and taken on many of the trappings and methods of private businesses. The strategies North Korea has used to evade sanctions, however, have often operated at cross-purposes with its foreign relations, leading to even greater diplomatic isolation.

A further wrinkle has come since North Korea shut its borders in January 2020 in response to the COVID-19 pandemic. The border closure appears to have caused significant damage to the country's economy—markets suffered from shortages of imported goods and price controls and food shortages were severe, although perhaps tempered by humanitarian aid shipments that were allowed into the country from May 2021.[58]

Despite its political isolation, much of North Korea's engagement with the outside world has been economic, and both formal and informal trade have been key for North Korea's survival, as well as the ability of Kim Jong-un to maintain the support of elites with the provision of business opportunities. North Korea's foreign policy practice as trade, and more specifically sanctions evasion, has thus been put under threat by the border closure. There has been some attempt by the North Korean government to rectify this situation: in its COVID-19 closure-related smuggling crackdown, the state seems to have allowed politically connected joint ventures to continue smuggling, and ship-to-ship oil transfers continued apace during the border closure.[59] Nonetheless, these efforts are unlikely to fully replace normalized trade across the China-North Korea border, and in the January 2021 Eighth Korean Workers' Party Congress, Kim Jong-un acknowledged economic challenges and laid out plans to move the state toward the center of the economy.[60]

While North Korea's formal trade was plummeting before COVID-19 (as seen in table 8.1), North Korea's self-imposed isolation to protect itself from COVID-19 is likely, if continued, to operate at cross-purposes with its general foreign policy objectives of global engagement through trade as a means of evading sanctions. A realignment of political and economic power within North Korea, where the central state takes control and attempts to pay off elites directly, may not be feasible in the long term for North Korea if there are no trade opportunities with which to garner support, and if sanctions no longer represent the primary excuse for North Korea being cut off from the outside world. For North Korea, surviving COVID-19 may not mean surviving (or at least thriving) economically.

NOTES

1. Sheena Chestnut Greitens, *Illicit: North Korea's Evolving Operations to Earn Hard Currency* (Washington, DC: Committee for Human Rights in North Korea, 2014).

2. Patrick McEachern. *Inside the Red Box: North Korea's Post-Totalitarian Politics* (New York: Columbia University Press, 2010).

3. Justin V. Hastings, *A Most Enterprising Country: North Korea in the Global Economy* (Ithaca: Cornell University Press, 2016), 32–47. Robert Collins, *Pyongyang Republic* (Washington, DC: American Enterprise Institute, 2016).

4. "Traitor Jang Song Thaek Executed," Korean Central News Agency, December 13, 2013, http://www.kcna.co.jp/item/2013/201312/news13/20131213-05ee.html.

5. "Koreas Restart Operations at Kaesong Industrial Zone," BBC, September 16, 2013.

6. "Resolution 2397 (S/RES/2397)," United Nations Security Council, December 22, 2017.

7. Zachary Keck, "How Japan and North Korea 'Use' Each Other," *The Diplomat*, May 21, 2014, https://thediplomat.com/2014/05/how-japan-and-north-korea-use-each-other/; Shannon Tiezzi, "The Renaissance in Russia-North Korea Relations," *The Diplomat*, November 22, 2014, https://thediplomat.com/2014/11/the-renaissance-in-russia-north-korea-relations/.

8. Kim Jong-un, "Kim Jong Un's 2018 New Year's Address," National Committee on North Korea, January 1, 2018, https://www.ncnk.org/node/1427.

9. "Trump Kim Summit: Full Text of the Signed Statement," BBC, June 12, 2018, https://www.bbc.com/news/world-asia-44453330; "Panmunjom Declaration for Peace, Prosperity and Unification of the Korean Peninsula (2018.4.27)," Ministry of Foreign Affairs, Seoul, April 27, 2018.

10. Julia Masterson, "North Korea Spurns Diplomacy with United States," *Arms Control Today*, May 2020, https://www.armscontrol.org/act/2020-05/news/north-korea-spurns-diplomacy-united-states.

11. Cheon Seong-Whun, "The Kim Jong-un Regime's 'Byungjin' (Parallel Development) Policy of Economy and Nuclear Weapons and the 'April 1st Nuclearization Law,'" Korean Institute for National Unification, Online Series 13–11, March 31, 2013, https://repo.kinu.or.kr/bitstream/2015.oak/2227/1/0001458456.pdf.

12. "Third Plenary Meeting of Seventh C.C., WPK Held in Presence of Kim Jong-un." Korean Central News Agency, April 21, 2018, https://www.ncnk.org /resources/publications/dprk_report_third_plenary_meeting_of_seventh_central _committee_of_wpk.pdf.

13. Kate O'Keeffe, "China Stymies Once-United U.N. Panel on North Korea Sanctions," *Wall Street Journal*, September 15, 2021, https://www.wsj.com/articles/china -stymies-once-united-u-n-panel-on-north-korea-sanctions-11631714247.

14. Andray Abrahamian, Geoffrey K. See, and Xinyu Wang, *The ABCs of North Korea's SEZs* (Washington, DC: US-Korea Institute, School of Advanced International Studies, The Johns Hopkins University, 2014); Heon Joo Jung and Timothy S. Rich, "Why Invest in North Korea? Chinese Foreign Direct Investment in North Korea and Its Implications," *Pacific Review* 29, no. 3 (2016): 307–30, https://doi.org /10.1080/09512748.2015.1022582.

15. Panel of Experts, *Final Report of the Panel of Experts Submitted Pursuant to Resolution 2515 (2020)*, (New York: United Nations Security Council, March 4, 2021).

16. United Nations Security Council, *Final Report of the Panel of Experts* 40–41, 51.

17. "On Your Marks: South Korean Firms Are Keen to Invest in the North," *The Economist*, September 22, 2018, https://www.economist.com/business/2018/09 /20/south-korean-firms-are-keen-to-invest-in-the-north; Nyshka Chandran, "South Korea's Economy Is Slowing. Its Leader Still Wants to Spend Millions on Pyongyang," CNBC, October 3, 2018, https://www.cnbc.com/2018/10/04/south-korea-aims -to-spend-millions-on-north-korea-projects.html.

18. Shunji Hiraiwa, "Japan's Policy on North Korea: Four Motives and Three Factors," *Journal of Contemporary East Asia Studies* 9, no. 1 (2020), https://doi.org/10 .1080/24761028.2020.1762300.

19. Yue Wang, "China's ZTE Faces Long-Lasting Damage from U.S. Trade Sanctions," *Forbes*, June 18, 2018, https://www.forbes.com/sites/ywang/2018/06/18 /chinas-zte-faces-long-lasting-damage-from-u-s-trade-sanctions/?sh=4943ac8f30ac.

20. James Reilly, "The Curious Case of China's Aid to North Korea," *Asian Survey* 54, no. 6 (2014).

21. Joe Byrne, "UN Panel of Experts Report on North Korea: More Advanced Weaponry, Better Sanctions Evasion," RUSI Commentary, April 27, 2021, https://rusi .org/explore-our-research/publications/commentary/un-panel-experts-report-north -korea-more-advanced-weaponry-better-sanctions-evasion.

22. Justin V. Hastings and Yaohui Wang, "Informal Trade along the China–North Korea border," *Journal of East Asian Studies* 18, no. 2 (2018).

23. Hastings and Wang.

24. Justin V. Hastings and Yaohui Wang, "Chinese Firms' Troubled Relationship with Market Transformation in North Korea," *Asian Survey* 57, no. 4 (2017); Stephan

Haggard, Jennifer Lee, and Marcus Noland, "Integration in the Absence of Institutions: China-North Korea Cross-Border Exchange," *Journal of Asian Economics* 23, no. 2 (2012).

25. Juan Zarate, *Treasury Wars: The Unleashing of a New Era of Financial Warfare* (New York: PublicAffairs, 2013).

26. "Sydney Man Receives Term of Imprisonment for Breaching North Korean Sanctions," Commonwealth Director of Public Prosecutions, Canberra, July 23, 2021, https://www.cdpp.gov.au/case-reports/sydney-man-receives-term-imprisonment-breaching-north-korean-sanctions. Interestingly, Choi, the defendant, was charged with violating both UN sanctions and separate Australian sanctions.

27. Bryan R. Early, "Unmasking the Black Knights: Sanctions Busters and Their Effects on the Success of Economic Sanctions." *Foreign Policy Analysis* 7, no. 4 (2011): 381–402.

28. See "North Korea Sanctions," Department of the Treasury, Washington, DC, December 10, 2021, https://home.treasury.gov/policy-issues/financial-sanctions/sanctions-programs-and-country-information/north-korea-sanctions.

29. Claire Ballentine, "U.S. Lifts Ban That Kept ZTE from Doing Business with American Suppliers," *New York Times*, July 13, 2018, https://www.nytimes.com/2018/07/13/business/zte-ban-trump.html.

30. "Summary of the North Korea Sanctions and Policy Enhancement Act of 2016," *National Committee on North Korea*, February 18, 2016.

31. See Hastings, *A Most Enterprising Country*, chapter 2.

32. Panel of Experts, *Report of the Panel of Experts Established Pursuant to Resolution 1874 (2009)* (New York: United Nations Security Council, February 24, 2016), para. 71.

33. Panel of Experts, *Final Report of the Panel of Experts Submitted Pursuant to Resolution 2345 (2017)* (New York: United Nations Security Council, March 5, 2018), para. 127.

34. Panel of Experts, para. 128.

35. Panel of Experts, para. 132.

36. Panel of Experts, *Report of the Panel of Experts Established Pursuant to Resolution 1874 (2009)* S/2020/151 (New York: United Nations Security Council, March 2, 2020), paras. 67–89.

37. Panel of Experts, *Report of the Panel of Experts established pursuant to resolution 1874 (2009)*, S/2019/1571 (New York: United Nations Security Council, March 5, 2019), paras. 5–10.

38. Kyu-ryun Kim, ed. *North Korea's External Economic Relations*, KINU Research Monograph. Seoul: Korea Institute for National Unification, 2008.

39. See, for example, Togzhan Kassenova, *Policy Forum 11–30: A "Black Hole" in the Global Nonproliferation Regime: The Case of Taiwan* (Berkeley, CA: Nautilus Institute, September 8, 2011); Center for Nonproliferation Studies, "Taiwan Further Restricts Trade to Iran, North Korea," *International Export Control Observer*, March/April 2007; "Treasury Sanctions Taiwan Proliferators Linked to North Korea," US Department of the Treasury press release, May 10, 2013.

40. For details of this case, see Panel of Experts, *Report of the Panel of Experts Established Pursuant to Resolution 1874 (2009)* S/2018/171" (New York: United Nations Security Council, 5 March 2018), paras. 63, 68–72. For free-on-board issues, see Panel of Experts, "*Report of the Panel of Experts Established Pursuant to Resolution 1874 (2009)* S/2019/1571, para. 11.

41. Panel of Experts, *Report of the Panel of Experts Established Pursuant to Resolution 1874 (2009)* S/2018/171, paras. 63, 68–72.

42. Panel of Experts, *Final Report of the Panel of Experts Submitted Pursuant to Resolution 2515 (2020)*, paras. 27–53.

43. "Resolution 2371," United Nations Security Council August 5, 2017.

44. M. C. Choy, "Ships Openly Admit to Buying Illegal Fishing Permits from North Korea," *NK News*, January 1, 2021.

45. J. S. Lee, J. G. Ryu, and H. K. Kee, "A Study on the Status of Chinese Fishing in the East Sea off North Korea and Directions for Countermeasures," *Journal of Fisheries Business Administration*, 48(3), 61–74.

46. Jaeyoon Park, Jungsam Lee, Katherine Seto, Timothy Hochberg, Brian A. Wong, Nathan A. Miller, Kenji Takasaki, et al., "Illuminating Dark Fishing Fleets in North Korea." *Science Advances* 6, no. 30 (2020): eabb1197, https://www.science.org/doi/abs/10.1126/sciadv.abb1197.

47. "Blue Crab Season? Chinese Fishing Vessels Are Engaging in Illegal Fishing Again," YTN, April 6, 2021, https://www.ytn.co.kr/_ln/0103_202104061640137711.

48. Rozanna Latiff and Ju-min Park, "North Korea Bars Malaysians from Leaving, in 'Diplomatic Meltdown,'" Reuters, March 7, 2017.

49. "Kim Jong-nam Killing: Senior N Korea Diplomat Named as Suspect," BBC, February 22, 2017, https://www.bbc.com/news/world-asia-39048658.

50. Panel of Experts, *Final Report of the Panel of Experts Submitted Pursuant to Resolution 2276 (2016)* (New York: United Nations Security Council, February 27, 2017)., para. 72.

51. Shahriman Lockman, "Malaysia and North Korea: A Peculiar Relationship Unravels," *Focus: Institute of Strategic and International Studies (ISIS) Malaysia*, no. 2 (2017):14–15.

52. Lockman, 14–15.

53. Abid Povera, "All North Koreans in Sarawak Have Been Sent Back," *New Straits Times*, September 21, 2017, https://www.nst.com.my/news/nation/2017/09/282406/all-north-koreans-sarawak-have-been-sent-back.

54. BenarNews, "Malaysia: Indonesian Suspect in Kim Jong Nam Murder Rewarded with Cambodian Trip," *Radio Free Asia*, February 9, 2018, https://www.rfa.org/english/news/korea/malaysia-kimjongnam-02092018173649.html.

55. Hyung-jin Kim, "North Korea Cuts Diplomatic Ties with Malaysia over US Extradition," *The Diplomat*, March 19, 2021, https://thediplomat.com/2021/03/north-korea-cuts-diplomatic-ties-with-malaysia-over-us-extradition/.

56. "Singapore Suspends Trade Ties with North Korea," BBC, November 17, 2017, https://www.bbc.com/news/business-42021273.

57. Eric Talmadge, "North Korea's 'Singapore Shops' Expose Gap in Sanctions Push," Associated Press, December 28, 2018, https://apnews.com/article/united

-nations-global-trade-north-korea-international-news-pyongyang-5816e8e32cc3478
6b79746a81c5c093c; Charmaine Ng, "Jail for Company Director Who Sold Luxury
Goods to North Korea, Cheated Banks of $130m," *Straits Times*, November 22, 2019,
https://www.straitstimes.com/singapore/courts-crime/jail-for-company-director-who
-sold-luxury-goods-to-north-korea-cheated-banks.

58. Kang Mi Jin, "N. Korean Rice Sellers Raking It In Thanks to Skyrocketing
Prices," *DailyNK*, February 26, 2020, https://www.dailynk.com/english/north-korean
-rice-sellers-raking-it-in-thanks-skyrocketing-prices/; Kang Mi Jin, "N. Korea Begins
Enforcing Price Controls in Local Markets," *DailyNK*, February 12, 2020; Josh
Smith, "N. Korea's Food Situation Appears Perilous, Experts Say," Reuters, October
8, 2021.

59. Ha Yoon Ah, "N. Korea's State-Run Smuggling Activities Continue Despite
Coronavirus," *DailyNK*, March 25, 2020, https://www.dailynk.com/english/n-koreas
-state-run-smuggling-activities-continue-despite-coronavirus/; Panel of Experts,
Final Report of the Panel of Experts Submitted Pursuant to Resolution 2515 (2020).

60. Benjamin Katzeff Silberstein, "Kim Jong-un's Congress Speech: Strengthening State Control Over the Economy," North Korean Economy Watch, January
12, 2021, http://www.nkeconwatch.com/2021/01/12/kim-jong-uns-congress-speech
-strengthening-state-control-over-the-economy/.

Chapter 9

North Korea's Evolving Cyber Strategies and Operations: Toward Weapons of Mass Effectiveness

Michael Raska

Over the past decade, North Korea has been expanding its cyber capabilities in conjunction with its nuclear weapons and ballistic missile programs to offset its strategic inferiority. Driven by the necessity to create freedom of action in an adversarial strategic environment, North Korea's cyber and information operations have provided Pyongyang with a range of relatively low-cost asymmetric options to demonstrate power without any visible military commitments. The use of cyber has bolstered the legitimacy of North Korean leader Kim Jong-un's rule by raising hundreds of millions of dollars to support the regime and its nuclear and ballistic missile programs, and ultimately, enabled Pyongyang to effectively counter stricter economic sanctions under the cover of plausible deniability.[1] In doing so, North Korea has effectively developed its cyber tactics, techniques, and procedures (TTPs) into cyber-enabled Weapons of Mass Effectiveness (WMEs), complementing its growing nuclear arsenal of Weapons of Mass Destruction (WMDs) in a unified asymmetric political strategy to induce the United States and the international community to recognize the sovereignty and legitimacy of North Korea under Kim Jong-un. As Kim reportedly declared in 2013, "Cyberwarfare, along with nuclear weapons and missiles, is an 'all-purpose sword' that guarantees our military's capability to strike relentlessly."[2]

In this context, this chapter aims to provide brief contours of North Korea's evolving cyber operations, strategies, and capabilities while ascertaining their implications for foreign policy behavior and international relations. The first part maps the historical overview and organizational structure of

North Korea's evolving cyber programs and units. The second part explores the forms of international cooperation necessary to enhance the reach of those capabilities, with a particular emphasis on how North Korean hacker groups have operated independently and covertly in Russia, China, and other countries. Finally, the chapter concludes with a discussion of the likely future paths of North Korean cyber operations as well as the mechanisms under development internationally in response to North Korean cyber capabilities. The chapter argues that North Korea's cyber capabilities have progressively evolved in four phases, or waves: "Precursors," or information warfare units in the late 1990s that established the initial cyber Unit 121 tasked with the research and development of cyber techniques, studying software engineering, cryptography, networking at top computer science programs in China and Russia, and preparing cyber operations from abroad; "First Generation" cyber units and operations (2009–2013) that developed North Korea's technological and organizational resources, assets, malware arsenals, and coding capabilities based on their experiences and lessons learned from attacking targets in South Korea; "Second Generation" cyber units and operations (2014–2019) targeting global cryptocurrency exchanges, conducting cyber espionage to obtain technologies needed for the development of North Korea's nuclear and ballistic missile programs; and "Third Generation" cyber units and operations (2020–present) focused on boosting the technological sophistication and creativity of hacking methods and conducting cyber espionage to obtain research data and intelligence on COVID-19 vaccine and treatment technologies.

North Korean hacker groups and units have demonstrated mixed skill sets—from very low to high levels of sophistication. In each phase, North Korea's cyber units have gradually advanced their capabilities by shifting their priority targets and objectives from baseline cyber espionage and distributing denial of service attacks (DDoS) on select South Korean political and socioeconomic targets to a much more significant strategic role focusing on cyber-enabled information and economic and political warfare globally. At the same time, North Korea has protected its critical infrastructure from potential reprisal cyberattacks by limiting its internet access and communication networks, relying primarily on China's internet infrastructure augmented by links to Russian networks and, more importantly, on the dispersion of its hacker groups across select countries worldwide. Pyongyang has gained the ability to mitigate the impact of international economic sanctions, generating financial resources that have advanced North Korea's military-technological development.

Prior to the analysis, however, *a caveat is in order*. Any assessment of North Korea's cyber operations poses a significant challenge because attribution is a recurring point of contention and because of the closed nature of the totalitarian government and society. Accordingly, the available open-source data about North Korea's cyber capabilities, technique patterns, strategies, and organizational structures are limited mainly to threat intelligence and investigations by global cybersecurity firms, select statements and publications by the US and South Korean governments, select North Korean defectors with partial knowledge of North Korea's cyber activities, secondary literature such as think-tank reports and academic articles, and references in international news media. Each source carries internal and external validity risks, including the potential outdated nature of data or possible politically motivated bias. To mitigate such risks to validity, this chapter synthesizes publicly available data with both primary and secondary open sources.

MAPPING THE TRAJECTORY OF NORTH KOREA'S CYBER OPERATIONS

Precursors: Information Warfare Units in the Late 1990s

North Korea's interest in cyberwarfare programs and training began in the mid-1990s when the Korean People's Army (KPA) studied the "electronic intelligence warfare" concepts formulated by China's People's Liberation Army (PLA). In particular, the KPA's conceptions of cyberwarfare seem to have adopted and adapted elements from the PLA's electronic intelligence warfare (EIW: 전자정보전), computer network warfare (CNW: 콤퓨터네트워크전), psychological warfare (심리전), military deception, and information warfare (IW: 정보전).[3] These in turn followed the conceptual and operational conduct of the US military's electronic warfare and cyber operation activities during the First Gulf War and the NATO campaign in the Balkans.[4] In 1995, North Korean leader Kim Jong-il issued a directive for the KPA General Staff Department (GSD: 총참모부) to develop "information warfare" capabilities, proposing to use the web for spying and attacking South Korea and the United States, while tightly controlling internet access in North Korea.[5]

Three years later, in September 1998, North Korea established Unit 121 (121소 or 121국) within the Staff Reconnaissance Bureau of the KPA, initially believed to be staffed with between five hundred and one thousand members. The initial Unit 121 was tasked with the research and development of cyber techniques, studying software engineering, cryptography, and networking at top computer science programs in China and Russia, as well as preparing cyber operations from abroad, according to public disclosures by two North Korean cyber-experts and defectors, Kim Heung-kwang and Jang Se-yul.[6] Most of the Unit 121 cadres sent abroad were selected from North Korea's top technology colleges such as the Pyongyang University of

Automation (formerly known as the Mirim College), Amrokgang College of Military Engineering, National Defense University, Pyongyang Computer Technology University, Korea Computer Center (KCC), and Pyongyang Informatics Center (PIC).[7]

In the following years, the GSD established its cyber operations under the Command Information Bureau and supporting units such as the Electronic Warfare Bureau and the Enemy Collapse Sabotage Bureau (Unit 204), reportedly tasked to develop electronic, information, and psychological warfare strategies in conjunction with cyber operations, primarily to counter the US–South Korea military operations.[8] The 2003 US invasion of Iraq, live-streamed across global news networks as a "shock and awe" campaign, further amplified North Korea's strategic priority to develop its cyberwarfare units. At that time, Kim Jong-il reportedly issued a warning to North Korea's military: "If warfare was about bullets and oil until now, warfare in the 21st century is about information."[9] At that time, however, much of North Korea's computer infrastructure and facilities were as rudimentary as the early phases of North Korean cyber programs, which were experimenting with basic cyberattack techniques, encryption programs, and malware research. In 2009, for example, the US National Intelligence Estimate dismissed North Korea's cyber capabilities, along with its long-range missile programs, noting that it would take years to develop them into a significant threat.[10] However, the establishment of Unit 121 provided the conceptual, technological, and organizational foundation for the subsequent three generations of North Korea's progressively evolving cyber operations and state-sponsored hacker groups.

First Generation Cyber Units: Targeting South Korea (2007–2013)

In 2007, global cybersecurity firms began to publicly identify and track select North Korean state-sponsored hacking groups, which deployed their first generation of malware in attributed cyberattacks known as "Operation Flame" and "1Mission" (2007–2012), "Operation Troy" (2009–2012), "Ten Days of Rain" (2011), and "Dark Seoul" (2013).[11] These attacks primarily focused on military and government targets in South Korea, hacking websites, stealing information, and distributing denial-of-service (DDoS) attacks.[12] For example, in March 2011 a major DDoS attack on forty South Korean media outlets, critical infrastructures, and financial websites, as well as US military entities in South Korea was attributed to a North Korean operation named "Ten Days of Rain."[13]

These cyber operations may have resulted from the revamp of North Korea's intelligence and internal security services in 2009, which brought varying North Korean intelligence and cyber units under the direct control of the National Defense Commission (NDC), principally to secure Kim Jong-un's position as successor to his father, Kim Jong-il. Under this revamp, the NDC merged intelligence organizations and its various cyber departments and bureaus from the Korean Workers' Party, the Operations Department and Office 35 (foreign operations), and KPA's military intelligence Reconnaissance Bureau into one Reconnaissance General Bureau (RGB) (정찰총국).[14] The RGB became North Korea's primary foreign intelligence service as well as headquarters for special and cyber operations.[15] The RGB, headed by General Kim Yong-chol (2009–2016), absorbed the initial cyber Unit 121, increased its size to three thousand persons, and upgraded its status to that of a "department" also known as Bureau 121—the Cyberwarfare Guidance Bureau (사이버전지도국).[16]

Closely intertwined with Bureau 121, the RGB's Computer Technology Research Lab, also known as Lab 110 (110호 연구소 or 110연구소), is believed to provide software engineering, technical reconnaissance, infiltration of computer networks, intelligence gathering through hacking, and planting viruses on targeted networks.[17] While the exact operational relationship and collaboration between Bureau 121 and Lab 110 is unknown, Lab 110 reportedly analyzes technological configuration and behavior patterns of targets and then develops tailored software and malware to be used in Bureau 121 cyberattacks.[18] In June 2018, the US Justice Department unsealed charges against an alleged hacker for the North Korean government in connection with a series of major cyberattacks, including the 2014 assault on Sony Pictures Entertainment and the WannaCry ransomware virus, which infected hundreds of thousands of computers in 150 countries and shut down dozens of emergency rooms in UK hospitals.[19] The complaint identified Park Jin-hyok as a member of Lab 110 responsible for "a wide-ranging, multi-year conspiracy to conduct computer intrusions and commit wire fraud by co-conspirators working on behalf of the government of the Democratic People's Republic of Korea, while located there and in China. . . . The conspiracy targeted computers belonging to entertainment companies, financial institutions, defense contractors, and others for the purpose of causing damage, extracting information, and stealing money, among other reasons."[20]

Open-source literature references also indicate that Bureau 121 established control over three leading units—Unit 91, Unit 180, and Lab 110—as core cyber components under the RGB's cyber operations along with its six intelligence bureaus—Operations, Reconnaissance, Foreign Intelligence, Inter-Korean Dialogue, Technical, and Rear Services.[21] It is likely that Unit 91, Unit 180, and Lab 110 include additional cyber intelligence-gathering and attack subunits and teams based on their changing mission-taskings, responsibilities, and skills. For example, these subunits may include system analysis teams, attack operations teams, code processing teams, development teams, inspection teams, network analysis teams, and battle planning teams.[22] Collectively, the primary mission of these units has focused on offensive cyber operations, including targeting critical information infrastructure—that is, communications, transportation networks, electricity grids, and aviation systems—in "unfriendly" nations, primarily in South Korea, while advancing cyber espionage against the government, military, defense industry, and media of other target countries.[23]

In 2013, under the order of Kim Jong-un, the RGB reportedly established a new cyber Unit 180 consisting of around five hundred members from the Bureau 121 specifically tasked with hacking global financial institutions to extract foreign currency in support of North Korea's nuclear and ballistic missile programs, as well as with installing malicious backdoors in the software development business in China and Japan, according to published interviews by North Korean defector Kim Heung-kwang.[24] In March 2013, following the passing of UN Security Council Resolution 2087 and B-52 strategic bomber overflights in South Korea, North Korea was attributed to have carried out cyberattacks dubbed "Dark Seoul" that destroyed the computer networks of South Korea's three major banks and two largest media broadcasters—the Korea Broadcasting System and Munhwa Broadcasting Corporation—infecting them with viruses and stealing and wiping information.[25] That year, North Korea intensified its cyber operations against South Korea with a cyber espionage campaign dubbed "Kimsuky" against South Korean think tanks and industries and varying DDoS attacks on South Korean media outlets, government websites, and financial companies.[26]

North Korea's first generation of cyber units and operations progressively developed their conceptual, technological, and organizational frameworks and prioritized their resources, assets, malware arsenals, and coding capabilities based on their experiences and lessons learned from attacking targets in South Korea. They also began to build relationships with other hacking groups outside North Korea, particularly by sending their most promising students to China and Russia. According to interviews by Sanger et al., by 2012 North Korea had sent the majority of its leading hacker teams abroad, establishing a high degree of plausible deniability.[27]

Second Generation Cyber Units: Global Rise (2014–2019)

During 2014–15, North Korea reportedly reorganized its cyber divisions further, with Unit 180 specializing in targeting cryptocurrency exchanges. For example, in January 2018 South Korea's National Intelligence Service (NIS) flagged Unit 180 as a likely perpetrator of a $530 million theft of the digital cryptocurrency NEM from the Tokyo exchange operator Coincheck.[28]

Meanwhile, Bureau 121 expanded its cyber operations beyond South Korea by attacking foreign nations' infrastructure such as transportation networks, telecommunications, electric and nuclear power grids, and aviation systems.[29] Part of the 2014–15 cyber revamp reportedly also included the elite Unit 91, initially tasked with conducting cyber espionage operations against South Korean government, corporate, and citizen targets, but since 2014–15 shifting its focus to "acquiring advanced technologies needed for nuclear development and long-range missiles from developed countries."[30] In 2016, all RGB's cyber units came under the direct control of the State Affairs Commission (SAC), which replaced the NDC as the supreme policy and power organization of the North Korean government (see figure 9.1).[31]

Meanwhile, KPA's military cyber warfare units also expanded in the GSD's Command Automation Bureau to include Unit 31, responsible for malware development; Unit 32, responsible for software development for military use; and Unit 56, responsible for software development for military command and control.[32] These units have provided software engineering and development teams responsible for developing the tools and capabilities, which are also used by the operational bureaus within the KPA as well as RGB. In 2016, the GSD established a new department for Command, Control, Communication, Computer, and Intelligence (C4I) in the military, which superseded the now-defunct Command Information Bureau.[33] The new C4I department's likely purpose has been to accelerate the integration of military cyber capabilities into conventional operations—that is, targeting critical infrastructures—and more importantly, to enhance the defensive cyber capabilities of the KPA's command and control systems. These have been reportedly compromised by a top-secret US military program aimed at disabling North Korea's ballistic missiles before lift-off ("left of launch") using cyberwarfare, directed energy, and electronic attacks.[34] To counter such measures, North Korea has been reportedly developing quantum encryption technology to build a highly secure command-and-control link between Pyongyang and strategic missile launching sites such as Wonsan, Tonghae, and Sohae.[35]

In November 2014, North Korean hackers gained global attention in a major cyberattack on Sony Pictures Entertainment, which destroyed 70 percent of Sony Picture's laptops and computers, in an attempt to coerce the company not to release the movie *The Interview*—a comedy about two journalists dispatched to North Korea to assassinate its new dictator.[36] Earlier in the same year, North Korean hacker groups targeted the computer networks of the British broadcaster *Channel Four*, which planned a drama series about a British nuclear scientist taken hostage in Pyongyang.[37] The attack was identified early before inflicting significant damage; however, it signaled North Korea's intent to use cyber means as part of its political and information warfare strategies.

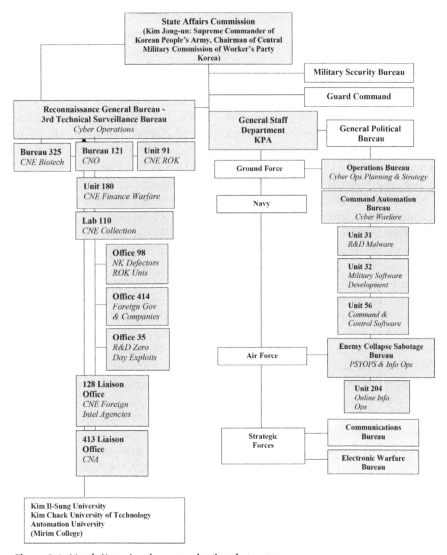

Figure 9.1. North Korea's cyber organizational structure

In 2015–16, North Korean cyber units intensified targeting of international banks connected to the SWIFT global financial messaging system, attempting to transfer $951 million from the Central Bank of Bangladesh.[38] They established a "backdoor" within the bank's internal electronic communication system, allowing them to learn about its communication, security, and operational protocols. On February 4, 2016, they sent instructions to the US Federal Reserve via the SWIFT network to make payments to various accounts in Sri

Lanka and the Philippines, using stolen usernames and passwords collected in the preceding months while operating in the Bank of Bangladesh network. They installed malware on the bank's network that blocked its employees from reading SWIFT messages. The Federal Reserve authorized the first five payment requests, totaling $101 million, but froze the following thirty payments of $850 million due to unrelated automated system alerts. Overall, North Korean hacker groups were able to transfer, divert, withdraw, and launder about $81 million using local contractors in the Philippines.[39]

Since then, North Korea's second-generation cyber units took part in a series of progressively evolving cyber operations, combining varying forms of cyber exploitation (espionage), cybercrime, and strategies of cyber disruption and destruction. In 2016, for example, North Korea was attributed as having successfully penetrated South Korea's military networks—hacking into South Korea's Cyber Command's Defense Integrated Data Center and extracting 235 gigabytes of classified military documents, including US–South Korea wartime operational plans.[40] From 2017 onward, North Korean hacker groups intensified their operations aimed at illicit financial gain—in February 2017, for example, several Polish banks were compromised as well as the South Korean cryptocurrency exchange Bithumb, from which North Korean hackers were able to steal $7 million.[41] In December 2017, the United States, United Kingdom, and Australia formally asserted that North Korea was behind the WannaCry 2.0 global ransomware attack, which infected more than two hundred thousand computers across 150 countries, including computers and devices of the National Health Service hospitals in England and Scotland, Boeing, and Germany's federal railway.[42] The hackers encrypted computers and then demanded payment in bitcoin to unlock the systems.[43] While the total amount of funds generated from the WannaCry ransom payments is unknown, the attack caused an estimated $4 billion in losses worldwide.[44]

According to a March 2019 report by the UN Panel of Experts on North Korean Sanctions Committee, North Korea "carried out at least five successful [cyber] attacks against cryptocurrency exchanges in Asia between January 2017 and September 2018, resulting in a total loss of $571 million."[45] Total proceeds from "widespread and increasingly sophisticated" North Korean cyberattacks on banks, cryptocurrency exchanges, and other forms of cybercrime until 2019 have been estimated at $2 billion.[46] Consequently, "cyberattacks by [North Korea] to illegally force the transfer of funds have become an important tool in the evasion of sanctions and have grown in sophistication and scale since 2016."[47]

At the same time, North Korea has conducted cyber operations to access and eavesdrop on critical infrastructure in the United States and other countries—for example, during the 2018 Trump-Kim Singapore Summit, North

Korea reportedly conducted a large-scale cyber espionage campaign in the United States designed to probe military, financial, energy, telecommunications, health care, and other networks for potential vulnerabilities.[48] While North Korea has rejected all accusations of involvement in illicit hacking activities, it has been arguably less concerned with attribution, using relatively simple false flags such as the "Guardians of Peace" in the wake of the Sony attack or other names such as the "New romantic Cyber Army Team" and the "WhoIs Team" in previous attacks on South Korean targets.[49]

With North Korean hacker groups conducting increasingly diverse and innovative cyber operations globally, there has been a significant overlap in external classifications of these groups based on their tactics, techniques, and procedures (TTPs). For example, some may refer to RGB's cyber units and to *any* activity attributed to North Korea, as "Lazarus Group," while other sources track North Korean clusters or groups such as Bluenoroff, APT37 (Reaper), and APT38 separately. In contrast, other sources refer to *some* activity associated with those group names by the RGB's Lazarus Group.[50] The US government, for example, refers to malicious cyber activity by the North Korean government as HIDDEN COBRA, reflecting the state's covert cyber operations and capabilities to target critical US financial and security infrastructure.[51] However, based on open-source government and private cybersecurity threat-intelligence reports, one could argue that there are a number of subgroups associated within the RGB, with distinct TTPs that should not be mistaken as all under the Lazarus Group. For example, according to an analysis of North Korean–attributed malware by McAfee Labs, "the North Koreans have groups with different skills and tools that execute their focused parts of cyber operations while also working in parallel when large campaigns require a mix of skills and tools."[52] For example, APT 37 (Reaper), Kimsuky, and Sun Team have distinct TTPs specializing in political cyber espionage when compared to the Lazarus-associated Andariel and APT 38 (Bluenoroff) groups focusing on financial extortion and cybercrime.[53]

In summary, the second generation of North Korea's cyber units has progressively developed their resources, assets, malware arsenals, and coding capabilities based on their experience and lessons learned from attacking targets worldwide and collaborating in attack campaigns by sharing networking infrastructure, social engineering skills, and continuously adapting malware code to avoid detection. With Unit 180 targeting cryptocurrency exchanges, Unit 91 focusing on cyber espionage for technologies needed to develop North Korea's nuclear and ballistic missile programs, and Bureau 121 focusing on cyber operations on critical foreign infrastructure, North Korea's hacking groups have expanded their cyber activities and operations beyond South Korea. Cybersecurity firms have identified North Korean cyber operations in India, Malaysia, New Zealand, Nepal, Kenya, Mozambique, Indonesia,

Table 9.1. North Korea's Cyber Activity Clusters Based on TTPs

APT Group	Target Sectors	Associated Malware	Attack Vectors
Lazarus Group *aka:* Labyrinth Chollima, Whois Hacking Team	Global— Information theft and espionage, disruption, sabotage, and financial gain. Lazarus Group activities center on achieving the political goals of the North Korean regime.	Lazarus has deployed multiple malware families across the years depending on targets and objectives. Lazarus uses various code obfuscation techniques, rewriting its own algorithms, applying commercial software protectors, and using its own underground packers. Most tools are designed to be replaced with a new generation as soon as they are used.	The Lazarus Group's attack vectors are continuously evolving. Its malware has been found in many serious cyberattacks, such as the massive data leak and file wiper attack on Sony Pictures Entertainment in 2014, the 2013 cyberespionage campaign in South Korea dubbed Operation Troy, and Operation DarkSeoul, which attacked South Korean media and financial companies in 2013.
APT 38/ Bluenoroff Lazarus subgroup *aka:* Stardust Chollima	Global—Exclusively focuses on financial institutions, casinos, financial trade software development companies, and cryptocurrency businesses. APT38 has conducted operations in over 16 organizations in at least 11 countries.	This large and prolific group uses a variety of custom malware families, including backdoors, tunnelers, dataminers, and destructive malware to steal millions of dollars from financial institutions and render victim networks inoperable.	ATP 38 is careful, calculated, and has demonstrated a desire to maintain access to victim environments for as long as necessary to understand the network layout, required permissions, and system technologies to achieve its goals.

Andariel – Lazarus subgroup *aka:* Silent Chollima	Initially, cyber espionage targeting South Korean military agencies, defense industries, political organizations, security companies, ICT companies, and energy research institutes. Now focuses on financial targets such as ATMs, banks, travel agencies, cryptocurrency exchanges, and online gambling users.	Andariel uses well-known backdoors, such as Aryan and Gh0st RAT, but also self-developed backdoors such as Andarat, Andaratm, Rifdoor, and Phandoor.	Spear phishing using macros, watering hole attacks exploiting Active-X vulnerabilities, vulnerability exploits on security and IT asset management systems, and supply chain attacks.
Kimsuky *aka:* Velvet Chollima	Since 2013, the Kimsuky group has pursued a cyber espionage campaign against South Korean government organizations and defense-related agencies as institutions and corporations related to South Korea's engagement with North Korea.	Kimsuky uses malware able to remote control PCs, logging keystrokes, stealing documents, and collecting directory listings. The name derives from the email account, "Kimsukyang," which was used as drop-point for stolen data in 2013.	Spear phishing methods—targeted cyber scams to lure users to malicious websites or to infect PCs via malicious attached files to access systems and sensitive data. Malicious emails disguised as an invitation to a press conference.

APT 37 *aka:* Reaper, Group 123, Ricochet Chollima, Scarcruft	From 2014 to 2017, APT37 targets concentrated primarily on the South Korean government, military, defense industrial base, and media sector. Since 2017, targets include Japan, Vietnam, and the Middle East in various industry verticals, including chemicals, electronics, manufacturing, aerospace, automotive, and healthcare.	APT37 employs a diverse suite of malware for initial intrusion and exfiltration. Their malware is characterized by a focus on stealing information from victims, with many set up to automatically exfiltrate data of interest. Along with custom malware used for espionage purposes, APT37 also has access to destructive malware.	Social engineering tactics tailored specifically to desired targets, strategic web compromises typical of targeted cyber espionage operations, and torrent file-sharing sites to distribute malware more indiscriminately.
Sun Team	Targets North Korean defectors and journalists in South Korea.	Sun Team uses Android malware that contains a backdoor file in the executable and linkable format. The malware poses as a legitimate app. Once the malware is installed, it copies sensitive information including personal photos, contacts, and SMS messages and sends them to the threat actors.	A highly targeted Sun Team campaign beginning in 2017 used Facebook and KakaoTalk, one of South Korea's most popular chat apps, to spread malware-laced phishing links to targets. Journalists were targeted with fake news stories directing them to infected websites.

Source: Adapted from Dmitry Tarakanov, "The 'Kimsuky' Operation: A North Korean APT?," Kaspersky Lab, *Kaspersky APT Reports*, September 11, 2013; FireEye, *APT 38—Un-usual Suspects*, FireEye Report, 2018; FireEye, "*APT37 (Reaper) The Overlooked North Korean Actor*, A FireEye Special Report, 2018; AhnLab, *Full Discloser of Andariel: A Subgroup of Lazarus Threat Group*, AhnLab Analysis Report, June 23, 2018; AhnLab, *Operation Kabar Cobra: Tenacious Cyber-Espionage Campaign by Kimsuky Group*, AhnLab Analysis Report, February 28, 2019; Trend Micro, "A Look into the Lazarus Group's Operations," *Trend Micro Cybercrime and Digital Threats Blog*, January 24, 2018; Jaewon Min, "North Korean Defectors and Journalists Targeted Using Social Networks and KakaoTalk," *McAfee Labs Blog*, January 11, 2018; Kasperksy Labs, *Lazarus under the Hood*, A Kaspersky Forensic Investigation Report, 2017; Novetta, *Operation Blockbuster: Unraveling the Long Thread of the Sony Attack*, Novetta Special Report, February 2016.

Chile, and other countries. While in some countries such as New Zealand, North Korean hacker groups used the country's computer infrastructure to virtually launch cyberattacks, in other countries such as China, India, and Russia, North Korean hackers have been covertly stationed, learning, training, and using social engineering techniques to disguise their identities.[54] At the same time, North Korea has protected its limited critical infrastructure from potential reprisal cyberattacks by restricting internal access, dependencies, and vulnerabilities on the internet and communication networks, relying instead primarily on China's internet infrastructure augmented only recently with a second internet link to Russian networks, and dispersion of its hackers abroad.[55]

Third Generation Cyber Units: Crisis Management and Adaptation (2020–Present)

Since 2016, North Korea has coped with progressive waves of tailored UN and US economic sanctions as a response to its nuclear and ballistic missile tests. These sanctions have precluded the country from accessing global financial markets, imposed strict import and export controls, and essentially banned banks, companies, and individuals outside North Korea from conducting economic activities that would support its nuclear programs. These sanctions, for example, include import restrictions of aviation fuel to North Korea (2016); coal, iron, and petroleum products (2017); export restrictions of North Korea's metals and agricultural products; and bans on the use of North Korean labor abroad.[56] While the sanctions have hindered North Korea's economy, evident in project delays and resource constraints, they have failed to deter or change North Korea's course in the development of its nuclear weapons programs. Indeed, North Korea has showcased its military-technological developments over the past five years, including an expanding catalog of advanced ballistic missiles and conventional weapons systems.[57]

During these five years, North Korea's political propaganda has embraced a counter-sanctions narrative that emphasizes selecting and concentrating resources, decreasing import dependencies, and expanding a "self-reliant" economic base.[58] However, cyber operations integrated with a "money-laundering" network of shell companies, joint ventures, and overseas banking representatives have provided North Korea's principal sanction evasion strategy and a financial lifeline for the Kim family, its surrounding elite circles, and the continuity of nuclear weapons programs. North Korean hackers, operating mainly outside North Korea, have spearheaded fraudulent cyber operations to circumvent sanctions, gaining access to the international financial system and illegally forcing funds transfers from financial institutions, SWIFT banking networks, and cryptocurrency exchanges worldwide.[59]

According to the blockchain analysis company Chainalysis, North Korean hacker groups were able to extract almost $400 million worth of digital assets in at least seven major attacks on cryptocurrency platforms in 2021 alone.[60]

Since 2020, however, the effects of the COVID-19 pandemic coupled with ongoing economic sanctions, severe environmental disasters, and mismanagement of social and economic policies have challenged North Korea's economy and political system. Kim Jong-un imposed a zero COVID-19 policy, meaning strict lockdowns and tight border controls, further restricting food and agricultural imports, remaining trade channels, and domestic travel. In 2020, Chinese exports to North Korea fell by 81 percent from 2019, while North Korea's exports to China declined by 78 percent.[61] According to the Bank of Korea, North Korea's economy declined by about 10 percent in 2020, a much more significant drop than any previous declines in economic output during the mid-1990s.[62] At the Party Congress in January 2021, Kim Jong-un noted that North Korea's economy "fell short of goals in almost every sector."[63] Consequently, ordinary North Koreans have faced price spikes, panic buying, and limited access to medical supplies and services.[64]

The COVID-19 crisis and resulting global border closures meant at least three developments for North Korea's cyber units. First, the pandemic likely increased internal political pressure on the cyber units to generate more financial resources for the Kim regime, which meant raising the technological sophistication and creativity in devising innovative hacking and wire fraud methods. In 2020, for example, North Korea's Lazarus Group was attributed with the most prominent cryptocurrency theft of the year, extracting about $275 million worth of cryptocurrency from the Singapore-based exchange KuCoin. While KuCoin eventually recovered about $204 million of the stolen funds, the crypto hack showed the creative ways North Korea's Lazarus Group exploited novel financial platforms such as decentralized finance (DeFi) to launder a portion of the stolen funds. DeFi platforms essentially enable users to swap one type of cryptocurrency for another without a centralized platform to facilitate the swap—meaning less user-specific information is linked to the transaction, providing greater anonymity when moving funds.[65] In the KuCoin case, North Korean hackers used the DeFi platform Uniswap. If the investigators hadn't known that the hackers controlled the specific wallet that sent and received the funds, it would have been nearly impossible to trace the funds' movements and identify the swap. According to findings by Chainalysis, Lazarus Group's reliance on DeFi platforms, which nearly doubled in 2020, represents a shift in money laundering strategy away from the previous focus on mainstream exchanges.[66]

The second trend in North Korean cyber operations during the COVID-19 crisis has been the expansion of cyber espionage to obtain research data and intelligence on vaccine and treatment technologies. In February 2021, for example, South Korea's NIS revealed at a regular closed-door hearing of the National Assembly's Intelligence Committee that North Korean cyber groups attempted to hack the servers of US drug manufacturer Pfizer as well as South Korean companies developing coronavirus vaccines and treatments.[67] While it is unclear whether these operations were successful, these intrusions have followed at least nine previous hacks by North Korean cyber groups into global pharma companies since 2019, including Johnson & Johnson, Novavax Inc, AstraZeneca, Genexine, Shin Poong, and Celltrion.[68] In October 2020, according to Microsoft research, one Russian and two North Korean hacker groups (Russia's APT28 or Fancy Bear, and North Korea's Lazarus and unknown group Cerium) jointly targeted seven leading pharma companies involved in COVID-19 research in the United States, Canada, France, India, and South Korea.[69] One of the groups, Cerium, used targeted spear-phishing emails to masquerade as actual representatives from the World Health Organization in charge of coordinating efforts to contain the COVID-19 pandemic.[70]

In January 2021, before the Eighth Party Congress, North Korea reportedly established a new elite hacking group, Bureau 325, nominally positioned under the RGB but directly reporting to Kim Jong-un. Bureau 325 is likely tasked with obtaining research data on vaccine technology related to COVID-19—targeting foreign biotechnology companies, research institutions, and government agencies.[71] According to *Daily NK* interviews with a high-ranking source, Bureau 325 comprises five groups—two research labs with about eight hundred personnel stationed in North Korea and three operating units stationed overseas. The overseas units likely conduct cyber operations, while the internal personnel in North Korea likely serve as their support, research, and logistical hubs. Bureau 325 can be seen as a next generation of North Korean cyber force, composed of elite members of existing hacking groups and newly hired top university graduates in computer science, biochemistry, mathematics, and related fields from top colleges such as the Kim Chaek University of Technology and Kim Il-sung University.[72]

These developments point toward the third trend that may characterize the next phase of North Korean cyber operations: strategic and operational consolidation in their capability development, meaning multiple hacker groups working together to conduct more advanced "full-spectrum" cyber operations. For nearly a decade, most North Korean leading hacker groups have been geographically dispersed in China, Russia, Southeast Asia, and even Europe, acting independently or mutually supporting each other based on their specific cyber-missions: from intelligence-driven cyber espionage and information manipulation (APT37, Kimsuky, Sun Team, Bureau 325) to covert financial extortion (APT38, Andariel) to various other disruptive and destructive cyber operations (Lazarus Group). As a result, North Korean hacker groups reflected a considerable variation in their tactics, techniques, and procedures—from very low to advanced-skills teams able to exploit cyber vulnerabilities. However, as cyber defenses become more advanced, integrating emerging technologies such as Artificial Intelligence (AI) systems capable of analyzing the behavior of threat actors and identifying anomalies and vulnerabilities within a system, costs have risen for cyber attackers. Hacker groups, including those working for North Korea, must also increase their level of technical sophistication, operational security, and funding, which may propel them to work together or even in selective alliances with other state-sponsored hacking groups, using novel multi-stage attack vectors.

INTERNATIONAL RESPONSES

International responses to North Korea's evolving cyber capabilities can be conceptualized along three dimensions, all showing considerable limitations. In the broader cyber landscape, North Korea's cyber activities are part of a rising global cybersecurity threat spectrum, which increases the imperative for international cooperation to develop ways and means to identify, counter, and ensure resilience of regional cyber ecosystems. North Korea's hacker groups such as RGB's Lazarus are on the list of Advanced Persistent Threats (APTs)—state-sponsored hacker groups that use sustained, covert, and sophisticated techniques to gain unauthorized access into networks and systems and remain inside for a prolonged time, with potentially destructive consequences. The list of tracked APTs, compiled by leading cybersecurity firms, governments, academic researchers, and policy analysts often include select Chinese, Russian, Iranian, Vietnamese, North Korean, and other hacker groups with different motivations, target sectors, and methods underlying their activities.[73] However, despite increasing global awareness about various APT groups, international cooperation on cybersecurity—including detecting, protecting, and responding to North Korean APTs—has been conditioned by different levels of threat perceptions and political and strategic interests. China and Russia, for example, have consistently denied providing a safe haven for North Korean hacker groups.[74] The reluctance to report, investigate, and share information on North Korean cyber activities by different states can be also seen in the experiences of the Panel of Experts at the UN Security Council (UNSC), tasked to assist the UNSC Sanctions Committee on North Korea with research and analysis on the status of sanctions and their implementation. According to one panel member, several member states strongly oppose panel investigations and reporting on cyber issues.[75] This could be attributed to multiple intervening internal and external variables shaped by ongoing tensions between great powers, which include global contestation and rivalry in critical areas of cybersecurity, ranging from infrastructure provision and data protection to global norms and conventions for fighting cybercrime.[76] Despite these constraints, however, the Panel has extensively reported on North Korean cyberattacks since 2019, identifying potential violations of provisions including UNSC Resolution 1718 (2006), Resolution 2094 (2013), and Resolution 2270 (2016).[77]

International responses to North Korea's covert cyber operations have been more visible in the efforts of "like-minded" countries to raise awareness, share technical information, and implement best practices. For example, in December 2017, Australia, Canada, New Zealand, the United States, and the United Kingdom publicly attributed the WannaCry 2.0 ransomware attack to North Korea and denounced its "harmful and irresponsible" cyber activities. Meanwhile, Denmark and Japan also issued supporting statements for the joint denunciation of the destructive WannaCry 2.0 ransomware attack.[78] In February 2021, the US Department of Justice released a detailed indictment of three North Korean military hackers—Jon Chang-hyok (전창혁), Kim Il (김일), and Park Jin-hyok (박진혁), as members of RGB units engaged in a broad array of criminal cyber activities worldwide, including using cyber means for political revenge and financial gain. According to the indictment:

> Throughout the investigation, the FBI and the Justice Department provided specific information to victims about how they had been targeted or compromised, as well as information about the tactics, techniques, and procedures used by the hackers with the goals of remediating any intrusion and preventing future intrusions. That direct sharing of information took place in the United States and in foreign countries, often with the assistance of foreign law enforcement partners. The FBI also collaborated with certain private cybersecurity companies by sharing and analyzing information about the intrusion TTPs used by the members of the conspiracy.[79]

The second layer of responses can be positioned in the political and strategic framework of the US-South Korea alliance. Since 2012, the foreign ministries of the United States and South Korea have held biannual meetings focused on cyber policy issues, including joint efforts to strengthen bilateral cooperation in tackling evolving cyber challenges and implementing measures to protect critical government infrastructure and online security.[80] In the alliance's defense diplomacy, the cyber domain has been discussed in the broader context of the US–South Korea alliance cooperative defense mechanisms, strategies, and capabilities. This is evident from the annual US-ROK Security Consultative Meetings and Joint Communiques, which list the need to strengthen cyber defense cooperation along with other issues and challenges shaping the direction and character of the alliance. In the most recent

53rd Security Consultative Meeting, the Communique notes the planned establishment in 2022 of a dedicated Cyber Cooperation Working group to "share trends of cyber threats and . . . to progressively develop cooperation and exchanges between the respective cyber commands with the aim of discussing and promoting mutual interests."[81]

In this context, one problematic aspect for the alliance is that the two sides have not clarified joint strategy, obligations, and appropriate responses to major disruptive or destructive cyberattacks. This may be particularly true in the context of interpreting a major cyberattack as an "armed attack" defined in the 1953 Mutual Defense Treaty, which would directly activate a US military response—for example, assuming wartime operational command and control of South Korean forces.[82] The alliance's ability to deter and effectively respond to North Korean cyber operations is also conditioned by internal South Korean political debates on the future of the alliance, US military presence in South Korea, and resulting political and strategic options. Over the past decade, the debate has reflected five themes in South Korea's defense planning and management: (1) how to balance and prioritize South Korea's current operational requirements vis-à-vis North Korea with future-oriented regional contingencies and potential conflicts; (2) how to ensure budgetary support and sustain defense resource allocation required for future defense reforms; (3) how to reduce the size of the South Korean force structure without diminishing its military effectiveness; (4) how and when to transfer current wartime operational command control (OPCON) from the US forces to South Korea; and ultimately (5) how to shape the future direction and strategic template of the US–South Korea alliance amid growing US-China strategic competition.[83] These internal political and external strategic challenges combined have precluded major organizational, conceptual, and operational innovation needed to develop joint cyber capabilities in the framework of the US–South Korea alliance.

This leads to the third response layer: individual country responses such as those by South Korea. Over the past decade, South Korea has aimed to develop multilayered cyber defense measures to protect its critical infrastructure and strengthen cyber resilience in its national security strategies, Defense White Papers, and specific policy documents such as the Comprehensive Countermeasures of 2009, 2013, and 2015, as well as the 2011 National Cybersecurity Master Plan.[84] South Korea has sought to adapt relevant laws to enable its cyber defenses, integrate cyber into military doctrine (the Joint Cyber Operations Manual), establish the ROK Cyber Command under the Joint Chiefs of Staff office, and create early warning and crisis management mechanisms for responding to cyber crises.[85] These measures, however, arose only in reaction to major North Korean cyberattacks during this period. It took another four years, until 2019, for South Korea to develop a comprehensive national cybersecurity strategy.[86] The strategy is built around six strategic pillars: secured national critical infrastructure, enhanced cyberattack defense capabilities, trust- and cooperation-based governance, cybersecurity industry growth, fostering a cybersecurity culture, and strengthened international cooperation. Since then, South Korea has aimed to implement civil-military cooperation in the cyber domain, including joint programs with the Ministry of Science, IT, and Future Planning and the NIS to create a possible cyber reserve force, and closer coordination of intelligence border monitoring, joint response to North Korea's electronic warfare and GPS jamming, and Special Forces. Taken together, these measures comprise South Korea's broader defense transformation aimed at redefining its strategic paradigms and military capabilities to allow for greater flexibility, adaptability, and autonomy under conditions of strategic uncertainty.

IMPACT OF CYBER ON NORTH KOREA'S FOREIGN POLICY BEHAVIOR

North Korea's evolving cyber capabilities in conjunction with its nuclear and ballistic missile programs provide a relatively low-cost but effective means to exert influence and political, economic, and military coercion without triggering a major armed conflict. Pyongyang's online activities and behaviors have an increasingly global impact, blurring distinctions between civil and military domains, state and nonstate actors, and principal targets and weapons used. The diverse character of these operations may increase the propensity for offensive and unrestricted cyber operations in the future given the prevailing perceptions of lesser risks of detection, the lack of accountability, and the resulting low probability of successful deterrence. Cyber operations enable and reinforce North Korea's political and strategic ambiguity and therefore can be used to create political outcomes without visible military commitments. Moreover, the country is still by and large unplugged from the global internet, and China's "Great Firewall" provides an "additional layer of protection, censorship, and surveillance for North Korea's cyberspace."[87] This reduces North Korea's dependencies and potential systemic vulnerabilities to retaliatory actions and, more important, mitigates risks of attribution. Consequently, North Korea can continue to target critical infrastructures of other states as well as private corporations and banks for varying political motivations, including retaliation, coercion, covert intelligence gathering, and increasingly also illicit financial gain to bypass stricter international sanctions and generate foreign currency. Cyber capabilities also enable North Korea to access information on emerging technologies such as electronic miniaturization, additive manufacturing, AI, space capabilities, and unmanned systems that can be absorbed into North Korea's future military development. Accordingly, North Korea's cyber capabilities will likely evolve further as Weapons of Mass Effectiveness, complementing the varying political and strategic effects of its Weapons of Mass Destruction.

NOTES

1. David Sanger, David Kirkpatrick, and Nicole Perlroth, "The World Once Laughed at North Korean Cyberpower. No More," *New York Times*, October 15, 2017, https://www.nytimes.com/2017/10/15/world/asia/north-korea-hacking-cyber -sony.html.

2. Hyungsoo Kim, "Kim Jong-Un Says 'Cyber Warfare Is an All-Powerful Tool,' Utilizes It as One of Three Major Means of Warfare," *Joongang Ilbo*, November 5, 2013.

3. Alexander Mansourov, "North Korea's Cyber Warfare and Challenges for the U.S.-ROK Alliance," KEI Academic Paper Series, December 2, 2014, http://keia.org /sites/default/files/publications/kei_aps_mansourov_final.pdf.

4. Daniel A. Pinkston, "Inter-Korean Rivalry in the Cyber Domain: The North Korean Cyber Threat in the Son'gun Era," *Georgetown Journal of International Affairs* 27, no. 3 (2016): 60–76.

5. Pinkston, 62.

6. Sangwon Yoon, "North Korea Recruits Hackers at School," *Aljazeera News*, June 21, 2011, https://www.aljazeera.com/indepth/features/2011/06/201162081543573839 .html.

7. Brian McWilliams, "North Korea's School for Hackers," *Wired*, February 6, 2003, https://www.wired.com/2003/06/north-koreas-school-for-hackers/.

8. Jenny Jun, Scott LaFoy, and Ethan Sohn, *"North Korea's Cyber Operations Strategies and Responses: A Report of CSIS Korea Chair* (Lanham, MD: Rowman & Littlefield, December 2015): 51, https://csis-website-prod.s3.amazonaws.com/s3fs -public/legacy_files/files/publication/151216_Cha_NorthKoreasCyberOperations _Web.pdf.

9. Sanger et al., "The World Once Laughed at North Korean Cyberpower."

10. Sanger et al.

11. Group IB, *Lazarus Arisen: Architecture, Tools, Attribution* (Group-IB, May 30, 2017), https://www.group-ib.com/blog/lazarus; Novetta, *Operation Blockbuster: Unravelling the Long Thread of the Sony Attack* (Novetta, February 2016), https:// www.usna.edu/CyberCenter/_files/documents/Operation-Blockbuster-Report.pdf.

12. Ryan Sherstobitoff, Itai Liba, and James Walter, "Dissecting Operation Troy: Cyberespionage in South Korea," McAfee White Paper, May 4, 2018, https://www .mcafee.com/enterprise/en-us/assets/white-papers/wp-dissecting-operation-troy.pdf.

13. McAfee, "Ten Days of Rain—Expert Analysis of Distributed Denial-of-Service Attacks Targeting South Korea," McAfee White Paper, July 2011. https://www

.mcafee.com/blogs/wp-content/uploads/2011/07/McAfee-Labs-10-Days-of-Rain-July-2011.pdf.

14. Joseph Bermudez, "A New Emphasis on Operations against South Korea? A Guide to North Korea's Intelligence Reorganization and the General Reconnaissance Bureau," *38 North Special Report*, June 11, 2010, https://www.38north.org/wp-content/uploads/2010/06/38north_SR_Bermudez2.pdf

15. Jun et al., "North Korea's Cyber Operations Strategies and Responses," 51.

16. Yoon, "North Korea Recruits Hackers at School."

17. Scott Tosi, "North Korean Cyber Support to Combat Operations," *Military Review*, July-August 2017, 26.

18. Duri Lee, "How to Improve the ROK and US Military Alliance against North Korea's Threats to Cyberspace: Lessons from NATO's Defense Cooperation" (master's thesis, Naval Postgraduate School, Monterey, CA, 2017), 22.

19. Hamish Mcdonald, "Fog of Cyberwar Spurs Virtual Arms Race on Korean Peninsula," *Nikkei Asian Review*, May 22, 2017, https://asia.nikkei.com/Politics/Fog-of-cyberwar-spurs-virtual-arms-race-on-Korean-peninsula.

20. United States of America v. Park Jin Hyok," United States District Court for the Central District of California, Case No. MJ18–1479, June 8, 2018, p. 3, https://assets.documentcloud.org/documents/4834314/Read-the-DOJ-s-criminal-complaint-against-an.pdf.

21. Bermudez, "A New Emphasis on Operations against South Korea?"; Joseph Bermudez, "North Korea Reorganizes Security Services," *IHS Jane's Report*, 2016.

22. Lee, "How to Improve the ROK and US Military Alliance," 22.

23. Jiro Yoshino, "North Korea's Cybertroops Span the Globe in Quest for Cash," *Nikkei Asian Review*, March 15, 2018, https://asia.nikkei.com/Politics/International-relations/North-Korea-s-cybertroops-span-the-globe-in-quest-for-cash.

24. Ju-min Park and James Pearson, "Exclusive: North Korea's Unit 180, the Cyber Warfare Cell That Worries the West," Reuters, May 21, 2017, https://www.reuters.com/article/us-cyber-northkorea-exclusive/exclusive-north-koreas-unit-180-the-cyber-warfare-cell-that-worries-the-west-idUSKCN18H020.

25. Choe Sang-Hun, "Computer Networks in South Korea Are Paralyzed in Cyberattacks," *New York Times*, March 20, 2013, https://www.nytimes.com/2013/03/21/world/asia/south-korea-computer-network-crashes.html; Michael Pearson, K. J. Kwon, and Jethro Mullen, "Hacking Attack on South Korea traced to China, Officials Say," CNN, March 21, 2013, https://edition.cnn.com/2013/03/20/world/asia/south-korea-computer-outage/index.html.

26. Dmitry Tarakanov, "The Kimsuky Operation: A North Korean APT?," Kaspersky Lab, *Kaspersky APT Reports*, September 11, 2013, https://securelist.com/the-kimsuky-operation-a-north-korean-apt/57915/.

27. Sanger et al., "The World Once Laughed at North Korean Cyberpower."

28. Cynthia Kim, "South Korean Intelligence Says N. Korean Hackers Possibly Behind Coincheck Heist—Sources," Reuters, February 6, 2018, https://www.reuters.com/article/uk-southkorea-northkorea-cryptocurrency/south-korean-intelligence-says-n-korean-hackers-possibly-behind-coincheck-heist-sources-idUSKBN1FP2XX.

29. Steve Miller, "Where Did North Korea's Cyber Army Come From?" *Voice of America*, November 20, 2018, https://www.voanews.com/a/north-korea-cyber-army /4666395.html.

30. Miller, "Where Did North Korea's Cyber Army Come From?"; Charlie Campbell, "Why We Shouldn't Be Surprised If North Korea Launched the WannaCry Ransomware Cyberattack," *Time*, May 17, 2017, https://time.com/4781809/ransomware -attack-north-korea-wannacry/.

31. "National Defense Commission (Defunct)," NK Leadership Watch, September 24, 2016, https://nkleadershipwatch.wordpress.com/dprk-security-apparatus/national -defense-commission/.

32. Jun et al., "North Korea's Cyber Operations Strategies and Responses," 47.

33. Lee, "How to Improve the ROK and US Military Alliance," 23.

34. David Sanger and William Broad, "Trump Inherits a Secret Cyberwar against North Korean Missiles," *New York Times*, March 4, 2017, https://www.nytimes.com /2017/03/04/world/asia/north-korea-missile-program-sabotage.html.

35. Martyn Williams, "Catch Me If You Can: North Korea Works to Improve Communications Security," *38North*, April 12, 2017, https://www.38north.org/2017/04/ mwilliams041217/.

36. Andrea Peterson, "The Sony Pictures Hack, Explained," *Washington Post*, December 18, 2014, https://www.washingtonpost.com/news/the-switch/wp/2014 /12/18/the-sony-pictures-hack-explained/; Greg Otto, "U.S. Charges North Korean Hacker over Sony, WannaCry Incidents," *Cyberscoop*, September 6, 2018, https:// www.cyberscoop.com/north-korea-indictment-sony-pictures-wannacry/.

37. Gordon Corera, "UK TV Drama about North Korea Hit by Cyber-Attack," BBC, October 16, 2017, https://www.bbc.com/news/technology-41640976.

38. Nalani Fraser, Jacqueline O'Leary, Vincent Cannon, and Fred Plan, "APT38: Details on New North Korean Regime-Backed Threat Group," FireEye Threat Research Report, October 3, 2018, https://www.fireeye.com/blog/threat-research /2018/10/apt38-details-on-new-north-korean-regime-backed-threat-group.html; "HIDDEN COBRA—FASTCash Campaign," Alert (TA18–275A), National Cybersecurity and Communications Integration Center, October 2, 2018, https://www.us -cert.gov/ncas/alerts/TA18-275A.

39. Ed Caesar, "The Incredible Rise of North Korea's Hacking Army," *New Yorker*, April 19, 2021, https://www.newyorker.com/magazine/2021/04/26/the-incredible -rise-of-north-koreas-hacking-army.

40. Kyongae Choi, "N. Korea Likely Hacked S. Korea Cyber Command: Military," Yonhap News, December 6, 2016, https://en.yna.co.kr/view/AEN20161205010451315; Christine Kim, "North Korea Hackers Stole South Korea-U.S. Military Plans to Wipe out North Korea Leadership: Lawmaker," Reuters, October 10, 2017, https:// www.reuters.com/article/us-northkorea-cybercrime-southkorea/north-korea-hackers -stole-south-korea-u-s-military-plans-to-wipe-out-north-korea-leadership-lawmaker -idUSKBN1CF1WT.

41. Eduard Kovacs, "Malware Attacks on Polish Banks Linked to Lazarus Group," *Security Week*, February 13, 2017, https://www.securityweek.com/malware-attacks -polish-banks-linked-lazarus-group.

42. Thomas Bossert, "It's Official: North Korea Is Behind WannaCry," *Wall Street Journal*, December 18, 2017, https://www.wsj.com/articles/its-official-north-korea-is-behind-wannacry-1513642537.

43. Caesar, "The Incredible Rise of North Korea's Hacking Army."

44. Jason Bartlett, "What Will North Korean Cybercrime Look Like in 2022?," *The Diplomat*, December 22, 2021, https://thediplomat.com/2021/12/what-will-north-korean-cybercrime-look-like-in-2022/.

45. *Final Report of the Panel of Experts Submitted Pursuant to Resolution 2464 (2019)*, United Nations Security Council, March 2, 2019, 51, https://www.undocs.org/S/2019/171.

46. *Midterm Report of the Panel of Experts Submitted Pursuant to Resolution 2464 (2019)*, United Nations Security Council, August 30, 2019, 26, https://undocs.org/S/2019/691.

47. *Final Report of the Panel of Experts Submitted Pursuant to Resolution 2464 (2019)*, 48.

48. Ryan Sherstobitoff, "Operation Sharpshooter Targets Global Defense, Critical Infrastructure," McAfee Labs, December 12, 2018, https://securingtomorrow.mcafee.com/other-blogs/mcafee-labs/operation-sharpshooter-targets-global-defense-critical-infrastructure/.

49. Andy Greenberg, "Russian Hacker False Flags Work—Even After They Are Exposed," *Wired*, February 27, 2018, https://www.wired.com/story/russia-false-flag-hacks.

50. "Lazarus Group," MITRE ATTACK Database, October 14, 2021, https://attack.mitre.org/groups/G0032/.

51. "HIDDEN COBRA—North Korean Malicious Cyber Activity," National Cybersecurity and Communications Integration Center (NCCIC), https://www.us-cert.gov/HIDDEN-COBRA-North-Korean-Malicious-Cyber-Activity.

52. Jay Rosenberg and Christiaan Beek, "Examining Code Reuse Reveals Undiscovered Links among North Korea's Malware Families," McAfee Labs Report, August 9, 2019, https://securingtomorrow.mcafee.com/other-blogs/mcafee-labs/examining-code-reuse-reveals-undiscovered-links-among-north-koreas-malware-families/.

53. "Treasury Sanctions North Korean State-Sponsored Malicious Cyber Groups," US Department of the Treasury, September 13, 2019, https://home.treasury.gov/news/press-releases/sm774.

54. Caesar, "The Incredible Rise of North Korea's Hacking Army."

55. Priscilla Moriuchi, "North Korea's Ruling Elite Adapt Internet Behavior to Foreign Scrutiny," *Recorded Future Blog*, April 25, 2018, https://www.recordedfuture.com/north-korea-internet-behavior/.

56. Eleanor Albert, "What to Know about Sanctions on North Korea," *Council on Foreign Relations*, July 16, 2019, https://www.cfr.org/backgrounder/what-know-about-sanctions-north-korea.

57. Chung Min Lee and Kathryn Botto (eds.), "Korea Net Assessment 2020: Politicized Security and Unchanging Strategic Realities," Carnegie Endowment for International Peace, March 18, 2020, https://carnegieendowment.org/files/Korea_Net_Assesment_2020.pdf.

58. Christy Lee, "As North Korea Reverts to Self-Reliance, Experts Urge Pressuring Elites," Voice of America, January 27, 2020, https://www.voanews.com /a/east-asia-pacific_north-korea-reverts-self-reliance-experts-urge-pressuring-elites /6183268.html.

59. *Final Report of the Panel of Experts Submitted Pursuant to Resolution 2464 (2019)*.

60. "North Korean Hackers Have Prolific Year as Their Unlaundered Cryptocurrency Holdings Reach All-Time High," Chainalysis Team, *Chainalysis Crypto Crime Report 2022*, https://blog.chainalysis.com/reports/north-korean-hackers-have-prolific -year-as-their-total-unlaundered-cryptocurrency-holdings-reach-all-time-high/.

61. Troy Stangarone, "Why Has North Korea Struggled to Normalize Trade with China?" *The Diplomat*, November 25, 2021, https://thediplomat.com/2021/11/why -has-north-korea-struggled-to-normalize-trade-with-china/.

62. Andrew Jeong, "North Korea's Economy Hit Harder Than It Has Been in Decades," *Wall Street Journal*, December 18, 2020, https://www.wsj.com/articles/ north-koreas-economy-hit-harder-than-it-has-been-in-decades-11608300202.

63. Sang-Hun Choe, "North Korea Party Congress Opens with Kim Jong-un Admitting Failures," *New York Times*, January 5, 2021, https://www.nytimes.com /2021/01/05/world/asia/north-korea-kim-jong-un-party-congress.html.

64. *Final Report of the Panel of Experts Submitted Pursuant to Resolution 2464 (2020)*, United Nations Security Council, March 4, 2021, 58, https://undocs.org/S /2021/211.

65. Chainalysis Team, "Lazarus Group Pulled Off 2020's Biggest Exchange Hack and Appears to be Exploring New Money Laundering Options," *Chainalysis Report*, February 9, 2021, https://blog.chainalysis.com/reports/lazarus-group-kucoin -exchange-hack/.

66. Chainalysis Team, "Lazarus Group Pulled Off 2020's Biggest Exchange Hack."

67. Simon Denyer, "North Korea Tried to Steal Pfizer Coronavirus Vaccine Information, South says," *Washington Post*, February 16, 2021, https://www.washingtonpost .com/world/asia_pacific/north-korea-pfizer-coronavirus-vaccine-hack/2021/02/16/ c09ec7fc-702e-11eb-8651-6d3091eac63f_story.html.

68. Sangmi Cha and Hyonhee Shin, "North Korean Hackers Tried to Steal Pfizer Vaccine Know-How, Lawmaker Says," Reuters, February 16, 2021, https://www .reuters.com/article/us-northkorea-cybercrime-pfizer-idUSKBN2AG0NI.

69. Tom Burt, "Cyberattacks Targeting Health Care Must Stop," *Microsoft on the Issues*, November 13, 2020, https://blogs.microsoft.com/on-the-issues/2020/11/13/ health-care-cyberattacks-COVID-19-paris-peace-forum/?2020-11-12.

70. Burt.

71. John Leyden, "Beyond Lazarus: North Korean Cyber-Threat Groups Become Top-Tier, 'Reckless' Adversaries," *Daily Swig—Cybersecurity News*, May 17, 2021, https://portswigger.net/daily-swig/beyond-lazarus-north-korean-cyber-threat-groups -become-top-tier-reckless-adversaries.

72. Seulkee Jang, "Kim Jong Un Is Directly Handling Results of new COVID-19 Hacking Organization's Work," *Daily NK*, February 5, 2021, https://www.dailynk

.com/english/kim-jong-un-directly-handling-results-new-COVID-19-hacking
-organization-work/.

73. "Advanced Threat Predictions for 2021," *Kaspersky Security Bulletin*, November 19, 2020, https://securelist.com/apt-predictions-for-2021/99387/.

74. Cory Bennett, "North Korean Hackers Test China's Patience," *Politico*, May 16, 2017, https://www.politico.com/story/2017/05/16/north-korean-hackers-test-china-patience-238473.

75. Eun DuBois, "Building Resilience to the North Korean Cyber Threat: Experts Discussion," Brookings Institution, December 23, 2020, https://www.brookings.edu/blog/order-from-chaos/2020/12/23/building-resilience-to-the-north-korean-cyber-threat-experts-discuss/.

76. George Christou and Michael Raska, "Cybersecurity," in *The European Union's Security Relations with Asian Partners*, ed. Thomas Christiansen, Emil Kirchner, and See Seng Tan (London: Palgrave Macmillan 2021), 209–30.

77. Keiko Kono, "An Overview of the Report of the UN Panel of Experts Established Pursuant to the Security Council Resolution 1874 (2009): Investigations into North Korean Cyberattacks Continue," NATO CCDCOE Law Branch, 2021, https://ccdcoe.org/incyder-articles/an-overview-of-the-report-of-the-un-panel-of-experts-established-pursuant-to-the-security-council-resolution-1874-2009-investigations-into-north-korean-cyberattacks-continue/.

78. "Guidance on the North Korean Cyber Threat," US Departments of State, the Treasury, and Homeland Security, and the Federal Bureau of Investigation, April 15, 2020, https://home.treasury.gov/system/files/126/dprk_cyber_threat_advisory_20200415.pdf.

79. "Three North Korean Military Hackers Indicted in Wide-Ranging Scheme to Commit Cyberattacks and Financial Crimes across the Globe," US Department of Justice, Press Release by the Office of Public Affairs, February 17, 2021, https://www.justice.gov/opa/pr/three-north-korean-military-hackers-indicted-wide-ranging-scheme-commit-cyberattacks-and.

80. "Korea, US Hold First Policy Consultation on Online Security," *Yonhap News*, September 13, 2012, http://www.koreatimes.co.kr/www/nation/2020/05/120_119884.html.

81. "53rd Security Consultative Meeting Joint Communique," US Department of Defense, December 2, 2021, https://www.defense.gov/News/Releases/Release/Article/2858814/53rd-security-consultative-meeting-joint-communique/.

82. Terrence Matsuo, "More Bilateral U.S.-ROK Cooperation Needed in Cyber Policy," *KEI Peninsula Commentary*, May 12, 2020, https://keia.org/the-peninsula/more-bilateral-u-s-rok-cooperation-needed-in-cyber-policy/.

83. Michael Raska, "Searching for Security, Autonomy, and Independence: The Challenge of Military Innovation in the ROK Armed Forces," in *Military Innovation of Small States: Creating a Reverse Asymmetry* (New York: Routledge, 2016): 121.

84. Hannes Ebert, "Cyber Resilience and Diplomacy in the Republic of Korea," *EU Cyber Direct—Digital Dialogue Report*, August 18, 2020, https://eucyberdirect.eu/research/cyber-resilience-and-diplomacy-in-the-republic-of-korea.

85. "Republic of Korea Cybersecurity Policy Documents," UNIDIR, UNIDIR Cyber Policy Portal, April 2021, https://unidir.org/cpp/en/state-pdf-export/eyJjb3Vud HJ5X2dyb3VwX2lkIjoiODgifQ.

86. So Jeong Kim and Sunha Bae, "Korean Policies of Cybersecurity and Data Resilience," Carnegie Endowment for International Peace, August 17, 2021, https://carnegieendowment.org/2021/08/17/korean-policies-of-cybersecurity-and-data-resilience-pub-85164#.

87. Mansourov, "North Korea's Cyber Warfare and Challenges for the U.S.-ROK Alliance," 2.

Chapter 10

North Korean Human Rights Diplomacy at the United Nations

Sandra Fahy

States use various methods to engage in diplomatic relations, including via the United Nations (UN). This chapter provides an overview of the relationship between North Korea and the UN, illustrating the UN's role as a venue for dialogue and criticism of human rights in North Korea, and for the North Korean state to respond to such concerns. UN agencies have served as a vehicle for North Korean engagement in technical cooperation through instruments such as the Panel of Experts and the Universal Periodic Review (UPR). This chapter examines North Korea's strategies toward the UN as a venue for promoting the state's perspectives and concerns on human rights issues to the international community. This chapter will identify what has changed, in terms of diplomacy and rights, since the publication of the UN Commission of Inquiry report of 2014. Finally, the chapter outlines how North Korea has engaged with the UN on human rights during Kim Jong-un's first decade of leadership.

THE HISTORY OF NORTH KOREA AND THE UN

The UN is an international organization intended to provide a platform for member states to express views and take actions on problems of global concern that impact individual member nations. As evidenced by contemporary calamities such as climate change and the COVID-19 pandemic, few if any issues today are truly contained by state borders. From its founding on October 24, 1945, the UN was, and remains, exceptional among the world's international organizations in its ambition to bring nations together to help the world's most vulnerable people, sustain development, protect human rights, and advance peace. While the UN is hardly immune from critique—whether in terms of ideology, policy, or representation—since its founding, it has continued to advance toward a progressive realization of peace and security.

The UN and the Korean Peninsula have a complex relationship. Though the UN granted South Korea observer status in 1948, it did not grant the same to North Korea until 1971. It wasn't until September 17, 1991, that the Forty-Sixth UN General Assembly admitted South Korea as a member state. North Korea was admitted as a member state the same day.[1] Summarized simply, the time gap between the two states' joining relates to the question, at that time, of whether the two states should join the UN as a single member state and if so, what the joint membership would mean for the future of the peninsula.

North Korea maintained that they should join the UN as one country with one joint seat. According to scholar Jie Dong, North Korea was concerned that separate membership and the resultant legitimization of each state at the international level would further entrench division.[2] In contrast, South Korea requested admission to the UN on January 19, 1949, as the legal government of the entire Korean Peninsula. South Korea's constitution, then as now, identifies the entire peninsula as the Republic of Korea, the official name of the government of South Korea.[3] Following South Korea's 1949 request to the UN, North Korea submitted an application contesting the South's submission.[4] The respective applications of North and South Korea were challenged by the United States and Soviet Union in their capacity as UN member states. Applications that followed during the Korean War were disqualified from the official UN agenda because of North Korea's invasion of South Korea. After the armistice that halted the Korean War in 1953, the United States and Soviet Union both rejected applications from "the other" Korean side. When the Soviets finally agreed to a policy of unilateral membership for each Korea in 1957, the United States rejected it. Then, under President Park Chung-hee, who held office from 1963 to 1979, South Korea proposed dual membership for the first time, as a route toward unification. By this time, North Korea's view of UN membership had changed, and they sought to join alone. The North Korean view at that time, under then-leader Kim Il-sung, set out a preferred order of requirements for how the Korean Peninsula would jointly join the UN:

(1) resolving the situation of the military confrontation between the South and the North to ease tensions, (2) establishing various joint cooperative enterprises and exchanges, (3) convening a large national conference composed of representatives from various political parties and social organizations, (4) forming

"a confederate republic of Goryeo" named after the Goryeo Dynasty, and (5) joining the UN under the single name of the Goryeo Confederated Republic.[5]

Many years followed during which neither Korea received official member status. During the 1970s and 1980s South Korea continued submissions for membership while North Korea, rather than applying for its own membership, sought to block those applications of the South.[6] According to Dong, North Korea saw South Korea's efforts to join the UN as a way to solidify the division of the peninsula. North Korea distrusted the UN—it saw the UN Command as responsible for much suffering during the Korean War, and for that reason didn't pursue its own admission with more rigor.[7]

With the reunification of Germany in 1990 and the collapse of the Soviet Bloc in 1991, relations between South Korea and these former states changed. North Korea began to reconsider its approach at the UN. According to Dong, China played an important role in persuading North Korea to request UN membership. Geopolitically, other changes were impacting South Korea and North Korea. China, internationally isolated, was undergoing internal struggles with the Tiananmen Square protests.[8] At the 46th UN General Assembly, on September 17, 1991, there were enough votes to admit North Korea as a member state. This was the same day of South Korea's admission.

The UN General Assembly and UN Security Council (UNSC) focus primarily on North Korean human rights issues and nuclear proliferation, respectively. In an effort to remedy these ongoing and seemingly intractable concerns, the UN has devised sanctions, technical exchanges, and cooperation through a variety of instruments. For example, the Panel of Experts operates through the United Nations Security Council and Universal Periodic Review operates through the United Nations Human Rights Council. In cases where member states raise concerns, the UN can gather a commission of experts to investigate allegations made about states. Galvanized by more than two decades of work by nongovernmental organizations (NGOs) based in South Korea and internationally, in 2013 the UN Human Rights Council assembled a commission to investigate allegations of crimes against humanity occurring within North Korea.[9] After a year of extensive research and investigation, the findings were published in a 2014 report. The Panel of Experts found that crimes against humanity were indeed taking place inside North Korea. North Korea has made only superficial changes to its human rights situation, mostly in the nature of submitting reports that accept the weakest, least costly recommendations. Notably, North Korea's nuclear proliferation and weapons of mass destruction (WMD) development continue to demand the greatest international attention, while the human rights situation continues without any improvement on the ground.

NORTH KOREA'S UNIQUE CHARACTERISTICS
AS A UN MEMBER STATE

Though UN membership grants legitimacy to states, it does not signify that a state always upholds and respects human rights as they are outlined in the United Nations Declaration of Human Rights. States such as North Korea that violate rights and engage in weapons proliferation are member states. Yet, even among those with an unfavorable reputation in this regard, North Korea is distinguished by its total absence of a civil society and free media. These two characteristics both strengthen the regime and weaken the effects of international pressure. Meanwhile, North Korea attempts to present the appearance of a civil society to the world, including recently through social media platforms such as YouTube. North Korea's efforts are stilted and obvious, particularly in comparison to more skilled states like China and Russia. Nevertheless, many states attempt to present as though they respect human rights when they do not.[10] North Korea also employs a tool used by other autocratic regimes: GONGOs, or Government Organized NGOs. North Korea, China, and Russia, among other autocratic states, employ GONGOs.[11] However, unlike China and Russia—which have some measure of a civil society—North Korea is the only state in the contemporary world with no known civil society. It is also the only state that has never had one. Without a civil society, the North Korean government has total control over what messages reach the international community and international bodies such as the UN from inside its borders—and vice versa.

North Korea also lacks free media. This is significant because free media acts as a check on government power, providing a means through which independent journalists can investigate and share insights critical of government power and whereby ordinary people can offer their views and gather insights from others in the public sphere. In North Korea, one cannot even keep a personal diary or speak candidly with a close friend if the content touches upon criticism of the government—such acts could land a person and their family in a political prison camp. North Korean people lack a safe venue for holding discourse on what kind of country governance they would like and thus lack knowledge on the inner worlds of their fellow citizens. The absence of civil society and free media has persisted since the country's founding. As such, one could argue that the North Korean regime has operated without input from its people since 1948.

North Koreans have never consumed free media made for them and by them. They have consumed Chinese, Japanese, South Korean, and other foreign media—albeit illegally—but nothing in which they see themselves represented by and for themselves. David Hawk, former executive director of Amnesty International and a former UN human rights official, writing in his 2021 report *Human Rights in the Democratic People's Republic of Korea: The Role of the United Nations*, states: "At the national, provincial, and local levels, there are *surely* numerous North Koreans who would very much like to curb the power of the internal security agencies and enlarge the sphere of fundamental rights, liberties, freedoms, and protections in the DPRK."[12] But because there are no genuine civil society organizations or free media within North Korea, we have never heard from these individuals while they remain inside the North. As Hawk elaborates, "even nations with terrible human rights records have in place elected and appointed officials who are tasked with addressing the human rights issues within their countries. These nation states have institutions designed to promote human rights through legal assistance, judges, prosecutors, and so on."[13] But there is no such thing in the North. Given these unique features of North Korea, the UN's task vis-a-vis the North is considerable and profoundly hindered.

Because North Korea has no domestic civil society, critique of North Korea's human rights can only reach North Korea's government representatives through the mechanisms and procedures of the United Nations, spurned by international civil society. All member states receive recommendations as to how they should improve human rights. The UN wields power on human rights issues through mechanisms such as: treaty bodies that review how states have implemented human rights conventions; Special Procedures that make use of thematic, for example LGBTQ+ or country-specific (North Korean), rapporteurs; and the UPR, which involves the periodic submission of reports from states demonstrating which recommendations they have adopted or rejected. Recommendations are also made via majority resolutions by voting UN member states at the UN General Assembly and Human Rights Council (HRC).

DECADES OF UN RECOMMENDATIONS

Since the 1970s, awareness at the UN and within the international community of North Korea's human rights violations has grown. Decades of recommendations related to access to food, medicine, and freedom of movement made to North Korea by UN officials, independent experts, and other member states "have been remarkably clear and consistent."[14] As the UN's Commission of Inquiry (COI) report noted in 2014, North Korea's human rights issues are "without parallel in the contemporary world." Pressure has increased, finally pushing North Korea into some, albeit limited, engagement.

Up until the publication of the COI Report in 2014, North Korea had refused to cooperate with the Universal Periodic Review. However, with the publication of the groundbreaking and condemning report, North Korea reversed that stance and began to respond to critique. The UN COI Report of 2014 was groundbreaking because it was the first time that North Korea's wide-sweeping and generational crimes against humanity were investigated. The investigation took one full year and involved work with more than 200 experts, survivors, and eyewitnesses. Although North Korea refused to participate with the UN COI investigation, the North's official representatives tried to finesse their state's public image through holding side events at the UN to present their side of the case. Pressured by the report, the North Korean government began to cooperate with the Universal Periodic Review, a key UN mechanism for monitoring human rights within applicable to all member states. To reach this stage took an enormous amount of work.

When a state ratifies a treaty, it agrees to the standards in the codified UN norm and is legally bound to protect those rights within its territory. This means that people can, in theory, expect those minimum standards from that state and that failure to uphold them will result in criticism and sanctions. Though these norms are a minimum standard of protection, many states still do not live up to them. UN mechanisms work, but they do so slowly and often only when there is great consensus. The most pressure on states tends to come when UN mechanisms are in concert with other instruments from the broader international community, such as investigative journalism and public campaigns. However, the UN is not a legal enforcer, and many states are feckless even when their failings are revealed and criticized. The UN has responded to such intransigence by endeavoring to pressure states through sanctions. Since the start of North Korea's nuclear and missile activity in 2006, the UNSC has adopted nine major sanctions resolutions on North Korea.[15] Sanctions take a range of forms, and more insights on these are available in the preceding chapter by scholar Justin Hastings on how sanctions have impacted North Korea.

When states ratify or cede to a treaty, they are obliged to submit periodic reports to the UN through the treaty bodies to demonstrate how they are meeting or attempting to meet the codified standards. These reports indicate what measures have been taken to implement rights related to particular conventions. The UN then makes recommendations on further measures that should be taken to bring the state into further compliance with the convention. North Korea's Universal Periodic Reports submitted to the UN Human Rights Council were inadequate.[16] According to Hawk, the UN remarked in particular on the paucity of information about *actual conditions* on the ground and expressed doubt about the veracity of claims made by North Korea in its report.[17] Hawk notes two distinguishing features of the first report: the absence of information on conditions inside North Korea, and the abundance of data on rights violations in South Korea. It was nearly two decades before

North Korea submitted an adequate report to the UN on its implementation of the International Covenant on Civil and Political Rights.

This pattern is endemic to North Korean state rhetoric: deflection, obfuscation, and whataboutism. It appears in North Korean state media, its outward facing international media, its side-event presentations at the UN, and its official documents submitted to the UN. After North Korea delivered its first report to the UN for review in 2009, it was clear that North Korea was incapable or unwilling to ameliorate the suffering of its people.[18] Throughout the 1990s, a preventable famine took place in the country, resulting in hundreds of thousands of deaths and leading many North Koreans to seek food outside their country, in China and elsewhere.[19] These refugees ended up, via China and other third countries, in South Korea and to a lesser extent in Japan. As they spoke about the famine, they also told stories about other conditions on the ground. A 1979 Amnesty International report had shed some light on North Korean political prison camps, but by the 2000s North Koreans who had left their homeland were sharing stories about reeducation centers, detention centers, public executions, and political prison camps.[20] The famine laid bare North Korea's rights violations. Political prison camp survivors began to organize in South Korea. One camp survivor, Kang Chol-hwan, worked with a French author to publish a memoir in French and then in English. The book, *Aquariums of Pyongyang: Ten Years in the North Korean Gulag* (2000), told the story of how generations of his family were thrown into the political prison camps and captured the attention of the international community.

Opting for more direct ways to improve the situation on the ground through the application of human rights norms, the UN decided to approach the matter through the UN's Human Rights Council and the General Assembly.[21] In 2003, the UN Human Rights Council singled out North Korea for its continual record of violating human rights by putting North Korea on a UN list of "gross violators" of human rights.

North Korea insisted it had no human rights problems. It also refused to cooperate with the UN to disprove the allegations of rights violations. It is not unheard of for states to deny that human rights violations are occurring—as I write this chapter, Russia's UN Ambassador Vasily Nebenzia sits at the UN Security Council repeatedly stating that the Russian bombing of Ukraine is a "special military operation" and not a matter of human rights.[22] It is rare, however, for states to entirely deny *any* violations at all or refuse to cooperate. Member states began to include North Korea's human rights situation in the UN HRC's yearly resolutions in 2003. In 2004, a Special Rapporteur (SR) on the situation of human rights in North Korea was appointed with the mandate of monitoring, raising awareness, facilitating global discussion, and taking action on the issue of North Korean human rights. The first SR, Vitit Muntarbhorn of Thailand, was appointed by the HRC (2004–2010).

Following his appointment, Marzuki Darusman of Indonesia was appointed (2010–2016); SR Darusman also served as one of the three Commissioners of Inquiry in 2013. Tomás Ojea Quintana of Argentina was appointed in 2016 and was succeeded by Elizabeth Salmon in 2022. None of these individuals have been invited to North Korea to monitor and observe human rights conditions on the ground. They have, however, visited South Korea and other countries to meet with North Korean refugees.

As mentioned, in 2014 the UN formed a COI to investigate allegations of crimes against humanity occurring inside North Korea. This decision came as the result of many decades of activism from civil society groups in South Korea and internationally, often in conjunction with North Korean refugee communities in those countries. Following a year of interviews with over two hundred North Korean refugees and experts, the Commission found that crimes against humanity were taking place in North Korea. Many of these oral testimonies are on the public record and can be viewed via the UN COI dedicated webpage.[23] The UN COI report identifies the earliest history of North Korea, from the Korean War to the present. North Korea was invited to participate in the investigation on several occasions, and Commissioners repeatedly sought access to the country—a norm for Commissions of Inquiry—but all Commission requests for participation and access were ignored. By ignoring the UN's invitations to participate with the inquiry, North Korea created a self-fulfilling prophecy when it came to the condemnation of the report. After its publication, North Korea accused the Commissioners of bias for not conducting an in-country investigation. As Michael Kirby, an international jurist, educator, former judge, and chairperson of the UN Commission of Inquiry on DPRK (2013–14), explains, the UN commissioners had said, "Let us come in, if any mistakes [in allegations] have been made we will acknowledge this. If not us, then let some other international trusted inspectors access the country."[24] But North Korea ignored the invitation out of a desire to undermine the findings. However, North Korea could not hide the wave of migration out of the country over the past thirty years. These waves of migration resulted in the eventual record of tens of thousands of oral and written testimonies by survivors of North Korea's rights violations, forming a growing basis of evidence against the regime.

North Korea countered the report's publication with its own human rights report and a slew of performative responses denouncing the Commission's findings, mostly online and via state media, with a familiar combination of obfuscation, deflection, and whataboutism. A detailed analysis of North Korea's denial campaign in the wake of the UN COI report can be found in Fahy's *Dying for Rights*.[25] North Korea submitted its human rights report to the UN on September 15, 2014, seven months after the COI report's publication. The *Report of the DPRK Association for Human Rights Studies* asserted that North Korea's history vis-à-vis "American Imperialism" was not a con-tributing factor for its current socioeconomic and geopolitical isolation.[26] The COI Commissioners had included—quite reasonably—the historic context for rights violations in North Korea: experiences of colonization, Korea's lib-eration from the Japanese, the early formation of the two Koreas, the Korean War, and the development of North Korea up to the present. The UN report therefore included punishment of colonial collaborators; prisoners of war and abductions, whether Japanese, Korean, or other nationalities; refoulement, or forced repatriation, from China and other countries; forced abortions in deten-tion facilities; torture-induced false confessions in political prison camps; and so on. It also identified China's role in thwarting North Koreans' access to refugee rights. North Korea's report, by contrast, is indifferent to the plight of its citizens and instead focuses on the criminality of enemy states (the United States, Japan, and South Korea), with an emphasis on US aggression during the Korean War. Wrongs committed against the state—namely, violations of state sovereignty—are erroneously highlighted as the primary human rights violation experienced by North Koreans.

At each stage, the UN has sought to bring North Korea's treatment of human rights into alignment with international norms through dialogue and accountability. While each stage added further pressure and contributed to a record of documentation, up until the 2014 COI report, little change had taken place. The period following the UN COI report can be classified as a slightly different type of engagement by North Korea at the UN, at least at the level of documentation and accountability. Minor changes occurred after the report was published. For example, North Korea invited the special rapporteur (SR) on the rights of persons with disabilities to visit North Korea on May 3–8, 2017. Ms. Catalina Devandas-Aguilar (Costa Rica), designated as the first to hold this position in June 2014, accepted the invitation from North Korea. Although her visit to North Korea did not grant her unlimited access to the country, she was nevertheless able to enter the country, and this alone was a considerable improvement to North Korea's previous engagement.

The greatest concern of North Korean state representatives is the fact that North Korean leader Kim Jong-un was recommended to the International Criminal Court (ICC) in 2014 for crimes against humanity taking place under his leadership. Evidence for Kim Jong-un's complicity in crimes against humanity were uncovered through the United Nation's Commission of Inquiry report of 2014. For allegations to reach the threshold of crimes against humanity, Commissioners had to find that violations were taking place on a widespread basis, causing widespread death and suffering, and, critically, occurring with the knowledge of the state. This final detail indicted Kim Jong-un and the regime's leadership. The UN COI recommended that steps be taken under international criminal law such as ensuring regime accountability for crimes against humanity, and the recommendation of the situation to the International Criminal Court.

Perhaps as a concession, North Korea began technical cooperation with the UN on human rights by submitting UPRs that accepted certain recommendations, rather than rejecting everything wholesale. North Korea's participation in the first (2008–11) and second (2012–15) UPR cycle shows that they consistently accept "weak" recommendations that are low-cost to the regime.[27] Analysis of North Korea's accepted and rejected recommendations could indicate areas where North Korea might be willing to improve. For example, Hawk points out that recommendations directly related to rights abuses were deemed "slanderous," while recommendations for more food production were supported.[28] At the current juncture, recommendations that they have accepted indicate that North Korea could engage with the UN on human rights mechanisms related to: ratification of additional human rights conventions; renewed cooperation with treaty committees for existing ratified conventions; and cooperation with thematic special rapporteurs—to their credit, North Korea did welcome an official visit from the SR for Disability Catalina Devandas-Aguilar to the country in May 2017.[29] During Devandas-Aguilar's visit, North Korea expressed its openness to inviting other thematic SRs in the future.[30] Further actions North Korea could take would include accepting more recommendations in future UPRs, inviting the UN High Commission for Human Rights to visit Pyongyang, the inclusion of a "rights-based approach" to development, and participation of North Korean representatives in training programs offered by the UN High Commission for Human Rights in Geneva as related to the UPR.[31]

NORTH KOREA'S POST-2014 UN ENGAGEMENT

In the years following the UN COI's 2014 publication, there was majority support among UN member states for the findings and recommendations, including the referral of the situation to the ICC. The UNSC voted in 2014 for the situation of human rights in North Korea to be on its "standing agenda."[32] As the member state under discussion, North Korea has the option to attend UNSC discussions, but has not done so. North Korean response to the human rights issue is motivated by the provision of recommendation of Kim Jong-un for referral to the ICC.

In 2014, North Korea's Foreign Minister Ri Su-yong was the first North Korean representative to attend the UN General Assembly. Ri also attended HRC sessions in 2015, 2016, and 2017. Ri addressed the UN General Assembly on September 27, 2014, calling the abuse of human rights issues for political purposes the biggest human rights violation of all. On September

15, a few weeks before Ri's address, the North sent a letter to the UN with its own 119-page human rights report attached. The document, written by North Korea's Association for Human Rights Studies, covered the earliest history of North Korea—from the foundation and ideology of the social system, through the Korean War, right up to the present.

North Korean state representatives threatened that unless the ICC-referral provision was removed, North Korea would expand its nuclear deterrent.[33] These threats were made at the Council on Foreign Relations in New York by North Korean Ambassador to the UN Jang Il-hun. They were made official in a letter from the North Korean Ministry of Foreign Affairs circulated to all Missions to the UN in New York. Ri again made this threat on the floor of the General Assembly in 2014. As Hawk writes, "It is inconceivable that co-sponsors of the resolution would have changed the language of a draft resolution in response to the threat of an action that was previously prohibited and condemned by multiple, unanimous Security Council resolutions."[34] To Hawk, this indicates how seriously the North Koreans took the findings of the UN COI. In my assessment, it shows how glib North Korea is in its concern for human rights. It further shows how easily North Korea blends the two major global security concerns of human rights and nuclear weapons.

In Marzuki Darusman's final report as the SR to the UN Human Rights Council in March 2016, he focused on increasing North Korea's accountability to the international community. Part of this recommendation involved the creation of an independent group of experts tasked with determining what further steps could be taken to build such accountability. The Group of Independent Experts on Accountability, pursuant to Human Rights Council Resolution 31/18 on the situation of human rights in the Democratic People's Republic of Korea, which included barrister Sara Hossain and former Commission of Inquiry member Sonja Biserko, sought to meet with North Korean representatives, but were unsuccessful. The Independent Experts produced a report in 2017 on the human rights situation in North Korea.[35] Critically, in this report they noted that North Korea had acceded to the Convention on the Non-Applicability of Statutory Limitations to War Crimes and Crimes Against Humanity in 1984. In this respect, they were able to outline an avenue of accountability for North Korea through the creation of an ad hoc international tribunal. This was important, given that the ICC referral has limited power due to the ICC having no jurisdiction over North Korea.

NORTH KOREAN STRATEGIES AT THE UN

It would be inaccurate to imagine that North Korea is unfamiliar with human rights theory, rhetoric, or norms. Indeed, North Korean state representatives are clearly schooled in international human rights norms, as demonstrated in the masterful way they leverage the delicate claims within rights language toward state ends. On September 15, 2014, North Korea wrote and submitted an assessment of their own human rights situation to the United Nations.[36] The report highlighted the existence of free speech and free press for citizens according to their Law on Protecting Intellectual Property Rights. The text also justified limitations on these rights under the "special duties and responsibilities" they command from the bearer, referring to Articles 19 and 20 of the UN International Covenant on Civil and Political Rights (ICCPR). Here North Korea operationalizes part of the ICCPR, which states that rights may "be subjected to certain restrictions." North Korea's report conveniently ignores the rest of this sentence: "these [restrictions] shall only be such as are provided by law and are necessary." North Korea picks and chooses what they are willing to adhere to by leveraging the second clause in Article 19: "[necessary] for the protection of national security or of public order." Article 20 also resonates with many authoritarian states, including North Korea: "Any propaganda for war shall be prohibited by law."[37] North Korea here interprets human rights as a mechanism of war propaganda.

To provide some elaboration on this feature of how North Korea interprets human rights rhetoric and practice, it is useful to look at some of the wider themes and historical approaches North Korea has taken to the phenomena of human rights. Political scientists Jiyoung Song and Robert Weatherly identified three main themes in North Korean human rights discourse across the country's history: rights are conditional (they must be earned, but only if you are the right type of person), collective rights supersede individual rights (the rights of the group are more important than individual rights), and welfare and subsistence rights have special importance. North Korea prioritizes collective rights and the interests of the family as the basic unit of society that enables the collective to function.[38]

Each of the three North Korean constitutions written after 1948 indicates the importance of collective principles over individualistic ones. The individual depends on the collective for their rights and can only have rights when the collective has them. Within this framework, it makes little sense for an individual to seek or demand their own rights, which could be seen as greedy, selfish, or as jeopardizing the collective interest. The notion of collective rights emphasizes national sovereignty. One of the fundamental arguments put forward by North Korea is that people cannot have human rights in a country that is not sovereign. Thus, no South Korean enjoys human rights because the country, according to North Korea, is a US colony.

The UN provides a convenient and legitimating forum through which North Korea can share its alternative interpretation of human rights through state representative speeches, side events, and through holding their submitted reports and documents online. North Korea, for its part, sees human rights as a matter of state sovereignty. If this sounds confusing, that is by design. North Korea views human rights as a private matter of domestic, private, concern. Criticism of the human rights situation in a foreign state is viewed as a matter of interference. Through its media and reports to the United Nations, North Korea shares these views. Some variation is offered between news for international and domestic consumption. In examining North Korean responses to the UN COI report both at the UN and in state media, the message is consistent and clear: North Korea has no human rights problems (best look at the United States) and is impervious to international efforts to force change through criticism. Close analysis shows that although North Korea claims to be impervious, it clearly has taken action in response to criticism—although possibly not to the betterment of rights. The international community might assume that North Korea categorically dismissed the UN COI. Indeed, North Korea has said as much. However, it has also gone much further. Just prior to and in the wake of the UN COI, North Korea was uncharacteristically outspoken on the topic of human rights, both domestically and internationally.

Prior to the publication of the UN COI report in 2014, an interactive dialogue—an informal private dialogue in order to enhance the participation—was held with COI members on September 17, 2013. At this meeting, Kirby stated that North Korea had been invited but declined to participate or cooperate with the Commission.[39] In the audience, North Korean representative Kim Yong-ho spoke from a prepared script, stating that North Korea "totally rejects" the oral update from the Commission because it was fabricated from "defectors and rivals" as part of a political plan to "sabotage our socialist system by defaming the dignified image of the DPRK . . . under the pretext of human rights violations."[40] Kim stated that the violations mentioned in the update "do not exist" in North Korea and claimed that the SR and UN commission were motivated by hostility. He concluded by saying that though the UN Commission would not result in any changes in North Korea, the country honors dialogue and cooperation on human rights.

Several months later, at another interactive dialogue with the Commission of Inquiry on March 17, 2014, North Korean representative So Se-pyong stated that his delegation "categorically rejects" the Commission because it was fabricated by the United States for "ill-minded political objectives." Based on the "fabricated stories" of "criminals," he claimed the report was "defective and unable to condemn" North Korea. So detailed the false documents used to support US-led wars in the Middle East and Balkans. Finally, he derided North Korea's referral to the ICC as a "desperate attempt to eliminate" their society. He asserted the North Korea's social system "protects human rights and fundamental freedoms both legally and in practice" and that North Korea will "faithfully fulfil its obligation in the international area of human rights." This is part of North Korea's international relations strategy. Representative So's response echoed the arguments employed by North Korea's state media: the lies used to justify the US war in Iraq and the "fabricated" testimony of defectors are often framed as discrediting the UN Commission of Inquiry's findings.[41]

Every four and a half years, all UN member states undergo a Universal Periodic Review of their human rights record that indicates what actions they have taken to improve the situation in their respective countries. After ignoring the process up until 2008, North Korea has engaged in three rounds of the UPR process in 2008–2011, 2012–2015, and most recently in 2019. North Korea's participation in the UPR represents a small, but not necessarily positive, change in their response to international rights norms.

In the first round of UPRs North Korea shocked the United Nations by rejecting all criticisms and accepting none of the recommendations proposed at the Human Rights Council. In its first review, North Korea received 167 recommendations and immediately rejected 50 of these recommendations, including many connected to civil, political rights and political prisons, on the basis that they were slanderous to the country. North Korea typically delays or fails to submit reports related to obligations (as they did with their first UPR). The North Korean state party report to the ICCPR was two years late (2004). Their submission to the Committee on Economic, Social and Cultural Rights was submitted ten years behind deadline.[42] Reporting obligations for other UN mechanisms are similarly delayed. The next—and, for North Korea, the third—UPR cycle took place in 2019.[43]

At a regular session of the Human Rights Council, North Korean state representative Y. Kim had the right of response as the concerned state representative. He addressed the panel, describing the claims as a political agenda. He quoted a Korean proverb that the panel should heed: "mind your own business."[44] During his allotted five minutes, the representative categorically rejected all allegations. He stated that the panel had nothing to do with human rights but rather was part of a political campaign aimed at eliminating North Korea. The speaker claimed that "even Western media" outlets had characterized the human rights report as not genuine and aimed at regime change. He further stated that the sponsors of the panel were "unqualified" to speak on issues related to its topic because they hailed from countries that had committed human rights violations. Here he referred to Japan's two year, non-permanent, elected seat (January 1, 2016) on the UNSC. North Korea interpreted Japan's presence in the UNSC as a historical and political contradiction, drawing upon Japan's historic crimes against the people of China and Korea during its occupation of those lands.

CONCLUSION

What is the impact of North Korea's human rights diplomacy at the UN? One of the goals of engagement with North Korea on its human rights violations is to generate change on the ground. Observers have yet to see improvement on the ground, by any minimum standard. However, North Korea is slowly moving in a positive direction in terms of rhetorical engagement on the subject of human rights, at least. North Korean responses to the international community, and to the UN, have evolved during the past decade under Kim Jong-un's leadership. They no longer always deny outright that rights violations exist (though they still deny doing this to a significant extent), and they have begun to acknowledge that domestic economic difficulties have impacted rights. There may be avenues through which the United Nations could engage North Korea to improve rights violations deemed related to economic difficulties. In my assessment, the biggest change since Kim Jong-un has taken office has been in terms of how North Korea responds to the international community. This can be seen in the increased rhetoric to the international community, both at the UN and via social media networks, on the topic of human rights (this is elaborated at length in Fahy 2019) and North Korea's continued testing of weapons delivery systems. In simple terms: North Korea talks a lot about rights but does little, and it spends elaborately on weapons delivery systems. The last two decades have seen greater global attention brought to these issues, resulting in increased pressure on North Korea.

Since North Korea's accession as a member state in 1991, the UN has played a role in maintaining technical exchange and relaying criticism between North Korea and the international community. However, advancements in these arenas have depended on the willingness to engage the North Korean state. For the majority of the North's time as a member state, it has participated little, often below a minimum standard of engagement. Still, the influence of UN instruments such as the Panel of Experts and the Universal Periodic Review on North Korea has improved at least at the level of engagement and dialogue. Current progress is indicated by the work of the Group of Independent Experts on Accountability, which has made recommendations such as "on-going consultation with such victims as are accessible; supporting relevant documentation by civil society groups, ensuring that such evidence gathering meet international norms and standards with regard to criminal procedure; and strengthening the ability of the Seoul Office of the UN High Commissioner for Human Rights to gather and preserve information."[45] While North Korea's involvement with the UN's human rights mechanisms has been slow and halting, continued engagement with North Korea has enabled the UN to develop and implement improved mechanisms such as the Group of Independent Experts to bring North Korea more into alignment with international human rights norms. Considering North Korea's engagement with the United Nations over the last three decades, it is possible to see some small improvements at least at the level of dialogue, reports, and country visits, which hopefully can be expanded and improved upon going forward.

NOTES

1. Robert King, "The Two Koreas Mark 30 Years of UN Membership: The Road to Membership," Korea Economic Institute, September 24, 2021, https://keia.org/the-peninsula/the-two-koreas-mark-30-years-of-un-membership-the-road-to-membership/.

2. Jie Dong, "North Korea's Changing Policy towards the United Nations," in *Korea and the World: New Frontiers in Korean Studies*, ed. Gregg A. Brazinsky (Lanham, MD: Rowman & Littlefield, 2019), 113.

3. Constitution of the Republic of Korea, https://www.law.go.kr/LSW/lsInfoP.do?lsiSeq=61603&viewCls=engLsInfoR&urlMode=engLsInfoR#0000.

4. Dong, "North Korea's Changing Policy Towards the United Nations," 113.

5. Dong, 113.

6. Dong, 111.

7. Dong, 111.

8. Dong, 111.

9. "Commission of Inquiry on Human Rights in the Democratic People's Republic of Korea," United Nations Human Right Council, https://www.ohchr.org/en/hr-bodies/hrc/co-idprk/commission-inquiryon-h-rin-dprk.

10. Sandra Fahy, *Dying for Rights: Putting North Korea's Human Rights Abuses on the Record* (New York: Columbia University Press, 2019).

11. Reza Hasmath, Timothy Hildebrandt, and Jennifer Hsu. "Conceptualizing Government-Organized Non-Governmental Organizations," *Journal of Civil Society* 15, no. 3 (July 2019): 267–84.

12. David Hawk, *Human Rights in the Democratic People's Republic of Korea: The Role of the United Nations* (Washington, DC: Committee on Human Rights in North Korea, 2021), 13.

13. Hawk, 13.

14. Hawk, 14.

15. "UN Security Council Resolutions on North Korea," Arms Control Association, January 2022, https://www.armscontrol.org/factsheets/UN-Security-Council-Resolutions-on-North-Korea.

16. "Universal Periodic Review—Democratic People's Republic of Korea," United Nations Human Rights Council, https://www.ohchr.org/en/hr-bodies/upr/kp-index.

17. Hawk, *Human Rights in the Democratic People's Republic of Korea*, 16.

18. Hawk, 16.

19. Sandra Fahy, *Marching through Suffering: Loss and Survival in North Korea* (New York: Columbia University Press, 2015).

20. Amnesty International, "Democratic People's Republic of Korea: Ali Lameda: A Personal Account of the Experience of a Prisoner of Conscience in the Democratic People's Republic of Korea," January 1, 1979, Index Number: ASA 24/002/1979, https://www.amnesty.org/en/documents/asa24/002/1979/en/.

21. Hawk, *Human Rights in the Democratic People's Republic of Korea*, 17.

22. "Russia Blocks UN Resolution Condemning Ukraine Invasion," Voice of America, February 25 2022, https://www.voanews.com/a/russia-blocks-un-resolution -condemning-ukraine-invasion/6460284.html.

23. "Report of the Commission of Inquiry on Human Rights in the Democratic People's Republic of Korea," United Nations Human Rights Council, https://www .ohchr.org/en/hrbodies/hrc/coidprk/pages/reportofthecommissionofinquirydprk.aspx.

24. Jed Lea-Henry, "Human Rights in North Korea—Looking Back on the Commission of Inquiry," *Korea Now* Podcast #21—Michael Kirby, August 30, 2018, https://www.jedleahenry.org/korea-now-podcast/2019/2/25/the-korea-now-podcast -21-michael-kirby-human-rights-in-north-korea-looking-back-on-the-commission-of -inquiry.

25. Fahy, *Dying for Rights*, 2019.

26. DPRK Association for Human Rights, *Report of the DPRK Association for Human Rights Studies*, DPRK Association for Human Rights, National Committee on Nort Korea, September 2014, https://www.ncnk.org/resources/publications/Report _of_the_DPRK_Association_for_Human_Rights_Studies.pdf.

27. Jonathan T. Chow, "North Korea's Participation in the Universal Periodic Review of Human Rights," *Australian Journal of International Affairs* 71, no. 2 (2017): 146–63.

28. Hawk, *Human Rights in the Democratic People's Republic of Korea*, 83–87.

29. Chow, "North Korea's Participation."

30. Catalina Devandas-Aguilar, "End of Mission Statement by the United Nations Special Rapporteur on the Rights of Persons with Disabilities," Taedonggang Diplomatic Club, Pyongyang, May 8, 2014.

31. Hawk, *Human Rights in the Democratic People's Republic of Korea*, 2.

32. "In Security Council, UN Officials Urge Renewed Engagement with DPR Korea on Human Rights," United Nations OHCHR, December 22, 2014, https://www.ohchr .org/en/stories/2014/12/security-council-un-officials-urge-renewed-engagement-dpr -korea-human-rights.

33. Hawk, *Human Rights in the Democratic People's Republic of Korea*, 79.

34. Hawk, 79.

35. "Group of Independent Experts on Accountability Pursuant to Human Rights Council Resolution 31/18 on the Situation of Human Rights in the Democratic People's Republic of Korea," United Nations OHCHR, https://www.ohchr.org/en/special -procedures/sr-dprk/group-independent-experts-accountability-pursuant-human -rights-council-resolution-3118-situation#:~:text=Click-,here,-to%20view%20an.

36. DPRK Association for Human Rights, *Report of the DPRK Association for Human Rights Studies*."

37. "No. 14668 Multilateral International Covenant on Civil and Political Rights, Adopted by the General Assembly of the United Nations on 19 December 1966," United Nations, United Nations Treaty Series, vol. 999, no. I-14668, https://treaties.un.org/doc/publication/unts/volume%20999/volume-999-i-14668-english.pdf.

38. Jiyoung Song, *Human Rights Discourse in North Korea: Post-colonial, Marxist and Confucian Perspectives* (New York: Routledge, 2014); Robert Weatherly and Song Jiyoung, "The Evolution of Human Rights Thinking in North Korea," *Journal of Communist Studies and Transition Politics* 24, no. 2 (June 2008): 272–96, https://doi.org/10.1080/13523270802003111.

39. Lea-Henry, "Michael Kirby—'Human Rights in North Korea.'"

40. Kim In Ryong, "Kim In Ryong (DPRK) on Human Rights—Press Conference (13 December 2016)," UN Web TV Video, 25:49, http://webtv.un.org/watch/kim-in-ryong-dprk-on-human-rights-press-conference-13-december-2016/5246257589001/?term=&lan=original. Note: North Korea's Representative Kim Yong-ho speaks at 00:17:39.

41. "ID Commission of Inquiry on DPRK—14th Meeting 24th Regular Session of Human Rights Council," UN Web TV, September 17, 2013, http://webtv.un.org/watch/id-commission-of-inquiry-on-dprk-14th-meeting-24th-regular-session-of-human-rights-council/2677214609001. Note: Kirby addresses the absence of North Korea in research at 1:26:15.

42. Ben Willis, "Scrutinizing North Korea's Record on Civil and Political Rights: The New ICCPR Reporting Cycle," *38 North*, September 2 2022, https://www.38north.org/2021/09/scrutinizing-north-koreas-record-on-civil-and-political-rights-the-new-iccpr-reporting-cycle/.

43. Willis.

44. Y. Kim, "North Korea on Human Rights, UN 150921," YouTube, September 21, 2015, https://www.youtube.com/watch?v=WpbXvlkwcnk.

45. Hawk, *Human Rights in the Democratic People's Republic of Korea*, 82

Chapter 11

North Korea's Track-II Knowledge Diplomacy

Kyung-Ae Park

After North Korean leader Kim Jong-un came to power in 2012, North Korea conducted four nuclear tests before Kim announced in November 2017 that the country had become a nuclear power. North Korea is undoubtedly a nuclear threshold country, if not a de facto nuclear power. Over the years, diplomacy between North Korea and the international community has focused on hard power issues involving North Korea's nuclear and missile capabilities. After North Korea conducted its fourth nuclear test in January 2016, the United States responded with a "maximum pressure" strategy, even signaling the possibility of launching a preventive military strike against North Korea. However, the tide began to turn in early 2018 when North Korea embarked on a charm offensive through a flurry of summit meetings. During an eighteen-month period, North Korea held twelve summit meetings with the leaders of major powers, including the United States, China, Russia, and South Korea. Summit diplomacy, however, suffered another turn of the tide after the failure of the Hanoi summit, and a breakthrough has yet to manifest. Since the initial eruption of the nuclear dispute in 2002, the pattern of ephemeral progress followed by severe setbacks in nuclear diplomacy has stubbornly persisted.

On the other hand, the Kim Jong-un regime has not shied away from Track-II unofficial interactions with the outside world, especially in efforts to enhance its knowledge diplomacy to build capacities by cultivating advanced ideas, partnerships, and relationships. This chapter explores Pyongyang's knowledge diplomacy under the Kim Jong-un regime, focusing on its cooperation in knowledge sharing initiatives with the Canada-DPRK Knowledge Partnership Program (KPP). The chapter examines Pyongyang's collaborative activities with the program in the last ten years. It also analyzes the driving forces behind and implications of North Korea's Track-II knowledge diplomacy.

NORTH KOREA'S TRACK-II KNOWLEDGE DIPLOMACY WITH THE KPP

The KPP is an academic exchange program with North Korea established in 2010 at the University of British Colombia (UBC). The KPP, which strives for human capacity building through knowledge sharing and knowledge diplomacy, was established with the belief that access to knowledge and education are universal human rights. The program emphasizes that educators are powerful agents for change, and that educational institutions possess inherent attractiveness and influence. The KPP also views knowledge sharing as a "high-culture" form of soft power and knowledge diplomacy as an important tool for soft power engagement. Working closely with North Korean academics and scholars is a unique aspect of the program. These individuals go on to transfer newly acquired knowledge to their students, most of whom will become the next generation of decision makers within the North Korean government and society.

North Korea has conducted knowledge diplomacy with the KPP since 2010 in a partnership that has spawned collaboration on many projects over the years. Together they launched a Visiting Scholar Program in 2011 as part of a long-term knowledge-sharing initiative. Through this program, North Korea has sent six professors annually for six-month periods of study at UBC. Participants have come from six major universities in North Korea: Kim Il-sung University, Kim Chaek University of Technology, University of National Economy, Wonsan Economic University, Pyongyang University of Foreign Studies, and Pyongyang University of Commerce. Scholars from the Academy of Forestry have also participated in the program. North Korean scholars have taken courses on business management, economics, finance, and international trade, as well as environment and forestry. In 2019, the KPP initiated a new Visiting Scholar Program for Joint Research at the suggestion of a North Korean partner. This program aims to increase the research capability of North Korean scholars and introduce them to innovative research conducted in the Western academic community. The program also aims to build a research network connecting the North Korean and North American academic communities.

In addition to the Visiting Scholar Program, North Korea has also partnered with the KPP to facilitate knowledge sharing through conferences, seminars, focused workshops, and field visits that gather international and

North Korean experts to participate in a productive exchange of ideas. The partnership first resulted in two international conferences in 2013 and 2014 in North Korea on Special Economic Zones (SEZs). These conferences brought together more than twenty foreign experts from the UN and nine different countries, as well as almost two hundred North Korean scholars and government officials.[1] Following the highly successful first conference, North Korea actively pursued a follow-up SEZ seminar with the KPP. In response, the KPP suggested visits by international conference participants to North Korea's newly announced SEZ sites before holding another conference, which North Korea enthusiastically accepted. These site visits in 2014 marked the first time that North Korea agreed to show SEZs throughout the country to a group of international experts. These conferences and the on-site visit were rare international events in North Korea, and as such, they garnered unprecedented media attention, with both local and international coverage. Many media outlets, including the Associated Press, *Financial Times*, *Kyodo News*, *Wall Street Journal*, Yonhap News Agency, and Xinhua News Agency published articles on the conferences. These articles were widely disseminated by other media outlets, including China Central Television, the *Globe and Mail*, and the *Washington Post*. The conferences also received unprecedented media coverage in Pyongyang, including in the *Rodong Sinmun* (Workers' Party newspaper) and *The Pyongyang Times*, as well as North Korea's state news agency, the Korean Central News Agency (KCNA). The Korean Central TV (KCTV) also reported on the conferences. The fact that all major North Korean news outlets reported on the two conferences strongly indicates Pyongyang's high level of enthusiasm regarding knowledge sharing on SEZs.

In 2016, North Korea again collaborated with the KPP to hold an international conference in Pyongyang on sustainable development. The conference brought together sixteen international delegates from the UN and eight countries across Asia, Europe, and North America. Also in attendance were 130 North Korean environmental experts, scholars, and government officials, as well as Pyongyang-based foreign diplomats. The conference fostered an active exchange of ideas and experiences on climate change adaptation, sustainable agriculture, and sustainable tourism, as well as forest, water, and waste management. This conference also received considerable international and local media coverage. In particular, a Xinhua News Agency article reporting on the conference appeared in over twenty Chinese media outlets.[2] To build on the conference theme of sustainable development, North Korea and the KPP organized two international workshops in 2017 on water and waste management, held at Mt. Paektu and in Pyongyang. *The Pyongyang Times* called the Paektu workshop "an important occasion in preventing pollution by sewage and solid waste in the development of the Samjiyon (Mt. Paektu) area and taking measures to conserve [*sic*] a healthy ecosystem."[3] North Korea's newly gained interest in Master of Business Administration (MBA) programs drove Pyongyang to seek further collaboration with the KPP in 2019. The KPP responded by holding a workshop in Pyongyang that examined the current landscape of MBA programs in North America and the opportunities and challenges of developing programs in North Korea. Pyongyang and the KPP also worked together in 2019 to launch the KPP Alumni Workshop and Field Trip Program in North Korea. The program is designed to allow KPP alumni to gain firsthand knowledge by engaging in active dialogue with experts in policy-making circles. The 2019 inaugural workshop was held at Mt. Chilbo, hosting KPP scholars and policy experts involved in Mt. Chilbo ecosystem conservation.

Another major collaboration between North Korea and the KPP involved holding study visits abroad and international workshops. The KPP and the North Korean government organized an economic study visit to Indonesia in 2015, holding workshops with Indonesian universities. Through these workshops, North Korean scholars and government officials interacted with Indonesian economic experts and administrators in active dialogue and gained firsthand knowledge of Indonesian SEZ management issues. The visit was extensively covered by both North and South Korean media, as well as Indonesian and North American news agencies. The *Pyongyang Times* credited the study visit with offering "a window of opportunity [for SEZ experts] to combine what they have learned at [KPP] conferences and training courses with practical experience."[4] Since 2015, the KPP and North Korea have focused their efforts on expanding the scope of knowledge sharing beyond the field of economics. In November 2015, they worked together in holding a week-long workshop on agriculture and livestock breeding in Switzerland, complete with field visits, in collaboration with the UN Institute for Training and Research (UNITAR). In 2018, North Korea actively collaborated with the KPP when the program hosted a twelve-member North Korean University presidents/vice presidents delegation comprised of representatives from six major universities, as well as officials from the Foreign Ministry and the Education Commission.[5] This historic visit marked an extremely rare occasion for a group of North Korean university presidents and vice presidents to visit a foreign university. The visit allowed North Korean educational stakeholders to engage with their Canadian counterparts, strengthening the foundations for deeper collaboration and partnership to advance the KPP's goal of knowledge sharing for constructive engagement with North Korean academic institutions. Many North American and South Korean news outlets covered this significant visit extensively. In particular, it represented the first time ever that South Korean media had interviewed North Korean university leaders. In a surprising move, North Korea responded positively to the KPP's initiative for the South Korean media to interview the delegation. The last study visit abroad before the COVID-19 pandemic took place in November 2018. The KPP organized an academic panel in China for the Annual Conference of the International Finance Forum (IFF), hosting prominent Chinese and North Korean speakers who shared their views on Sino–North Korean economic cooperation. North Korea, after some debate over the KPP's proposal, sent a delegation including a representative from Department 18 of the Presidium of the Supreme People's Assembly, which had existed for several years but remained unknown to outsiders. This visit marked the first time that North Korean economic experts participated in the IFF.

Since the inception of the partnership for knowledge sharing with the KPP, North Korea has cooperated enthusiastically, suggesting details and plans for implementation and actively seeking to expand the scope of cooperation. Pyongyang has also given considerable media attention to the outcome of the collaboration through its major media outlets, although the KPP has pursued a strategy of minimal media contact over the years. In addition, North Korea has shown its full support for KPP efforts to monitor the effectiveness and impact of its program by conducting follow-up evaluation meetings with program participants, leaders of participating universities, and senior government officials. These meetings were held in Pyongyang to ascertain participants' acquired abilities and future goals regarding the diffusion of received knowledge upon their return home. Since 2020, COVID-19 and the resultant strict travel restrictions have limited KPP program activities. Nevertheless, the collaboration between the KPP and North Korea has continued with a discussion of possible knowledge sharing through virtual methods, including virtual seminars and lectures for academics and experts in North Korea.

DRIVING FORCES OF PYONGYANG'S
TRACK-II KNOWLEDGE DIPLOMACY

Resuscitating the Economy by Building Powerful Human Capital

The two largest challenges North Korea has faced over the years are the protection of state survival by building a strong military and of regime survival by achieving solid economic performance. To overcome these dual challenges, in 2013 North Korean leader Kim Jong-un announced the *byungjin* policy (simultaneous development of North Korea's nuclear capability and economy), soon after assuming power in 2012. The rationale was that a credible nuclear deterrent would create a secure external environment and reduce defense spending, opening the way for more concentrated efforts to build the economy. In the following years, North Korea conducted several nuclear tests until Kim finally announced the completion of a state nuclear power in November 2017. Nuclear capabilities secured, Pyongyang's *byungjin* policy shifted toward a focus on resuscitating its economy to improve people's living standards. North Korea has tolerated the expansion of private economic activities to stimulate its economy, as reflected in the rapid increase of *jangmadang*, or privately owned markets. There were more than six hundred *jangmadang* before the COVID-19 period where local as well as foreign residents visited frequently. Some markets in Pyongyang even reserved parking spots for foreign diplomats. According to a survey of North Korean defectors living in South Korea, 70 percent were engaged in personal business in North Korea, and of these, 70–80 percent of their total income came from such informal sources.[6] The number of private businesses has also increased tremendously. As private business activities have increased, the number of cell phones, which are essential for conducting business transactions, also jumped to over six million, with around 18 percent of the population estimated to have mobile phones.[7] As a result of the expansion of private businesses, North Korea witnessed the emergence of a new middle-class, nouveau riche, known as *donju*.

North Korea's efforts to stimulate its economy also resulted in a construction boom, especially in the Pyongyang area. Since 2015, Pyongyang has been transformed with the construction of new, towering buildings and streets including Future Scientist Street and Ryomoung Street. With many new high-rise buildings, Pyongyang has become "Pyonghattan," as described by many foreign observers. Many welfare and entertainment facilities such as the Children's Hospital, the Women's Clinic, shopping centers, ski resorts, water parks, and horse-ride tracks were also built during this period. At the same time, many new restaurants opened to serve foreign foods such as pizza and sushi, which have become quite popular among North Koreans. In fact, in 2016 North Korea recorded an economic growth rate of 3.9 percent, the highest in seventeen years since 1999.[8] However, with ever-increasing international sanctions, recurring natural disasters, and COVID-19, the overall economy deteriorated in the following years, as shown by growth rates of -3.5 percent, -4.1 percent, 0.4 percent, and -4.5 percent in 2017, 2018, 2019, and 2020, respectively.[9] Under the 2020 COVID-19 lockdown, North Korea recorded its biggest contraction in twenty-three years since 1997 and is expected to record a growth rate of -1 percent by the end of 2021.[10]

In his endless struggle with North Korea's dire economy, Kim Jong-un has put much emphasis on human capital since coming into power, giving notable attention to quality of education and pushing for research and development. At the 2012 Supreme People's Assembly meeting, the first such meeting of Kim's regime, North Korea adopted a law for universal twelve-year compulsory education, which extended compulsory schooling from eleven to

twelve years, one of the highest in the world. Stressing that economic construction would be unthinkable without the rapid development of education,
North Korea fully implemented the law in 2017. At the Fourteenth National
Conference of Teachers held in 2019, Kim emphasized that those who had
studied abroad should be appointed as university faculty members, saying,
"They have to be placed in the university education field so that one can grow
ten talents who can nurture 100 talents."[11] Again, in his New Year's speech
in 2019, Kim called on educators "to improve the quality of training talented
personnel, who will shoulder the socio-economic development."[12] He stressed
that such improvements should be "in conformity with the world trend of
developing education and pedagogical requirements."[13] North Korea's long-
term goal is to gain spots for its universities on the world top-ranking university list. In this context, the importance of quality education for human capital
building fostered throughout the Kim Jong-un era undoubtedly drove North
Korea to make concerted efforts for consistent knowledge diplomacy with the
KPP to gain knowledge of the Western academic community.

North Korea has also pushed for the development of science and technology as strategic assets for a knowledge-based economy, regarding education as the "mother of science and technology." Pyongyang announced its
fourth five-year plan for the development of national science and technology in 2013 and opened the Science and Technology Complex in 2016 to
disseminate knowledge on research and development. According to Kim,
North Korea should develop new technologies and concentrate its efforts
"on research into core technologies of great practical and economic significance, so as to secure the leading force of economic growth."[14] At the April
2018 plenary session of the Seventh Party Central Committee, North Korea
set forth the strategic slogan "Let us make a leap forward through science
and guarantee our future through education!" The goal was to bring about a
revolutionary turn in scientific research and education. Over the years, North
Korea has increased investment in education, reflecting its position as "the
most important state affair" while suggesting that all state institutions become
sponsoring bodies for educational units. At the same time, several preferential
policies for educators, scientists, and experts were introduced under Kim.
In assigning newly built high-rise apartments, Pyongyang gave them a top
priority, built recreation centers exclusively for them, and granted special
privileges and favorable treatment in distributing food, arguing that they will
shoulder socioeconomic development in the future.

Likewise, education has received notable attention throughout the Kim
Jong-un era, as he has put much emphasis on human capacity building through education. North Korea's need to invest in human capital to
strengthen its economy, especially involving those who would study abroad,
facilitated its participation in the KPP, a human capacity-building program

focused on training talented human capital. North Korea has sent over fifty university professors to the KPP's Visiting Scholar Program, and more than 80 percent of these scholars hailed from the fields of business and economics. In addition, the rare visit of North Korean university leaders to UBC in 2018 for a KPP event reflected North Korea's concerted efforts toward knowledge diplomacy with the Western academic community.

Economic Development Strategy through Special Economic Zones (SEZs)

After the collapse of the socialist market, North Korea demonstrated an interest in developing its economy through the expanded use of SEZs. SEZs are distinct and separate economic areas generally segregated from the domestic economy. They often are markedly different from domestic economic regimes and may establish different laws and regulations. In China and Vietnam, SEZs were used in part as an experiment to gain experience with capitalism. Over time, the two countries gained sufficient understanding of and experience with the capitalist market to transfer elements of SEZ economic policies into their domestic economies. As such, SEZs represent laboratories for alternative economic policy experimentation. In North Korea, this initiative began with a few earlier SEZs, including the implementation of new administrative policies and foreign investment agreements in Rason SEZ in 2010 and continuing with the creation of Hwanggumpyong and Wihwado SEZs the following year.

In line with these new policy initiatives, North Korea and the KPP convened an international conference on SEZ development in Pyongyang in 2013. North Korea expressed a great deal of enthusiasm, fully supporting the conference and inviting participants from across the country. The conference took a broad-based approach to knowledge sharing on SEZs, highlighting best practices in SEZ development and operation as well as country-specific case studies, providing North Korea with a basis from which to begin planning the development of its SEZs.[15] During the conference, North Korean experts showed keen interest in many SEZ issues, including public-private partnership financing methods, especially Build-Operate-Transfer (BOT) and Build-Own-Operate (BOO), cooperation with international financial institutions, qualifications for receiving overseas development assistance, the rights and responsibilities of joint venture enterprises, land management methods, and tax laws, among others. They hoped to make SEZ development plans based on international practices and standards to attract the foreign investment essential for economic development through SEZ experimentation. After the conference, all presented papers were distributed to experts throughout the country who could not attend the conference so that they

could also benefit from sharing knowledge on SEZs. Following the conference, North Korea announced that it would establish thirteen new SEZs in
eight provinces with the goal of developing its local economy and promoting
economic exchange and cooperation with other countries. Since then, North
Korea has continued to revise SEZ-related laws and increase the number of
new SEZs. Today, North Korea has twenty-seven SEZs throughout the country and is eager to attract investment, especially in building infrastructure for
these SEZs, science and technology, and producing goods competitive in the
international market.[16] However, these plans are not progressing smoothly,
mainly due to international sanctions.

As noted earlier, North Korea's enthusiastic response to knowledge diplomacy initiatives, built on the great success of the first SEZ conference, persuaded the KPP to hold another SEZ seminar in 2014. North Korean experts
were eager to absorb cutting-edge knowledge and insights from the international participants. For the follow-up conference, Pyongyang organized
meetings with provincial leaders and field visits to all provinces in the country with SEZs in operation. The site visits were to provide the international
participants with localized observations so that they could present specific
feedback and guidance based on their observations of North Korean SEZs
and experiences in other SEZs around the world. The remarkable cooperation
from Pyongyang was driven by their efforts to revive the economy through
SEZ experimentation and to gain more knowledge of international market
operations and regulations. Conference participants revealed their particular
interests in legal measures and strategies to create a more favorable climate
for foreign investors and tax and land-lease incentives for potential investors.
North Korean participants found a special session on the BOT model particularly informative. The BOT model benefits the government in question,
as it makes use of private corporate investment, thus reducing the need for
government borrowing of large sums of money and expenditure on infrastructure. It helps improve the operational effectiveness of infrastructure projects
by allowing profit-oriented, experienced firms to take the lead in development. These infrastructure projects were attractive to North Korea, as these
firms are able to contribute to technology and skills transfer, as well as the
development of capital markets. North Korea's desire for a thorough understanding of international practices on SEZs is well reflected in the concluding
remarks by a North Korean authority at the conference, who articulated the
country's action plan for SEZs based on the issues discussed in both SEZ
conferences.[17] He included creating master zone plans in line with global
standards, sending North Korean delegations on field trips to other SEZs to
gain firsthand experience in successful zone development and management,
and establishing the education infrastructure for training the future experts
responsible for the country's SEZs. According to him, North Korea would

explore training programs with other countries to facilitate the development of its SEZs. He even called on the international experts and diplomats in attendance to share with their colleagues what is happening in North Korea, and to act as a bridge between the world and North Korea's SEZ program. He affirmed North Korea's need for membership in the Asian Development Bank and other financial institutions, asking for the international experts' help in assisting with and negotiating for North Korea's entry. Having pursued an economic development strategy tied to SEZs, North Korea is well aware that it must educate a generation of young people in market economics and allow them the global exposure necessary to understand, connect with, and monitor fluctuations and trends in the global economy. Along the same line, the 2019 MBA workshop held in Pyongyang also reflected the country's enthusiasm to obtain knowledge on international practices of conducting business and to prepare their students for international business and market operations.

Earning Hard Currency and Defying Sanctions through Tourism Development

Another driving force behind North Korea's knowledge diplomacy that led to its collaboration with the KPP is the country's need to earn hard currency and overcome international sanctions and pressure by developing its tourism industry. Tourism has received tremendous attention since Kim Jong-un took power. It is regarded as a measure to circumvent sanctions and a reliable source of revenue and foreign currency. UN sanctions prohibit bulk cash transfers from business activities, but do not directly ban tourism. It was reported in 2018 that North Korean tourism had generated revenues as much as $44 million annually, and that between 2014 and 2019, up until North Korea closed its borders in January 2020 due to COVID-19, the amount had increased by 400 percent.[18] In 2019 alone, Chinese tourists were estimated to have brought $175 million into the country.[19] Hard currency earning through tourism is vital for North Korea considering the great economic pressure from UN and US sanctions since 2014, and thus, the tourism industry has become a key area in the North Korean economy.

Over the years, North Korea has developed several tourism projects and introduced new tourist attractions such as the Pyongyang marathon and concerts. Such projects include the Wonsan-Kalma Coastal Tourist Zone, Masikryong ski resort, the Mt. Paektu development of Samjiyon and the Mubong tourism zone, and the Yangdok Hot Springs zone, among others. In 2019, Pyongyang planned to target medical tourism and link it to leisure tourism, establishing the Treatment Tourism Exchange Corporation and health clinics in its tourism facilities.[20] North Korea's efforts in the tourism industry attracted many tourists, especially from China and Europe, to the degree that it became difficult to find seats on flights and trains from Beijing to Pyongyang or rooms in hotels, causing a severe strain on North Korea's tourism infrastructure. In 2018, the number of tourists jumped to two hundred thousand, while at least three hundred fifty thousand Chinese entered the country the following year in 2019.[21] The tourism boom is expected to resume once the COVID-19 pandemic ends. Moreover, progress in inter-Korean relations and a resumption of tourism at Mt. Kumgang, which received almost two million South Korean visitors between 1998 and 2008 when tourism was halted, could constitute a major stepping-stone for the North Korean tourism industry.

North Korea's most ambitious flagship tourism project is the Wonsan-Kalma Coastal Tourist Zone development, which began construction in 2012 soon after Kim Jong-un assumed power. Upon multiple visits to the site to encourage progress, Kim stressed that the zone would be key in defying international sanctions by demonstrating that North Korea could build its economy in spite of international pressure. After the opening date was delayed several times, the project was finally slated to finish in April 2020 by Kim Il-sung's birthday. However, the project still remains under development. The successful completion of the site would have significant implications for North Korea's self-reliant economic development strategy amid a hostile external environment of sanctions and the COVID-19 pandemic. One of the main political slogans of North Korea's "new path" for 2020 was making "head-on breakthroughs," which Kim declared at the Fifth Plenary Meeting of the Seventh Party Central Committee held at the end of December 2019. He called for an offensive approach to making head-on breakthroughs politically, diplomatically, and militarily, while describing the economy as the key front in the offensive.[22] Kim perceived the current US–North Korea confrontation as a clear stand-off between sanctions and self-reliance and emphasized that North Korea should make a breakthrough head-on through the power of self-reliance: "In other words, we should never dream that the US and other hostile forces will leave us to live in peace. Rather, we must make a breakthrough head-on through the strength of self-reliance."[23] The tourism projects received much attention, as they are closely linked to Kim's emphasis on making head-on breakthroughs based on self-reliance.

Against the backdrop of strengthening its tourism industry, North Korea enthusiastically participated in the KPP's 2015 study visit to Indonesia held in Jakarta and Bali for seminars on SEZs and tourism. North Korea has shown great interest in issues relating to ecotourism, cultural tourism, hotel management, the role of SEZs in the success of the tourism industry, infrastructure financing, and the role of universities in enhancing tourism training and providing skills to the local industry. Participants also held an interest in how different types of tourism worked in Bali, from mass tourism with large numbers and smaller revenues to high-end, sustainable ecotourism that could bring in higher revenues. The North Korean delegation was also eager to examine the impact of tourism on the environment, the role of Balinese culture in the success of the tourism industry, and the types of incentives or preferential treatment provided to foreign investors in tourism. In addition, tourist-related regulations, including whether tourists can stay at private homes in addition to hotels, stimulated participant interest, as North Korea has allowed several homestay programs to host tourists, including the program at Mt. Chilbo. The delegation also wanted to examine the allocation of responsibility across various levels of government, inquiring about who undertakes land use planning, and about how decisions are coordinated among the central government Tourism Ministry, the provincial government Tourism Council, and local governments and village leaders. Given that North Korea has set up several economic development zones for tourism under the supervision of provincial governments, the level of government undertaking strategic planning for the tourist industry was an important issue for the participants. In addition, realizing that development and education of human capital relate closely to tourism, much attention was given to the establishment of a university by an Indonesian SEZ. In fact, North Korea opened the Pyongyang Tourism College in 2015 for training tourism experts. These issues eagerly raised by the delegation reveal that North Korea's economic development efforts centered around tourism, which is regarded as a reliable source of foreign currency and means to combat international pressure and sanctions. After the study visit, the delegation mentioned to the author that many aspects of their observations in Bali applied to the Wonsan-Kalma zone development plan and other tourism projects. The panel on sustainable tourism at the 2016 sustainable development conference held in Pyongyang also emerged from their strong interest in tourism industry development. North Korea will likely continue knowledge diplomacy in the tourism area to learn from the experiences of other countries and obtain new approaches to the tourism industry.

Efforts to Overcome Food Shortages and Malnutrition

North Korea is a very mountainous country, with 80 percent of its land composed of mountains and uplands and only about 17 percent arable land. Combined with an unfavorable climate and poor soil quality, North Korea's endeavors for self-sufficient food production have faced constant challenges, leading to chronic food shortages and a serious malnutrition problem. In its 2020 Humanitarian Situation Report, UNICEF reported that "more than ten million people are considered food insecure and an estimated 140,000 children under five suffer from acute malnutrition."[24] To cope with chronic food insecurity and malnutrition, North Korea initiated a "Let's Turn the Grass into

Meat" campaign and began in 2012 to expand livestock farms in the Sepo area of Kangwon Province. In a January 2015 speech, Kim Jong-un urged the development of animal husbandry to produce large amounts of good-quality protein, including meat and eggs, while also "solving the problem of procuring animal feed rich in protein."[25] To improve soil quality and create pastures, Kim urged his country to "adopt the good experiences other countries have gained in cultivating pastures" and to conduct with foreign countries "brisk scientific and technological exchanges" so that North Korea could import "domestic animals of superior breeds and raise them after going through the stage of performance testing."[26] From the very beginning of the Sepo Zone development, it was emphasized that North Korean experts should "keep abreast of world trends in stockbreeding development" to introduce scientific knowledge and skills.[27] In October 2017, efforts in developing animal husbandry led to the opening of the Sepo Stockbreeding Zone, which according to then Premier Pak Pong-chu, "will be greatly helpful to the improvement of the people's standard of living."[28]

In this vein, there was a critical need to build capacity in agricultural processes and livestock breeding, which drove North Korea to engage in knowledge diplomacy in these fields. North Korea enthusiastically cooperated with the KPP in planning a 2015 study visit to Switzerland, which included workshops and field visits on sustainable agriculture and livestock breeding, including of dairy animals. North Korea's Ministry of Agriculture joined the visit to obtain advanced knowledge and glean the experiences of other countries. In addition, training in agricultural productivity and sustainable food systems was essential for North Korea to achieve the goals set forth in the 2030 Agenda for Sustainable Development adopted by the UN General Assembly in September 2015. In light of the global priority of sustainable development, the Agenda outlined clear goals and indicators for sustainable development worldwide, including a goal for sustainable agriculture and food production. Goal 2 of the Agenda articulates an intention to end hunger, achieve food security and improved nutrition, and promote sustainable agriculture. North Korea also stated that it highly prioritized agriculture and food self-sufficiency in its 2021 Voluntary National Review (VNR) on the 2030 Agenda submitted to the UN Economic and Social Commission for Asia and the Pacific.[29] The Switzerland study visit was a timely opportunity for North Korea to obtain substantive insights into the best practices in sustainable organic agriculture and livestock breeding developed by Swiss researchers and producers. During the visit, the cross-cutting issues of climate change and the environment and their impact on agriculture and food security were of great interest to the North Korean delegation members. In addition, workshops on pasture creation and management issues applicable to the Sepo Zone, the selection of feed-grass seeds suitable to the zone's climate, and the creation of windbreakers on grasslands were of particular importance in the North Korean context. Field visits to laboratories, farms, and research centers allowed participants to gain a better understanding of and further enquire into practices and technologies used in Switzerland's agricultural and veterinary industries. North Korea's knowledge diplomacy in this area was facilitated by its need to cooperate with the global community to achieve food security and nutritional improvement.

Achieving Sustainable Development Goals

In line with collective global efforts toward the Millennium Development Goals (MDGs) and the successor Sustainable Development Goals (SDGs) in the economic, social, and environmental sectors, the Kim regime has been moving to a more sustainable model of development. For the 2017–2021 period, North Korea developed with the UN the new UN Strategic Framework, incorporating the global SDGs into its national goals. Expressing its full support of the 2030 Agenda, North Korea has set up a National Task Force (NTF) to implement the agenda with priorities placed on 17 goals, 95 targets, and 132 indicators. According to North Korea, its SDGs aim to consolidate its economy "by upholding the line of prioritizing science and education."[30] It also emphasized strengthening collaboration with the international community to achieve the SDGs.[31] In the environmental sector, North Korea admitted that one of the biggest challenges in environmental education was that "professional knowledge of academics and others is not keeping pace with global best practices," which "necessitates capacity-building by academics and other experts."[32] In this context, North Korea and the KPP worked together to hold the 2016 international conference in Pyongyang on sustainable development. The conference provided an important capacity-building opportunity for North Korean experts in the areas of climate change, forestry, water, waste, agriculture, and tourism. North Korean scholars found the knowledge gained at the conference indispensable in devising evaluation methods of sustainability, especially in the areas of air pollution, water crisis and disaster management, and forest ecosystems. Learning from the environmental experiences of other countries proved highly valuable and the North Korean participants suggested several follow-up knowledge-sharing activities. These activities included joint research and publications, workshops for major conference themes, study visits abroad to sustainably managed sites, and academic training at foreign universities. In response to North Korean requests, the KPP and North Korea again engaged in knowledge diplomacy for follow-up activities in the ensuing years, including the publication of conference papers and additional workshops. A publication plan for selected papers presented at the sustainable development conference generated strong enthusiasm, leading to an agreement with the Kim Il-sung University Press to publish a book. Unfortunately, however, sanction measures prevented publication of international scholars' research papers in North Korea.

Despite this setback, plans for an additional workshop the following year on water and waste management forged ahead. One of Kim Jong-un's signature development projects is the reconstruction of Samjiyon, located at the foot of Mt. Paektu. The Samjiyon area is regarded as a sacred place where Kim Il-sung staged anti-Japanese guerrilla warfare during the Japanese colonial rule and the birthplace of Kim Jong-il. With three-stage development plans started in 2013, the reconstruction of the city was declared complete in December 2019, featuring new apartments, hotels, a ski resort, and commercial, cultural, and medical facilities.[33] In October 2021, North Korea announced the building of one thousand more houses in the city. With the development plan under way, North Korea and the KPP held an international workshop in Samjiyon to share knowledge on the environmental protection of Mt. Paektu. The focus was to address measures for preventing pollution caused by sewage and solid waste and maintaining a healthy ecosystem in the development of the Samjiyon area. According to the VNR on the SDG goals, North Korea assigns top priority to the effective use of water resources and the improvement of water quality to ensure safe drinking water on a sustainable basis. North Korea acknowledged that industrial and household wastewater were released into rivers and drained into soil without full treatment, causing water pollution.[34] The workshop analyzed wastewater disposal treatment technology to improve water quality in the development of the Samjiyon area. An additional workshop held in Pyongyang focused on waste treatment technologies and the recycling industry, addressing environmental pollution caused by solid waste. North Korea has vigorously pushed ahead in the reuse and recycling of industrial and household wastes such as wastepaper, wood, and plastics, adopting recycling laws including the most recent "Law on Recycling in the DPRK" enacted in 2020. The recycling campaign has gained more importance during the COVID-19 pandemic as North Korea has tightly closed its border and blocked all imports. Furthermore, economic incentives continue to drive the government to enforce the campaign. The import of plastic goods and rubber totaled $338 million in 2019, accounting for 12.5 percent of total imports and surpassing the country's total exports of $308 million that year.[35] The continuing recycling push could save Pyongyang much needed hard currency reserves. However, the national recycling rate remains inadequate, and Pyongyang acknowledged that it is necessary to "exchange with other countries on experiences, technologies, and methods related to waste listing, surveying, and recycling."[36] In this context, the workshop provided an opportunity for North Korean experts to broaden their perspectives and learn from the experiences of other countries through knowledge shared by foreign speakers, particularly on the issues of circular economies and preferential treatment for recycling industries.

Another important example of follow-up cooperation for knowledge sharing occurred in the area of sustainable forestry management. North Korea has long suffered from a high level of deforestation caused by the clearing of forests for planting crops or obtaining wood for fuel. North Korea's forest cover has declined by 12 percent between 1990 and 2018, and the country faces major ecological challenges yearly, including floods and landslides, which further exacerbate food and energy shortages.[37] These challenges necessitate forest recovery, and led Kim Jong-un to declare a "war against deforestation" in late 2015. The North Korean Workers' Party even declared forest restoration "a matter of crucial importance vital to [the] existence of the State and the people."[38] The reforestation campaign has urged a "patriotic mind" to "transform all the mountains of the fatherland into mountains of gold and treasure, lush with green forests."[39] Kim's reforestation efforts brought notable success and gained international attention by decreasing non-forest land area from 10.6 percent in 2010 to 5.5 percent in 2019; Pyongyang has forged ahead with plans to afforest about 1.4 million hectares of mountain by 2024.[40] To effectively address one of the most important policy issues of the Kim regime, North Korea set up the National Forestation Strategy (2015–2044) and sought expanded international cooperation to join the global fight against deforestation. Given the national priority on forestry, the Kim Il-sung University created a new College of Forest Science in April 2017. Upon its establishment, the University and the KPP engaged in knowledge diplomacy and began active cooperation to train scholars of the new college through the KPP Visiting Scholar Program. These efforts resulted in the visits of nine North Korean experts to UBC for six-month programs of study in 2018 and 2019. In addition, in 2019 the two sides conducted a workshop and field visit to Mt. Chilbo, which was designated in 2014 for inclusion in the World Network of Biosphere Reserves, along with four other mountains: Paektu, Kuwol, Myohyang, and Kumgang. Over the years, North Korea has sought to increase the acreage of biosphere reserve areas. The workshop assessed Mt. Chilbo biosphere reserve's forest management information system, and scholars and policy experts exchanged their academic and practical perspectives. Pyongyang has also attempted to transform forests by introducing tree species that produce various raw materials with high economic value, including fiber, pulp, oil, wild fruits, and medical herbs. In the field of forest management, North Korea has actively sought to advance knowledge, especially in biodiversity, the economics of forests, and the prevention of massive insect outbreaks.

IMPLICATIONS OF NORTH KOREA'S
TRACK-II KNOWLEDGE DIPLOMACY

For a decade, North Korea has conducted Track-II knowledge diplomacy under the Kim Jong-un regime and continuously cooperated with the KPP by sending scholars and policy experts for university education, international seminars and workshops, and study visits abroad. North Korea's pursuit of academic cooperation is deeply rooted in its quest for new and advanced knowledge in areas closely linked to major domestic policy initiatives under Kim. North Korean participation in knowledge sharing initiatives rests on rational calculations that such programs serve to practically benefit policies pursued by the government. In particular, Pyongyang was motivated to engage in knowledge diplomacy to: sustainably and durably boost its economy, especially through SEZs; earn hard currency and defy sanctions through tourism development; overcome food shortages and chronic malnutrition; and achieve sustainable development, especially in the areas of environment and forestry. Pyongyang did not hesitate to reach out to the international community to understand global standards and best international practices, taking great interest in expanding international cooperation at the Track-II level. During the pandemic, North Korea has stressed regaining government control over the economy by repressing market activities and renewing ideological education to root out foreign culture and "capitalist tendencies." It is debatable whether this policy shift from previous years represents a tactical retreat due to COVID-19 or more of a fundamental strategic reorientation of Kim's economic policy. Nevertheless, North Korea's search for advanced knowledge for Kim's ambitious flagship policies discussed above will likely continue in the post-COVID period. Prioritizing a knowledge-based economy, North Korea will continue to push for the capacity building of human capital unless it chooses to pursue a policy of complete autarky. In dealing with difficult domestic policy imperatives in the development of tourism, agriculture, and sustainability, North Korea is well aware of the pivotal role of advanced knowledge. North Korea has in fact continued to reach out to foreign partners during the pandemic with the expectation that it would not undo the knowledge exchanges it had built up during previous years. Its knowledge diplomacy will likely resume in due course.

Knowledge diplomacy constructed through academic dialogue has certainly impacted North Korea through the dissemination of cutting-edge knowledge to its scholars and experts. Over the years, KPP scholars have unanimously credited their KPP experience with greatly broadening their academic horizons, helping them better understand the current landscape of their fields of study, and thus having a far-reaching impact on their teaching, research, and policy advising to the North Korean government. Their newly gained expertise and valuable knowledge diffuses beyond the academic context into the policy-making realm, fostering development in domains beyond education. This ripple effect will benefit generations of North Koreans, including future academic leaders and policy makers.

The impact of knowledge diplomacy goes well beyond simply sharing innovative ideas and global knowledge. It also presents a unique channel for cross-cultural communication, builds mutual understanding among institutions across national boundaries, and in turn develops durable relationships based on trust, confidence, and patience. By inviting North Korean scholars to interact with their North American counterparts, the KPP has opened a rare window for both sides to obtain a deeper understanding of the other and strengthen the foundation for further mutuality and trust. Such engagement can contribute a great deal to confidence building, which can in turn facilitate constructive engagement between states locked in conflict and even play a significant role in eliminating such conflict. For North Korea, a state with a long history of entrenched conflicts with other states, Track-II knowledge exchanges can present an alternative route to conflict de-escalation and reconciliation.

Knowledge diplomacy also has important implications for peacebuilding beyond the realm of hard power. According to Krause and Oliver, peacebuilding "implies something more positive and dynamic than simply creating stability . . . and revolves around notions of capacity-building, good governance, inclusion, economic opportunity and individual well-being."[41] Likewise, the understanding of peacebuilding actors has evolved from a limited view of state actors in "high politics" to a more inclusive understanding involving "low politics" actors who build cooperative relationships through Track-II contacts.[42] Strategic peacebuilding encourages and supports capacity building, which knowledge diplomacy ultimately aims to promote, especially at the Track-II level. Capacity building through knowledge sharing serves as a vital instrument of foreign policy and tool of engagement, which could lead to conflict prevention and peacebuilding. For a global issue such as sustainability that defies territorial boundaries, the international community does not have the luxury to choose its cooperative partners. Even isolated North Korea is a key stakeholder in solving global challenges, and it has sought to join in global cooperation efforts through knowledge diplomacy. It is therefore of the utmost importance for the international community to encourage and support North Korea's Track-II knowledge diplomacy so that it may continue into the future.

NOTES

1. Also in attendance were foreign diplomats stationed in Pyongyang from China, Germany, Great Britain, India, Indonesia, Iran, Malaysia, Mongolia, Russia, Sweden, Switzerland, and Vietnam, as well as representatives from the European Union and the UN Development Program.

2. These outlets include CCTV, Beijing TV, Southeast TV, *People's Daily*, China News Service, *China Youth Daily*, *Shangluo Ribao*, *Wuijing Ribao*, *Luoyang Daily*, *Xianning Daily*, China Radio International, Phoenix New Media, and others.

3. "Workshop Contributes to Protecting Environment of Mt. Paektu Area," *Pyongyang Times*, August 3, 2017.

4. "SEZ Experts Visit Indonesian Economic Zones," *Pyongyang Times*, June 20, 2015.

5. University leaders came from Kim Il-sung University, Kim Chaek University of Technology, Pyongyang University of Foreign Studies, University of National Economy, Wonsan University of Economy, and Pyongyang University of Commerce.

6. Philo Kim, "Recent Social Changes in North Korea: Based on North Korean Refugees Survey," *Bukhan Yeonku Hakhoebo* [*North Korean Studies Review*] 18, no. 2 (2014): 153.

7. "18 Percent of North Koreans Now Thought to Own Mobile Phones," *Korea JoongAng Daily*, August 11, 2020.

8. "Gross Domestic Product Estimates for North Korea in 2020," Bank of Korea, July 30, 2021, 1, file:///C:/Users/Kyung%20Ae%20Park/Downloads/GDP_of_North_Korea_in_2020_F.pdf.

9. "Gross Domestic Product Estimates for North Korea in 2020," 1.

10. "North Korea GDP Annual Growth Rate," Trading Economics, https://tradingeconomics.com/north-korea/gdp-annual-growth-rate#:~:text=GDP%20Annual%20Growth%20Rate%20in%20North%20Korea%20is%20expected%20to,macro%20models%20and%20analysts%20expectations.

11. Dagyum Ji, "North Korean Education still 'Lags Far Behind' Global Trends, Kim Jong Un Says," *North Korea News*, September 3, 2019.

12. Kim Jong-un, "Kim Jong-un's 2019 New Year Address," January 1, 2019, https://www.ncnk.org/resources/publications/kimjongun_2019_newyearaddress.pdf/file_view.

13. Kim Jong-un.

14. Kim Jong-un.

15. The conference explored fundamental characteristics of zone planning, SEZ management and governance, SEZ and investment and the domestic economy, and SEZ evolution. International speakers examined both general trends and case studies in other countries including China, India, Indonesia, Malaysia, Myanmar, Singapore, and Vietnam.

16. This presentation was made by the North Korean delegation at the KPP panel, "China-DPRK Economic Cooperation Dialogue," Annual Conference of the International Finance Forum, Guangzou, China, November 25, 2018.

17. Concluding remarks by a participant from the Korea Economic Development Association, International Conference on "SEZs in the DPRK," Pyongyang, North Korea, May 2, 2014, Notes taken by the author.

18. Alberto Ballesteros, "The Pandemic and North Korea's Tourism Industry: Another Shock for the Regime," *38 North*, April 8, 2021, https://www.38north .org/2021/04/the-pandemic-and-north-koreas-tourism-industry-another-shock-for-the -regime/.

19. Chad O'Carroll, "As Chinese Tourism to North Korea Soars, Local Operators Feel the Strain," *North Korea News*, October 31, 2019, https://www.nknews.org/2019 /10/as-chinese-tourism-to-north-korea-soars-local-operators-feel-the-strain/.

20. "North Korea Plans to Target Visitors from China for Medical Tourism," *Japan Times*, December 7, 2019, https://www.japantimes.co.jp/news/2019/12/07/asia -pacific/north-korea-plans-target-visitors-china-medical-tourism/.

21. Ballesteros, "The Pandemic."

22. National Committee on North Korea, *Report of the Fifth Plenary Meeting of the 7th Central Committee of the WPK*, January 1, 2020, https://www.ncnk.org/resources /publications/kju_2020_new_years_plenum_report.pdf/file_view.

23. National Committee on North Korea.

24. "DPRK Humanitarian Situation Report, End of Year 2020," UNICEF, February 20, 2021, 2, https://www.unicef.org/media/93821/file/DPRK-End-Year-SitRep -2020.pdf.

25. "Guidelines Set Forth to Develop Nation's Animal Husbandry," *Pyongyang Times*, February 3, 2015, http://www.pyongyangtimes.com.kp/?bbs=19797.

26. "Guidelines Set Forth."

27. "Guidelines Set Forth."

28. "Sepo Stockbreeding Zone Opened," North Korea Leadership Watch, October 3, 2017, http://www.nkleadershipwatch.org/.

29. *DPRK Voluntary National Review on the Implementation of the 2030 Agenda for Sustainable Development* (Pyongyang: Government of the DPRK, June 2021), 15, https://sustainabledevelopment.un.org/content/documents/282482021_VNR_Report _DPRK.pdf.

30. *DPRK Voluntary National Review*, 5.

31. *DPRK Voluntary National Review*, 50.

32. *DPRK Environment and Climate Change Outlook* (Pyongyang: DPRK Ministry of Land and Environment Protection, 2012), 98, https://wedocs.unep.org/ bitstream/handle/20.500.11822/9679/-Environment_and_Climate_Change_Outlook -2012ECCO_DPRK_2012.pdf.pdf?sequence=3&amp%3BisAllowed.

33. "North Korea's Kim Jong-un Opens New City and 'Socialist Utopia' of Samjiyon," *The Guardian*, December 3, 2019, https://www.theguardian.com/world/2019 /dec/03/north-koreas-kim-jong-un-opens-new-city-and-socialist-utopia-of-samjiyon.

34. *DPRK Voluntary National Review*, 25.

35. Martyn Williams, "Turning Waste into Treasure: North Korea's Recycling Push," *38 North*, June 15, 2021, https://www.38north.org/2021/06/turning -waste-into-treasure-north-koreas-recycling-push/#:~:text=North%20Korea%20is %20undergoing%20something,than%20bottles%2C%20cans%20and%20paper.

36. *DPRK Voluntary National Review*, 39.

37. "State of the Climate in Asia 2020, No. 1273," World Meteorological Organization (WMO), 2021, 29, https://library.wmo.int/index.php?lvl=notice_display&id =21977#.YXxJEZ7MJPY.

38. Benjamin R. Young, "How North Korea Has Waged 'a War to Improve Nature,'" *NK News*, June 2, 2021, https://www.nknews.org/2021/06/how-north-korea -has-waged-a-war-to-improve-nature/.

39. Andrea Valentino, "Widespread Deforestation Threatens to Leave North Korea Buried in the Pines," *NK News*, July 19, 2021, https://www.nknews.org/2021/07/ widespread-deforestation-threatens-to-leave-north-korea-buried-in-the-pines/.

40. *DPRK Voluntary National Review*, 44.

41. Keith Krause, and Oliver Jütersonke, "Peace, Security and Development in Post-Conflict Environments," *Security Dialogue* 36, no. 4 (2005): 454.

42. Annie Young Song and Justin V. Hastings, "Engaging North Korea: Environmental Cooperation in Peacebuilding," *Third World Quarterly* 41, no. 11 (2020): 1812.

Bibliography

Abrahamian, Andray, Geoffrey K. See, and Xinyu Wang. *The ABCs of North Korea's SEZs*. Washington, DC: US-Korea Institute at Johns Hopkins University's School of Advanced International Studies, 2014.

"After Tests in the North, Conservatives in South Korea Call for a Nuclear Program." *New York Times*, February 19, 2016.

Agence France Presse. "Pakistan Supplied North Korea with Nuclear Weapons Technology: Daily." October 18, 2002.

———. "US and North Korea Sign Historic Nuclear Accord." October 2, 1994.

"Agreement on Reconciliation, Non-Aggression, and Exchanges and Cooperation between North and South Korea." UN Peacemaker, December 13, 1991.

"Agreement on the Implementation of the Historic Panmunjom Declaration in the Military Domain." National Committee on North Korea, September 19, 2018.

Ahlander, Johan, and Philip O'Connor. "North Korea Breaks Off Nuclear Talks with U.S. in Sweden." Reuters, October 5, 2019.

AhnLab. *Full Discloser of Andariel: A Subgroup of Lazarus Threat Group*. AhnLab Analysis Report, June 23, 2018.

———. *Operation Kabar Cobra: Tenacious Cyber-Espionage Campaign by Kimsuky Group*. AhnLab Analysis Report, February 28, 2019.

Albert, Eleanor. "What to Know about Sanctions on North Korea." *Council on Foreign Relations*, July 16, 2019.

Amnesty International, "Democratic People's Republic of Korea: Ali Lameda: A Personal Account of the Experience of a Prisoner of Conscience in the Democratic People's Republic of Korea," January 1, 1979, Index Number: ASA 24/002/1979.

Arms Control Association. "Chronology of U.S.-North Korean Nuclear and Missile Diplomacy."

———. "The North Korean Missile Crisis." November 2017.

———. "UN Security Council Resolutions on North Korea," January 2022.

Baker, Peter, and Choe Sang-Hun. "Trump Threatens 'Fire and Fury' against North Korea If It Endangers U.S." *New York Times*, August 8, 2017, sec. World.

Ballentine, Claire. "U.S. Lifts Ban That Kept ZTE from Doing Business with American Suppliers." *New York Times*, July 13, 2018.

Ballesteros, Alberto. "The Pandemic and North Korea's Tourism Industry: Another Shock for the Regime." *38 North*, April 8, 2021.

Bank of Korea. "Gross Domestic Product Estimates for North Korea in 2016." July 13, 2017.

———. "Gross Domestic Product Estimates for North Korea in 2020." July 30, 2021.

Bartlett, Jason. "What Will North Korean Cybercrime Look Like in 2022?" *Diplomat*, December 22, 2021.

BBC. "Kim Jong-nam Killing: Senior N Korea Diplomat Named as Suspect." February 22, 2017.

———. "Kim Jong-un Left Russia Seven Hours Earlier Than Initially Planned." April 26, 2019.

———. "Koreas Restart Operations at Kaesong Industrial Zone." September 16, 2013.

———. "North Korea Blows Up Joint Liaison Office with South in Kaesong." June 16, 2020.

———. "North Korea to Decide Soon Whether to Continue Denuclearization Negotiations with US." March 16, 2019.

———. "North Korea's Kim Jong-Un Visits China's Xi Jinping." *BBC News*, January 8, 2019.

———. "Singapore Suspends Trade Ties with North Korea." November 17, 2017.

———. "Trump Kim Summit: Full Text of the Signed Statement." June 12, 2018.

BenarNews, "Malaysia: Indonesian Suspect in Kim Jong Nam Murder Rewarded with Cambodian Trip." *Radio Free Asia*, February 9, 2018.

Bennett, Bruce W., Kang Choi, Myong-Hyun Go, Bruce E. Bechtol, Jiyoung Park, Bruce Klingner, and Du-Hyeogn Cha. *Countering the Risks of North Korean Nuclear Weapons*. Santa Monica, CA: RAND Corporation, 2021.

Bennett, Cory. "North Korean Hackers Test China's Patience." *Politico*, May 16, 2017.

Berger, Andrea. *Target Markets: North Korea's Military Customers in the Sanctions Era*. London: Routledge, 2017.

Bermudez, Joseph. "A New Emphasis on Operations against South Korea? A Guide to North Korea's Intelligence Reorganization and the General Reconnaissance Bureau." *38 North Special Report*, June 11, 2010.

Bermudez, Joseph. "North Korea Reorganizes Security Services." *IHS Jane's Report*, 2016.

Bezik, Igor. "The Participation of DPRK Nationals in the Economic Development of the Soviet Far East (1950s–early 1960s)." *Oriental Institute Journal*, no. 1 (2011).

Bikmurzina, Ella. "The North Korean Attack on Oceanographers." *Vokrug Sveta*, November 30, 2010.

Bolton, John. "Lessons from Libya and North Korea's Strategic Choice." Speech at Yonsei University, July 21, 2004.

Bolton, John. *The Room Where It Happened: A White House Memoir*. New York: Simon & Schuster, 2020.

Bossert, Thomas. "It's Official: North Korea Is Behind WannaCry." *Wall Street Journal*, December 18, 2017.

Brunnstrom, David, and Chris Gallagher. "Biden Imposes First Sanctions over North Korea's Missiles Program after Missile Tests." Reuters, January 13, 2022.

Burt, Tom. "Cyberattacks Targeting Health Care Must Stop." *Microsoft on the Issues*, November 13, 2020.

Byrne, Joe. "UN Panel of Experts Report on North Korea: More Advanced Weaponry, Better Sanctions Evasion." RUSI Commentary, April 27, 2021.

Byrne, Leo. "N. Korea, Russia Sign Military Agreement." *NK News*, November 13, 2015.

Caesar, Ed. "The Incredible Rise of North Korea's Hacking Army." *New Yorker*, April 19, 2021.

Campbell, Charlie. "Why We Shouldn't Be Surprised If North Korea Launched the WannaCry Ransomware Cyberattack." *Time*, May 17, 2017.

Carlin, Robert L. "The Real Lessons of the Trump-Kim Love Letters." *Foreign Policy*, August 13, 2021.

CBS News. "Transcript: CIA Director Mike Pompeo on *Face the Nation*, March 11, 2018."

Center for Nonproliferation Studies. "Taiwan Further Restricts Trade to Iran, North Korea." *International Export Control Observer*, March/April 2007.

Cha, Myung Soo, and Nak Nyeon Kim. "Korea's First Industrial Revolution, 1911–1940." *Explorations in Economic History* 49, no. 1 (2012).

Cha, Sangmi, and Hyonhee Shin. "North Korean Hackers Tried to Steal Pfizer Vaccine Know-How, Lawmaker Says." Reuters, February 16, 2021.

Cha, Victor. "Hawk Engagement and Preventive Defense on the Korean Peninsula." *International Security* 27, no. 1 (2002): 40–78.

Chainalysis Team. "Lazarus Group Pulled Off 2020's Biggest Exchange Hack and Appears to be Exploring New Money Laundering Options." *Chainalysis Report*, February 9, 2021.

———. "North Korean Hackers Have Prolific Year as Their Unlaundered Cryptocurrency Holdings Reach All-Time High." *Chainalysis Crypto Crime Report 2022*.

Chandran, Nyshka. "South Korea's Economy Is Slowing. Its Leader Still Wants to Spend Millions on Pyongyang." CNBC, October 3, 2018.

"Chaoxian jiangyu 23ri zhi 25ri zeqi feiqi beibu he shiyanchang" [North Korea to abandon northern nuclear testing site between 23rd and 25th]. *People's Daily*, May 12, 2018.

"Chaoxian lingdaoren de zhongguo zuji: Jin richeng zhuxi shengqian 40duoci fanghu" [Footprints in China by North Korean leaders: Kim Il-sung Chairman visited China over 40 times]. *Huanqiu Renwu* [*Global Figure*], March 31, 2018.

Cheng, Jonathan, and Andrew Jeong. "Kim Reaffirms Korean Denuclearization Push, Looks Forward to Trump Meeting, Moon Says." *Wall Street Journal*, May 27, 2018.

Cheon, Seong-Whun, "The Kim Jong-un Regime's 'Byungjin' (Parallel Development) Policy of Economy and Nuclear Weapons and the 'April 1st Nuclearization Law.'" Korea Institute for National Unification, Online Series 13–11, March 31, 2013.

Cherkashin, Pavel. "Current Russian-North Korean Relations and Prospects of Their Development." *Russian International Affairs Council*, August 24, 2015.

China and the Democratic People's Republic of Korea." Marxist.org, accessed October 16, 2021.

"China-North Korea Normal State Relationship." *Daily NK*, May 27, 2013.

Cho, Youngwon. "Method to the Madness of Chairman Kim: The Instrumental Rationality of North Korea's Pursuit of Nuclear Weapons." *International Journal* 69, no. 1 (2014): 5–25.

Choe, Sang-Hun. "Computer Networks in South Korea Are Paralyzed in Cyberattacks." *New York Times*, March 20, 2013.

———. "Kim Jong-un's Absence and North Korea's Silence Keep Rumor Mill Churning." *New York Times*, April 26, 2020.

———. "North Korea Accused of Shooting and Burning South Korean Defector." *New York Times*, September 24, 2020.

———. "North Korea Party Congress Opens with Kim Jong-un Admitting Failures." *New York Times*, January 5, 2021.

Choe, Sang-Hun, and Sharon LaFraniere. "Carter Wins Release of American in North Korea." *New York Times*, August 27, 2010.

Choi, Jung Hoon. "Advancement of North Korea's Nuclear Weapons and Survivability under the Kim Jong Un Regime: An Assessment based on Nuclear Deterrence Theory." *Journal of the Asia-Japan Research Institute of Ritsumeikan University* (2019).

Choi, Kyongae. "N. Korea Likely Hacked S. Korea Cyber Command: Military." Yonhap News, December 6, 2016.

Choi, Song Min. "China Electrifying Border Fencing." *DailyNK*, October 11, 2012.

Chow, Jonathan T. "North Korea's Participation in the Universal Periodic Review of Human Rights." *Australian Journal of International Affairs* 71, no. 2 (2017): 146–63.

Choy, M. C. "Ships Openly Admit to Buying Illegal Fishing Permits from North Korea." *NKNews*, January 1, 2021.

Christou, George, and Michael Raska. "Cybersecurity." In *The European Union's Security Relations with Asian Partners*, edited by Thomas Christiansen, Emil Kirchner, and See Seng Tan. London: Palgrave Macmillan 2021.

"A Chronology of U.S. Relations with North Korea, 1970–February 1985." *Korea and World Affairs* 9, no. 1 (1985): 129–73.

Chung, Young-chul, Yong-hyun Kim, and Kyungyon Moon. "State Strategy in the Kim Jong-Un Era: The 'Byongjin' Policy of Pursuing Economic and Nuclear Development." *Korea Observer* 47, no. 1 (2016): 1–34.

Clinton, Bill. *My Life*. London: Arrow Books, 2005.

CNN. "Transcript: Kim Jong Un's Letters to President Trump." September 9, 2020.

———. "World Leaders React to North Korea's Nuclear Test." February 12, 2013.

Collins, Robert. *Pyongyang Republic*. Washington, DC: American Enterprise Institute, 2016.

The Commission on Presidential Debates, "September 26, 2008 Debate Transcript."

The Committee for Human Rights in North Korea. "Socialist Constitution of the Democratic People's Republic of Korea."

Commonwealth Director of Public Prosecutions. "Sydney Man Receives Term of Imprisonment for Breaching North Korean Sanctions." Canberra, July 23, 2021.

Connection Denied: Restrictions on Mobile Phones and Outside Information in North Korea. London: Amnesty International, 2016.

Cooperman, Alan. "Stalin Approved Start of Korean War, Documents Show." AP, January 13, 1993.

Corera, Gordon. "UK TV Drama about North Korea Hit by Cyber-Attack." BBC News, October 16, 2017.

"Dear Leader Kim Jong Un Did Field Guidance at Onpo Greenhouse Factory in Kyungsung County, North Hamgyong Province." *Rodong Sinmun*, August 8, 2018.

"Dear Leader Kim Jong Un Did Field Guidance at Yangduk Spa Tourist District." *Rodong Sinmun*, August 31, 2019.

"Dear Supreme Leader Comrade Kim Jong-un Conducted an On-the-Spot Guidance to Mt. Kumgang Tourism District." *Rodong Sinmun*, October 23, 2019.

"Declaration for Advancing Inter-Korean Relations and Peace and Prosperity." National Committee on Korea, October 4, 2007.

"De-dollarization of North Korean Economy: Realities, Implications and Prospects." *Korea Development Institute North Korea Economy Review*, November 2021.

Defenseweb. "Pakistan Denies It Was Bribed by North Korea." July 8, 2011.

Democratic People's Republic of Korea and Republic of Korea. "The July 4 South-North Communiqué." July 4, 1972.

Denyer, Simon. "North Korea Tried to Steal Pfizer Coronavirus Vaccine Information, South says." *Washington Post*, February 16, 2021.

Devandas-Aguilar, Catalina. "End of Mission Statement by the United Nations Special Rapporteur on the Rights of Persons with Disabilities." Taedonggang Diplomatic Club, Pyongyang, May 8, 2017.

"The Direct Control of the State over Permission of Market Prices and Economic Activities." *DailyNK*, February 6, 2020.

"Dmitry Medvedev and Kim Jong-il Resolved the Problem of DPRK's Debt to Russia." *Rossiyskaya Gazeta*, August 24, 2011.

"Docs Shed Light on Scope of N. Korean Development Strategy through 2020." *Mainichi*, April 20, 2019.

"Dollarization of North Korean Economy: Causes and Effects." *Korea Development Institute North Korea Economy Review*, November 2019.

Dong, Jie. "North Korea's Changing Policy Towards the United Nations." In *Korea and the World: New Frontiers in Korean Studies*, edited by Gregg A. Brazinsky. Rowman & Littlefield, 2019.

DPRK Association for Human Rights, *Report of the DPRK Association for Human Rights Studies*. National Committee on North Korea, September 2014.

DPRK Ministry of Land and Environment Protection. *DPRK Environment and Climate Change Outlook*. Pyongyang: DPRK, 2012.

"DPRK Net—Encyclopedia: Science Technology Research Institutions." *Joongang Ilbo*.

DuBois, Eun. "Building Resilience to the North Korean Cyber Threat: Experts Discussion." Brookings Institution, December 23, 2020.

Early, Bryan R. "Unmasking the Black Knights: Sanctions Busters and Their Effects on the Success of Economic Sanctions." *Foreign Policy Analysis* 7, no. 4 (2011): 381–402.

Easley, Leif-Eric. "Trump and Kim Jong Un: Climbing the Diplomatic Ladder." *North Korean Review* 16, no. 1 (2020): 103–10.

Ebert, Hannes. "Cyber Resilience and Diplomacy in the Republic of Korea." *EU Cyber Direct - Digital Dialogue Report*, August 18, 2020.

"18 Percent of North Koreans Now Thought to Own Mobile Phones." *Korea JoongAng Daily*, August 11, 2020.

Embassy of Hungary in DPRK. *Report, Embassy of Hungary in North Korea to the Hungarian Foreign Ministry*. History and Public Policy Program Digital Archive, Wilson Center, March 9, 1985, Accessed October 8, 2021.

Embassy of the People's Republic of China in the Democratic People's Republic of Korea. "Chaoxian dangzhongyang juxing jinian jin zhengri fanghua 25 zhounian zhaodaihui" [North Korean Central Party leadership hosts reception on 25th anniversary of Kim Jong-il's visit to China]. June 11, 2008.

———. "Zhongguo tong chaoxian de guanxi" [China's relations with North Korea].

Erdağ, Ramazan. *Libya in the Arab Spring: From Revolution to Insecurity*. New York: Palgrave Macmillan, 2017.

Fahy, Sandra. *Dying for Rights: Putting North Korea's Human Rights Abuses on the Record*. New York: Columbia University Press, 2019.

———. *Marching through Suffering: Loss and Survival in North Korea*. New York: Columbia University Press, 2015.

Feng, Zhu, and Nathan Beauchamp-Mustafaga. "North Korea's Security Implications for China." In *China and North Korea: Strategic and Policy Perspectives from a Changing China*, edited by Carla P. Freeman. New York: Palgrave Macmillan, 2015.

FireEye. *APT 38—Un-usual Suspects*." FireEye Report, 2018.

———. *APT37 (Reaper) The Overlooked North Korean Actor*. A FireEye Special Report, 2018.

Foreign Ministry of the People's Republic of China. "2019nian 1yue 8ri waijiaobu fayanren lu kang zhuchi lixing jizhehui" [January 8, 2019 Foreign Ministry spokesperson Lu Kang hosts press conference]. January 8, 2019.

———. "Shuangbian guanxi: Zhonghua renmin gongheguo waijiaobu" [Bilateral relations: The Ministry of Foreign Affairs of the People's Republic of China]. Accessed October 16, 2021.

Frankel, Max. "Nixon Arrives in Peking to Begin an 8-Day Visit; Met by Chou at Airport." *New York Times*, February 21, 1972.

Fraser, Nalani, Jacqueline O'Leary, Vincent Cannon, and Fred Plan. "APT38: Details on New North Korean Regime-Backed Threat Group." FireEye Threat Research Report, October 3, 2018.

Freeman, Carla. "Developments in China's North Korea Policy and Contingency Planning."

"Full Text of Statement by Kim Kye-gwan on 'the Possibility of Reconsidering the North Korea–US summit.'" *Hankyung*, May 16, 2018.

Gabuev, Alexander. "Dmitry Medvedev Is Building a Bridge from Seoul to Skolkovo." *Kommersant*, November 11, 2010.

"Game-Changing Agricultural Policies for North Korea?" *38 North*, February 26, 2014.

Garamone, Jim. "Bombers Show U.S. Resolve to Defend South Korea, Spokesman Says." American Forces Press Service, March 18, 2013.

Gills, Barry. *Korea Versus Korea: A Case of Contested Legitimacy*. London: Routledge, 1996.

Global Security. "OPLAN 5015 [Operation Plans]."

Gorbachev Foundation. *Final Report on the Project "Russia-Korea Relations in the Architecture of Northeast Asia and the Asia-Pacific*. February 2003.

"The Gorbachev-Roh Breakthrough." *Washington Post*, June 6, 1990.

Gordon, Michael R., Jonathan Cheng, and Michael C. Bender. "Trump, Kim Begin New Phase of Diplomacy." *Wall Street Journal*, June 15, 2018.

Gordon, Michael R., Jonathan Cheng, and Vivian Salama. "U.S., North Korea Trade Blame for Failed Summit." *Wall Street Journal*, February 28, 2019.

Government of the DPRK. *DPRK Voluntary National Review on the Implementation of the 2030 Agenda for Sustainable Development*. Pyongyang: Government of the DPRK, June 2021.

"The Great Combat Platform Leading Our-Style Socialist Construction to a New Victory: On Dear Comrade Kim Jong-un's Report Delivered at the Eighth Congress of the WPK." *Rodong Sinmun*, January 9, 2021.

Greenberg, Andy. "Russian Hacker False Flags Work—Even After They Are Exposed." *Wired*, February 27, 2018.

Greitens, Sheena Chestnut. *Illicit: North Korea's Evolving Operations to Earn Hard Currency*. Washington, DC: Committee for Human Rights in North Korea, 2014.

Group IB, *Lazarus Arisen: Architecture, Tools, Attribution*. Group-IB Investigation Report, May 30, 2017.

Grzelczyk, Virginie. "From Balancing to Bandwagoning: Evaluating the Impact of the Sanction Regime on North Korea–Africa Relationships." *North Korean Review* 15, no. 1 (2019): 9–33.

———."Going at It Alone? North Korea's Adaptability as a Small Power in a Changing World." *Third World Thematics* 1, no. 1 (2016): 63–78.

———. "Six-Party Talks and Negotiation Strategy: When Do We Get There?" *International Negotiation* 14, no. 1 (2009): 95–119.

Guancha. "Jin zhengen 7ri kaishi dui zhongguo jinxing fangwen" [Kim Jong-Un Begins China Visit on the 7th]. Guancha.cn, January 8, 2019.

"Guidelines Set Forth to Develop Nation's Animal Husbandry." *Pyongyang Times*, February 3, 2015.

Ha, Yoon Ah. "N. Korea's State-Run Smuggling Activities Continue Despite Coronavirus." *DailyNK*, March 25, 2020.

Haggard, Stephan, and Marcus Noland. "Sanctioning North Korea: The Political Economy of Denuclearization and Proliferation." *Asian Survey* 50, no. 3 (2010): 539–68.

Haggard, Stephan, Jennifer Lee, and Marcus Noland. "Integration in the Absence of Institutions: China-North Korea Cross-Border Exchange." *Journal of Asian Economics* 23, no. 2 (2012): 130–45.

Halle Institute for Economic Research (IWH). *The Economic Integration of East Germany*. November 2016.

Han, Ki-beom. *North Korea's Economic Reform and Bureaucratic Politics* [북한의 경제개혁과 관료정치]. Seoul: North Korea Research Institute, 2019.

Han, Tak Sung, and Jeon Kyung Joo. "Can North Korea Catch Two Rabbits at Once? Nuke and Economy. One Year of the Byungjin Line in North Korea and Its Future." *Korean Journal of Defense Analysis* 26, no. 2 (2014): 133–53.

Han, Un-il. "Victory of Socialism Lies in Living and Fighting Our Own Way" [우리 식대로 살며 투쟁하는데 사회주의승리가 있다]. *Rodong Sinmun*, May 20, 2020.

Hasmath, Reza, Timothy Hildebrandt, and Jennifer Hsu. "Conceptualizing Government-Organized Non-Governmental Organizations." *Journal of Civil Society* (2019): 267–84.

Hassig, Ralph, and Oh Kongdan. "Kim Jong-un Inherits the Bomb." *International Journal of Korean Unification Studies* 20, no. 1 (2011): 31–54.

Hastings, Justin V. *A Most Enterprising Country: North Korea in the Global Economy*. Ithaca: Cornell University Press, 2016.

Hastings, Justin V., and Yaohui Wang. "Chinese Firms' Troubled Relationship with Market Transformation in North Korea." *Asian Survey* 57, no. 4 (2017): 618–40.

———. "Informal Trade along the China–North Korea Border." *Journal of East Asian Studies* 18, no. 2 (2018): 181–203.

Hawk, David. *Human Rights in the Democratic People's Republic of Korea: The Role of the United Nations*. Washington, DC: Committee on Human Rights in North Korea, 2021.

Hayes, Peter, and Roger Cavazos. "North Korea in 2015." *Asian Survey* 56, no. 1 (2016): 68–77.

Hiraiwa, Shunji. "Japan's Policy on North Korea: Four Motives and Three Factors." *Journal of Contemporary East Asia Studies* 9, no. 1 (January 2, 2020): 1–17. https://doi.org/10.1080/24761028.2020.1762300.

Human Rights Watch. *2019 World Report*.

Hwang, Shin-ryul. "The External Exploits of Establishing a Basis for Completing the Great Deed of Juche Under the Banner of Songun" [선군의 기치높이 주체혁명위업완성의 근본담보를 마련하신 불멸의 업적]. *Rodong Sinmun*, August 25, 2016.

Interfax. "Russia Supplied 50,000 Tons of Wheat as Humanitarian Aid to the DPRK." September 12, 2020.

International Atomic Energy Agency. "Implementation of the NPT Safeguards Agreement of the Socialist People's Libyan Arab Jamahiriya." GOV/2004/27.

International Broadcasting in North Korea: North Korean Refugee/Traveler Survey Report. April–August 2009. Washington, DC: InterMedia, 2009.

International Finance Forum. "China-DPRK Economic Cooperation Dialogue." Annual Conference, Guangzou, China, November 25, 2018.

Jang, Seulkee. "China Intensifies Security along Sino-North Korean Border." *DailyNK*, July 19, 2019.

———. "Kim Jong Un Is Directly Handling Results of new COVID-19 Hacking Organization's Work." *Daily NK*, February 5, 2021.

Jeong, Andrew. "North Korea's Economy Hit Harder Than It Has Been in Decades." *Wall Street Journal*, December 18, 2020.

———. "One Small Step for Moon, One Large Stride for Korean Harmony." *Wall Street Journal*, April 27, 2018.

Jeong, Chang-heong. "Wages of North Korean Workers Reportedly Increased by One Hundredfold" [북한 노동자들의 월급이 100배 인상됐다는데]. *Tongil News*, December 2, 2013.

Ji, Dagyum. "North Korean Education still 'Lags Far Behind' Global Trends, Kim Jong Un Says." *North Korea News*, September 3, 2019.

"Jin zhengen dui zhongguo jinxing fangwen" [Kim Jong-Un visits China]. *People's Daily*, January 8, 2019.

Johnson, Alex, and Arata Yamamoto. "Japan Nominated Trump for Nobel Peace Prize after White House Asked, Newspaper Reports." NBC, February 18, 2019.

"Joint Statement of President Donald J. Trump of the United States of America and Chairman Kim Jong Un of the Democratic People's Republic of Korea at the Singapore Summit." June 12, 2018.

"Joint Statement of the Fourth Round of the Six-Party Talks." U.S. Department of State Archive, September 19, 2005.

Jones, Charles O. *An Introduction to the Study of Public Policy*. Monterey, CA: Brooks/Cole Publishing Co., 1984.

Joung, Eun-lee. "Analysis on Change of Property and Development in North Korea" [북한 부동산 개발업자의 등장과 함의에 관한 분석]. *KDI Review of North Korean Economy*, no. 9 (2016).

Jun, Jenny, Scott LaFoy, and Ethan Sohn. "*North Korea's Cyber Operations Strategies and Responses: A Report of CSIS Korea Chair*. Lanham, MD: Rowman & Littlefield, December 2015.

Jung, Heon Joo, and Timothy S. Rich. "Why Invest in North Korea? Chinese Foreign Direct Investment in North Korea and Its Implications." *Pacific Review* 29 no. 3 (2016): 307–30. https://doi.org/10.1080/09512748.2015.1022582.

Kang, Chul-Hwan, and Pierre Rigoulot. *Aquariums of Pyongyang: Ten Years in the North Korean Gulag*. New York: Basic Books, 2001.

Kang, Dong-wan. "The Status of North Koreans' Access to Foreign Culture and Policy Measures from the Standpoint of North Koreans living in China" [중국 체류 북한 주민을 통해서 본 외래문화 접촉실태와 정책방안]. *Journal of Political Science and Communication* 24, no. 1 (February 2021), 41–72.

———. "A Study on the Introduction of Foreign Culture into North Korea and Changes to the North Korean Society: With an Interview Survey with North

Koreans in a Third Country" [북한으로의 외래문화 유입 현황과 실태: 제3국에서의 북한주민면접조사를 중심으로]. *The Institute of Humanities for Unification* 60 (December 2014), 167–202.

Kang, Dong-wan, and Park Jung Ran. *Hallyu: The Wind of Unification* [한.류: 통일의 바람]. Seoul: Myungin Books.

Kang, Mi Jin. "N. Korea Begins Enforcing Price Controls in Local Markets." *DailyNK*, February 12, 2020.

———. "N. Korean Rice Sellers Raking It In Thanks to Skyrocketing Prices." *DailyNK*, February 26, 2020.

Kaspersky Labs. "Advanced Threat Predictions for 2021." *Kaspersky Security Bulletin*, November 19, 2020.

———. *Lazarus under the Hood.* A Kaspersky Forensic Investigation Report, 2017.

Kassenova, Togzhan. *Policy Forum 11–30: A "Black Hole" in the Global Nonproliferation Regime: The Case of Taiwan.* Berkeley, CA: Nautilus Institute, September 8, 2011.

KBS. "Inter-Korean Summit." June 15, 2000.

KCNA. "DPRK Gov't on Successful Test-Fire of New-Type ICBM." November 29, 2017.

———. "Foreign Ministry Spokesman Denounces U.S. Military Attack on Libya." Korea Central News Agency, March 22, 2011.

———. "Kim Jong Un Makes Report on Work of WPK Central Committee at Its 7th Congress," Korea Central News Agency, May 7, 2016,

———. "Kim Yo Jong Rebukes S. Korean Authorities for Conniving at Anti-DPRK Hostile Act of 'Defectors from North.'" Korean Central News Agency, June 4, 2020.

———."National Defense Commission Proposes to Hold a High-Level Meeting between the DPRK and the United States." Korean Central News Agency, June 16, 2013.

———. "On Report Made by Supreme Leader Kim Jong Un at Eighth Party Congress of WPK." Korean Central News Agency, January 9, 2021.

———. "Statement of the Spokesperson of the Foreign Ministry of the DPRK." Korean Central News Agency, March 7, 2013.

———. "Third Plenary Meeting of Seventh C.C., WPK Held in Presence of Kim Jong-un." Korean Central News Agency, April 21, 2018.

———. "Traitor Jang Song Thaek Executed." Korean Central News Agency, December 13, 2013.

Keck, Zachary. "How Japan and North Korea 'Use' Each Other." *The Diplomat*, May 21, 2014.

Khoo, Nicholas. "Retooling Great Power Nonproliferation Theory: Explaining China's North Korea Nuclear Weapons Policy." *Pacific Review* 34, no. 4 (2019): 523–46.

Kim, Bomi. "North Korea's Siege Mentality: A Sociopolitical Analysis of the Kim Jong-un Regime's Foreign Policies." *Asian Perspective* 40, no. 2 (2016): 223–43.

Kim, Byung-Yeon. "Marketization during Kim Jong-un's Era: Policies and the Sanctions." The Korea Development Institute Working Paper. February 24, 2022.

———. "North Korean Economy in Kim Jong-un's Era." In *Today's North Korea*, edited by Youngkwan Yoon. Seoul: Neulpoom Plus, 2019.

———. *Unveiling the North Korean Economy*. Cambridge: Cambridge University Press, 2017.

Kim, Christine. "North Korea Hackers Stole South Korea–U.S. Military Plans to Wipe out North Korea Leadership: Lawmaker." Reuters, October 10, 2017.

Kim, Cynthia. "South Korean Intelligence Says N. Korean Hackers Possibly Behind Coincheck Heist—Sources." Reuters, February 6, 2018.

Kim, Dae-jung. *Conscience in Action: The Autobiography of Kim Dae-jung*, translated by Jeon Seung-hee. London: Palgrave Macmillan, 2018.

Kim, Dawool. "Determinants of Regional Economic Performance in North Korea: Evidence from Satellite Nighttime Lights." PhD Dissertation, Seoul National University, 2021.

Kim, Hyung-jin. "North Korea Cuts Diplomatic Ties with Malaysia over US Extradition." *The Diplomat*, March 19, 2021.

Kim, Hyungsoo. "Kim Jong-Un Says 'Cyber Warfare Is an All-Powerful Tool,' Utilizes It as One of Three Major Means of Warfare." *Joongang Ilbo*, November 5, 2013.

Kim, In Ryong. "Kim In Ryong (DPRK) on Human Rights—Press Conference (13 December 2016)." UN Web TV.

Kim, Jack. "Bill Clinton in North Korea, Meets Kim Jong-il." Reuters, August 4, 2009.

Kim, Ji-eun. "'National Intelligence Service—United Front Department' Emerged as Informal Channel for Communication." *Hankyoreh*, February 22, 2018.

Kim, Jihee, Kyoochul Kim, Sangyoon Park, and Chang Sun. "The Economics Costs of Trade Sanctions: Evidence from North Korea." *Social Science Research Network*, November 15, 2021.

Kim, Jong-un. "Kim Jong Un's 2018 New Year's Address." Korea Central News Agency, January 1, 2018.

———. "Kim Jong-un's 2019 New Year Address." January 1, 2019.

———. "New Year's Address." January 1, 2018.

Kim, Kyu-ryun, ed. *North Korea's External Economic Relations*. KINU Research Monograph. Seoul: Korea Institute for National Unification, 2008.

Kim, Patricia. "Failure in Hanoi Doesn't Mean Peace Is Dead." *Foreign Policy*, March 1, 2019.

Kim, Philo. "Recent Social Changes in North Korea: Based on North Korean Refugees Survey." *Bukhan Yeonku Hakhoebo* [*North Korean Studies Review*] 18, no. 2 (2014).

Kim, So Jeong, and Sunha Bae. "Korean Policies of Cybersecurity and Data Resilience." Carnegie Endowment for International Peace, August 17, 2021.

Kim, Soohyon, and Sohn, Wook. "Economic Policy Changes in North Korea: A Text Mining Approach to Economic Research." BOK Economic Research, 2020.

Kim, Y. "North Korea on Human Rights, UN 150921." YouTube, September 21, 2015.

Kim, Yo-jong. "First Vice Department Director of WPK Central Committee Issues Statement." Korean Central News Agency, June 13, 2020.

———. "Honeyed Words of Impudent Man Are Disgusting: Statement of the First Vice Department Director of WPK Central Committee." Korean Central News Agency, June 17, 2020.

Kim, Yongho. "North Korea's Threat Perception and Provocation under Kim Jong-un: The Security Dilemma and the Obsession with Political Survival." *North Korean Review* 9, no. 1 (2013): 6–19.

King, Lawrence, and Ivan Szelenyi. "Post-Communist Economic Systems." In *Handbook of Economic Sociology*, edited by Neil Smelser and Richard Swedberg. Princeton, NJ: Princeton University Press, 2005.

King, Robert. "The Two Koreas Mark 30 Years of UN Membership: The Road to Membership." Korea Economic Institute, September 24, 2021.

Kirschenbaum, Joshua. "Operation Opera: An Ambiguous Success." *Journal of Strategic Security* 3, no. 4 (2010): 49–62.

Kiryanov, Oleg. "South Korea Has Missed a Chance for Diplomacy in Sochi." *Rossiyskaya Gazeta*, February 8, 2014.

Kono, Keiko. "An Overview of the Report of the UN Panel of Experts Established Pursuant to the Security Council Resolution 1874 (2009): Investigations into North Korean Cyberattacks Continue." NATO CCDCOE Law Branch, 2021.

Korea Economic Development Association. "SEZs in the DPRK." Korea Economic Development Association, International Conference, Pyongyang, North Korea, May 2, 2014.

Korean Central Television. "Statement of the DPRK: On the Success of Test-Firing of New Type of ICBM." November 29, 2019.

Korostikov, Mikhail. "Sergey Lavrov Made a Visit to Pyongyang." *Kommersant*, May 31, 2018.

Kovacs, Eduard. "Malware Attacks on Polish Banks Linked to Lazarus Group." *Security Week*, February 13, 2017.

Krause, Keith, and Oliver Jütersonke. "Peace, Security and Development in Post-Conflict Environments." *Security Dialogue* 36, no. 4 (2005): 454.

Krechetnikov, Artem. "The Korean War: Another Mystery of Stalin." BBC, July 26, 2013.

Kremlin. "Beginning of Conversation with DPRK State Affairs Commission Chairman Kim Jong-un." Kremiln.ru, April 25, 2019.

———. "Joint Russian-Korean Declaration." July 19, 2000.

———. "Meeting with Journalists Following Talks with Chairman of the State Defence Commission of the Democratic People's Republic of Korea Kim Jong Il." Kremlin.ru, August 24, 2011.

———. "Russian President Vladimir Putin Held Talks with His Visiting North Korean Counterpart, Kim Jong Il." Kremlin.ru, August 4, 2001.

———. "Vladimir Putin Took Part in a Meeting of G8 Heads of State and Government." Kremlin.ru, July 22, 2000.

Kretchun, Nat. "The Need for a New US Information Strategy for North Korea." *United States Institute of Peace Special Report* No. 451, June 2019.

Kristensen, Hans M., and Robert S. Norris. "A History of US Nuclear Weapons in South Korea." *Bulletin of the Atomic Scientists* 73, no. 6 (2017): 349–57.

———. "North Korean Nuclear Capabilities, 2018." *Bulletin of the Atomic Scientists* 74, no. 1 (2018): 41–51.

Kroeber, Arthur. *China's Economy.* New York: Oxford University Press, 2016.

Kwon, Edward. "Policies of Last Resort for Dealing with North Korea's Nuclear Weapons Programme." *Asian Affairs* 49, no. 3 (2018): 402–32.

Kyodo News International. "Kim Jong Il Says Missile Remarks 'Laughing Matter.'" August 14, 2000.

Lankov, Andrei. "North Korean Refugees in Northeast China." *Asian Survey* 44, no. 6 (2004).

———. "North Korean Workers in the USSR and Russia." *Polit.ru*, May 21, 2021.

———. "Pyongyang Strikes Back: North Korean Policies of 2002–08 and Attempts to Reverse 'De-Stalinization from Below.'" *Asia Policy* 8, no. 1 (2009): 47–72.

Latiff, Rozanna, and Ju-min Park, "North Korea Bars Malaysians from Leaving, in 'Diplomatic Meltdown.'" Reuters, March 7, 2017.

Lea-Henry, Jed. "Human Rights in North Korea—Looking Back on the Commission of Inquiry." *Korea Now* Podcast #21—Michael Kirby, August 30, 2018.

Lee, Christy. "As North Korea Reverts to Self-Reliance, Experts Urge Pressuring Elites." *Voice of America*, January 27, 2020.

———. "US, South Korea to Launch Joint Working Group on North Korea." Voice of America, November 3, 2018.

Lee, Chung Min, and Kathryn Botto (eds.). "Korea Net Assessment 2020: Politicized Security and Unchanging Strategic Realities." Carnegie Endowment for International Peace, March 18, 2020.

Lee, Duri. "How to Improve the ROK and US Military Alliance against North Korea's Threats to Cyberspace: Lessons from NATO's Defense Cooperation." Master's thesis, Naval Postgraduate School Monterey, CA, 2017.

Lee, Hong Yung. "North Korea in 2012." *Asian Survey* 53, no. 1 (2013): 176–83.

Lee, Il-young. "To What Extent Are the Sanctions Effective." *Kyunghayng Shinmun*, February 7, 2018.

Lee, J. S., Ryu, J. G., and Kee, H. K. "A Study on the Status of Chinese Fishing in the East Sea off North Korea and Directions for Countermeasures." *Journal of Fisheries Business Administration* 48, no. 3 (2017): 61–74.

Lee, Jong-seok. "Kim Jong-un Wants Reform and Open-Up as Deng Xiaoping Did for China." Yonhap News Agency, November 28, 2019.

Lee, Jong-suk. "The Sanctions Are Not a Universal Talisman." *Hankyoreh*, July 16, 2017.

Lee, Michelle Ye Hee. "North Korea's Latest Missile Test May Not Have Been What It Claimed." *Washington Post*, March 28, 2022.

Lee, Ming. "Seoul's Searching for '*Nordpolitik*': Evolution and Perspective." *Asian Perspective* 13, no. 2 (1989): 141–78.

Leyden, John. "Beyond Lazarus: North Korean Cyber-Threat Groups Become Top-Tier, 'Reckless' Adversaries." *Daily Swig—Cybersecurity News*, May 17, 2021.

Li, Zhongfa. "Xi Jinping tong chaoxian laodongdang weiyuanzhang jin zhen-gen juxing huitan" [Xi Jinping holds talks with North Korean Worker's Party Commissioner Kim Jong-Un]. *People's Daily*, June 20, 2018.

Liptak, Kevin. "Trump Says Singapore Summit with Kim Is Back On." CNN, June 1, 2018.

Lockman, Shahriman. "Malaysia and North Korea: A Peculiar Relationship Unravels." *Focus: Institute of Strategic and International Studies Malaysia*, no. 2 (2017).

Lukin, Artyom. "North Korea Stuck Between a Rock and a Hard Place: One Year After the Hanoi Summit." *Foreign Policy Research Institute*, March 10. 2020.

———. "The Putin and Kim Rendezvous in Vladivostok: A Drive-By Summit." *38 North*, May 2, 2019.

———. "Russia's Policy toward North Korea: Following China's Lead." *38 North*, December 23, 2019.

———. "Will North Korea's Squid Poaching Strain Its Ties with Russia?" *World Politics Review*, October 8, 2019.

Lukin, Artyom, Georgy Toloraya, Ilya Dyachkov et al. "Nuclear Weapons and Russian—North Korean Relations." *Foreign Policy Research Institute*, November 2017.

Maksimenkov, Leonid. "A Korean Tango of Three." *Kommersant*, September 9, 2017.

Mansourov, Alexander. "North Korea's Cyber Warfare and Challenges for the U.S.-ROK Alliance." *KEI Academic Paper Series*, December 2, 2014.

"Markets Burgeon in N. Korea." *Chosun Ilbo*, October 26, 2015.

Martin, Tim, and Andrew Jeong. "North Korea Fires Unidentified Short-Range Weapon." *Wall Street Journal*, May 4, 2019.

Martin, Timothy W., Dasl Yoon, and Nancy A. Youssef. "North Korea's ICBM Intrigue: Is Latest Missile New or Old Technology?" *Wall Street Journal*, April 1, 2022.

Masterson, Julia. "North Korea Spurns Diplomacy with United States." *Arms Control Today*, May 2020.

Matsuo, Terrence. "More Bilateral U.S.-ROK Cooperation Needed in Cyber Policy." *KEI Peninsula Commentary*, May 12, 2020.

McAfee. "Ten Days of Rain—Expert Analysis of Distributed Denial-of-Service Attacks Targeting South Korea." McAfee White Paper, July 2011.

McCune, George. *Korea*. Cambridge, MA: Harvard University Press, 1950.

Mcdonald, Hamish. "Fog of Cyberwar Spurs Virtual Arms Race on Korean Peninsula." *Nikkei Asian Review*, May 22, 2017.

McEachern, Patrick. "Centralizing North Korean Policymaking under Kim Jong Un." *Asian Perspective* 43, no. 1 (2019): 35–67.

———. *Inside the Red Box: North Korea's Post-totalitarian Politics*. New York: Columbia University Press, 2010.

McGrath, Matthew, and Daniel Wertz. *North Korea's Ballistic Missile Program*. Washington: The National Committee on North Korea, 2013.

McWilliams, Brian. "North Korea's School for Hackers." *Wired*, February 6, 2003.

Mearsheimer, John. *The Tragedy of Great Power Politics*. New York: W.W. Norton & Company, 2001.

Migheli, Matteo. "Do the Vietnamese Support the Economic Doi Moi?" *Journal of Development Studies* 48, no. 7 (July 2012): 939–68.

————. "Supporting the Free and Competitive Market in China and India: Differences and Evolution Over Time." *Economic Systems* 34, no. 1 (2010): 73–90.

Miller, Steve. "Where Did North Korea's Cyber Army Come From?" *Voice of America*, November 20, 2018.

Min, Jaewon. "North Korean Defectors and Journalists Targeted Using Social Networks and KakaoTalk." *McAfee Labs Blog*, January 11, 2018.

————. "Panmunjom Declaration for Peace, Prosperity and Unification of the Korean Peninsula (2018.4.27)." April 27, 2018.

Ministry of Foreign Affairs "The Statement of the Ministry of Foreign Affairs in Connection with the Conduct of Another Nuclear Test in the DPRK." Seoul, February 12, 2013.

MITRE ATTACK Database. "Lazarus Group." October 14, 2021.

Moon, Jae-in. "Address at the Körber Foundation, Germany." Office of the President, July 6, 2017.

————. "Report to the People on the Result of the Second North-South Summit of 2018." May 27, 2018.

Moriuchi, Priscilla. "North Korea's Ruling Elite Adapt Internet Behavior to Foreign Scrutiny." *Recorded Future Blog*, April 25, 2018.

"Moscow Declaration of the Russian Federation and the DPRK." August 4, 2001.

Mount, Adam. "How China Sees North Korea." *The Atlantic*, August 29, 2017.

Mozzhuhin, Andrey. "The Foundling Dictator." *Lenta.Ru*, December 25, 2018.

Mufson, Steven. "Albright, N. Korea's Kim Meet for Historic Talks." *Washington Post*, October 24, 2000.

National Committee on North Korea. *DPRK Report on the Third Plenary Meeting of the Seventh Central Committee.* April 21, 2018.

————. *Report of the Fifth Plenary Meeting of the 7th Central Committee of the WPK.* January 1, 2020.

————. "Summary of the North Korea Sanctions and Policy Enhancement Act of 2016." February 18, 2016.

National Cybersecurity and Communications Integration Center. "HIDDEN COBRA—North Korean Malicious Cyber Activity."

————. "HIDDEN COBRA—FASTCash Campaign." Alert (TA18–275A), National Cybersecurity and Communications Integration Center, October 2, 2018.

Ng, Charmaine. "Jail for Company Director Who Sold Luxury Goods to North Korea, Cheated Banks of $130m." *Straits Times*, November 22, 2019.

Nikitin, Mary Beth Dunham and Samuel D. Ryder. "North Koreas Nuclear Weapons and Missile Programs." *Congressional Research Service*, January 5, 2021.

"North Korea Diary." *Chosun Ilbo*, Accessed October 14, 2021.

"North Korea Is Not Able to Print Money." *DailyWill*, October 5, 2021.

North Korea Leadership Watch. "National Defense Commission (Defunct)." September 24, 2016.

————. "Sepo Stockbreeding Zone Opened." October 3, 2017.

"North Korea Plans to Target Visitors from China for Medical Tourism." *Japan Times*, December 7, 2019.

"North Korea Resumes Foreign Currency Control." *The Freedom and Life*, September 6, 2021.

"North Korean Authorities Ban Use of Foreign Currencies at Markets." *Maeil Kyungje*, December 29, 2020.

"North Korea's Choe Son-hui 'Pence is a dumb idiot.'" BBC, May 24, 2018.

"North Korea's Kim Jong-un Opens New City and 'Socialist Utopia' of Samjiyon." *The Guardian*, December 3, 2019.

"North-South Joint Declaration." UN Peacemaker, June 15, 2000.

"North-South Joint Statement." UN Peacemaker, July 4, 1971.

Novetta. *Operation Blockbuster: Unraveling the Long Thread of the Sony Attack.* Novetta Special Report, February 2016.

Nuclear Threat Initiative. "The CNS North Korea Missile Test Database." NTI, April 24, 2017.

————."Kori Nuclear Power Complex."

————. "North Korea Submarine Capabilities."

Nuland, Victoria. "U.S.-DPRK Bilateral Discussions." US Department of State, February 29, 2012.

O'Carroll, Chad. "As Chinese Tourism to North Korea Soars, Local Operators Feel the Strain." *North Korea News*, October 31, 2019.

O'Keeffe, Kate. "China Stymies Once-United U.N. Panel on North Korea Sanctions." *Wall Street Journal*, September 15, 2021.

Oberdorfer, Don. "North Korean Leader Promotes Son." *Washington Post*, January 24, 1992.

Oberdorfer, Don, and Robert Carlin. *The Two Koreas: A Contemporary History*. New York: Basic Books, 2001.

"On Your Marks: South Korean Firms Are Keen to Invest in the North." *The Economist*, September 22, 2018.

Otto, Greg. "U.S. Charges North Korean Hacker over Sony, WannaCry Incidents." *Cyberscoop*, September 6, 2018.

Ouellette, Dean. "The Tourism of North Korea in the Kim Jong-un Era: Propaganda, Profitmaking, and Possibilities for Engagement." *Pacific Focus 31*, no. 3 (2016): 421–51.

Pacheco Pardo, Ramon. *North Korea–US Relations from Kim Jong Il to Kim Jong Un*. London: Routledge, 2019.

————. "Pyongyang's Failure: Explaining North Korea's Inability to Normalize Diplomatic Relations with the United States." *Asia Policy* 16, no. 1 (2021): 97–117.

Paik, Haksoon. "Changes and Continuities in Inter-Korean Relations." In *North Korea in Transition*, edited by Kyung-Ae Park and Scott Snyder. Lanham, MD: Rowman & Littlefield, 2013.

————. "North Korea's Choices for Survival and Prosperity since 1990s: Interplay between Politics and Economics." *Sejong Policy Studies* 3, no.2 (2007): 250–77.

Panda, Ankit. "North Korean Human Rights Abuses on the Agenda at UN Security Council." *The Diplomat*, December 23, 2014.

Panel of Experts. *Report of the Panel of Experts Established Pursuant to Resolution 1874 (2009).* S/2020/151. New York: United Nations Security Council, March 2, 2020.

———. *Report of the Panel of Experts Established Pursuant to Resolution 1874 (2009).* S/2019/1571. New York: United Nations Security Council, March 5, 2019.

———. *Report of the Panel of Experts Established Pursuant to Resolution 1874 (2009).* S/2018/171. New York: United Nations Security Council, March 5, 2018.

———. *Report of the Panel of Experts Established Pursuant to Resolution 1874 (2009).* New York: United Nations Security Council, February 24, 2016.

———. *Final Report of the Panel of Experts Submitted Pursuant to Resolution 2345 (2017)* (New York: United Nations Security Council, March 5, 2018).

Park, Han S. "Military-First Politics (Songun): Understanding Kim Jong-il's North Korea." *Korea Economic Institute Academic Paper Series* 2, no. 7 (2007).

Park, Jaeyoon, Jungsam Lee, Katherine Seto, Timothy Hochberg, Brian A. Wong, Nathan A. Miller, Kenji Takasaki, et al. "Illuminating Dark Fishing Fleets in North Korea." *Science Advances* 6, no. 30 (2020): eabb1197. https://doi.org/doi:10.1126/sciadv.abb1197.

Park, Ju-min, and James Pearson. "Exclusive: North Korea's Unit 180, the Cyber Warfare Cell That Worries the West." Reuters, May 21, 2017.

Park, Seong-Yong. "North Korea's Military Policy under the Kim Jong-Un Regime." *Journal of Asian Public Policy* 9, no. 1 (2016): 57–74.

Park, Yong Soo. "Policies and Ideologies of the Kim Jong-un Regime in North Korea: Theoretical Implications." *Asian Studies Review* 38, no. 1 (2014): 1–14.

Park, Yong-chae. "Kim Jong-un Becomes Deng Xiaoping and Wonsan Does Shanghai." *Kyunghyang Shinmun*, June 19, 2018.

Pearson, Michael, K. J. Kwon, and Jethro Mullen. "Hacking Attack on South Korea traced to China, Officials Say." CNN, March 21, 2013.

Pellerin, Cheryl. "Carter Reaffirms U.S. Commitment to South Korea." American Forces Press Service, March 18, 2013.

Perlez, Jane. "Kim's Second Surprise Visit to China Heightens Diplomatic Drama." *New York Times*, May 8, 2018, sec. World.

Peterson, Andrea. "The Sony Pictures Hack, Explained." *Washington Post*, December 18, 2014.

Pinkston, Daniel A. "Inter-Korean Rivalry in the Cyber Domain: The North Korean Cyber Threat in the Son'gun Era." *Georgetown Journal of International Affairs* 27, no. 3 (2016): 60–76.

Pleasance, Chris, and Tim Stickings. "South Korean Ministers Say They KNOW Kim Jong Un's Location and the Dictator Is Laying Low, Not Because He Is Ill, but to Avoid Coronavirus, amid Rumours He Had Died." *Daily Mail,* April 28, 2020.

Povera, Abid, "All North Koreans in Sarawak Have Been Sent Back." *New Straits Times*, September 21, 2017.

"Press Conference by President Trump." National Committee on North Korea, June 12, 2018.

Putin, Vladimir. "News Conference Following Russian-North Korean Talks." Kremlin.ru, April 25, 2019.

————. "Remarks at Eastern Economic Forum. Vladivostok." Kremlin.ru, September 7, 2017.

————. "Remarks at Saint Petersburg Economic Forum." Kremlin, June 2, 2017.

————. "Remarks at the meeting of the Valdai International Discussion Club." Kremlin, October 19, 2017.

————. "Replies to Russian Journalists' Questions about Talks with Kim Jong-il, Chairman of the Defence Committee of the Democratic People's Republic of Korea." Kremlin, July 19, 2000.

————. "Statement to the Press after the Talks with the Chairman of the State Defence Committee of the DPRK Kim Jong Il." Kremlin, August 23, 2002.

"Pyongyang Joint Declaration of September 19, 2018." National Committee on North Korea.

"Questions and Answers on New U.S. Guidelines Governing Contact between U.S. and North Korean Diplomats, during Briefing by U.S. State Department Spokesman Charles Redman Washington, March 9, 1987." *Korea and World Affairs* 11, no. 1 (1987): 172–74.

Quinones, C. Kenneth. "The Six Party Talks: Going in Circles." *World & I* (April 2016).

Radio Liberty. "The DPRK Leader Kim Jong-un Will Come to Russia at the End of April." Svoboda, April 18, 2019.

Rampton, Roberta, and Hyonhee Shin. "After Surprise Trump-Kim Meeting, U.S. and North Korea to Reopen Talks." Reuters, June 30, 2019.

Raska, Michael. "Searching for Security, Autonomy, and Independence: The Challenge of Military Innovation in the ROK Armed Forces." In *Military Innovation of Small States: Creating a Reverse Asymmetry*. New York: Routledge, 2016.

Reilly, James. "The Curious Case of China's Aid to North Korea." *Asian Survey* 54, no. 6 (2014): 1158–83.

RIA Novosti. "The First Summit of Putin and Kim Jong-un Lasts Three and a Half Hours." April 25, 2019.

Rich, Timothy S. "Deciphering North Korea's Nuclear Rhetoric: An Automated Content Analysis of KCNA News." *Asian Affairs* 39, no. 2 (2012): 73–89.

Roehrig, Terence. "North Korea's Nuclear Weapons Program: Motivations, Strategy, and Doctrine." In *Strategy in the Second Nuclear Age*, edited by Toshi Yoshihara and James Holmes. Washington, DC: Georgetown University Press, 2012.

Romanian Ministry of Foreign Affairs. "Telegram from Pyongyang to Bucharest, No.76.121, TOP SECRET, April 8, 1967." History and Public Policy Program Digital Archive, Archive of the Romanian Ministry of Foreign Affairs, April 8, 1967.

Rosenberg, Jay, and Christiaan Beek. "Examining Code Reuse Reveals Undiscovered Links among North Korea's Malware Families." McAfee Labs Report, August 9, 2019.

"Russia and the DPRK Step Up the Contacts of Law-Enforcement Agencies." *Izvestiya*, April 2, 2019.

Sagan, Scott D. "Why Do States Build Nuclear Weapons? Three Models in Search of a Bomb." *International Security* 21, no. 3 (1996): 54–86.

Sanger, David. "Carter Visit to North Korea: Whose Trip Was It Really?" *New York Times*, June 18, 1994.

Sanger, David, and William Broad. "Trump Inherits a Secret Cyberwar against North Korean Missiles." *New York Times*, March 4, 2017.

Sanger, David, David Kirkpatrick, and Nicole Perlroth. "The World Once Laughed at North Korean Cyberpower. No More." *New York Times*, October 15, 2017.

Sciutto, Jim, Joshua Berlinger, Yoonjung Seo, Kylie Atwood and Zachary Cohen. "US Monitoring Intelligence That North Korean Leader Is in Grave Danger after Surgery." CNN, April 21, 2020.

Seong-hun, Jeon. "Kim Jong-un's Byungjin Policy of Simultaneous Nuclear and Economic Development and 'April 1 Declaration of Nuclear Status'" [김정은 정권의 경제핵무력 병진노선과 "4.1 핵보유 법령"]. Korea Institute of the National Unification, 2013.

Seong-joo, Kim. "Analysis on the Contents and Changes in Logical Structure of Line of Simultaneous Economic and Defense Build-ups (Byoungjin Line)" [북한 병진노선의 내용 및 논리구조 변화 분석]. *Quarterly Journal of Defense Policy Studies* 32, no. 2 (2016).

Seong, Yeon-cheol. "Moon Encourages Trump to Continue Making 'Bold Decisions' for Peace on the Korean Peninsula." *Hankyoreh*, March 1, 2019.

"SEZ Experts Visit Indonesian Economic Zones." *Pyongyang Times*, June 20, 2015.

Shen, Zhihua. "Features and Future of Sino-DPRK Alliance." Chahar Institute, June 29, 2017.

———. *Zuihou de "tianchao": Mao zedong, jin richeng yu zhongchao guanxi* [*The Final dynasty: Mao Zedong, Kim Il-sung, and Sino-North Korean relations*]. Hong Kong: The Chinese University of Hong Kong, 2018.

Sherstobitoff, Ryan, Itai Liba, and James Walter. "Dissecting Operation Troy: Cyberespionage in South Korea." McAfee White Paper, May 4, 2018.

———. "Operation Sharpshooter Targets Global Defense, Critical Infrastructure." McAfee Labs, December 12, 2018.

Shim, Elizabeth. "China Rejects North Korea Request to Join Asian Infrastructure Investment Bank," United Press International, March 31, 2015.

———. "CIA Korea Head Paved Way for Kim Jong Un, Mike Pompeo Meeting." UPI, May 15, 2018.

Shin, Gi-Wook, and Rennie J. Moon. "North Korea in 2018: Kim's Summit Diplomacy." *Asian Survey* 59, no. 1 (2019): 35–43.

Shiner, Josette. "Kim Il-sung Asks for a Thaw in Ties with the U.S." *Washington Times*, April 15, 1992.

Silberstein, Benjamin Katzeff. "Kim Jong-un's Congress Speech: Strengthening State Control Over the Economy." *North Korean Economy Watch*, January 12, 2021.

"The 6th Politburo Meeting of the 8th Central Committee of the WPK in Progress." *Rodong Sinmun*, January 20, 2022.

Smith, Josh. "N. Korea's Food Situation Appears Perilous, Experts Say." Reuters, October 8, 2021.

Snyder, Scott. *Negotiating on the Edge: North Korean Negotiating Behavior*. Washington DC: United States Insitute of Peace Press, 1999.

"Society and Power in the Russian Far East in 1960–1991." In *History of the Russian Far East*. Vol. 3. Book 5, edited by Victor Larin and Angelina Vashchuk. Vladivostok: Institute of History, Archaeology and Ethnography of the Peoples of the Russian Far East of the Far Eastern Branch of the Russian Academy of Sciences, 2016.

Song, Jiyoung. *Human Rights Discourse in North Korea: Post-colonial, Marxist and Confucian Perspectives.* New York: Routledge, 2014.

Stangarone, Troy. "Why Has North Korea Struggled to Normalize Trade with China?" *The Diplomat*, November 25, 2021.

Sterngold, James. "Seoul Gets Some Diplomatic Backing in China." *New York Times*, September 30, 1992.

"Striking Demonstration of Great Military Muscle of Juche Korea: Successful Test-Launch of New-Type ICBM Respected Comrade Kim Jong Un Guides Test Launch of ICBM Hwasongpho-17." *Rodong Sinmun*, March 25, 2022.

"Strong Control on Individual Commercial Activities Started Eventually. Is It Part of Kim Jong-un's Anti-Market Policies?" Asia Press, April 26, 2021.

Supreme People's Assembly of the Democratic People's Republic of Korea. "The Letter to the Congress of the United States of America." March 25, 1974.

Talmadge, Eric. "Deciphering the Body Language at the Kim-Putin Summit, from Hearty Handshakes to Manspreading." *National Post*, April 25, 2019.

———. "North Korea's 'Singapore Shops' Expose Gap in Sanctions Push." Associated Press, December 28, 2018.

Tan, E. W., and G. Govindasamy. "From Kim Jong Il to Kim Jong Un: Nuclear Impasse or Diplomatic Opportunity?" *Asia Europe Journal* 10, no. 4 (2012): 301–16.

Tarakanov, Dmitry. *The "Kimsuky" Operation: A North Korean APT?* Kaspersky Lab, Kaspersky APT Reports, September 11, 2013.

TASS. "The DPRK Ambassador Says Peace on the Korean Peninsula Is Impossible without the Withdrawal of US Troops." August 12, 2021.

———. "The History of the Visits by the Leaders of the DPRK to the USSR and Russia." April 24, 2019.

———. "Matvienko: Kim Jong-un Hopes That the Russian Federation Could Assist in Easing the Sanctions Imposed on the DPRK." September 10, 2018.

Testimony before the US-China Economic and Security Review Commission, Washington, D.C, April 12, 2018.

Tiezzi, Shannon. "The Renaissance in Russia-North Korea Relations." *The Diplomat*, November 22, 2014.

Toloraya, Georgy. "Korean Peninsula and Russia: The Problems of Interaction." *Mezhdunarodnaya Zhizn* [International Affairs], November 2002.

Toloraya, Georgy, and Lyubov Yakovleva. "Russia and North Korea: Ups and Downs in Relations," *Asian Politics and Policy* 13, no. 2 (2021).

Tosi, Scott. "North Korean Cyber Support to Combat Operations." *Military Review*, July–August 2017.

Trading Economics. "North Korea GDP Annual Growth Rate."

"Treaty of Friendship, Cooperation and Mutual Assistance between the USSR and the DPRK." July 6, 1961.

"Treaty of Friendship, Good Neighborliness, and Cooperation between the Russian Federation and the DPRK." February 9, 2000.

Trend Micro. "A Look Into the Lazarus Group's Operations." *Trend Micro Cybercrime and Digital Threats Blog*, January 24, 2018.

Troianovski, Anton, and David Sanger. "Rivals on World Stage, Russia and U.S. Quietly Seek Areas of Accord." *New York Times*, October 31, 2021.

Trump, Donald J. "I too have a Nuclear Button, but it is a much bigger & more powerful one than his." Twitter, January 2, 2018.

Trump, Donald J., and Kim Jong-un. "Joint Statement of President Donald J. Trump of the United States of America and Chairman Kim Jon Un of the Democratic People's Republic of Korea at the Singapore Summit." June 12, 2018.

"Trump's Letter to Kim Jong-un." *Korea Times*, May 24, 2018.

Understanding North Korea. Seoul: National Institute for Unification Education, 2021.

UNICEF. "DPRK Humanitarian Situation Report, End of Year 2020." February 20, 2021.

United Nations. "Agreed Framework between the United States of America and the Democratic People's Republic of Korea." Geneva, October 21, 1994.

———. "No. 14668 Multilateral International Covenant on Civil and Political Rights, Adopted by the General Assembly of the United Nations on 19 December 1966." United Nations Treaty Series, vol. 999, no. I-14668.

United Nations Institute for Disarmament Research (UNIDIR). "Republic of Korea Cybersecurity Policy Documents." UNIDIR Cyber Policy Portal, April 2021.

United Nations OHCHR. "Group of Independent Experts on Accountability Pursuant to Human Rights Council Resolution 31/18 on the Situation of Human Rights in the Democratic People's Republic of Korea."

———. "In Security Council, UN Officials Urge Renewed Engagement with DPR Korea on Human Rights." December 22, 2014.

———. "Report of the Commission of Inquiry on Human Rights in the Democratic People's Republic of Korea." United Nations Human Rights Council.

United Nations Security Council. *Final Report of the Panel of Experts Submitted Pursuant to Resolution 2515* (2020). March 4, 2021.

———. *Final Report of the Panel of Experts Submitted Pursuant to Resolution 2276 (2016)*. February 27, 2017.

———. *Final Report of the Panel of Experts Submitted Pursuant to Resolution 2464* (2019). March 2, 2019.

———. *Final Report of the Panel of Experts Submitted Pursuant to Resolution 2464 (2020)*. March 4, 2021.

———. "ID Commission of Inquiry on DPRK—14th Meeting 24th Regular Session of Human Rights Council." UN Web TV, September 17, 2013

———. *Midterm Report of the Panel of Experts Submitted Pursuant to Resolution 2464 (2019)*. August 30, 2019.

———. "Resolution 2371" August 5, 2017.

———. "Resolution 2397 (S/RES/2397)." December 22, 2017.

———. "Security Council Committee Established Pursuant to Resolution 1718 (2006)."

United States of America and Democratic People's Republic of Korea. "Agreed Framework between the United States of America and Democratic People's Republic of Korea 1994." October 21, 1994.

United States of America v. Park Jin Hyok. United States District Court for the Central District of California, Case No. MJ18–1479, June 8, 2018.

"U.S. and North Korea Meet for First Cabinet-Level Talks." *New York Times*, January 23, 1992.

US Department of Defense. "53rd Security Consultative Meeting Joint Communique." December 2, 2021.

US Department of Justice. "Three North Korean Military Hackers Indicted in Wide-Ranging Scheme to Commit Cyberattacks and Financial Crimes across the Globe." Press release by the Office of Public Affairs, February 17, 2021.

US. Department of State. "Secretary of State Madeleine K. Albright Press Conference, Koryo Hotel." October 24, 2000.

US Departments of State, the Treasury, and Homeland Security, and the Federal Bureau of Investigation. "Guidance on the North Korean Cyber Threat." April 15, 2020.

US Department of the Treasury. "North Korea Sanctions." December 10, 2021.

———. "Treasury Sanctions North Korean State-Sponsored Malicious Cyber Groups." September 13, 2019.

———. "Treasury Sanctions Taiwan Proliferators Linked to North Korea." Press release, Washington, DC, May 10, 2013.

"U.S.-DPRK Joint Communique." October 12, 2000.

"U.S.-ROK Leaders' Joint Statement." White House, May 21, 2021.

"US Will Not Accept Nuclear North Korea Despite North Korean Ambitions: US Official." *Korea Times*. August 4, 2021.

"USSR–North Korea Agreement on Economic and Cultural Cooperation," Encyclopedia of Korean Culture.

Valentino, Andrea. "Widespread Deforestation Threatens to Leave North Korea Buried in the Pines." *NK News*, July 19, 2021.

"The Value of Dollars Drops by 20% for Two Weeks Because of Ban of Use of Foreign Currencies." *Hankyung*, November 28, 2020.

Van Diepen, Vann H. "North Korea's March 24 ICMB Launch: What If It Was the Hwasong-17?" *38 North*, April 7, 2022.

Voice of America. "Russia Blocks UN Resolution Condemning Ukraine Invasion." February 25, 2022.

Volynets, Alexey. "Number-One Persons Visiting the Far Eastern Border." *DV.Land*, November 23, 2020.

Voznesensky, Mikhail. "The Secret Summit of Brezhnev and Kim Il-sung."

Waltz, Kenneth. "The Spread of Nuclear Weapons: More May Be Better." *Adelphi Papers* no. 171. London: International Institute for Strategic Studies, 1981.

———. *Man, the State, and War*. New York: Columbia University Press, 1959.

Wang, Junsheng. "Zhongchao 'teshuguanxi' de luoji: Fuza zhanlve pingheng de chanwu" [The logic of the Sino-DPRK special relationship: The complex product of strategic balancing]. *Dongbeiya Luntan [Northeast Asia Forum]*, no. 1 (2016): 51–65.

Wang, Yue. "China's ZTE Faces Long-Lasting Damage from U.S. Trade Sanctions." *Forbes*, June 18, 2018.

Ward, Peter. "Kim Jong Un's Battle with Teen Spirit, Foreign Media and Bureaucracy Goes Public." *NK News Pro*, May 4, 2021.

———. "Market Reforms with North Korean Characteristics: Loosening the Grip on State-Owned Enterprises." *38 North*, December 21, 2017.

———. "North Korea Continues to Claw Back Control from the Private Economy." *NK News Pro*, May 17, 2021.

Weatherly, Robert, and Jiyoung Song. "The Evolution of Human Rights Thinking in North Korea." *Journal of Communist Studies and Transition Politics* 24, no. 2 (2008): 272–96, https://doi.org/10.1080/13523270802003111.

Wehrey, Frederic. "NATO's Intervention." In *The Libyan Revolution and Its Aftermath*, edited by Peter Cole and Brian McQuinn. New York: Oxford University Press, 2015.

Whang, Taehee, Michael Lammbrau, and Hyung-min Joo. "Talking to Whom? The Changing Audience of North Korean Nuclear Tests." *Social Science Quarterly* 98, no. 3 (2017): 976–92.

Williams, Martyn. "Catch Me If You Can: North Korea Works to Improve Communications Security." *38 North*, April 12, 2017.

———. *Digital Trenches: North Korea's Information Counter-Offensive*. Washington DC: Committee for Human Rights in North Korea, 2019.

———. "Turning Waste into Treasure: North Korea's Recycling Push." *38 North*, June 15, 2021.

Willis, Ben. "Scrutinizing North Korea's Record on Civil and Political Rights: The New ICCPR Reporting Cycle." *38 North*, September 2, 2022.

Wit, Joel S., Daniel B. Poneman, and Robert L. Gallucci. *Going Critical: The First North Korean Nuclear Crisis*. Washington, DC: Brookings Institution Press, 2004.

Woo, Seongji. "Pyongyang and the World: North Korean Perspectives on International Relations under Kim Jong-il." *Pacific Focus* 26, no. 2 (2011): 188–205.

Woodward, Bob. *Rage*. New York: Simon & Schuster, 2020.

"Workshop Contributes to Protecting Environment of Mt. Paektu Area." *Pyongyang Times*, August 3, 2017.

World Bank Group. "GDP per Capita (Current US$)—Korea, Republic."

World Meteorological Organization (WMO). "State of the Climate in Asia 2020, No. 1273."

Wroughton, Lesley, and David Brunnstrom. "Exclusive: With a Piece of Paper, Trump Called on Kim to Hand Over Nuclear Weapons." *Reuters*, March 30, 2019.

Wuddun, Sheryl. "North Korea Fires Missile over Japanese Territory." *New York Times*, September 1, 1998.

Xinhua News Agency. "Xi jinping dui chaoxian jinxing guoshifangwen" [Xi Jinping visits North Korea for state]. June 10, 2019.

———. "Xi jinping tong chaoxian laodongdang weiyuanzhang jin zhengen juxing huitan" [Xi Jinping holds talks with North Korean Worker's Party Commissioner Kim Jong-un]. *People's Daily*, June 20, 2018.

———. "Xi jinping tong chaoxian laodongdang weiyuanzhang guowu weiyuanhui weiyuanzhang jin zhengen juxing huitan" [Xi Jinping holds talks with North Korean Workers Party Commissioner Kim Jong-un]. June 20, 2019.

———. "Xi jinping tong chaoxian laodongdang weiyuanzhang jin zhengen zaidalian juxing huiwu" [Xi Jinping holds meeting in Dalian with North Korean Worker's Party Commissioner Kim Jong-un]. May 8, 2018.

———. "Xi Jinping tong jin zhengen juxing huitan" [Xi Jinping holds talks with Kim Jong-un]. March 28, 2018.

———. "Xi jinping zongshuji lishixing fangchao huanying changmian chao zhen-han!" [General Secretary Xi Jinping historical visit to North Korea, the welcome scene is very shocking]. June 20, 2019.

Yang, Moon-Soo. *The Economic Reform of North Korea in the Kim Jong-un Era: Status & Evaluation*, KDI Working Paper. Seoul: Korea Development Institute, 2021.

Yang, Xiangfeng. "Disenchanted Entanglement: The North Korean Shades of Grey on the Chinese Mind." *Journal of Contemporary China* 29, no. 123 (2019): 462–67.

Yim, Eul-chul. "Kim Jung-un Regime's Economic Development Zone Policy: Characteristics, Assessments, and Prospect" [김정은 시대의 경제개발구 정책: 특징, 평가 및 전망]. *Journal of Northeast Asian Economic Studies* 27, no. 3 (2015).

Yonhap News Agency. "According to National Intelligence Service, Kim Jong-un Executed a Major Player in Currency Markets." November 27, 2020.

———. "Biden Says Will Meet N.K. Leader If He Agrees to Draw Down Nuclear Capacity." October 23, 2020.

———. DPRK Minister of Foreign Affairs Ri Yong-ho, Press Conference, March 1, 2019.

———. "Korea, US Hold First Policy Consultation on Online Security." September 13, 2012.

———. "Moon to Stay in Paekhwawon Guest House Known for Hosting VIPs." September 18, 2018.

———. "N. Korea Hints at Lifting Moratorium on ICBM, Nuclear Tests, Citing U.S. 'Hostile Policy.'" January 20, 2022.

———. "N. Korea Says It Wants Partial Sanctions Relief." March 1, 2019.

———. "N. Korean Leader's Visit Highlights 'Charm Offensive.'" February 9, 2018.

———. "Remarks by Ri- Yong-ho and Choe Sun-hee at Late-Night Press Conference." March 1, 2019.

Yoon, Sangwon. "North Korea Recruits Hackers at School." *Aljazeera News*, June 21, 2011.

Yoshino, Jiro. "North Korea's Cybertroops Span the Globe in Quest for Cash." *Nikkei Asian Review*, March 15, 2018.

Yost, David "The Budapest Memorandum and Russia's Intervention in Ukraine." *International Affairs* 91, no. 3 (2015): 505–38.

Young, Benjamin R. "How North Korea Has Waged 'a War to Improve Nature.'" *NK News*, June 2, 2021.

Young Song, Annie, and Justin V. Hastings. "Engaging North Korea: Environmental Cooperation in Peacebuilding." *Third World Quarterly* 41, no. 11 (2020).

YTN. "Blue Crab Season? Chinese Fishing Vessels Are Engaging in Illegal Fishing Again." April 6, 2021.

Yu, Hongjun. "Lengzhan suiyue de zhongchao guanxi (1976–1991)" [Sino-DPRK relations during the Cold War (1976–1991)]. *US-China Perception Monitor*, June 25, 2019.

Zarate, Juan. *Treasury Wars: The Unleashing of a New Era of Financial Warfare.* New York: PublicAffairs, 2013.

Zhelev, Zhelyu. "Is Communism Returning?" In *The Revolutions of 1989*, edited by Vladimir Tismaneanu. London: Routledge, 1999.

Zoubir, Yahia H. "Libya in US Foreign Policy: From Rogue State to Good Fellow?" *Third World Quarterly* 23, no. 1 (2002): 31–53.

Index

Page references for figures are italicized.

Afghanistan, 8, 116, 128
Agreed Framework, 45, 71, 110
Albright, Madeline, 71, 110, 130

Biden, Joe, 76, 118, 154
Bolton, John, 7
byungjin policy, xi, 46, 50, 154, 223–24;
    components of, 6–10, 12, 16–17, 20,
    50; goals under, xxiv, 9–10, 223–24;
    Kim Il-sung, original policy of, 46;
    launch of, 111, 154, 223

Carter, Jimmy, 109, 111
China: economic development in,
    10–13, 29–30; North Korea, bilateral
    relations with, xix, 18–19, 88–91,
    92–102, 203; North Korea, border
    with, 15–16, 153, 156–57; sanctions,
    enforcement of, 156–158
Clinton, Bill, 110–11, 118, 130
Cold War, 45, 139
Comprehensive Military Agreement
    (CMA), 69, 76
constitution: of China, 30; of North
    Korea, 30, 43, 49, 212; of South
    Korea, 202

coronavirus. *See* COVID-19 pandemic.
COVID-19 pandemic, xii, 18,
    33–34, 38–39, 167–68, 187–88,
    223, 229, 235

Democratic People's Republic of Korea
    (DPRK). *See* North Korea.
Deng Xiaoping, 10, 90, 91, 109
denuclearization, xvii, 38–39, 51,
    56–57, 75, 113, 150, 154; agreements
    on, 67–69, 81–82; negotiations
    for, 45, 48, 80, 114, 138; obstacles
    toward, 54–57, 82, 100, 102, 116
diplomacy: between China and North
    Korea, xix, 88–92, 94–100; between
    North Korea and Russia, xx,
    125–138; between North Korea and
    the United States, xix–xx, 78–79,
    108–112, 115–19; inter-Korean,
    xviii–xix, 66–69, 77–78, 108, 110;
    multilateral, xx–xxi, 45, 48, 201–3,
    210–11, 220–23
DMZ. *See* Korean Demilitarized
    Zone (DMZ).

economic reforms: of China, 10, 12–13;
    of North Korea, xii, xv, 13–17,
    27–29; of Vietnam, 11

About the Contributors

Sandra Fahy is a former visiting fellow with the Human Rights Program at Harvard Law School. She holds a PhD from SOAS University of London. She is the author of *Marching through Suffering: Loss and Survival in North Korea* (2015) and *Dying for Rights: Putting North Korea's Rights Abuses on the Record* (2019). She is currently writing *States, Lies and Video: A Century of States Using Video to Deny Allegations of Rights Abuses.* She is an associate professor with the Bachelor of Global and International Studies at Carleton University's Kroeger School of Public Affairs.

Virginie Grzelczyk is a reader/associate professor in international relations at Aston University and head of the School of Social Sciences and Humanities. She holds an MA and PhD in government and politics from the University of Maryland, and an MA in diplomacy and security from Ewha University. Her research focuses on security relationships over the Korean Peninsula, especially regarding North Korea, with publications spanning the Six-Party Talks process, North Korea's energy security dilemma, Korean identity in the context of reunification, the concept of crisis in Northeast Asia, and North Korea's foreign relations. Her latest project focuses on the politics of toys in conflict and post-conflict spheres, and she has been supported by a Leverhulme Research Fellowship to conduct fieldwork in both the ROK and the DPRK.

Justin V. Hastings is professor of international relations and comparative politics at the University of Sydney. His research focuses on the geography and political economy of clandestine groups, including organized criminals, maritime pirates, terrorists, insurgents, nuclear traffickers, and black and gray market participants, particularly in Southeast Asia, Northeast Asia, and the Indian Ocean. He is the author of *No Man's Land: Globalization, Territory, and Clandestine Groups in Southeast Asia* (2010) and *A Most Enterprising Country: North Korea in the Global Economy* (2016). Hastings holds degrees from the University of California, Berkeley (MA, PhD) in political science, and from Princeton University (AB) in public and international affairs.

Byung-Yeon Kim is director of the Institute for Peace and Unification Studies and professor in the Department of Economics at Seoul National University (SNU). His research interests lie in the fields of transition economics and the economies of North Korea as well as former socialist countries. He received his BA and MA from SNU and a PhD from the University of Oxford. He has published a number of articles in international journals and wrote a book on the North Korean economy (*Unveiling the North Korean Economy*, 2017). He was awarded with Excellence in Academic Achievements by the National Academy of Sciences and the T. S. Ashton Prize, and he has been recognized as distinguished researcher by SNU. He has served as a member of various government committees including the National Economic Advisory Council, the Presidential Committee for Unification Preparation and the Advisory Committee for the Korean Summit, and the Policy Advisory Committee for the Ministries of Unification and Foreign Affairs.

Andrei Lankov was born in 1963 in Leningrad (now Petersburg). He completed his undergraduate and graduate studies at Leningrad State University (PhD in 1989). From 1996 to 2004, he taught Korean history at the Australian National University, and since 2004 he has been teaching at Kookmin University, currently at the College of Social Studies, and also serves as the director of Korearisk.com group. His major research interest is North Korean history and society. His major English-language publications on North Korea include: *From Stalin to Kim Il Sung: The Formation of North Korea, 1945–1960* (2003); *Crisis in North Korea: The Failure of De-Stalinization, 1956* (2004), *North of the DMZ: Essays on Daily Life in North Korea* (2007), and *The Real North Korea* (2013). He has contributed to the *Wall Street Journal, New York Times, Financial Times*, and *Newsweek*, and has published a number of academic articles, including articles in *Foreign Affairs* and *Foreign Policy*. In 2017, *Foreign Policy* magazine included him in its list of Global Thinkers. He also writes extensively in Korean and Russian.

Artyom Lukin is deputy director for research at the Oriental Institute–School of Regional and International Studies, Far Eastern Federal University, in Vladivostok. He is also professor of international relations there. Lukin earned his PhD in political science from Far Eastern State University in 2002. Lukin has authored numerous chapters, papers, and commentaries, in Russian and English, on Asia-Pacific international politics and Russia's engagement with Asia. His latest book (coauthored with Rens Lee) is *Russia's Far East: New Dynamics in Asia Pacific and Beyond* (2015). Artyom Lukin's research interests include international relations and security in the Asia-Pacific and Northeast Asia; Russian foreign policy; Russia's engagement with the Asia-Pacific; and politics and economics in the Russian Far East. Lukin has authored and coauthored multiple scholarly publications in Russian and English. He has been involved in numerous research and publication projects both in Russia and abroad. He is a regular commentator for Russian and international news media.

Haksoon Paik is executive director of the "Kim Dae-jung Peace Forum" and a member of the Board of Directors of the Kim Dae-jung Peace Center. Most recently, he was president of the Sejong Institute, a leading think tank in South Korea. He was formerly an advisor in various capacities to South Korea's Ministry of Unification, Ministry of Foreign Affairs, and National Assembly. He was vice president of the Korean Political Science Association and also vice president of the Korean Association of North Korean Studies. He has written extensively on North Korean politics, inter-Korean relations, North Korea–US relations, North Korean nuclear and missile issues, and East Asian international relations. He is author of numerous books and monographs written in Korean, including: *The Korean Peninsula Peace Strategy* (coauthor, 2022), *Park Geun-hye Administration's Policy on North Korea and Unification: Comparison with Previous Administrations* (2018), *North Korean Politics in the Kim Jong Un Era, 2012–2014: Ideas, Identities, and Structures* (2015), *The U.S.–North Korea Relations during President Obama's Second Term, 2013–2014: Threat of the Use of Nuclear Weapons and the Collapse of Relations* (2014), and *The History of Power in North Korea: Ideas, Identities, and Structures* (2010). He earned his PhD in political science from the University of Pennsylvania and was a postdoctoral fellow at Harvard University.

Ramon Pacheco Pardo is professor of International Relations at King's College London and the KF-VUB Korea Chair at the School of Global Governance of Vrije Universiteit Brussels. He holds a PhD in International Relations from the London School of Economics and Political Science (LSE). Prof. Pacheco Pardo is also adjunct fellow (nonresident) with the Korea Chair at CSIS and committee member at CSCAP EU. He has held visiting positions at Korea University, the Lee Kuan Yew School of Public Policy, and Melbourne University. Dr. Pacheco Pardo has been editor of *Millennium: Journal of International Studies* and currently sits on the editorial boards of *East Asia: An International Quarterly*, *EU-China Observer*, and *Global Studies Journal*. His publications include the book *North Korea–US Relations from Kim Jong Il to Kim Jong Un*, published in 2019, and peer-reviewed articles with *Asia Europe Journal*, *Asia Policy*, *Asian Studies*

Review, *Global Governance*, *Global Policy*, *International Relations of the Asia-Pacific*, *Journal of Contemporary China*, and *New Political Economy*, among others.

Kyung-Ae Park holds the Korea Foundation Chair at the School of Public Policy and Global Affairs at the University of British Columbia. She is the founding director of the Canada-DPRK Knowledge Partnership Program (KPP), which is a long-term knowledge sharing and academic exchange initiative with North Korea. The KPP has been hosting six North Korean professors annually since 2011 for their study at UBC. Since the mid-1990s, she has made numerous trips to Pyongyang and hosted North Korean delegation visits to Canada, playing a key role in promoting Track II exchanges and diplomacy between the two countries. She is the author, coauthor, and editor of many scholarly publications, including *Non-Traditional Security Issues in North Korea*; *North Korea in Transition: Politics, Economics, and Society*; *New Challenges of North Korean Foreign Policy*; *Korean Security Dynamics in Transition*, and *China and North Korea: Politics of Integration and Modernization*. She also authored articles in a number of journals, including *Comparative Politics*, *Journal of Asian Studies*, *Pacific Affairs*, *Asian Survey*, and *Pacific Review*.

Michael Raska is the coordinator of the Military Transformations Program at the S. Rajaratnam School of International Studies, Nanyang Technological University, Singapore. His research interests focus on theoretical and policy-oriented aspects of military innovation, emerging technologies, and cyber conflicts in East Asia. He is the author of *Military Innovation and Small States: Creating Reverse Asymmetry* (2016) and coeditor of *Defence Innovation and the 4th Industrial Revolution Security Challenges, Emerging Technologies, and Military Implications* (2022). He has published in peer-reviewed academic journals such as the *Journal of Strategic Studies, Strategic Studies Quarterly, PRISM—Journal of Complex Operations*, and *Korea Journal of Defense Analysis*. His contributions include chapters in edited volumes in research collaboration with the Norwegian Institute of Defense Studies, International Institute for Strategic Studies, European Union Institute for Security Studies, Center for New American Security, and Swedish Defense University. He holds a PhD from the National University of Singapore.

Scott A. Snyder is senior fellow for Korea studies and director of the program on US-Korea policy at the Council on Foreign Relations (CFR). His program examines South Korea's efforts to contribute on the international stage; its potential influence and contributions as a middle power in East

Asia; and the peninsular, regional, and global implications of North Korean instability. Mr. Snyder is the author of *South Korea at the Crossroads: Autonomy and Alliance in an Era of Rival Powers* (January 2018) and coauthor of *The Japan-South Korea Identity Clash: East Asian Security and the United States* (May 2015) with Brad Glosserman. He is also the coeditor of *North Korea in Transition: Politics, Economy, and Society* (October 2012), and the editor of *Global Korea: South Korea's Contributions to International Security* (October 2012) and *The U.S.-South Korea Alliance: Meeting New Security Challenges* (March 2012). Mr. Snyder served as the project director for CFR's Independent Task Force on policy toward the Korean Peninsula. He currently writes for the blog *Asia Unbound.*

Yun Sun is a senior fellow and codirector of the East Asia Program and director of the China Program at the Stimson Center. Her expertise is in Chinese foreign policy, US-China relations and China's relations with neighboring countries and authoritarian regimes. From 2011 to early 2014, she was a visiting fellow at the Brookings Institution, jointly appointed by the Foreign Policy Program and the Global Development Program, where she focused on Chinese national security decision-making processes and China-Africa relations. From 2008 to 2011, Yun was the China analyst for the International Crisis Group (ICG) based in Beijing, specializing on China's foreign policy toward conflict countries and the developing world. Prior to ICG, she worked on US-Asia relations in Washington, D.C., for five years. Yun earned her master's degree in international policy and practice from George Washington University, as well as an MA in Asia Pacific studies and a BA in international relations from Foreign Affairs College in Beijing.

ASIA IN WORLD POLITICS

Series Editor: Samuel S. Kim

Made in the USA
Las Vegas, NV
09 November 2022

59090955R00177